Readings in
ZERO INVENTORY

Complete transcripts of papers
on the topic of
Zero Inventory
presented at the
APICS 27th Annual International Conference

October 9–12, 1984
Las Vegas, Nevada

1984
CONFERENCE COMMITTEE

NICK TESTA, CPIM*
Newport Electronics, Inc.
Santa Ana, CA

ED JACKS, CPIM
Endevco
San Juan Capistrano, CA

NICK MRAOVICH
Emporium Capwell
Pacifica, CA

RAY YBARRA
Hewlett Packard
Los Angeles, CA

PROGRAM REVIEWERS

George P. Adams, CPIM
Martin Adduci
Ali Bakhtiar
David Barsocchini
Jeri D. Baumgardner, CPIM
Kenneth Berkowitz, CPIM
Jim Bernstein, CPIM*
Jan Bindewald, CPIM
Robert C. Brackett, CPIM*
William F. Braun, CPIM
Thomas L. Brescia, CPIM
Jim Brown
Dewey H. Burkett, Jr., CPIM
James K. Burns
Thomas V. Cerri, CPIM
Chao-Hsien Chu, CPIM
Robert Clark, CPIM*
George V. Colby, III, CPIM
William T. Darnton, CPIM*
Bruce M. Didsbury, CPIM
Richard C. Dixon
John Draxler, CPIM
Steven C. Dunn, CPIM

Merle L. Ehlers, CPIM*
David Epps, CPIM
Walter L. Ernst, CPIM*
Fredric R. Fish, CPIM
William O. Foelker, CPIM*
Howard Forman, CPIM
Chester H. Frame, CPIM
Evan Francis, CPIM
Bob Frerichs, CPIM*
Frederick E. Fry
William A. Geist, CPIM
Harry J. Golowen, CPIM
Daniel S. Grummersch
Michael Hecker
Richard L. Hoffman, CPIM
Thomas R. Hoffmann, CPIM*
Kenneth J. Holden, CPIM
Philipp R. Hornthal, CPIM
Richard R. Jesse, CPIM*
Richard A. Johnson, CPIM
Bernadyne Kaknavich, CPIM
Daniel J. Karp
John Kashmer, CPIM

Nancy E. Keller, CPIM
James Kirkpatrick, CPIM*
Monty Kisslinger, CPIM*
G. Samantha Knoerr
James A. G. Krupp, CPIM*
Paul Lavallee, CPIM*
Robert Leach, CPIM
Marsha Lehman, CPIM
Eriks Leimanis, CPIM
Thomas P. Leonard
Randall K. Love, CPIM
Tim Lyons, CPIM*
Michael A. Manna, CPIM
C. Donald McCullough, CPIM
John Meaker, CPIM
E. Douglas Moore, CPIM
Paul H. Moore, CPIM
Kenneth D. Mroczek, CPIM
C. K. Nelson
Horace R. Norfleet, Jr., CPIM
Edward N. O'Rourke, CPIM
Steve Pavlik, CPIM*
Lorin L. Peterson, CPIM*

James A. Pope
James M. Powell, Jr., CPIM
William F. Pritchard, CPIM
Balasubramanian Ram, CPIM
Michael Rosiak, CPIM
Bill Sebastian, CPIM
John Charles Shearer, CPIM
Mark L. Silverberg
Daniel J. Smith, CPIM
Ron Staples, CPIM
Michael J. Stefanics
Bob Stockwell, CPIM*
George H. Stoebel, CPIM
David J. Storm, CPIM*
Georgana Thompson, CPIM
George A. Tusa
Duane R. Walker
W. James Walker, CPIM
Mary Kay Wells, CPIM
George Willson, CPIM*
Donald E. Wilson, Jr., CPIM*
David L. Wood, CPIM*
William Zuellig, CPIM*

TABLE OF CONTENTS

ZERO INVENTORY: PROVIDING FOCUS FOR THE CONVERGING MANUFACTURING STRATEGIES OF THE 80S

Kenneth J. McGuire, CPIM*
Kenneth J. McGuire, Inc.

"In war, let your great object be victory, not lengthy campaigns. Thus it may be known that the leader of armies is the arbiter of the people's fate..."

Sun Tzu 500 B.C.
The Art of War

Zero Inventory is the pursuit of an ideal in a quest for manufacturing excellence. It requires a war on waste in our manufacturing processes in order to achieve and maintain higher levels of manufacturing performance. The Zero Inventory/Just-in-Time challenge is to combine all known methodologies and techniques in our body of knowledge while expanding our skills into disciplines which we must understand in order to integrate all manufacturing efforts towards the same goal.

The subject of this presentation is how the various manufacturing strategies might be converged into a vehicle providing focus for our manufacturing companies. The object of victory is a genuine competitive superiority for our manufacturers, most of whom entered the decade of the eighties sharing a common problem. The problem was an abrupt end to thirty plus years of relative affluence where some degree of waste could be conditionally tolerated. That era has ended. Even the companies on the edge of technology entered the eighties more vigilant of the narrowing margin of error that world competition has brought about. Zero Inventory/Just-in-Time is important to every manufacturing company because our competitors in the world are pursuing it and the competitive pressures can only increase, both at home and abroad. We can no longer afford fragile ego and cynical arrogance on approaches we didn't invent. The last recession hopefully taught us that at least.

America is a manufacturing based economy. Without a strong manufacturing base we will need patronage to provide our freedoms. That is the pragmatic reason to preserve our economic strength.

THE ECONOMICS OF MANUFACTURING

Manufacturing companies differ from all other categories in the business world because they alone create the wealth which others trade on. Manufacturers create the wealth by converting raw materials into saleable products for consumption by "adding value" to otherwise worthless materials. The premature report in the 1950's that the manufacturing problem was a technical one which had already been solved erred by presuming that the conversion process was only a technical task. It was and is not. The most important, and the most difficult task of manufacturing is the efficient allocating of resources, not just their conversion. That allocating process is most effectively measured by the quantity of resources used to produce products of equivalent quality and value. This is where many American manufacturing companies have suffered competitive failings to foreign suppliers. This is where a Zero Inventory/Just-in-Time focus can provide a correction to manufacturing strategies which no longer are appropriate to the economics of the eighties.

The fundamental economics of manufacturing have not really changed since the 1950's when most of our current practices were born. Then, as now, the manufacturing companies that are the most successful at allocating their resources usually are those with the lowest costs for equal delivered quality and value. These companies then enjoy the largest profits both for reinvestment and distribution. Short tern profitability is not necessarily an accurate measure of genuine resource allocating superiority, but it is a clear indication of momentary superiority when compated to competitors less efficient at allocating resources.

The resources which manufacturing companies most frequently relate to are the quantitative measures of men, machines, materials, and money. The most efficient producers are considered to be using "just enough" while the least efficient are thought to be using "too much." The decade of the eighties has enlightened us to at least two more resources to be allocated, time and skills.

The time resource has always been a factor in production but our practices have never really treated it as if it were in scarce supply. Time has most often been stated as a given that needed to be managed around. The introduction to the Japanese practice of Just-in-Time production has awakened us to the tremendous leverage on production cost that is available in the better management of time, as in lead times. The skills resource has been around to be managed too, but our focus has been narrowly concentrated only on direct labor skills. The expansion of skills to indirect tasks in a factory were considered a separate issue entirely. Again, the examination of Just-in-Time has exposed the potential which direct labor can leverage in the area of indirect cost.

So while the fundamental economics of manufacturing have not changed, the introduction of two formerly insignificant factors has altered the proportionage values substantially. The rules governing the allocation process need to be re-examined to see if they still apply and, if not, how should they be changed to accomodate the efficient allocation of resources.

HISTORICAL PERSPECTIVE

The best way to evaluate how changes can be most effective is to examine the way they became conventional wisdom. For the most part, the traditions are rooted most deeply in metalworking companies. The newer, high tech growth businesses suffer only from their degree of adoption of the prevalent conventional wisdom, which may explain why Just-in-Time production is having its early successes with those industries first.

In the immediate post World War II era the United States began its rise to the zenith of industrial might. While Americans shared the grief of the terrible war, our territory was spared its ravages. The industrial base, already energized by wartime production, shifted to peacetime production of consumer goods. The pent up demand provided a manufacturing priority to drive the machinery to the maximum in order not to lose sales opportunities. Volume increases and revenue growth covered most problems for a time. And as volume growth leveled the American knack of superior marketing delivered continuing revenue growth with segmentation, clever differentiation of goods, and use of the new media for articulated selling.

The success of demand management in always clearing the shelves allowed neglect to go unnoticed in production. Resource costs that mildly ratcheted upwards could easily be passed along using marketing finesse. When the growth cycle flattened and price resistance surfaced financial skills became an equally effective tool in maintaining the earnings patterns of the past. Practices in manufacturing concentrated on reducing the labor content of production while material cost inflation was only partially contained. Product proliferation complicated the managing process and caused overhead to grow to cope with expanding varieties of features, options, and styles.

The first oil crunch in 1973 marked the first recognition of global shifts in industrial power. Without cheap energy, whole industries became obsolete almost overnight. The second oil shock confirmed the inevitable. The high cost of waste made Americans less competitive and failure to compete began to take its toll on our companies.

CURRENT OUTLOOK

The economics of manufacturing now requires that a new approach be adopted in order to compete effectively in a global market. Partly because our past efforts with direct labor have been so effective and partly because the proportionate values have changed there is no longer much leverage to be gained concentrating on the direct labor component of our product costs. Labor rarely amounts to more than 15% of cost and often accounts for 5% or less. There is 40% to 60% cost to improve on in material content and 25% to 45% of product cost available to be maximized in the overhead content. Yet in many traditional settings the structure has burden functions accounting for 25% of the cost poised to concentrate on absolute control over the 5% to 10% of the direct labor cost. The manufacturing practices must be changed to address this fact of manufacturing economics.

MANUFACTURING STRATEGY AS A COMPETITIVE TOOL

For the most part, top management has looked upon the task of manufacturing as a nuts and bolts function, largely a technical and mechanical function that is a pretty straightforward procedure of getting what is needed and putting it together for customer orders. That may be changing. Our foreign competitors, led by the Japanese, have shown that manufacturing competence can be an effective competitive weapon (not tool) which can penetrate markets, alter buying preferences, and command economic leverage on future growth. How? Remember when Honda only made motor cycles and Sony only made cheap transistor radios? Better yet, remember when Toyota only made funny little cars?

Of all the measures of economic wealth the productive capability of manufacturing claims the most prodigious proportions of future risk free potential. And, with correct incorporation into a company growth strategy, a JIT manufacturing strategy can provide an unequalled opportunity for immediate improvement with the most direct, tangible benefit because of past inattention to the vital asset base of manufacturing resources.

Using manufacturing strategy as a competitive weapon has two prerequisites. They are:
1. Top management must believe executing the strategy is possible; and
2. An uncompromising dedication to achieving the strategy.

The first requirement is perhaps the most difficult because of an established intuition based on an acceptance of negatives and confirmed by experience which is an enormous attitude obstacle to overcome.

The second requirement is popularized by the characteristic of success "A Bias towards Action" from In Search of Excellence. By actually trying new things the learned experience of failure clarifies the direction of the next moves. The habit of continuous trials for learning, combined with a firm conviction that achieving the strategy is realizable with enough successful tries, creates the favorable environment in which the strategy likely will succeed.

THE STRATEGY ROLE OF MATERIALS MANAGEMENT

The role of production and inventory control has not often included setting, much less developing a manufacturing strategy for the company. Even when the position is elevated to materials manager and includes the purchasing, shipping and receiving functions the ability to effect a manufacturing strategy is still limited. What then can be done to bring about change?

There are three things of a tactical nature which can be done to prove that uncompromising dedication can make a ZI/JIT strategy work and also to convince top management that a Zero Inventory/Just-in-Time manufacturing strategy can be a reality for your company.
1. Attack Work in Process Inventory
2. Attack Material Cost
3. Attack the Cost Adding Overhead

All three of these areas are to a large degree controllable in the production and inventory control function, and to the extent that they are not, the P&IC influence can be the most profound in objectively evaluating the potential cost benefits for the company as a whole.

ATTACKING WORK IN PROCESS INVENTORY

Experience with Just-in-Time is consistantly proving that work in process is the throttle which activates the lever on productivity. The usual experience has been that a 40% to 60% reduction in work in process generates a 25% to 35% improvement in productivity. In a plant wide program, 70% or more of the productivity increase is caused by changing practices with little or no outlay of significant expense or capital monies. Any broad based JIT program must address these areas to achieve those gains:

    Set-up Reduction
    Material Handling Efficiencies
    Flow Pattern Improvements
    Multifunctional Skills
    Quality at the Source
    Lot Size Reductions
    Leveling Production
    Pull Signalling Controls

On a broad scale any practitioner would be foolish to institute a wholesale experiment with JIT production without addressing each of these issues. But as a trial to prove to yourself and possibly a few close peers from other functions its worth the risk. Every P&IC practitioner can think of one product or part family or isolated work center or department where, with a few daring colleagues, an experiment might be tried. Finding something or somewhere where the set-ups are not too bad, the quality is pretty good, the schedule is fairly level, the opera-

tions are arranged in a reasonable flow pattern with common types of skills required just could be an easy task. The only thing to do then is to reduce the lot sizes dramatically, and babysit the experiment. Observation as with every experiment should be accompanied by copious notes of detailed events as they unfold.

The surprises just might be that it works pretty well with significantly less inventory in process. That should not be too surprising because most JIT projects show that 50% of the set-up reduction comes from preparedness for the set-up; eliminating adjustments cuts it 15% to 25% more. Another surprise may be that set-ups are not always a problem anyhow except as a factor in unit cost, which presumes there is something equally productive to be doing instead of setting up, which an observer might be able to conclude would have been idle time. Some surprises might unfold in the quality as well. The claim that 15% of the defects are operator controllable and 85% of them are in the realm of management control could become a bit more realistic from the experiment. And the observer could also discover the informal flow pattern devised in the workplace along with the "real" part routing.

The experiment is sure to excite some new ideas at the minimum. And if one experiment is not enough, try another. Unless your factory is very unusual, the evidence gained ought to be very convincing to management to take the experiment to a broader base.

ATTACK MATERIAL COST

The plan of attack against material cost needs to begin with a rule that disallows beating on the vendor for a price reduction. That is the old fashioned way of reducing material costs which presumes every supplier to be a chiseler attempting to cheap his way to prosperity. Years of doing it the old fashioned way have honed experts in negotiating finesse in the astute buyer who regularly challenges the forces of clever, articulate sales representatives. Little is said about it but the adversarial relationships between these specialists of our companies pales the much heralded labor/management frictions.

The real material cost reductions probably cannot be gotten until we begin to bond a partnership relationship with our suppliers. Fundamental to really getting at the meat of material cost reductions is beginning to assemble all the parties of your company who have responsibility for material cost. As a production and inventory control functionary, the potential will be obvious from the fragmented exercise of the material selection process which takes place between sales, product design, purchasing, manufacturing engineering, and manufacturing. As a third party to the process, after the fact, but with the sole interest in facilitating a supplier partnership, you will be able to knowledgeably ask some crucial "what if" questions which will be the beginning of substantive cost reduction breakthroughs.

A serious endeavor into cooperative non-leveraged price concessions is characterized by the constantly recurring use of the interrogative "why". Why a casting? Why not an investment casting? Why is the volume so low? Why is this part different from that one which as the same function? Why is this part so heavy? Why round? Why are we such an insignificant portion of this supplier's business? Why don't we do this some other way? Why, why, why?

Selection of only a small segment of one product family can lead to some real avenues of substantial cost reduction, which is of mutual benefit to both you and your supplier. Sometimes the pursuit will lead to longer, larger commitments with the supplier. And sometimes the mutual benefit will be terminating a relationship where changing design benefits your cost while the supplier's benefit comes from ridding his company of a genuine nuisance quantity of special variety item. Remember, your supplier probably has many of the same cost problems that you have. A genuine effort to cooperate for mutual benefit with a supplier by discarding the arms length netotiating posture has these opportunities for material cost reduction:
  - Standardization of supply/materials/processes/ products
  - Exposure to the ideas of a dedicated specialist
  - Assessment of mutual procedure compromises (packaging, order/invoicing)
  - Familiarization of technology upgrading potential
  - Cooperation in demand/supply requirements (leveling)
  - Potential substitution of materials processes
  - Mutual understanding of problems/opportunities of interrelationship

The experience has shown that a 20% improvement can be
accomplished on a 60¢ material cost base.

ATTACK COST ADDING OVERHEAD

When production and inventory control practitioners
plan to attack the overhead areas it may almost seem as if
they are sharpening the razor to cut their own throat.
Considering the growth of overhead relative to the other
factors of production cost, that may be true unless the
competitive advantage is used as leverage on volume. But
it is probably better to do it yourself instead of waiting
for a competitor to do it for you.

It is interesting to note that the most mentioned
reason in a recent study for factory shutdowns was obsolete
production technology. That reason was followed closely by
price competition, severe market loss, cost pressures, and
labor productivity problems. But all these problems were
mainly from domestic competitors. Most factories don't
develop mediocrity overnight, they slide into it over time.
Among the major causes for the slide are:
- Generations of product proliferation
- Accumulated "Lean to" expansions of facility
- Excessive Overhead structure
- Deteriorating Mgt/Workforce relationships
- Dated production technology - Struggling to cope
  with complexity

All of these causes combine to create an uncompetitve
manufacturing environment with rampant waste. A simplistic
way to demonstrate the potential benefits to be achieved in
overhead areas is to construct an inventory flow model.
The model is based on the premise that during the manufacturing cycle there are only two possible activities:

      Value Adding operations

      Cost Adding operations

Since the specific value adding operations can be easily
identified through manufacturing route sheets and process
documentation the exact timing and duration can be pin-
pointed in colored bar chart fashion along the horizontal x
axis with the accumulating cost buildup plotted on the
corresponding vertical y axis. All areas under the profile
where value adding is not indicated can thus be assumed to
be potential cost adding activities.

The result is a graphic pictorial of where the leverage exists against cost adding operations during manufacture. It is quite common to admit to a 95% idle 5% value
adding proportion existant in the manufacturing lead times.
The graphic of this, however, brings focus to how and where
the most effective use of the elements of a Just-in-Time
production system can be applied to reduce overhead costs.
Also evident is the payback leverage on product redesign
and the application of automation for manufacturing cycle
reduction.

Another useful tool is a roadmap of movement for a
product line through the factory. Every direction change
and every brokering transaction through the stockroom is an
opportunity to reduce cost adding elements from the process.
Manufacturing concepts initiated at the outset of product
design that have crept into obsolescence are prime targets
for reconsolidation into efficient flow patterns with less
cost adding opportunity. And the surprising element is
just how much more effective manufacturing control systems
like MRP can operate when the flow is simplified. No administrative planning system can compensate for a process
that is too complex or has no pattern. The detailed reporting simply cannot keep up with the action in manufacturing.

The overhead costs that can be trimmed usually amount
to 30% to 40% and by leveraging direct labor into indirect
operations instead of into idle time waiting for parts,
materials, and inspections, the gains can be even higher.
Quality at the source is a perfect example of how to systematically incorporate this leveraging potential. The
fact is that in direct comparisons of U.S. to Japanese
manufacturers where quality at the source is widely practiced, the U.S. manufacturers have 3 to 15 times more inspectors with still 5 times the defects. Are those inspectors adding cost or value?

The evidence is mounting and the imperative is clear:
a move towards Zero Inventory/Just-in-Time is providing
focus for converging the strategies for manufacturing ex
cellence in the 1980's.

KENNETH J. MCGUIRE

KENNETH J. MCGUIRE, INC.

BACKGROUND PROFILE

Ken McGuire is the President of the management consulting firm of Kenneth J. McGuire, Inc., which specializes in
the field of Manufacturing Control and Systems Development.
The firm serves the needs of the manufacturing company in
the design and installation of manufacturing controls,
especially the implementation of Just-in-Time Production
Systems, Manufacturing Resource Planning, and other related
systems improvements.

Mr. McGuire has had extensive experience in manufacturing and systems. He served in both line and staff positions for over 15 years prior to establishing his own firm.

He received his formal education at Canisius College
where he earned a B.S. in Economics, and at Syracuse University, School of Management MBA program. He is an active
member of the American Production and Inventory Control
Society (APICS) Hartford Chapter, and has received APICS
certification at the Fellow Level. He has participated in
several APICS sponsored and other study missions to Japan
to study Japanese Productivity, Production and Inventory
Control techniques.

Mr. McGuire serves on the APICS Zero Inventory Steering Committee at the national level.

APPLYING JUST-IN-TIME IN A LARGE NORTH AMERICAN ELECTRONICS PLANT

K. I. Powell
J. C. Weddell, CPIM*
Northern Telecom Canada Ltd.

Northern Telecom Ltd., the second largest telecommunications manufacturer in North America, builds a diverse portfolio of high technology electronic products to satisfy constantly evolving and expanding international requirements. With the move into the Information Age, the Company has made a commitment to remain on the leading edge of technology in new and existing products. In keeping with this policy, the technology of manufacture must keep pace to ensure that these products are produced to high quality levels, on time, to customer needs and at the lowest cost possible. This is particularly true of the A&R Transmission Division where a variety of factors from specific customer needs to weather at installation sites influence manufacturing.

THE ENVIRONMENT

As North America is going through the transition from the traditional smokestack industries to the more high technology businesses, such as state of the art electronics we find the move taking place in manufacturing from high volume process-related operations to complex make-to-order or low volume job shop type operations. In the scramble for companies to be competitive, especially in light of the pressure being applied from overseas competitors, conditions which are less than optimal for Just-In-Time inventory management to work are at play.

A&R Transmission Division is part of the Transmission Group of Northern Telecom Ltd. The Division is located in St. Laurent, Quebec, and has responsibility worldwide for the manufacture of analog and digital microwave transmission equipment and systems. In addition, the plant manufactures a wide array of other products from analog and digital multiplex systems, private networks to voice frequency equipment.

The Division is currently working exceedingly hard at increasing penetration and market share in the U.S. market, particularly as a result of the AT&T divestiture and deregulation. In this marketing effort, primary competition is coming from the Japanese as well as the already entrenched supply sources. This strategy is forcing us toward J-I-T. Our definition of J-I-T says move faster with new product introduction, do things right the first time, at just the right moment while keeping costs in line to meet our profit targets. This environment, however, creates a series of factors which are less than conducive to a J-I-T philosophy. They are:

- Changing Product Mix & Volume,
- Proliferation of Product Options,
- Leading Edge Design Technology,
            Production Processes,
            Componentry,
- Reduced Design-To-Customer Leadtime,
- Large Portfolio,
- No Fixed MPS Time Fence,
- Large, Widespread Supplier Base.

To determine the impact of these factors on the use of J-I-T, we must take a closer look at the Just-In-Time philosophy itself.

J-I-T PRINCIPLES

The use of J-I-T, as reported by observers who have visited Japan and seen it in operation, embodies a set of rules for the conduct of business quite different from past practice in North America. These apply to relationships within the business as well as outside.

For example, consider our traditional approach to each of these components of our business environments:

- Labor,
- Vendors,
- Customers.

We have strived for flexibility in each of these areas; yet J-I-T's success is based upon stability.

Conversely, stability has been the watchword for the following:

- Equipment,
- Systems,
- Skills.

Again, the J-I-T experience is just the reverse, emphasizing flexibility.

Increasing inventory has been the universal solution for reducing problems to below the level of consciousness, though never solving most of them. Reducing inventories is the J-I-T technique for exposing problems so that they can be solved. With Pareto in mind, the J-I-T companies in Japan use the entire workforce - organized in Quality Circles - to resolve the "trivial many" problems while leaving the "vital few" to absorb management's attention.

J-I-T INVOLVES MORE THAN INVENTORY REDUCTION

Too often, the initial view of Just-In-Time, as reducing inventories on hand and in process, becomes the lasting impression. Much is missed in this simplistic view that deserves closer attention.

To highlight some of these ideas, let's return to the business components considered earlier with a J-I-T frame of mind.

- Labor (People) benefit from a stable level of employment, but also contribute more when the longer range objectives of both employee and company are seen as one.

- Vendors, likewise, enjoy the fruits of long term relationships and can adapt their practices as well as their facilities to your needs.

- Customers, the Japanese have taught us, will buy a reasonably priced quality product that is well-equipped without insistence upon custom-configuration or any of 999 color schemes.

- Equipment takes on a new meaning when terms like FMC (Flexible Manufacturing Cells) and SMED (Single Minute Exchange of Dies) are introduced.

- Systems, in the global sense, can be simplified and reduced in paperwork along the much discussed lines of KANBAN.

- Skills can be seen in a team sense, where the mix of people, their roles and capabilities respond to the needs of the occasion not an iron-clad job-descriptive straight-jacket.

J-I-T

These are some of the lessons we have seen which the Just-In-Time philosophy teaches. Putting them into action in our environment is obviously not an off-the-shelf application. The potential benefits, which include preservation of the business, are sufficient reason to make the necessary effort. The question is "how to implement J-I-T?"

THE J-I-T STRATEGY

The Division has a large and diversified product portfolio comprised of 3000 end item assemblies and a component data base approaching 45,000 items. Procurement of the majority of this material is achieved currently from about 2500 suppliers spread across most of the world, but focused in North America.

With this size of operation, it is inconceivable to launch into Just-In-Time in an uncontrolled fashion.

We settled upon a J-I-T strategy focused around three areas:

- Purchased Material,
- Manufactured Assemblies,
- Employee Involvement.

In each of these areas, we can strive for excellence in quality, flexibility, productivity, a commitment to people and communication.

PURCHASED MATERIAL

Purchased material accounts for approximately 70% of the product cost, therefore, this was and continues to be the area of focus. A stratification of material on the basis of forward annual dollar usage was performed and, using a Pareto distribution, determined that 3% of the items accounted for 80% of the dollar volume. These then were the items which could be scheduled to be available just in time while maintaining modified policies on the remaining low cost but not necessarily low volume components. In order to operate with J-I-T policies on this material, we had to address equipment and systems to handle material flow. In addition, we had to begin working more closely with our suppliers through a program we call V.I.P. - Vendor Integration Program.

MANUFACTURED ASSEMBLIES

The focus then on manufactured assemblies centered around product quality/productivity and reduced cycle times. To achieve quantum improvements in quality, the only answer is to automate, particularly as product size reduces and component densities increase. The ensuing quality improvement through automation also leads to better productivity through improved repeatability.

In order to be responsive to the market, drastically reduced cycle times are required. To achieve this, clean production flows are necessary, bottleneck work centers need to be addressed and material release must be carefully controlled.

EMPLOYEE INVOLVEMENT

Without people, nothing happens but, without people's commitment, nothing happens effectively. To achieve employee commitment in the traditional North American environment, born out of management-union conflict, takes and will continue to take considerable effort and time on the part of both sides. It is, we feel, management's responsibility to initiate the process and begin building the confidence that is the first step to operating in the spirit of mutual trust and cooperation. Through this spirit, we can look toward safeguarding all our jobs while continuing to support the lifestyles to which we have become accustomed.

Making a start in this area has been challenging, and we have just scraped the surface on this issue. We have begun a series of programs aimed at fostering communication in all directions, crossfunctional team-building through the use of value engineering/value analysis and employee involvement in problem-solving in the workplace.

To see how these activities relate to our earlier points, we should consider some of the efforts we have made in the Division.

LABOR

Improvements in our people-relationships will take longer than some other areas to bear results. We have to build faith in one another and that is not a fast process for humans. Communication is a vital ingredient. We've set up courses to train our Managers, at all levels, to be better managers. Through an Employee Involvement Program, our people are successfully learning about their role in product and service quality and the impact these have on jobs. Value analysis teams provide opportunities to employees, specialists and managers to participate in joint efforts to improve our environment and practices. Included in this process is senior divisional management, with the General Manager and Director of Manufacturing conducting information sessions for all employees.

VENDORS

The objectives of the Vendor Integration Program (VIP) include building closer relationships with fewer vendors. Progress is easier to achieve here because the two-way benefits are readily apparent very early in the process. Through Value Analysis/Value Engineering sessions, cost improvements have been created with mutual gain. We have even taken our people on-site to conduct VA/VE sessions for VIP vendors. Even some geographic gains have been made with a significant vendor selecting a new plant site nearby.

CUSTOMERS

This will be the hardest area to tackle for, let's face it, having encouraged the customer to "have it your way", we cannot just cut back to three flavors without causing offence. It will take time and skill in product design to move toward greater standardization of product features while keeping customer satisfaction at a high level. The increasing ability to use soft and firmware to set final product configuration in the electronics world will doubtless play a role in this direction. There is, however, a recognition that the customer is "king" and we must meet his needs first and foremost.

EQUIPMENT

The emphasis here has been on improved quality hand-in-hand with productivity. Automation of highly repetitious activity has been the key. Being able to repeat many small tasks precisely is a prime consideration in quality production of many products, particularly electronic ones. The resultant reduction in cycle times not only reduces inventories, it greatly simplifies the obstacles to flexibility and thus aids scheduling. Lot sizes can be kept low due to the adaptability of the automated assembly equipment.

SYSTEMS

We have to overcome the "new theory" mystique of Just-In-Time. Rather than a new theory, it's a philosophy that ties together many of the basic concepts of our existing MRPII systems. J-I-T implies a higher level of coordination between the inter-related events controlled by the materials people and systems. Like a touchdown pass or a triple-play, it's all in the precision timing. Computer systems have provided us with the opportunity to reduce our prior reliance on paper and thus reduce cycle times for our activities. New on-line Purchasing, Stockroom, Data Base Management and Receiving/Inspection systems are coupled with advanced material handling systems that emphasize flow. The simplicity of Toyota's Kanban cards represent an ideal to strive for. We are using bar coding of shop transactions as a step in this direction. Shop floor applications in automated and manual test areas are another paperless achievement.

SKILLS

Our production processes tend to emphasize individual activity rather than team work. To help bring people together and utilize their brainpower in team efforts, we have established VA/VE groups that have already tackled several substantial aspects of process improvement. Material supply to production, supplier packaging, handling of sensitive materials are all areas that have benefitted from this effort. Office routines have also benefitted from this type of analysis, for example product documentation routines.

OTHER ASPECTS OF J-I-T

INVENTORIES

The thrust of J-I-T philosophy may cover many areas, but the impact on inventory levels is too substantial to ignore. When you can get substantially better control on virtually 60% of your cost of product by using Just-In-Time-based policies on 5% of the purchased material, you know you're onto something good. Though, as we have seen, the benefits are not isolated to inventory.

SCHEDULES

A reliable schedule has always been the key to
successful MRP. This is very much the case with J-I-T.
Syncronization of the many variables affecting the schedule
has always been the problem. The Kanban is Toyota's solution to the problem of syncronization. In North America,
for all the reasons we have cited and more, we must rely on
reduced cycle times for all activity (not just WIP) along
with better systems to achieve this syncronization.

DATA ACCURACY

Reducing inventory levels brings out the formerly
hidden problems in our processes and practices. It also
exposes us, especially as our materials activity cycle
times reduce, to the hazards of unreliable data. Accuracy
is the key ingredient in reliable material management
decision-making. We cannot afford to be unreliable.

THE FUTURE

As we continue along the problem finding and fixing
path to Just-In-Time, what do we expect to find? That
progress will continue to be made in bite-sized portions.
That constant monitoring and feedback - bottom to top and
back - will be needed to avoid slipping back in those areas
where gains have been made. That management must not only
be committed but must remain committed. You can't let
success spoil you.

What challenges lie ahead? Well, the latest thinking
centers on Zero Inventories!

KEITH I. POWELL is currently Director of Materials for the
A&R Transmission Division of Northern Telecom Canada Ltd.
Keith has over 16 years of experience in materials, production and inventory control in high tech industries
such as aerospace and telecommunications. He has been a
speaker at the APICS Conference as well as at CAPIC
National & Chapter meetings. He holds a B.Sc. degree
from Sir George Williams University (Concordia) and an
M.B.A. from McGill Unversity in Montreal.

J. CLARK WEDDELL CPIM* is currently Manager of Manufacturing Systems Development for the A&R Transmission Division
of Northern Telecom Canada Ltd. Clark, who has held
various senior materials positions in the electronics,
food and pharmaceutical industries over the past twenty
years, was one of the first two Canadians recognized as a
CPIM Fellow by APICS. He holds a B.A. degree from Loyola
of Montreal (Concordia) and a diploma in Management from
McGill University. A speaker at the APICS and CAPIC
Conferences, Clark has also addressed a number of CAPIC
Chapter meetings as well as various other groups. A past
president of Montreal Chapter, he has served as a Director
on the Region VIII Board and is currently a member of the
Advisory Council of Montreal Chapter.

TOTAL INVENTORY PLANNING: FROM MRP I TO MRP II AND ON TO JIT/TQC

Robert H. Murphy, Jr., CPIM*
Charles G. Andrew & Co.

Abstract

Let's stop asking for commitment and saying we need more discipline to make our information systems work! We need to examine our systems and determine if a reasonable manager would use them. This paper examines these support systems and comes to the conclusion that those which generate isolated solutions are doomed to fail. We must develop systems which are not suboptimizing but assist the management team to increase the organization's profits. This presentation explains not only the what to do, but also the how to for achieving positive results.

The exciting part of this process is that we are almost there. Our existing information systems can be integrated to help the management team on a coordinated basis. The focal point for that coordination is the inventory plan and current performance in relation to planned actions. Everyone on the management team has a responsibility for a part of the inventory plan. By encouraging their working together (commitment!), the organization can achieve increased productivity and profitability.

Applying the Total Inventory Planning concept is itself a progressive journey and this paper describes in step-by-step fashion how to make that journey successfully--first from MRP to MRP II at a company level and then on to Just-In-Time P&IC at the shop floor level.

Introduction

"Watch your inventory as you watch your weight. A sudden or unexpected change in either is a sign of potential serious trouble." This sage piece of advice from Peerless Topman in George Plossl and Evert Welch's book, The Role of Top Management in the Control of Inventory, has prompted many managers to take a closer look at their inventory, how it is controlled and how it is changing.

Historical Perspective

During the 1960's and 1970's, manufacturing management attempted to replace its order-point-based production and inventory control systems with formal material requirement planning systems (MRP I). Although there were spectacular successes, the vast majority of management saw only minor improvements in inventories, customer service or profits. In fact, in many areas, these key performance factors moved in the wrong direction! In order to remedy these failures, some manufacturing managers started on their own personal (and frustrating) odyssey to find the perfect MRP system for their companies. A few implementation checklists and guidelines were developed by consultants to improve the probability of successful MRP implementation.

By the mid-1970's, enough experience had been gained using, or misusing, MRP that the importance of the Master Production Schedule was realized. Consultants, educators, and practitioners reasoned that MRP is a planning process which starts with items having independent demands and rigorously calculates demands for all dependent items. Consequently, the Master Production Schedule, as the statement of future demand for the independent items, is the critical controlling factor on the entire process.

Again, the manufacturing managers started on a search for the perfect master production scheduling system which would solve all their problems. Unfortunately, the results were mixed.

By the late 1970's, the educators and consultants reminded us that the material requirements plan was only one of many plans in a manufacturing company and that all of the plans should be coordinated if management expected to realize any of them. They renamed MRP to mean Manufacturing Resource Planning (MRP II) and proposed that it be expressed in financial terms so that it could also function as the major budgeting tool for the company.

Later, the Business Requirements Planning (BRP) concept was developed which recommended starting with the company's overall business plan and gradually progressing through the marketing plan, the manufacturing plan, the master schedule, the materials plan, and the capacity plan until all of the major plans for the company were developed and coordinated.

The power of the computer to enhance the planning process was being felt throughout the organization. The only problem was that results continued to be mixed with minimal successes and "business as usual" in most companies. Of the companies with successes, there seemed to be a common set of circumstances.

First, top management was interested in the project and used the system to actively lead the company. Second, a major crisis or series of crises arose which made it obvious that drastic change was required. Third, once major successes were achieved, the formal system received legitimacy to such a level that the managers applied peer pressure to their compatriots to attend the educational sessions on the new concepts and to achieve additional or continued successes.

In summary, the system was used to develop a coordinated set of plans but, more importantly, management worked to achieve those plans or explain why not. Consequently, the plans were better, and more achievable to begin with, and everyone expected them to be followed/realized.

What about the other companies, the non-successes? These companies were not really failures. In many cases, they made large profits. They just did not completely achieve the planned benefits from the MRP projects. APICS seminars and P&IC literature is full of presentations blaming the managers of these companies for not being "committed." If asked, each of the managers would disagree. They would talk about the money they spent, the educational sessions they attended, the people they hired, and the meetings they ran. However, if asked which part of the systems they used, we would get blank stares. As Plossl and Welch told us, they should have been watching their inventory levels and investigating any sudden unexpected change.

Analysis of the Problem

We believe that the MRP/MRP II theory is correct. The leading consultants and educators usually present a closed loop model which includes both planning and control. The facts are that the applications of the MRP and MRP II theory were not entirely successful. Since we are embarking on an even more difficult leg of the productivity journey, JIT/TQC (Just-in-Time/Total Quality Control), we should take a closer look at the MRP/MRP II application to determine what was lacking.

MRP was developed as a better demand planning technique under the responsibility of the Production and Inventory Control Department. As evidenced by the MRP reports produced by most software packages, the emphasis is only on planning (see Exhibit 1). None of the reports provide any analysis which compares actual performance to plans. "Closing the Loop" was interpreted as meaning: check the material availability; check the capacity availability; confirm that the plan is feasible in relation to planned material availability or capacity. As long as the planned load was within the planned capacity then the "loop" was "closed" even if the company had not realized the plan in the past.

Exhibit 1

Order Quantity = Lot for Lot   Lead Time = 2   On Hand = 0

		1	2	3	4	5	6	7	8
Week No.		1	2	3	4	5	6	7	8
Required				30		25		35	
Scheduled Receipt				30					
Available	0	0	0	0	0	−25		−35	
Planned Due						25		35	
Planned Release				25		35		20	

MRP II expanded on the MRP theory by expressing the plan in financial terms and potentially providing a forecast to top management for the profitability of the entire business. Few members of top management used the projections. The reports were typically used by the Materials Manager, the Master Scheduler and the Marketing Manager during the master schedule meeting. The MRP II report showed projections with no comparison of actual performance in relation to the plan. Few financial managers trusted the projections. The reason seems obvious as soon as we evaluate the financial managers' management reports.

Most financial reports (Exhibit 2) present actual results in relation to historical results and plans. The financial managers analyze the differences as variances and attempt to determine the causes without knowing the details.

In summary, the Materials Manager focuses on planning to the extent that performance against plan, although recognized as important, is not analyzed in detail to

<u>Exhibit 2</u>

INVENTORY PLAN
FORECAST REPORT
GENERAL LEDGER SYSTEM
Month Ending Nov. 30, 1984

	Beg. Bal	Year to Date Actual	Year to Date Plan	Budget to Year End	Forecast at Year End Forecast	Forecast at Year End Plan
Inventory	100					
Purch.		50	40	10	60	50
Labor		30	25	5	35	30
Overhead		20	15	5	25	20
Sales		(90)	(100)	(15)	(105)	(115)
Inventory		110	80	5	115	85

determine causes and to improve performance in the future. In contrast, the Financial Manager focuses on performance against the plan assuming that the plan was valid. Frequently, the financial plan is based on historical product mixes or ratios which are not consistent with the current facts.

<u>Proposed Solution</u>

Let's review what we have said and determine where it leads us.

1. MRP/MRP II theory is valid. Most plans are dependent on a few (independent) plans. Once the major assumptions concerning sales and inventory levels have been made, then other plans for production, purchasing, personnel, cash flow, etc., can be derived from the master plans.

2. Top management must be able to use the few (independent) plans to manage the business. The concept of "Planning the work and working the plan" is valid. Top management must be able to "Close the Loop" in terms of not only validating that the original plans are feasible but also achieving the tasks/results specified by the plan. Unfortunately, many top managers are concerned only with making profit plans and sales/shipment plans. They feel that other plans are details delegated to their staff and do not require executive attention. This viewpoint is rapidly changing as more emphasis is being placed on management's ability to produce a reasonable return on investment and a major controllable portion of that investment is inventory.

3. Every manager should have the following understanding:

   o His plan supports the major business plan
   o He has the resources and authority to achieve the plan
   o He feels responsible for achieving the plan.
   o He is measured/evaluated/rewarded for meeting the plan.

Given these observations, we need a plan which is important to top management, that we can relate to all other plans, and that can be used to assign responsibility for its realization. The Inventory Plan discussed by Plossl and Welch (Exhibit 3) satisfies these prerequisites.

<u>Exhibit 3</u>

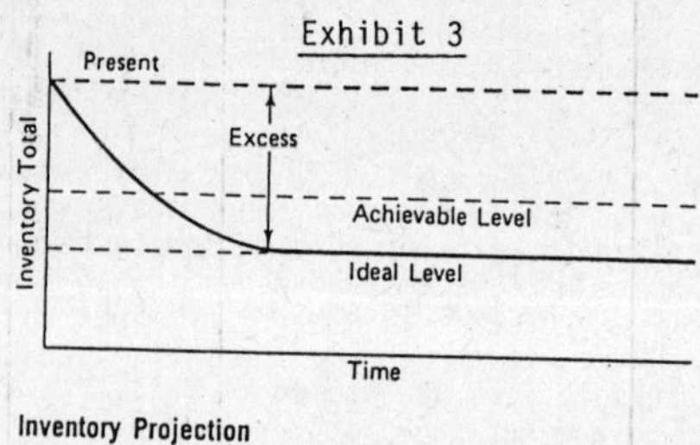

Inventory Projection

The level of inventory is a key performance indicator for top management. Whenever anything goes wrong, inventory tends to increase whether it be from errors in sales forecasting, missed production schedules, excessive absenteeism or poor vendor performance. An unexpected increase in inventory hurts return on investment. An unexpected decrease in inventory decreases sales and profits. In all cases, top management's performance is adversely affected.

The inventory plan is easily shown as the result of lower level plans. How to develop/prepare these lower level plans is covered by many readings/seminars. My only intent is to show that in total they produce the Inventory Plan. Exhibit 4 shows that inventory at the end of each period is equal to the sum of the beginning inventory balance plus material, labor, and overhead minus shipments and adjustments. Each of these lower level factors or functions requires a plan. The power of this concept is that the plans can be tied together and a manager can be assigned the responsibility for achieving each plan. Some of the plans directly relate to one manager, for example, Direct Labor or Purchasing. Other plans require two or more managers to work together. For example, the forecast of customer orders and the production plan must work together and be achieved in order to meet the Sales Plan.

<u>Exhibit 4</u>

```
Month - Starting Inventory
Inputs
    Purchased Materials & Parts
    Direct Labor
    Burden
    Decreases in Reserves
    Total Inputs

Outputs
    Sales
    Indirect Materials
    Increases in Reserves
    Total Outputs

Month-Ending Inventory
```

Even more important than the ability to correlate the plans and assign responsibilities is the ease with which the inventory plan can be used to evaluate actual results versus planned. The Inventory Projection, Exhibit 3, is simply the "Month-Ending Inventory" from the Inventory Plan, Exhibit 4. Most MRP II systems provide the data to prepare the Inventory Projection. In order to show the supporting plans, it is best to present the data in a cumulative fashion. Exhibit 5 shows outputs (sales), and inputs (labor, overhead and purchases) respectively. Exhibit 5 shows that the difference between cumulative graphs of outputs and inputs is the graph of planned inventory. The planned inventory is the responsibility of top management. This is the only level at which all of the lower level plans come together. Up until this point, we have done nothing other than graph information which was available for our MRP II system. However, learning from our previous analysis, we can improve on these graphs as a management tool by showing actual performance against past plans. Exhibit 6 shows the past six months of experience and the next six months of planned inventory level. With this tool in front of the top management group, and the understanding that inventory levels are a key factor in monitoring performance to plan, we should be able to get their attention and <u>commitment</u>!

Exhibit 5

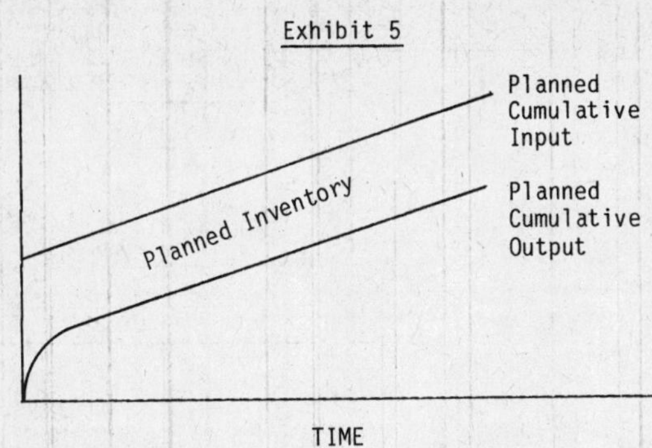

We can provide the same graphs for sales, production, and purchasing respectively. These graphs should get the attention of these managers as they prepare to report on their performance to top management.

Exhibit 6

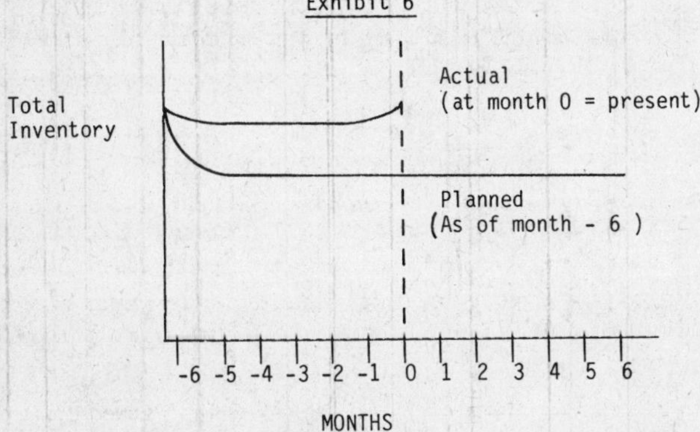

Let's see where we are. We have developed a management tool which coordinates all plans in terms of responsible managers for use by top management. We will most likely use the skills of the financial analyst to help us to identify the causes of the variances. However, we still have one basic problem, the plan. The planned inventory is based on the MRP II system. There are two factors at work which may mean that the inventory plan from MRP II is not the correct base to measure performance. First, data may not be correct. This is so basic that most practitioners will immediately dismiss it. I only include it at this time because most of the systems I review have a huge amount of past due customer orders, manufacturing orders and purchase orders. No manager truly expects these orders to be completed on schedule; they are already past due! Therefore, any inventory plan based on this data will be incorrect. Second, top management has plans for the inventory which are not reflected in the formal system. They either overstate the sales plan or master schedule to give middle management <u>incentive</u> or they arbitrarily set an inventory goal without making the proper adjustment to the system inputs. In either case, management has a different inventory level in mind than that shown by the formal system; therefore, they do not feel committed to meeting the formal goal. In order to receive the benefits from MRP II, top management must believe in the Inventory Plan and lead its company's effort to achieve it.

The previous section explained the importance of the Company's Inventory Plan in achieving the benefits of MRP II. The next section will present the need for extending the Total Inventory Plan concept to the shop floor in order to realize the benefits of JIT/TQC.

Implications for JIT/TQC - For MRP Users

As we join the Zero Inventory Crusade, we are not only increasing the benefits of performing to schedule but also increasing the penalty for missing the schedule. MRP removed the safety stock at interim levels and delayed production until the standard (usually inflated) lead time. MRP II increased the stakes by generating the financial plan for the entire company from the operating plan. Now

the Zero Inventory Crusade and the JIT/TQC (Just-in-Time/ Total Quality Control) movement is reducing the inventory even further and converting the manufacturing operations from batch production to flow production. This latest change drastically increases the importance of performing to schedule because there is no inventory buffer to rely on.

Before we discuss why the Total Inventory Planning concept is needed in a JIT environment, it might be helpful to briefly describe how a typical JIT system works and identify its shortcomings for all manufacturing managers, not just those in the U.S.

The APICS sponsored booklet, "Driving the Productivity Machine-Production Planning and Control in Japan" by Robert W. Hall, 1981, presents an excellent but simple description of Toyota's JIT system, Kanban, and the overall approach for production methods improvements, KANBAN. At the risk of oversimplifying this paper, I will concentrate on the Kanban system itself and assume that the overall KANBAN improvements to reduce setups, relayout the factory, improve quality and generally convert from batch production to flow production are in place and operating. The Kanban system uses a "pull" approach to control the production and movement of parts through the manufacturing process. Authorization to produce more of a particular part is given only after that part is consumed at the next work station. The parts are "pulled" through the production process by actual events. If production stops at an assembly work station, no parts are consumed and no parts are manufactured. This system is in contrast to a typical MRP system which is based on a "push" concept. Parts are produced and moved through the manufacturing process based on the weekly schedule. Parts are "pushed" through the process according to the schedule without any consideration as to circumstances at assembly work centers until the next MRP run is processed.

Both Kanban and MRP users have "blind spots" in their systems. The Kanban users will be told to stop production but will not be told what else to make until the next planning run. MRP users will continue to make the excess inventory until the next planning run. We need something in between our planning system, MRP, and our execution system, Kanban.

Most managers have realized that their existing shop floor control systems must be replaced by a "Kanban" type system to support the JIT concept, however they have tried to adapt their existing planning systems and procedures, which were designed for the MRP/MRP II control concept, to JIT. Few people are talking about the major change which has to occur in their shop floor planning and measurement system. We are told by the gurus: "It's easy! Inventory in total, especially on the shop floor, is intentionally reduced to create problems. When you find a problem, solve it and reduce the inventory again!" The example is given of a boat (the company) on a lake filled with water (inventory) and occasional rocks (problems). No skipper would intentionally wait to hit a rock! He would send someone forward to warn him of problems which he could not see from his position in the stern.

Our shop floor planning systems have to warn us <u>ahead of time</u> that we are out of control. They have to be <u>excellent</u> predictors of pending difficulties. Our product is flowing too fast to do otherwise. Our shop floor planning, execution and performance measurement systems have the same requirements discussed previously. They have to be of interest to multiple levels of management; they have to be used to hold managers accountable for performance; and they have to be expressed in the same terms as higher level plans. The Total Inventory Planning concept has the capability to support JIT. An Inventory Plan for a work center on the shop floor can warn of impending difficulties and help to manage the area. The Inventory Plan will look like the well-known Input-Output Control Analysis (Exhibit 7) presented by a number of authors.

The adaptation which we have made is to convert hours of work into "days of supply" of inventory in order to support the JIT concept.

The best way to illustrate how an inventory plan for a work center would help a foreman to anticipate problems and maintain control of his production process is to use two graphs (Exhibits 8 and 9). Exhibit 8 shows the planned

Exhibit 7

	Work Center 15				All Data in Standard Hours	
			Week No.			
	27	28	29	30	31	32
Input:						
Planned	170	170	170	170	170	170
Actual	175	165	130	155		
Cum. Diff.	+5	—	−40	−55		
Output:						
Planned	200	200	200	200	170	170
Actual	205	160	180	195		
Cum. Diff.	+5	−35	−55	−60		
Work-in-process						
Planned	240	210	180	150	150	150
Actual	240	245	195	155		

cumulative inputs and outputs for the particular work
center's output storage area. To simplify the illustration, we have shown one line for each. However we could
also have a number of supporting graphs for each product
which passes through the work center if it made multiple
products. We have also assumed a fixed rate of flow, in
and out, whereas most work centers have minimum and maximum
rates for both production and moves. Exhibit 9 represents
the inventory at the work center which is merely the difference between the cumulative production less the cumulative moves. Exhibit 9 is the shop planner's control
device. The cumulative graphs answer his questions when
the inventory graph tells him he has a problem. Here is
where the power of the concept becomes apparent. MRP would
tell him when to order one lot of material if he needed
only one piece at some time in the future. Kanban tells
him to make one piece as he needs it with minimal information about the future. By using the inventory planning
technique at the work center, the shop planner can obtain
some flexibility by setting upper and lower guidelines for
the inventory. As his inventory plan tells him

Exhibit 8

Work Center No. 9 Storage Area

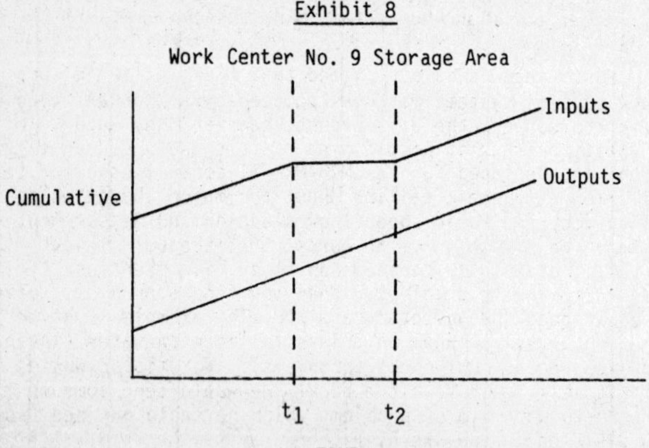

that he will be approaching his lower limit at a specific
time in the future, he can decide whether to increase production or allow the inventory to run out if he determines
that his future need for this item is also decreasing.
With existing JIT systems, he had only one option, increase
production. With existing MRP systems, he would have been
told to make another lot or make nothing. <u>The inventory
plan easily shows him his options in time to plan the
solution.</u> There are no stopped lines, no red lights, no
"rocks in the inventory lake" and no emergency situations
which have to be solved right away.

Conversely, as the inventory plan tells the shop
planner that the inventory at the work center will exceed
the upper limit at a future point in time, he has the
option to increase the production at the next work center
or decrease the production at this work center. If he
decides to decrease the production at this work center, he
can tell how much to decrease it and for how long (Exhibit
10). This is a major advantage over the existing Kanban
system which just notifies manufacturing to stop production
now! The inventory planning technique can be used by the
shop planner to determine when to stop production and, more

important, how long it will be stopped. With this information, the shop planner can schedule a second item to be
produced in the interval. This forward planning capability
is very important because, although he may have "single
digit set-ups" for machine change over, he still needs to
have some warning to prepare his set-up teams to switch
from one product to another.

Exhibit 9

Work Center No. 9 Storage Area

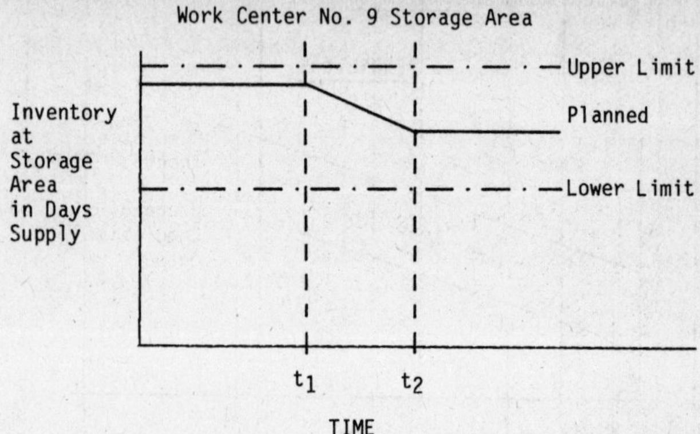

Exhibit 10

Work Center No. 9 Storage Area

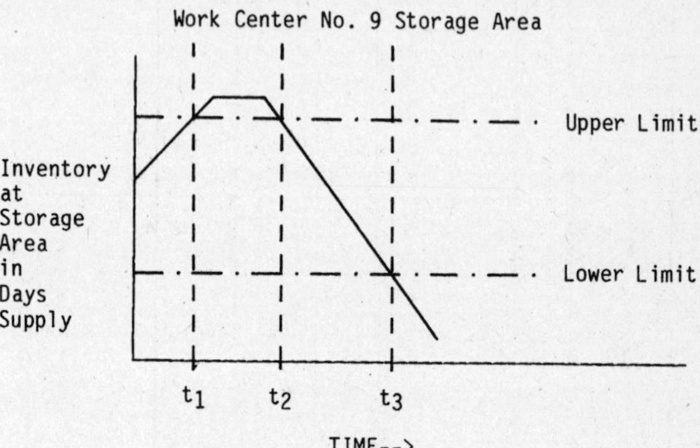

t_1 = latest date to stop/slow production
t_2 = earliest date to start production
t_3 = latest date to start production

The exciting thing about this whole concept is that
the technology is here. The problem is that the technology
is in pieces: the MRP plans are usually on a business computer; the JIT concepts are manual procedures known to
management and manufacturing managers; and the personal
computers are available to act as terminals to obtain the
data from the business computer and present it to management in graphic format. Does this mean that the inventory
plan is a computer concept? No! Just as MRP and the Zero
Inventory Crusade focused on techniques for tools but
depended on management for results, the Total Inventory
Planning concept is a management concept which provides
each level of management, from the executive suite to the
shop floor, with a closed loop management system to plan
and control its area of responsibility to achieve planned
results. The common language is inventory whether we're
talking about the total inventory for the company or merely
the inventory at a work center. Let's look at the Inventory Plan for a work center as a closed loop presentation.

The work center's inventory plan should show plan
versus actual for the last few weeks and the plan and projected actual for the future. The inventory plan satisfies
the closed loop concept because it provides the shop planner with the feedback information to control the process
and achieve the planned results. The planner would not
have to look at every part going through every work center,
just those parts which are exceeding the inventory limits
at their work centers. Exhibit 11 shows an inventory plan
with four weeks of history and four weeks of future. The
trend is disturbing since inventory is increasing. If we

had been on plan, we would have been in good shape. Our projection shows that we will exceed our upper limit by the third week.

Exhibit 11

Work Center No. 9

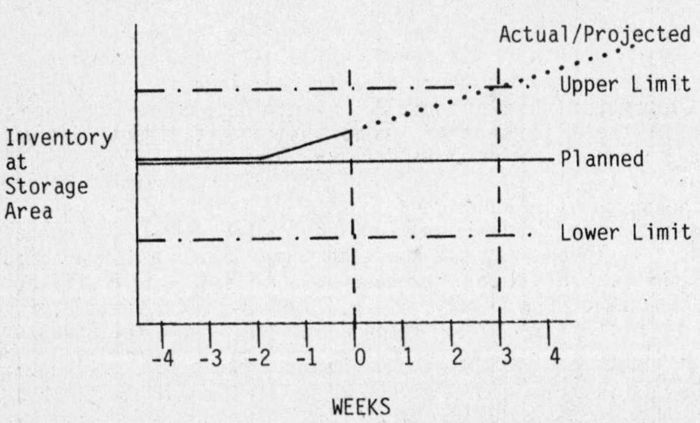

The cumulative graph (Exhibit 12) shows what happened.

Exhibit 12

Work Center No. 9

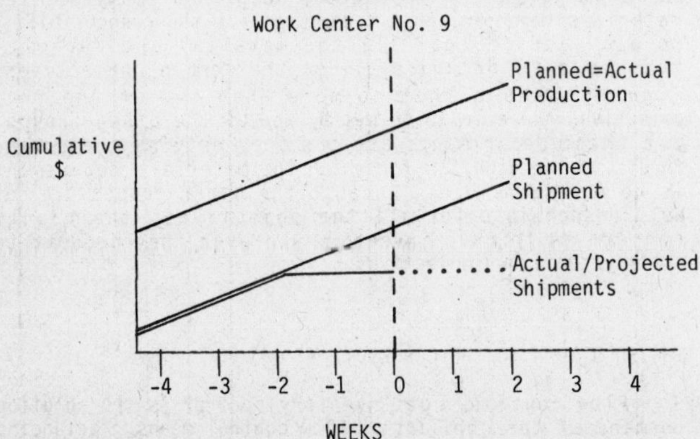

Receipts are progressing according to plan but moves/ shipments have stopped. We need to look at the next work center, because the moves at work center number 9 are directly related to production at work center number 10. Work center number 10 (Exhibit 13) shows that production has stopped and will remain stopped for two weeks. Knowing the planned consumption rate from work center number 10, the shop planner can tell that production of this part at work center number 9 will be stopped for four weeks. He can then review his other work for work center number 9 and select a job which is needed but will run less than four weeks, or he can decide to schedule a major overhaul for the machine or tools.

Exhibit 13

Work Center No. 10

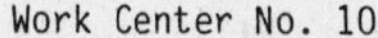
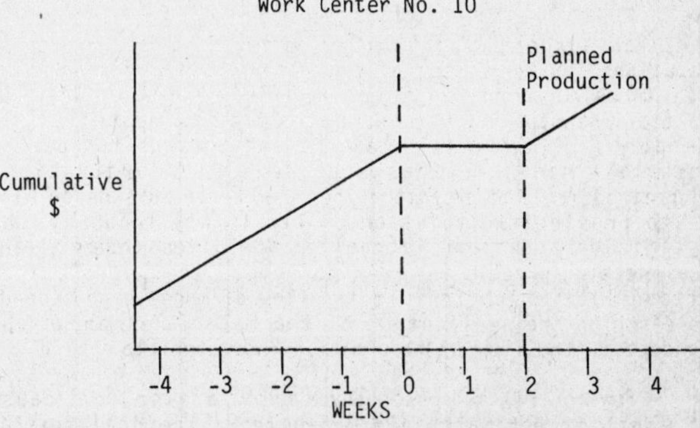

Our MRP systems have been criticized as being too nervous. We have tried to reduce the fluctuation by adding filters to the planning logic. Kanban systems, on the other hand, allow fluctuations, up to +10%, by having excess capacity; however, when the fluctuations exceed 10%, they give no guidance as to what to do. The Total Inventory Planning logic allows fluctuation within the agreed upon inventory limits and provides warnings when the limits will be exceeded in time for the planner to take action.

<u>Summary</u>

1. MRP and MRP II are excellent planning systems but provide poor support to operations.

2. JIT/TQC is an excellent operating system but does not always do a good job of handling changes to the short range plan.

3. Few of the existing systems satisfy the closed loop concept of helping management to "Plan the work and work the Plan".

4. The Total Inventory Planning concept closes the loop from MRP to MRP II to JIT.

5. Total Inventory Planning provides managers with complete, consistent information to plan their work and measure (evaluate) their results.

<u>ROBERT H. MURPHY, JR., CPIM*</u>

Mr. Murphy is Vice-President of Charles G. Andrew & Co., a management counseling and education firm specializing in the manufacturing industry. He has had 16 years of experience in the field of Production and Inventory Control, including positions as Production Control Manager, Project Leader and Consulting Manager. Mr. Murphy has designed, implemented and worked with systems in various environments, including make-to-stock, assemble-to-order and make-to-order manufacturing companies.

Mr. Murphy is active in APICS having served as Co-chairman of the 1981 International Conference. He is Past President of the Hartford County Chapter and was Chairman of the Region I Chapter President's Council. He is certified at the Fellow level and is an active speaker at Chapter meetings, seminars, and certification sessions. Mr. Murphy graduated from Stanford University with a major in Industrial Engineering and received his M.B.A. from the University of Connecticut.

FLOW CONTROL, NOT INVENTORY CONTROL! THE ROLE OF MATERIALS MANAGEMENT IN THE EIGHTIES

Dennis R. Fisher, CPIM
The Gus Berger Group

PURPOSE

The purpose of this paper is to identify and propose solutions for the causes of conflict caused by misguided attempts to control inventory levels rather than to control inventory flow in manufacturing organizations. It proposes to address a major trend towards the use of materials management as a concept of coordination, organization, and profits. The results of this paper will be to provide two solutions: first, how to apply the Optimized Production Technology (OPT) techniques to the goal-setting process in order to remove the basic causes of conflict which inhibit the flow of money, and second, to describe the application of the materials management concept to the flow of information and materials.

Flow control addresses three basic areas: the cause of conflict for materials management; the goal-setting processes that drive the materials organization; and the organizational aspects of authority, delegation and measurements of performance.

THE CONFLICTING OBJECTIVES

It is common practice in most manufacturing organizations to have a set of the following objectives.

1. Reduce product cost
2. Increase customer service
3. Reduce inventory
4. Increase facilities utilization

These goals are obviously valid. However, this apparently innocent looking set of goals creates a considerable set of conflicts within four major functional areas of the organization; manufacturing, marketing, finance and materials management. Figure 1 illustrates these conflicting objectives.

A close look at the manufacturing department's performance to the objectives would reveal that it is actually the ability to make long runs without breaking set-ups that is the primary requirement for the department to reduce product cost and increase facilities utilization. Naturally, this will require raw material inventories in front of those long-running machines. However, as demands change for customer service, these long runs inhibit the ability of the company to provide all products to the customer when needed. Also, inventory

is being built at the same time. The marketing group has the responsibility for maximizing customer service, but in order to do so they must have more finished goods inventory whenever required. This means shorter runs for the manufacturing group, along with higher product costs and even lower facilities utilization.

The general accounting group in the finance department has a goal to reduce costs throughout the company. This requires an overall reduction of inventories from every department. It's easy to see what a conflict this produces. Within the same financial department is another group that is at direct odds with the general accounting group - cost accounting. Their goals are to reduce product cost which inevitably forces the purchasing department to buy larger lots in order to get favorable discounts which reduce the unit purchase cost in inventory. At the same time, they want long runs from manufacturing for the same reason. Thus, if cost accounting were to have its way, product cost would drop and facilities utilization would go up, but the inventory levels would increase and the customer service would go down.

The role for materials management in this conflicting goals scenario becomes one of considerable consequence to the entire organization. The major goal of the materials department is to set and maintain valid schedules which must balance the demands for inventory made by the other functional groups. Much to the chagrin of many a fired Materials Manager, this department has the responsibility to plan and control all the material and capacity resources to optimize all of the company objectives. Figure 1 shows that no more than two of the four objectives are able to be met by any of the other groups, yet these departments are the ones driving the demand inputs to the schedule for which the materials department is held responsible. Because the other groups are not held responsible for all the objectives, their only concern is to have inventory wherever they need it to satisfy their own objectives.

THE SOLUTIONS TO THE CONFLICT

Flow control, not inventory control is the solution to many of the conflicts. Flow control means: <u>balancing the priorities which control the utilization of capacity and materials.</u> Priorities are driven by decisions about what comes first. If the flow of inventory is the objective which drives the company, then flow control must begin with a set of logical objectives.

The Optimized Production Technology (OPT) approach to goal-setting will be the guidelines for defining objectives in this paper. Simply stated, the only goals that are valid for a manufacturing organization are to:

REDUCE INVENTORY
INCREASE THROUGHPUT

Throughput is defined as "money generated as a result of selling product." As a consequence, any inventory that is generated that is not part of an inventory plan will be considered as an expense and will be charged to the department whose actions caused it to be generated. This clearly changes the definition of the conflicting objectives mentioned previously. It states that any actions not directly tied to the flow of materials will be considered as a cost of doing business which can be applied to any of the functions in a company and most importantly, can be used as a measurement of performance.

The guiding philosophy for OPT, Just-in-Time, and Zero Inventory is the control of the flow of materials (Figure 2).

The flow of money is usually seen as the results of the actions presented after the fact. Usually it is represented by variances to budget, adjustments to inventory levels or even getting loans from the bank to support high inventory levels. Inventory control is perceived by many companies as something that is a stand-alone activity. This misconception cannot be further from the truth. No function in an organization is a stand-alone activity. All activities are integrated by the nature of the flow of materials.

THE CONFLICTING OBJECTIVES

OBJECTIVE	PRODUCT COST	CUSTOMER SERVICE	INVENTORY	FACILITY UTILIZATION
COMPANY	↓	↑	↓	↑
-MANUFACTURING LONG RUNS	↓*	↓**	↑	↑
-MARKETING MAX. CUST. SERVICE	↑	↑	↑	↓
-FINANCE MIN. ASSET COST	↑	↓	↓	↓
-FINANCE LOW PRODUCT COST	↓	↓	↑	↑

*MET THE OBJECTIVE   **MISSED THE OBJECTIVE

THE GUS BERGER GROUP, INC.

(Figure 1)

(Figure 2)

The management of inventory flows requires several good business practices. The business practices listed in Figure 3 represent the basic building blocks for flow control and will be the format for the balance of this paper.

THE MANAGEMENT OF INVENTORY

REQUIRED BUSINESS PRACTICES INCLUDE:

1. CLEAR CUT LOGICAL OBJECTIVES

2. AN INVENTORY PLAN

3. VALID SCHEDULES

4. DATA INTEGRITY

5. MEASUREMENTS OF PERFORMANCE

6. SOMEONE TO DO IT

(Figure 3)

THE MANAGEMENT OF INVENTORIES

1. Clear-cut Logical Objectives

The Opt techniques for goal-setting were established earlier. The practical issue of setting an inventory plan which support the OPT definition of throughput starts with the definition of inventory management. Inventory management is now more clearly defined as the determination of inventory throughput objectives and to plan and control the inventory flows and balances to achieve those objectives.

(Figure 4)

2. An Inventory Plan

The simple answers to the three questions of inventory management shown in Figure 4 grow very complex with the addition of the conflicts listed earlier. Without an inventory plan that sets out the guidelines for inventories for the entire company, the conflicts will still exist. Without a reasonably consistent input of demand for inventories from all departments an, inventory plan will not be valid. This self-defeating cycle can be devastating. So, a new definition is required: All managers who make decisions affecting the flow of materials are inventory managers. This includes almost everyone in the company: those who do the forecast, the quotations department, the shop floor supervisor, the master scheduler, the quality control manager, the purchasing agent, etc.

As long as the changes to inventory flow are done within the plan guidelines, all managers are seen to be performing their jobs effectively. However, these managers must understand another tenet of flow control: any unplanned change to schedules will result in excess inventory costs. These can result for many reasons. Someone decides not to cycle count this week, allowing errors to creep into the system; the sales department decides it's too much trouble to update the rolling forecast this period; the president decides to expedite a special order, etc. Under the OPT rules, the excess inventories will be charged to their departments.

3. Valid Schedules

<table>
<tr><td>

MANAGEMENT QUESTION #1:

DO YOU WANT YOUR

PEOPLE TO PERFORM ?

</td><td>

MANAGEMENT ANSWER #1:

IF YOU WANT THEM

TO PERFORM

GIVE THEM REALISTIC

SCHEDULES

</td></tr>
</table>

(Figure 5a)   (Figure 5b)

The master production schedule is the integration of all the diverse organizational functions within the company. It is the single schedule that drives all activities within the organization. Even if a company

doesn't have a formal master schedule, the same precepts
apply: anyone causing an unplanned change to scheduled
activities is going to create excess inventory costs. The
only difference between the formal and the informal
schedules is that the formal one is much easier to monitor
and measure performance against. The effects to the
schedules are so subtle in some cases as to hide the
causes for shortages, poor performance of the
manufacturing manpower, high expediting costs and many
other of the apparently mundane activities of daily life
in the plant. Emphasis by all managers on schedule
adherence is the key to this essential tool. The master
schedule is the focal point of the supply demand balance
and it must represent manufacturing management's strategy
for meeting forecasted demand. It sets the priorities for
all actions to be performed. Figure 6 illustrates the
supply-demand balance represented in the master schedule.
Each small box on the supply side of the system is offset
by a demand on the MPS side of the system.

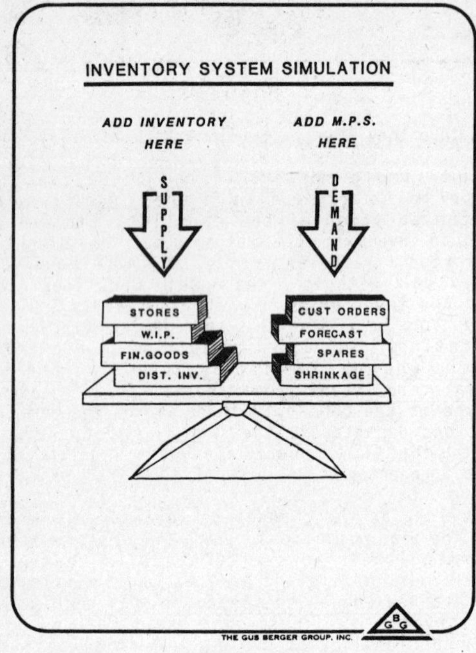

(Figure 6)

Peter Drucker, when addressing management priorities
stated...: "the crucial difference is: 'What comes
first?' Rather than 'what should be done?'... The normal
human reaction is to evade the priority decision by doing
a little bit of everything." The point is that many
decisions are made which effect inventory flows which are
never integrated with scheduled priorities. The proper
phrasing should be: "what should be done first?" The
answer must be: "whatever has the highest due date
priority." Note: Due date and priority have the same
meaning. There is no such thing as "ASAP" in a good
planning system. Also note that priority is not equal to
dollars shipped! Most companies using this second
definition of priority tend to look like the cartoon in
Figure 7.

The scheduling system sets the priorities based on
due date and the control functions below that are
responsible for maintaining those priorities. This
parent-component relationship is identical to the bill of
material relationships upon which MRP nets requirements
for materials. Any missing or undefined links in a
multi-level bill structure will create false
recommendations for resources at the bottom level. Each
level of the management structure from top to bottom sets
the priorities for the next level to control which in turn
sets the priorities for the next subordinate level, etc.
When conflicting priorities are driven down through this
structure, the output will not be very effective for
controlling resource utilization.

4. DATA INTEGRITY--CONTROLLING THE FLOW

There are four areas in which data integrity has the
most input on the flow of materials:

(Figure 7)

1.   Master Production Schedule
2.   Inventory Records
3.   Shop Floor Data
4.   Open Order Status

Information is the raw material for decision making.
It is the representation of the company's assets if it
shows the status of materials in the company. The master
schedule is the focal point of all activities and it must
be accurate. The rule is: <u>The flow of information is the
flow of materials.</u> Thus, the data must be accurate, or it
will not properly represent the flow of money. When
something moves, the data or the paperwork moves in
sequence with it. When changes to dates (ie. priority)
occur, the system must know. Remember, data integrity is
not just accuracy, but timing and discipline.
Responsibility for data integrity must be assigned for the
data collection, data entry, auditing, and timeliness.
Please note that since the evolution of computers as data
tools that there is a new way to view resources in today's
business-that is: Data is an asset! It costs money to
collect, collate, post, process, report and analyze it.
It should be considered the third resource in a company
after materials and capacity.

5. MEASUREMENTS OF PERFORMANCE

Measurement is an established routine that reports
performance to plan. The established routine for any
system of measurement must be based on a set of
procedures. It is the body of procedures that make up a
company's operating system that keep the priorities in
balance. Without valid and up-to-date procedures, there
is no way to hold people responsible for such things as
discipline, accountability or performance to due date
priorities. The procedures define the observable actions
expected by management, maintain the system integrity and
train new people. Procedures must be simple, logical, and
integrated to the other functions with which they
interface. They must be basically usable. Procedures are
worthless without a strong foundation based on the
previous points mentioned in Figure 3.

WHO IS SUPPOSED TO DO ALL THIS ?

This is one of the missing links in much of the
literature about MRPII, Just-in-Time, Zero Inventory and
OPT. With the advent of these modern concepts, the issues
have shifted to "how are we going to get it done?",
instead of "what are we going to do?" The role of
materials management in the 1980's will be to answer the
challenge of these new concepts of flow control.
Materials management is a business management concept that
began in 1832 when Charles Babbage wrote of a "materials
man". The concept of materials management grew slowly
until relatively recent times. As late as 1968 a survey
by Harvard Business Review showed that only about three
percent of those companies had tasks or jobs which had
been assigned the title of material manager or equivalent.
But in 1979 Harvard Business Review conducted the same
survey again and found that well over fifty per cent of

those companies had job titles of that description within their organization. This growth indicates the tremendous surge in the concept of flow control. Figure 8 provides the definition of materials management.

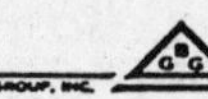

(Figure 8)

(Figure 9)

Most important, materials management is a method to assign responsibility and authority. In essence, the materials management function acts like a traffic cop. (Figure 9)

Materials management is a concept for "c"oordination, "o"rganization and "p"rofit. It is a coordination and control concept that balances conflicting departmental interests through planning and controlling the materials flow to achieve the most profitable combination of costs and service to the company. It is an organizational concept that centralizes the responsibility for the flow of materials through the company and it recognizes that individual sub-systems are all interrelated and interactive. It can create highly leveraged increases in profit through improved inventory positions reductions in purchasing costs and higher production efficiencies.

So, the "cop" has the responsibility to direct the flow of materials. This new definition must be recognized as one of the most powerful and useful tools in the modern manufacturing world. Significant facts about inventory and materials management highlight this fact: (1) Annual inventory carrying costs may account for 30% to 50% of the inventory cost in an organization; (2) In some industries the total cost for material, its storage, movement and waste, runs from 50% to 70% of the total factory cost of finished product; (3) Improvements in materials management can be a factor of profit as much as 4 to 1, that is, for every dollar saved in materials costs there is a resulting four dollar increase in profits to the bottom line. Instead of assassinating a Materials Manager because he was unable to satisfy everyone in the company, he should be applauded for surviving the lack of understanding for all these years.

SUMMARY

In summary, the materials management concept is a profitable way to do business. The control of flow, not inventory levels, is the best way to manage costs in a company. Flow control, like cash flow, will require greater discipline and understanding by management in order to reap the greatest benefits from the concept. It all starts with those items listed in Figure 3: properly defined goals, balanced objectives, a material manager with clear cut authority and responsible to create and maintain valid materials and capacity plans for which others will be held responsible, and proper procedures that provide a basis for measurement. Adherence to these tenets of flow control will help resolve the conflicts which drive the materials managers crazy and tie up the profits in piles of excess inventories. Remember, the flow of materials is the flow of money!

BIOGRAPHY

Mr. Dennis R. Fisher is a Senior Manufacturing Consultant with The Gus Berger Group, Inc. He has served as Vice-President of Education for the Los Angeles Chapter of American Production and Inventory Control Society (APICS) and has also been Chairperson of the Materials Management Committee of the Los Angeles Purchasing Management Association.

He has been Materials Manager in Aerospace, Electronics and Computer Industries; Project Manager for MRP installations in many domestic and international companies. He has designed and implemented Material Control Systems, Preventative Maintenance and Plant Engineering Systems; Planning and Purchasing Programs; Warehouse Layouts; and Personnel Evaluation Methods/Techniques.

Mr. Fisher's education encompasses an M.B.A. from Pepperdine University; a Bachelor of Arts in Sociology and Communications; and certificates in Production Planning and Control, Purchasing Management, Paint Technology, Nuclear Technology, Electronics, Inventory Management and Materials Requirements Planning. He is an Assistant Professor at the California State University, Dominguez Hills. He is the author of "Using the MPS for Business Planning," Auerbach Publishers, Inc., New Jersey.

Mr. Fisher presents lectures, seminars, workshops, educational and certification programs throughout the West. He is certified both by APICS as a CPIM, and by the National Association of Purchasing Management as a CPM.

DRAINING THE INVENTORY SWAMP

Robert W. Hall, Ph.D., CPIM*
Indiana University

Inventory hides problems, and removing inventory reveals problems. So goes the logic of zero inventories, and the process of identifying and removing problems in manufacturing has been likened to the process of locating and removing rocks from a river. Reducing the water level helps us to see the rocks, but if nothing else is done, they are still there.

This process is somewhat like that old adage about draining the swamp. It is hard to maintain attention on it. It is also useful to remember that reducing the swamp level by half has the short term effect of doubling the concentration of alligators. A few of them may crawl elsewhere of their own volition, but some of them must be subdued. The objective is not just to reduce the inventory, but to overcome the problems which require it.

It is easy to be in favor of reducing waste -- any unnecessary use of labor, material, equipment, space or energy. Most of us are also in favor of displacing all alligators from the swamp. It is a matter of finding them and overcoming them, something not done without being prepared. First we have to see them. Then we have to cage them, kill them or run them away. If there are very many, it is a good idea to have a systematic way to overcome alligators.

Problems come in many forms, and many of the real sources of difficulty are unseen at first. Problems in two different categories are very often undetected by industrial cost systems as those are usually constructed:

1. <u>Quality and rework</u>. Quality implies that we understand what to do and do it without rework or hesitation so there are no defects created. That is much more than conformance to specification in the final product.

2. <u>Material handling</u>. Everyone who touches material for any reason is engaged in material handling. Inspectors, stock clerks and machine operators are all engaged in material handling -- manually or through automatic equipment. In this sense the movement of material for any purpose is material handling. There is usually a great deal of wasted effort in moving and positioning material in addition to the wasted time represented by material just sitting, not being moved at all.

These notions are related. The idea is to move material through the operations which are necessary to transform it with no unnecessary stops, rework or movements, and to make it complete, extend the idea to tools, instruments, supplies, and even computation and paperwork.

There are several reasons why problems go unnoticed. We become accustomed to them. The wasted effort is included in the standards so that they do not appear as cost variances unless they are abnormally wasteful. Organizations become structured to handle waste. Repair bay work on very expensive computers is highly skilled, important work, for example.

Of course, some of the problems can be easily overcome while others are the "old dog" problems that seem to have been born with the industry, and never are all of them solved. The important issue is the intensity with which all of the problems are attacked. When digging for the root source of a problem, it can be found in many places. Three categories of location are:

1. <u>Plant floor</u>. These can be eliminated by better organizing the workplace, by modifying equipment or tooling and by increasing the skills of the operators.

2. Support activities. These can be eliminated by improved practice in tool rooms, instrument calibration, maintenance, and so on. This requires the inclusion of these groups in the program.

3. <u>Management organization and practice</u>. These are only overcome by changes in performance measurement methods, how responsibility is divided (or avoided), in cost systems P&IC systems, order entry systems, product design methodology, engineering change systems, and on and on.

With anything this broad in scope, it is obvious that top management must be involved. Lower level management may try a few experiments, but they cannot create a revolution in how the company operates as a whole. The wider the scope in which the company creates an atmosphere of constant improvement, the better the results. After a time, the result is an organization which can take a brand new product into excellent, low cost production in record time.

As broad as it may be in scope, the true test of whether a problem has been solved by this philosophy is whether production runs with very low inventory on the plant floor. Just as one of the key phrases summarizing <u>In Search of Excellence</u> was "close to the customer," one of the key phrases which would summarize the "zero inventories" approach is "close to the production process."

<u>HOW TO START</u>

The purpose of incrementally reducing inventory is to stimulate ourselves to improve production as much as possible as fast as possible. Therefore, the reductions in inventory need to be accompanied by systematic methods of identifying the true cause of the problems which required the inventory and incorporate the solutions into permanent practice. If one is going to start a major program to do this, one must build the capability and willingness to find and subdue the biggest alligators in the swamp. Of course, one can be content to cut setup times a bit here and smooth the layout a bit there without having much fuss about it. Most plants do engage in some of that as people experiment and gain confidence. However, when starting in a major way, the priority of work is as follows:

1. PEOPLE
2. PHYSICAL PLANT AND EQUIPMENT
3. SYSTEMS

Note that this is a priority, not a chronological sequence. Many actions will take place at once.

The factor which distinguishes an outstanding program from one which produces only modest gains is the preparation of people. The best American programs have spent time up front preparing people to overcome problems. Omark Industries, one of the better examples so far, spent considerable time explaining to everyone in the company what the methods were about and why. They even adopted a corporate philosophy statement which incorporated just-in-time principles, and which stressed dedication to excellence, and which further gave indication of how the company would treat its employees and other constituencies as a result. Some of Omark's biggest gains have come from employee suggestions.

Then start on the factory floor with a program to organize the workplace -- housekeeping with a purpose. That in itself should provide the basis for considerable problem solving if vigorously pursued. The intial deep cuts of work-in-process inventory come by the removal of excess inventory from the floor as a part of this. Many of the problems uncovered will be quality problems and material handling problems so to carry this very far we need problem solving in those areas.

As one example of how workplace organization provokes attention to problems, one company began by removing the excess stock from the floor. Much of the excess was boxes of material on quality hold, some of which had been on hold for several weeks. The foreman sent the boxes to the quality department, but that created a great clutter in that department, so the boxes were returned to sender. The problem want to the plant manager for resolution. Part of it was that Quality Control had too large a backlog, but that was only a symptom. The real problem was that the engineering methods for establishing specifications for the parts left too much ambiguity in practice.

This was only the first in a long series of problems which would arise, but it is typical. What started as a small inventory problem became a foray into how to set specifications for a particular class of parts.

Third, make major revisions in how systems work -- cost systems and other systems, not just P&IC systems. The current P&IC system is adequate in the beginning if it is possible to control inventory enough to assure that a reduction is being made. If an MRP system is in place, the initial reductions in inventory can be done just by making incremental reductions in lot sizes or lead times. As more and more progress is made, the planning bills of material may be revised to reflect it, usually by

simplifying them. Most companies do at some point begin
to have problems because the reporting from the plant
floor is no longer possible in the way originally designed
in the system. Material issues or counts are done more
frequently than the system updates, and so on. The usual
procedure is to work around the system for a time. Make a
systems change when the plant changes reveal what will be
useful on a more permanent basis.

The reason for not trying to design a systems change
too far ahead is that it is usually difficult to see
exactly what will be required. Neither does one want to
stall the improvements in the plant because the system
does not "permit them." This sounds a bit vague, but
actually the development of a P&IC system to fit what a
plant can do is not the hardest part of zero inventories
if the production planners and controllers have some skill
in the field. The hard part is in overcoming the tough
quality and material handling problems -- and especially
in upgrading the management practices to make a permanent
change. A systematic approach to problem solving is a
very key factor.

DEVELOPING THE PLANT AS A PRODUCTION LABORATORY

Just thinking of a plant as a production problem
laboratory helps to set the atmosphere. Then think of the
components of this laboratory in three categories:
(1) Tools and methods, (2) Practice, and (3) Organization.

TOOLS AND METHODS

A five-step logic pattern is very useful for
structuring an overall approach. The form of the logic
steps shown in Figure 1 is familiar to many people as one
more variant of the scientific method. The name suggests
closed-loop MRP, or MRP II, but the importance is in
applying this logic to structure a concerted attack on
basic manufacturing problems.

Table 1.

Closed Loop Method of Improvement

1. Seek problems aggressively by plan.

2. Determine the true causes of problems.

3. Determine countermeasures.

4. Check to be sure countermeasures work.

5. Incorporate into actual practice the
   successful countermeasure.

Seeking problems by plan begins with the customers.
The most important place to seek problems with quality,
delivery or price is there. The most important
communication into the factory concerns the products in
use. Most manufacturers respond to customer complaints,
but not so many have programs to gather data on field use
and relate that to production problems.

Selectively reducing inventory by an increment is
another way to seek problems. That is done in conjunction
with observation and data gathering to identify what
happens. Relate the amount of inventory to time by
expressing the measurement of it as days on hand, or
perhaps even hours or minutes on hand is some cases if the
flow is fast enough. Then flow chart the path of material
through all operations. Often just measuring the overall
travel distance of a part number through a plant is enough
to provoke ideas on how to improve. It is relating the
reduction in inventory to specific ways to change layout,
reduce machine breakdowns or otherwise improve that is the
objective.

Over time, a regular habit of observation and data
collection makes this into a way of life. Each operation
will have logbooks or charts to prompt observations by
operators in a way they can manage.

Determining the true causes of the problems begins
with pure logic. Asking the question "why" over and over
leads to the root cause of problems seen in production.
Devise a systematic search process to do this for each
operation. Look in the easiest places first. This is
particularly applicable to quality problems -- existence
of defects. One search hierarchy which is effective is:

1. First, search for the location of a defect in the
   workpiece itself; the pattern of holes in porous
   castings, the location of defective components on
   a printed circuit board.
2. Next relate the occurrence of a defect to the time
   it is produced. This associates defects with tool
   wear, heat build up, deterioration of lubrication,
   or other time related factors which may be readily
   identified by those familiar with the operation.
3. Then trace the defects to the location where they
   may originate -- to a specific machine, tool,
   operator or container. The traceability is made
   easier by having less work-in-progress inventory
   and the ability to do this when required is one of
   the objectives of workplace organization and
   layout.

This is something of a detective job, a pattern of
fault free analysis familiar to repairmen. It is enhanced
by adding the measurement tools necessary; control charts,
cause and effect diagrams and any other form of analysis
that readily contributes to answering why questions.

Developing countermeasures may or may not be
difficult. It is usually made easier if a good job has
been done making sure that the source of the problem has
been found. This is very much like repairing a car. One
can replace parts by guesswork until the defective one is
found, or one can try to be smarter about it.

Checking to see that the countermeasure worked is no
great added burden, but it is important not to just assume
that the correct fix has been made.

Incorporating into actual practice the countermeasure
which is effective is a frequent weak link. Instructions
are not passed on, operators, foremen or suppliers change,
or an improvement adopted later undoes one made earlier.
It is the stimulus imposed by having to work with a low
amount of inventory that maintains attention on the
details of work, but more than just vigilance is
required. It takes method. Both among operators and
among staff, it generally requires people to regularly
explain how and why they perform certain jobs. In a plant
which is making a daily habit of high quality and
improvement, one sees a great deal of visible operator
instruction at the worksite. Some of that is prepared by
the operators themselves and is done so that operators can
rotate jobs without adverse consequences.

It is one thing to make improvement. It is another to
preserve it. A great deal of basic effort must go into
the preservation of what has been gained.

PRACTICE

None of the tools and methods are so complex that they
cannot be used and mastered by most people who work in
manufacturing -- including the operators. It is a matter
of practice. The idea of zero inventories is to stimulate
constant practice. Good workplace organization and
reduction of inventory stimulates practice. Begin there.

A good way to think about workplace organization is in
five categories: (1) Simplification, (2) Organization,
(3) Discipline, (4) Cleanliness, and (5) Participation.
Think about problems and overcome them while doing this.

Simplification is the process of removing from the
work areas anything which is not needed for immediate
use. That first requires a definition of immediate for
each work center -- today, this week, this month? What is
the cycle period for planning, and if that is vague, why
is that true?

The seemingly simple decisions can become big.
Removing extra material requires decisions about
disposition. Removing extra equipment requires
determining why it is there, and if it is used as a backup
because of equipment or tooling failure, there is a design
or maintenance problem to look into. The source of the
problems can reach into the procedures used in staff and
support areas, and they usually do.

Remove the "government jobs" and excess personal
effects. That can lead to an issue of where to put them,
and designation of locations for personal items.

The housekeeping certainly extends to tooling,
fixtures and supplies. It is not possible to execute
rapid setups on equipment without having these items
positioned for it, and the beginning point is to decide
which ones should be nearby and which ones stored away.
If the method of classifying and storing tools, dies and
fixtures is inadequate, this initiates a project to
correct that.

Organizing is the process of assigning a location for everything. Items used constantly in specific locations, items used together kept together and so on. Developing this and maintaining it generally require assigning responsibility for the organization of each area to someone, and it may require revising how the work centers or work stations are defined. At the lowest level, each operator will be responsible for their area once this is carried far enough.

If workers rotate jobs (and they should) or if there are multiple shifts, the workplace organization becomes a vehicle for communicating the details of how work is performed. If two different people want the same area organized differently, is that for significant or non-significant reasons? Problems of standardization and quality can emerge from this activity -- and some should. In order to do this well, those organizing the workplace (usually workers on the floor, in maintenance, etc.) need basic instruction on work simplification and motion economy.

One other basic objective of this sorting out process is to develop visibility of conditions on the floor. It should become possible to spot excess material because it overflows the area designated for it. If stockpoints are to be used, the locations should be marked. If material is to be left in queue, the location for inbound material should be marked. Problems are not only exposed by having a low level of inventory, but by it being in a specified location. The same goes for tooling and supplies.

On assembly lines the sequencing and positioning of material is especially important, but this also applies to fabrication work centers. Even in a job shop with a variety of work, positioning the workpieces for future work in order lets everyone know by sight what is to be run next. There is almost always some difficulty doing this, but trying to develop a way to do it is very instructive of the problems in a plant.

Discipline is a matter of practice so that everyone becomes accustomed to the methods of layout and workplace organization and understands their purpose. That will not happen quickly, and the housekeeping program will likely have to take place in stages. If programs to improve quality and to reduce setup times are initiated, the reasons for the housekeeping begin to become evident.

Cleanliness is important to have everything ready for action at any time, and it is also important to quality. Dirt is an important factor in many problems with quality, as in painting. Making a fetish of cleanliness serves no purpose. The idea is to prevent dirt from being a source of production problems. Cleaning is also a fundamental part of a preventive maintenance program. Those who clean a machine observe what others miss, and that is the reason why having those who are responsible for equipment and a work station also responsible for cleaning it. It should not be regarded as a low status task, but as an extension of being observant about the job and its surroundings.

Participation by everyone is important. It becomes obvious that worker involvement is necessary, and it is also important that everyone else have a basic knowledge of the "housekeeping" rules. If someone is held responsible for the organization of a work area, others should not mess it up. That includes supervisors, repairmen, engineers and others. It should be understood that people do not walk into a work area and do whatever they want -- something that is sure to provide some problems in the modus operandi of various service functions in many plants.

In addition to the effect coming from workplace organization taking place generally, quality problems are likely to be overcome quicker if professional attention is directed to the "key points" in material flow. Examples: Painting operations in most fabrication shops, or wave solder operations in most factories loading components in printed circuit boards. These are points at which defects show up, and from which it should be possible to trace the source of many defects rapidly.

ORGANIZATION

If the plant is to become a production laboratory, the entire organization of the factory must be shaped for it, beginning with the top management. Their leadership is essential for reconstituting of how people work together, because teamwork is obviously required along with rethinking the basis of many common, everyday procedures.

A project team, or implementation team, with at least one or more full time members is necessary, depending on the size plant. Something less than that assures that only a few improvements will be made before the effort becomes swallowed by the momentum of everyone rushing to continue with the current modus operandi. The leadership of line management is critical. Some minimal degree of participation is needed from the workforce, and to get this takes no small amount of revision in the usual ways in which workers and management interact.

In the various staff groups there are generally a number of forward planning projects along with the duties of support for existing manufacturing operations. Often the support duties are considered less important. When the inventory is reduced, support for existing operations cannot be slighted, and that requires some adjustments in staff priorities. (In one single-shift plant, the daily downtime was cut nearly in half by having all staff personnel report for work half an hour before line workers. Their first duty each morning was to be sure everything was ready for start up.) Such attention is necessary when the material and tools immediately at hand and the only items which provide work.

Worker involvement groups are the organizational innovation which has received the most attention, whether called quality circles or something else. These are voluntary participation groups. In American plants there are usually some enthusiastic participants, but not a large percentage of participation. One of the usual problems is maintaining a useful direction for them. Left entirely to themselves, interest wanders to many areas, some of which are outside the expertise of the people in the groups. For all the benefit which has come from them, there have also been many failures.

There are many ways to obtain worker support. They all require constant interaction with the workforce. Hewlett-Packard in several plants has not had success with quality circles. They ask each supervisor to have a daily meeting with the group. That ensures full participation, and it focuses the energy of the group on the problems of concern. In addition, management can form temporary task forces, committees -- all the familiar methods of concentrating on specific problems and issues.

There are several ways to prompt worker groups to concentrate on the work before them in which they are truly expert. One is to ask them to describe a problem which they touch every day with their own hands, and suggest a remedy if possible. Another is to have them describe their own job, or parts of it, in detail. That is a very useful way to start communication and prompt ideas.

Probably the most important part of organization is that ethereal quality called management attitude. Changes in physical plant and in system provides some benefit, but without any major change in how management works together these are limited by lack of cooperation and understanding.

BASIS OF STANDARDIZATION

This is a major ingredient in a vision of where a plant is headed even if the details cannot be foreseen. A repetitive manufacturer standardizes by making the same things -- repeated production of the same parts. That provides the basis for the "pull system" of control, if the other conditions for it can be developed.

Most manufacturers have some common factors among all the products they make -- common materials, geometries, tests and so on. The big advances come from finding the way to apply the greatest standardization to the production task -- a simple generality. The design of a new plant or for the revision of an old one has to be guided by some vision which comes from this.

THE P&IC SYSTEM AS A PROBLEM

At some point in the progress of the plant, the P&IC system will be seen as a problem. This has happened in several cases. Subsequent to reducing the inventory, but before a system revision is in place, the inability to generate pick lists fast enough or inability to report as designed will create a problem. Each specific P&IC system is designed with application to a given plant and its existing production methods.

A P&IC system in a plant with a major zero inventories program is a system in transition. The system which exists must plan and control production as it is -- bad as well as good. As the manufacturing process itself improves, the planning and control should also improve, frequently by simplifying. Less attention must be given

to checking, rechecking and expediting, and more attention
can be given to planning. The specific changes and the
way in which they take place is a function of each case:
job shop, repetitive, mostly fabrication or mostly
assembly, degree of customization of the product, and so
on. The important point is not to allow the system to be
the permanent obstacle to progress. It will be at times
because it is necessary to maintain control of the
material, but one cannot make great improvement merely by
having control.

A machining process statistically in control may still
run many rejects. An operation which is in cost control
may still not be competitive. A plant which has 99%
inventory accuracy and ships 90% on time may still be too
wasteful in doing it. The major objective is constant
improvement.

REFERENCE

Peters, Thomas J. and Waterman, Robert H. Jr.; In
Search of Excellence, Harper & Row, New York, 1982.

ROBERT W. HALL

Prof. Hall has taught Operations Management at the
Indianapolis Campus of Indiana University for 14 years.
Before that he worked for Eli Lilly, Inc. and Union
Carbide Corp.

He is a certified fellow of the American Production
and Inventory Control Society, and a past president of the
Central Indiana Chapter. He has made numerous
presentations at national and local conferences, and he
has written material for the APICS Repetitive
Manufacturing Group. He has made comparative studies of
Japanese and American manufacturing methods, and is the
author of:

Driving the Productivity Machine (APICS)
Kawasaki, U.S.A. (Case study, APICS)
Zero Inventories, (Dow Jones-Irwin and APICS)

JIT ACCOUNTING
Julie A. Heard
Plossl & Heard

FOREWORD

Many manufacturing installations have Zero Inventory or Just-In-Time programs under way. Several of these efforts have run head on into conflicts with their finance or accounting groups over current cost accounting and performance measurement methods. Some traditional performance measures are inconsistent with JIT and have to be replaced or discarded. Some JIT operating methods appear to be inconsistent with current manufacturing accounting procedures. In many cases, the inconsistencies are only superficial and can be easily resolved. The purpose of this paper is to shed some light on a poorly understood subject. This presentation describes what changes must take place, why they are necessary, how they can be accomplished, who will be responsible for them, and where they will have the greatest impact on manufacturing operations.

FUNCTIONAL ORGANIZATION

In many plants, machines and workers are organized along functional lines. Machines are grouped into work centers based on the similarity of their functional capabilities. (See the top half of Figure 1.) The usual rationale is that this type of organization provides maximum leverage for technical expertise. Operators are typically assigned to one machine or in some cases to multiple machines of the same type. In many cases, these work centers are also designated as cost centers for cost accounting purposes.

Work centers are usually planned and scheduled as a group. Supervisors have broad responsibilities for work center operation. They are charged primarily with the efficient operation of their units. Various measurement schemes are used to evaluate supervisory performance. Most such measurement schemes rely exclusively on data collected for payroll and cost accounting purposes.

PUSH SYSTEMS

Each manufactured part has a designated routing. The routing specifies what is to be done to the part, where it is to be done, the sequence for individual operations, how long each operation should take for each piece, the setup time required to produce the part, etc. This information is used for material and capacity requirements planning, performance measurement, and for cost control, among other things.

Dispatch lists from production control are used to set priorities for work orders at the work centers. Given work to do and machine, material, tool and operator availability, the supervisor is obligated to maximize machine utilization even if that means operating ahead of schedule and producing unnecessary inventory.

When all work center operations on a work order are complete, that work order is turned over to materials handling. The material is then moved to stores or to the next work center on the routing as required. No consideration is given to whether the next work center is ready to work on the material or not. Hence, the use of the term—push system.

DATA COLLECTION

Data collection occupies considerable time and resources in a functionally grouped plant. Virtually every time material moves from one operation to the next, data is collected reflecting how long the operation required, who performed it and how many parts were involved. This information is used to drive payroll, cost accounting and inventory systems.

Move tickets are often used to request and authorize

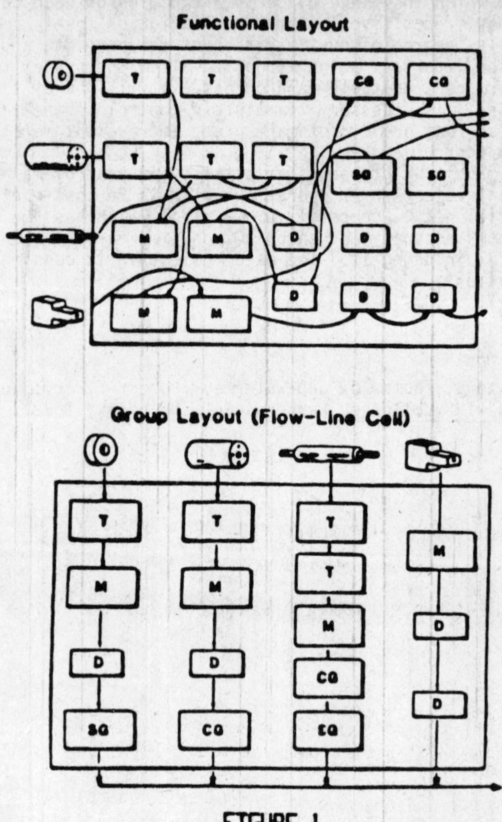

movement of materials between work centers. Even when tickets are issued with the work order packet, time is required to find the necessary ticket and verify that it is in fact the right one. Likewise, the material handler must check the move ticket to identify the proper destination.

When materials have to be returned to or brought from stores, other inventory transactions must also be completed. These transactions drive work order costing and, hence, the cost accounting as well as the inventory system. Not only does the variety of transactions require time and resources, but they also multiply the chances for error.

GROUP TECHNOLOGY CELLS

JIT manufacturing involves fundamental rethinking of many practices that have previously been accepted as inevitable. One of these is the functionally based work center. JIT encourages the development of Group Technology work cells. (See the bottom portion of Figure 1.) GT work cells consist of groups of dissimilar machines that function like an assembly line.

GT work cells are dedicated to the production of a limited number of parts or products requiring similar sequences of operations. The parts are produced in small lots. Since processing requirements are so similar, a limited number of fixtures are needed and setups are both fast and frequent.

Cell managers are responsible for throughput in their cells. Due to the highly focused nature of the work cell, their responsibilities are readily apparent. Consequently, they may be given a great deal of operational authority over a broader spectrum of functions than is normal under functional work center organization. See Figure 2 for the contrasting characteristics of work centers and work cells.

PULL SYSTEMS

Under full JIT operation, work cells function under pull

system control. Consumption of parts at using operations is monitored and various types of signaling systems are used to authorize production and movement of the part to the using location.

WORK CENTER VS. WORK CELL

DISSIMILAR MACHINES

    WIDELY DISBURSED OPERATIONS

    EACH MACHINE PROCESSES MANY PARTS

    ORDERS MOVE IN BATCH LOTS

    MULTIPURPOSE EQUIPMENT

GT LAYOUT

    CELLS OF DISSIMILAR MACHINES

    FUNCTION LIKE ASSEMBLY LINES

    PROCESS A LIMITED NUMBER OF PARTS

    USE A LIMITED NUMBER OF FIXTURES

    FREQUENT SETUP REPETITION

    OPERATIONAL AUTONOMY

FIGURE 2

Unless the producing cell has proof of authorization to produce, standing instructions are not to run more parts. Naturally this can result in substantial idle time for those cells currently staffed above true capacity requirements. The belief is that it is more beneficial to absorb short run idle time than to add to inventory during these periods.

STANDARD CONTAINERS

Under JIT operation, materials are pulled through the shop in standard containers. Every part has one and only one container in which it is moved. The same type of container may be shared by more than one part, but no part is ever moved in more than one type of container.

There is method in this madness. Ideally, the container is deliberately matched to the run lot size and vice versa. The objective is to provide a quick visual means of work in process control. Cards or some other physical device is required to authorize movement and temporary storage of any container of parts. Strictly limiting the number of cards for a specific part number combined with the standard containers provide a strict upper limit on the quantity of each part that can be on the floor at once.

GT CELL DATA COLLECTION IMPLICATIONS

Conversion to GT work cells has several implications for data collection. Under work center operation, part count and labor had to be collected after every operation for two reasons. One was to feed the payroll and cost accounting systems. The other was to feed work order and inventory tracking systems.

Within a GT cell, parts flow from machine to machine one piece at a time. There is no need or opportunity to track labor and count parts at each machine. The process is simply occurring too fast for that to be viable. Since parts are obviously not being returned to a storeroom between machines, many inventory transactions are avoided and along with them the potential for transaction errors.

If parts are to be counted and labor measured in a GT cell, the only logical places to perform these operations is at the beginning and end of the cell. Critical measurements would be how many parts were processed and how much of a run interval was dedicated to a specific part number.

STANDARD CONTAINER DATA COLLECTION IMPLICATIONS

How difficult is it to count parts when every container that a part can exist in contains the same quantity? Not only does the container hold the same quantity, but that quantity doesn't vary from day to day. Now suppose that an additional stipulation is imposed that only full containers of parts are allowed to move.

Clearly the use of standard containers can greatly simplify inventory data collection. Since parts are only transferred in standard quantities, tracking inventory flows is highly simplified. All that is required is physical inventory stockpoints on the shop floor such that inventory can be plussed in to one stockpoint and minused out of the previous stockpoint at the same time. This assumes, of course, that there is a need or desire to track inventory from physical location to physical location on the floor. If lead times are short enough, that may not even be the case.

INCENTIVE SYSTEMS

In work centers, individual incentives are often used to encourage individual efficiency. Each operator has, in effect, a budget for the lot of parts to be processed. If that lot can be processed under budget, pay for the individual worker is increased. The negative side of incentive pay is that there is no concern for capacity imbalances between successive operations. As a result, the incentive system encourages the fast operator to overdrive the station or work center that uses the parts he produces. Because successive operations may take place at widely separate locations, such imbalances can exist for long periods of time. The result is work in process accumulation.

Under JIT operation, when a processing operation completes a batch and has no further work authorizations, it is supposed to stop until such an authorization is received. As a result, capacity imbalances are obvious to the most casual observer. Clearly, individual incentive systems are inconsistent with JIT operations. Not only is the necessary data not collected but the results would be counterproductive since the worker would be penalized for capacity imbalances over which he has no control.

If individual incentives aren't feasible with GT cell operation, then what is? Some authorities recommend straight salaries. Others suggest group incentives. Even when group incentives are in place the idea is not to pay for excess production but to pay bonuses for producing the requested items using less resources. This type of incentive does not lend itself to short run measurements or reimbursement.

What does need to be tracked is the number of people hours required in a given cell during extended intervals. This type of information is usually readily available from payroll records and does not require elaborate data collection on the floor. Cell output can be tracked by counting, recording and transmitting the number of parts of each type leaving the cell. In truly repetitive environments, this is not even necessary. Since parts are not being produced for inventory, ouput can be backed out from finished goods production records and bills of material.

SUPERVISORY PERFORMANCE MEASUREMENT

Several mechanisms are used to measure supervisory performance in work centers—cost variances, indirect/direct ratios, labor utilization and machine utilization. Utilization measures often lead to the same sort of inventory buildup encouraged by individual incentive systems.

Variance analyses may be useful for GT cell supervisory performance evaluation under two conditions. First, the cost accounting system and data collection system has to reflect the reality of JIT operation. Standards used for work center operation of the same machines will be inappropriate for use as basis for variance calculation in a GT cell. The other requirement is that variances be communicated to the cell manager while the conditions creating the out of tolerance condition still exist. Unless the information is received by the cell manager quickly, it simply is not very useful. This condition alone rules out variance analysis as an effective tool for supervisory performance evaluation in most plants.

JOB COSTING PROCEDURES

Job costing is the typical method of cost accumulation and assignment in plants that process readily identifiable units or batches of products through multiple work centers. The job costing process attempts to specifically identify and assign all the costs of processing a batch of parts through an operation to a specific work order.

Work center costs usually assigned to production batches include direct labor and materials, production supplies and manufacturing overhead. Materials and production supplies costs are usually assigned based on the issuance of parts for a specific work order. Direct labor is assigned to individual work orders based on individual worker job/operation cards or tickets. Since GT cell workers do not report operation labor, it is clear that job costing may be unworkable for GT cells.

Manufacturing overhead is usually assigned to individual work orders in direct proportion to consumption of direct materials or direct labor. This assignment is typically based on time standards and a predetermined absorption rate. The absorption rate is reviewed and modified periodically based on estimated expenses and forecast utilization of the work center in question. Once again, since pre-existing standards may be irrelevant or inappropriate under GT cell operation, this procedure may have to be modified to account for costs under JIT.

PROCESS COSTING PROCEDURES

Process costing is at the opposite end of the spectrum from job costing. It concentrates on flow rates or volumes per time interval and deals primarily with averages as opposed to specific, determinable batch or unit costs. Plants that use process costing exclusively are generally involved in continuous process manufacturing. There is generally little or no variation in individual units and batch processing costs may differ only because of larger or smaller batch sizes. Costs are typically assigned by spreading total production costs and manufacturing overhead over the volume produced during the period.

Process costing systems require relatively minimal data collection. Labor is accumulated through the payroll system. Materials cost accumulation is based on withdrawals from inventory. Cost assignment to individual portions of the manufacturing process is usually limited to allocation of labor costs to the area to which specific personnel are assigned.

COST CENTER REDEFINITION

JIT operation requires cost center redefinition in line with any changes made to the physical layout. The most natural cost center unit under JIT is the GT work cell. Other cost centers would include final assembly lines and, during the evolution toward total JIT operation, some traditional work centers would likely remain in place.

Perhaps more important than the actual redefinition of cost centers is a change in the way cost centers are perceived. Under JIT, each cell, assembly line, etc. becomes a miniature factory. That is, it starts with materials and produces a finished product. Since all production is in response to a pull signal from the next user, it is easy to visualize cells and assembly lines as continuous processes. This perception is extremely important since it facilitates the adaptation of process costing procedures to the JIT environment.

JIT PRODUCT COSTING

One school of thought claims that JIT operations are so highly simplified that one simply counts finished units and spreads all costs across them without regard to the cost of individual parts. Another school of thought says that the financial people in North America are in such firm control that there is no way they will accept such a procedure. Others say auditors and the IRS won't buy it.

Still others question whether anybody will throw away computerized cost systems that it has taken two or three decades to develop.

Some critics worry that prices for component parts sold as spares will become uncompetitive unless existing cost systems are maintained by ongoing data collection programs. It is theoretically possible to operate under the previously cited procedure even when some component parts are sold as spares. To avoid the pricing problem, costs should be based on engineered standards. The tradeoff is between continuous data collection and continuous updating of engineering standards for salable components.

JIT LABOR COSTING

As was mentioned previously, labor standards used in work centers may be inappropriate for use in GT work cells. This is true because of the continuous process nature of cell operation. In a multiple station process like the one in Figure 3, standard times for the respective operations on multiple parts may be as shown. Notice that

STANDARD TIMES PER PIECE*

| ITEM | MACHINE | | |
	1	2	3
A	20	10	20
B	10	20	15
C	15	0	12.5

OUTPUT

A	50
B	100
C	40

* IN MINUTES

FIGURE 3

each piece has, in effect, a bottleneck operation. It is the times for those bottleneck operations that limit flow through the process.

Consequently, when part A is being run and there is one operator at each machine, the time requirement for each operator for each piece is 20 minutes. Each piece consumes 60 minutes of the labor resource rather than the sum of the standard times which is 50 minutes.

To further complicate matters, under JIT operation there may be more machines than workers. The problem then is that standard times may become totally irrelevant. In the extreme case, an entire cell may operate with only one worker. In that case, each machine simply waits until the operator gets to it. Provided the standards shown are still appropriate, the time consumed for one piece of A with one opertor running the cell would be 50 minutes. In other words, the important variable is cycle time rather than standard time. Cycle time is a function of the cell staffing level. Any cell may have multiple cycle times. When a cell processes multiple parts as shown in Figure 3, it becomes necessary to track the length of time the cell operates on a given day. It is also necesssary to determine what percentage of that operating time was dedicated to each part during that time period. That information can be combined with the number of each part produced and the appropriate cycle times to compute the cost attributable to the respective parts produced during that period.

The question then becomes what has to be tracked to develop the necessary information. Three things: 1) the length of time the cell ran; 2) the number of operators in the cell during the period; and 3) the quantity of each part completed during the period. Cycle times for each part don't have to be tracked, as they can be determined from specially constructed computerized cycle time tables or from the records kept by the cell manager.

JIT AND MANUFACTURING OVERHEAD

Manufacturing overhead allocation under both traditional job costing and process costing is based on estimated expenses and forecast utilization for a work center. Actual manufacturing overhead dollars are then assigned based on time standards and a predetermined absorption rate which is in direct proportion to the consumption of direct materials or direct labor. Assignment of manufacturing overhead for a GT cell for a GT cell operates in a similar manner.

Historically, overhead costs have been assigned based on the percentage of direct labor used for a part or batch produced in proportion to total direct labor usage. Under JIT operation, overhead assignment based on direct labor usage is valid; however, the percentage of direct labor attributable to a given part should be based on the cycle time concept described in the JIT Labor Costing section above rather than on the basis of standard times.

Refer again to Figure 3. If standard time per piece were used to allocate manufacturing overhead, Part A would absorb approximately 31% of total overhead, part B 56%, and part C 13%. Using the cycle time concept described earlier, part A would absorb 27%, part B would absorb 56% and part C would absorb 17% for the period in question. A basic accounting principal is that of matching revenue to expense — the cycle time concept for both labor and manufacturing overhead allocation more nearly meets this need.

JIT AND INVENTORY VALUATION

Inventory valuation is a widely debated topic that has provided many an accountant and auditor with hours of work. One school of thought tracks all costs of operation and specifically assigns them to parts produced during the period. Inventory is broken down by categories—raw materials, work in process and finished goods—and recorded in the financial accounting system. This system requires extensive record keeping, data manipulation, and frequent, costly physical inventories.

Under JIT operation, lead times are extremely short. This allows raw materials to be acquired, processed and transferred directly to finished goods inventory in the financial accounting system. Using this system, work in process inventory accounts would not be maintained. Consequently, all labor and manufacturing overhead for a period would simply be allocated to the number of units produced during that period.

The approach to inventory valuation described above suffers from the same deficiency recognized in both labor and overhead allocation. That is, all finished units of different types are not necessarily created equal. Because of that deficiency, a procedure analagous to that described as the cycle time concept should be used to properly allocate labor and overhead among parts produced.

An alternative procedure would be to adopt an inventory valuation method that has long been used successfully in repetitive manufacturing plants. This process involves setting up checkpoints (or tollgates) on the shop floor at various stages of product completion. Each checkpoint has and maintains its own specific inventory accounts. The physical location (checkpoint) inventory balances are maintained by "plussing" completed units into the appropriate in-process inventory account and "minusing" (backflushing) components out of feeder checkpoint inventory accounts as products cross each checkpoint. All period labor costs and manufacturing overhead between physical locations are allocated to period completions (plusses) using conventional accounting procedures.

Under JIT operation, the entry and exit points to individual GT cells make ideal checkpoints. Inventory balances could be maintained by plussing completions and minusing components based on starts at each individual cell.

SUMMARY AND CONCLUSION

Implementing Just In Time in a manufacturing environment almost certainly means major changes throughout a company. Many of those changes impact on the cost accounting systems currently in place. Some "experts" have advocated throwing out these conventional cost accounting systems. This paper has attempted to detail some of the changes necessary, state the logical reasons for them, and explain the impacts of these changes. JIT and conventional cost accounting systems CAN work together. It takes dedicated effort to implement JIT AND dedicated effort to make JIT and conventional cost accounting systems work together.

ABOUT THE AUTHOR

Julie Heard is a consultant with Plossl and Heard, a manufacturing management counseling and educational services company based in Columbia, South Carolina. In addition, she operates her own firm which provides accounting, tax and financial counseling services to a variety of corporations. She has a background in accounting, finance and manufacturing systems developed over the last ten years. Julie is an active member of APICS and the National Association of Accountants. She has appeared on the International APICS Conference Program and has spoken at a number of APICS chapter meetings. In addition, she has published in a national accounting magazine. Julie is Past President of the Mid-Carolina Chapter of APICS, and is currently serving as Assistant Director of Education and Research for Region XI. She holds a Bachelor's Degree in Accounting from the University of South Carolina.

OPT(IMIZING) JUST-IN-TIME—LEAPFROGGING THE JAPANESE

Robert E. Fox, CPIM*
Creative Output, Inc.

The Japanese manufacturing machine rolls on. They own the consumer electronics business, - while our approach to automotive manufacturing has proven to be second rate. The Japanese are now making new inroads into the machine tool business, as well as other industrial goods markets. Our aircraft manufacturers are comforted by the fact that the bulk of their contracts come from the defense department, but even they are beginning to realize that this advantage may not be enough. The pride and joy of our technical genius - the computer industry - has braced itself for a head-on assault by Japanese manufacturers. There no longer seems to be an industry that is safe from the Japanese manufacturing machine. It has quickly become evident that _meeting_ the Japanese machine is no longer a sufficient strategy. If we want to survive as a major manufacturing nation, we must _beat_ the competition!

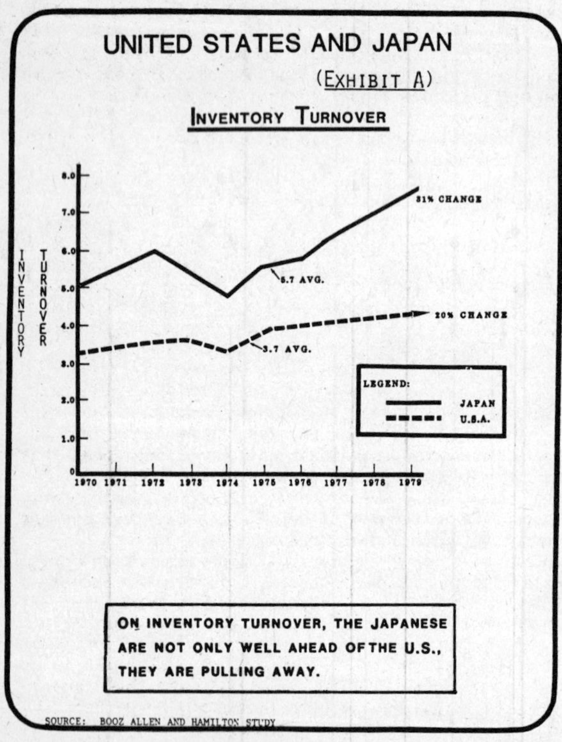

Four years ago at the Los Angeles convention, I presented versions of the Exhibit A and B charts illustrating the results of a Booz, Allen & Hamilton survey. The survey indicated that the Japanese approach to manufacturing management was clearly out stripping us. To highlight this point, I presented the study results which showed that the Japanese were turning their inventory much faster than their counterparts in the U.S. At that time, there was much skepticism about the validity of these survey findings. Few were willing to accept the fact that the Japanese were that far ahead. They were certain some information had been left out of the survey and that the results were not comparable. Today there remains a skepticism about these numbers, but a different kind. Some people now feel the Japanese were even further ahead than these results depicted and, more importantly, the numbers did not show with sufficient clarity the huge gains that the Japanese had made in the last years of the 1970's. It is unfortunate that Booz, Allen did not continually update their survey as I believe it would today show the gap widening even more rapidly than was recognized four years ago.

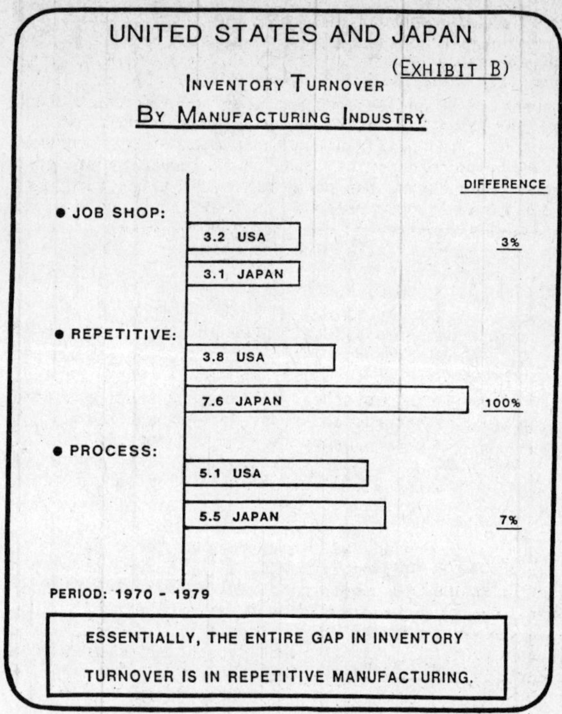

Several years after recognizing the Japanese threat, most U.S. industries are still without an effective strategy to combat it. Yes, we are moving. We now have zero inventory, Just-In-Time, and statistical process control programs. Industries are investing in robotics and reindustrialization. However, I firmly believe that most of these efforts will simply delay our losing, but they will not enable us to win. We need a coherent strategy that has the possibility of not only catching the Japanese but leapfrogging them. I believe also that such an approach is within our reach. We can yet win the game, and I hope that enough of our companies have the foresight and courage to recognize and take the necessary steps.

The key, I believe, lies in not working harder, but smarter. The Japanese are defeating us, not because of low cost labor, modern equipment, wartime loans or other such myths. They have been defeating us because they have a better system for managing manufacturing - a better technology of management - their Just-In-Time system. The electronics industry has learned very well that you do not defeat your competition by copying his technology, you do it by leapfrogging to the next level of technological development. That is what we must do with our management systems. Copying the Just-In-Time system will not do it. The Japanese have a 10-20 year lead and they are moving forward. We are not very likely to catch them, let alone surpass them by copying what they have done. We must move to the next technology - the OPT Management System - the OPT Way of Thinking! This approach will allow us to utilize the Just-In-Time techniques in a much more effective way than the Japanese have been able to do so. OPT (Optimized Production Technology), as will be illustrated, will allow us to go much, much further with the Just-In-Time approach.

Ironically, one of the inspirations for a leapfrog strategy comes to us from the father of the Just-In-Time approach - Dr. Taiichi Ohno. At his presentation entitled "The Origin of Toyota('s) Production System and Kanban System" at the International Conference on Productivity and Quality Improvement in Tokyo - 1982, Dr. Ohno recounted the post World War II strategy of the Japanese automakers. The survival of the Japanese auto industry would not come from copying the industry of competitive countries, he said, but "we had to develop our own system to produce low cost autos... It was apparent that we would not be able to compete with the European and American nations if we followed the same method as they did. Therefore, our only possibility to survive in this industry was to develop a unique production system of our own". Ohno's exhortation to the Japanese Auto Industry has relevance to us today. _Our_ next generation of technology is OPT.

The Japanese approach to manufacturing management has been described in a variety of ways by many authors. One useful description is to look at the 14 elements or thrusts that typically comprise the Just-In-Time approach (Exhibit C). A brief examination of several of these principles helps us to understand why it has taken the Japaneses 20-30 years to implement their now highly effective system.

EXHIBIT C

ELEMENTS OF JUST-IN-TIME

ELIMINATION OF WASTE
- FOCUSED FACTORY NETWORKS
- GROUP TECHNOLOGY
- QUALITY CONTROL
- JUST-IN-TIME PRODUCTION
- UNIFORM PLANT LOADING
- KANBAN SYSTEM
- MINIMIZED SETUP TIME

RESPECT FOR PEOPLE - "JIDOKA"
- LIFETIME EMPLOYMENT
- COMPANY UNIONS
- ATTITUDE TOWARD WORKERS
- AUTOMATION/ROBOTICS
- BOTTOM ROUND MANAGEMENT
- SUBCONTRACTOR NETWORKS
- QUALITY CIRCLES

Many of these elements involve establishing an ongoing program and attitude of improvement in almost every area of the business. A mindset or culture that constantly strives to squeeze out the last bit of waste. Such programs were clearly not established in a brief period of time and the significant benefits achieved required many years of sustained effort. This has clearly been the Japanese experience. They have <u>continually</u> tried to reduce the amount of time required for setup, to reduce the number of defects, to eliminate any possible variation in the manufacturing process. They have invested heavily in time and dollars and are now achieving enviable results. Persistence, faith, tenacity and a dogged determination have driven Japan to be one of the world's great industrial powers.

THE ACHILLES HEEL OF JUST-IN-TIME OR PARETO: THE FORGOTTEN ITALIAN

The basic concepts upon which Just-In-Time rests are sound. They are the same concepts that Henry Ford used nearly 80 years ago in developing assembly line manufacturing. The assembly line and the Just-In-Time approach are simply two procedures for implementing the correct rules of manufacturing. Maybe what we need to do is to better understand these rules to see if we can determine a better procedure for implementing them, a procedure that will give us a greater return with less effort. I believe there is such a procedure, but first let us understand the weakness of the Just-In-Time system, its Achilles' heel. Just-In-Time suffers from not always knowing to focus effort. The famous Italian Pareto told us that in life there are a few important things (the "vital few") and many that are relatively trivial. We often record his observation as the 80/20, or the ABC rule. Properly understood the Pareto principle can direct us to where we should make improvements first, those areas where a given effort will yield the most benefit.

In the typical factory there is wide variety of opportunities for improvement. As shown by Exhibit D, each opportunity has an implementation cost and a Return on Investment. The key to success is in identifying those opportunities yielding the greatest benefit for a given expenditure, those with the greatest return on investment.

In contrast to the Japanese Just-In-Time approach, OPT inherently recognizes Pareto in that it:

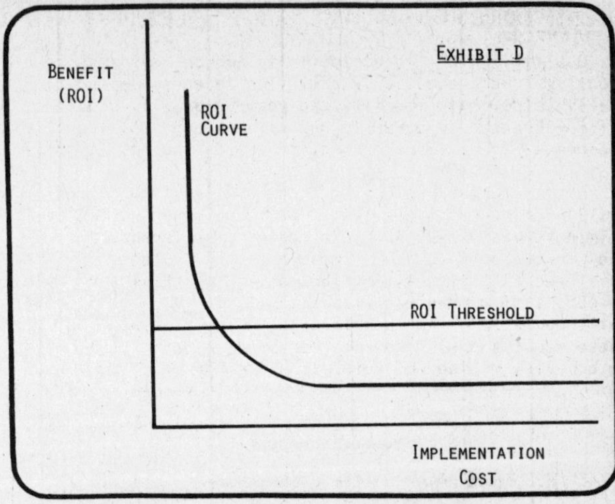

- focuses the effort toward the problem areas. Those areas where the greatest return on investment may be expected.
- serves as a simulation tool to test the results of an investment.

The results of this twofold modification of the Just-In-Time approach can be best illustrated by example. The following examples concentrate upon the "elimination of waste" elements of Just-In-Time to show how OPT can accelerate the implementation effort through a Pareto based focused approach.

FOCUSED FACTORY NETWORKS

Instead of building a large factory that is highly vertically integrated, the Japanese build highly specialized small plants. Smaller, more specialized facilities are less bureaucratic and easier to manage. Plants designed and built for a specific purpose are more economical to operate than "general purpose" plants.

OPT can be used to project capacity requirements, while OPT's highly flexible modeling language can be used to simulate plant loading. Plant proposals can be thoroughly tested to avoid the trial and error approach. The use of multiple simulations can focus efforts on the best configuration alternative. Brute and costly experience can be substituted by iterative simulations. The final product - a small, highly efficient plant - can be achieved without hard won experience.

Analysis of capacity boosting alternative routings using OPT can preclude the necessity of building additional plants. Again, the highly flexible language of OPT is the key, giving OPT the capability of modeling virtually any machine - fixture - workcenter - worker, etc. relationship within the plant. The elimination of waste through process changes can be driven and proven through simulations using OPT. A lifetime of hard won experience can be simulated in weeks or months. What took the Japanese years to achieve can be accomplished in a fraction of the time.

GROUP TECHNOLOGY

Like many of the Japanese approaches, Group Technology was invented here. The approach refers to the practice of grouping all of the operations required to produce a part together. Studies have shown that 90% of the time in a part's "life" within the plant is spent moving or waiting to be worked on. Reducing move and wait time through group technology can have a dramatic impact upon worker productivity as well as causing a reduction in work in process inventories.

The analysis required to develop the group technology aproach can be accelerated by OPT. Through its modeling capability, OPT can highlight manufacturing cell configuations with the potential of greatly reducing wait and move time. Work in process inventory reductions can be effected quickly through the use of simulations to configure the manufacturing cells. Again, this precludes the necessity of exhaustive trial and error. The Japanese success was hard won and took a good deal of time. Their success can be replicated through simulation using OPT at a fraction of the time and effort.

Quality is an objective with which everyone can identify. But quality where? The Japanese depend upon quality circles to identify and resolve quality problems. OPT may be used in a Pareto based approach to identify the areas where improved quality yields the most benefit – at the bottleneck.

Bottleneck identification is the key to focusing quality improvement as well as our other efforts to eliminate waste. Bottlenecks control the inventory level and throughput of a manufacturing plant. The bottlenecks' effect may be shown by dividing the resources of a manufacturing plant into two categories: bottlenecks and non-bottlenecks. The interaction of these two types of resources can be further illustrated by a review of the OPT Rules (see Exhibit E).

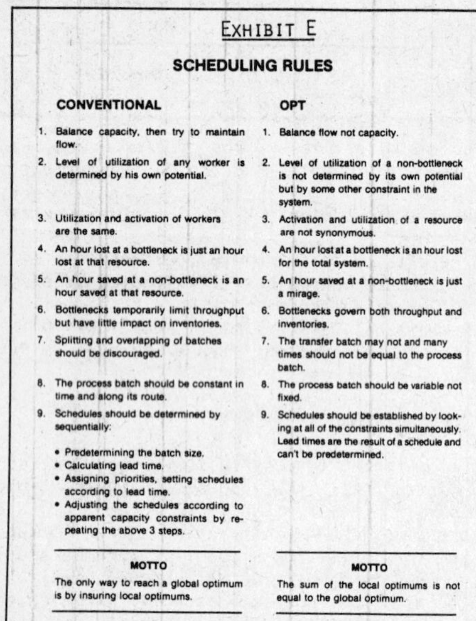

Exhibit E

SCHEDULING RULES

CONVENTIONAL	OPT
1. Balance capacity, then try to maintain flow.	1. Balance flow not capacity.
2. Level of utilization of any worker is determined by his own potential.	2. Level of utilization of a non-bottleneck is not determined by its own potential but by some other constraint in the system.
3. Utilization and activation of workers are the same.	3. Activation and utilization of a resource are not synonymous.
4. An hour lost at a bottleneck is just an hour lost at that resource.	4. An hour lost at a bottleneck is an hour lost for the total system.
5. An hour saved at a non-bottleneck is an hour saved at that resource.	5. An hour saved at a non-bottleneck is just a mirage.
6. Bottlenecks temporarily limit throughput but have little impact on inventories.	6. Bottlenecks govern both throughput and inventories.
7. Splitting and overlapping of batches should be discouraged.	7. The transfer batch may not and many times should not be equal to the process batch.
8. The process batch should be constant in time and along its route.	8. The process batch should be variable not fixed.
9. Schedules should be determined by sequentially: • Predetermining the batch size. • Calculating lead time. • Assigning priorities, setting schedules according to lead time. • Adjusting the schedules according to apparent capacity constraints by repeating the above 3 steps.	9. Schedules should be established by looking at all of the constraints simultaneously. Lead times are the result of a schedule and can't be predetermined.
MOTTO	**MOTTO**
The only way to reach a global optimum is by insuring local optimums.	The sum of the local optimums is not equal to the global optimum.

Since bottlenecks control throughput, a quality check before the bottleneck can assure that none of the bottlenecks' precious capacity is expended processing defective goods. All operations after the bottleneck containing material processed by the bottleneck likewise represent time at the bottleneck. Maybe our quality improvement efforts should focus from the bottleneck and upward as shown by Exhibit F. Poor quality in the critical resource network portion of Exhibit F impacts total plant throughput. As stated by OPT Rule 4, "An hour lost at a bottleneck is an hour lost for the total system." While the Japanese have been effective at improving overall quality, using OPT to focus in on those areas where quality is critical to plant throughput gives us the biggest return on investment. While the Japanese quality effort to obtain Just-In-Time benefits is a "shotgun approach", OPT zeros in on the key quality improvement areas with pinpoint accuracy. Using OPT _every_ action taken to improve quality has a positive impact on throughput.

The American approach to inventory is to stock material Just In Case something goes wrong. The Japanese approach is to drive queues toward zero in order to:
- minimize inventory investment. Cutting batch sizes in half cuts WIP inventory substantially.
- uncover anyy quality problems. The concept here is that lowering the level of water in the lake uncovers the hidden rocks. Running with less and less inventory reveals the problem areas so they may be addressed.
- reduce lead times. Since 90% of the time in a part's life is queue and wait time, reducing inventory by reducing batch size also reduces the amount of time parts must wait in queues to be processed.
- reduce reaction time. Faster cycle times allow a plant to react faster to changes in demand.

If the Just-In-Time approach is to be successful we must have good quality. Inventory is a hedge against

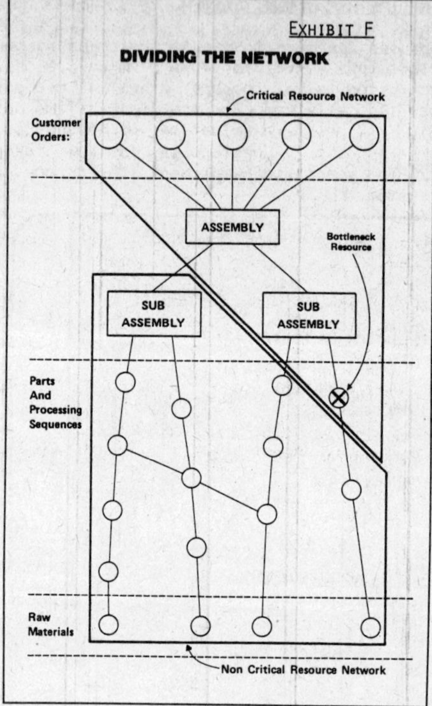

poor quality. The absence of inventory means that there are no backup parts to replace the defective ones.

The Japanese accomplish Just-In-Time production through a gradual reduction of inventory. Increasing the number of setups can be a good or bad move in accomplishing Just-In-Time production. If a work center is a bottleneck - where total time is equal to process and setup time - increasing the amount of setups reduces the amount of process time available. Since bottlenecks govern the total plants throughput, reducing the processing capacity of a bottleneck will have a negative impact on the entire plants throughput.

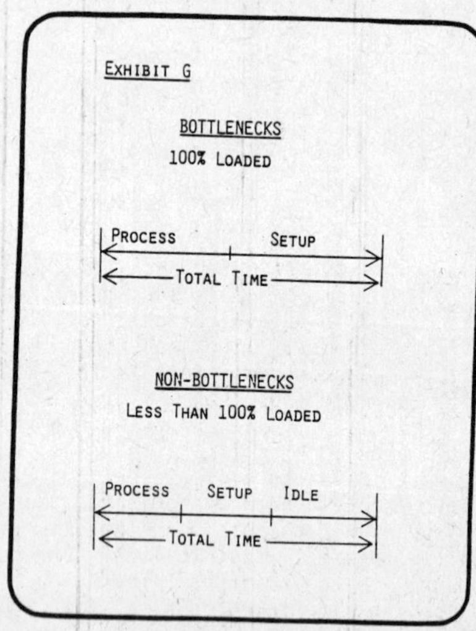

In a non-bottleneck work center the opposite is true. In the non-bottleneck, where the work center is not 100% utilized, total time is equal to process time, setup time and a third time component. That third time component is a dirty four letter word - idle time. Increasing setups at a non-bottleneck work center will increase the total amount of time spent on setups - cutting into the idle time. Thus, processing time stays the same while increased setups afford us the advantages of Just-In-Time production.

The Japanese have sorted out the bottlenecks and non-bottlenecks and focused their activity accordingly over a good deal of time. While the concepts are sound

and proven in practice, the knowledge required to
implement this approach in Japan was hard won through
years of effort. OPT can be used as the tool to identify
bottleneck versus non-bottleneck work centers.

The OPT ability to work with transfer batches and
process batches can further reduce inventories. This is
done by advancing small transfer quantities of material
to the next operation before the batch quantity at the
current operation is completed. The net effect is
splitting and overlapping production batches. There is a
key difference between the Japanese and OPT approach at
accomplishing this Just-In-Time aspect of production.
That difference is _speed_. While the Japanese approach is
trial and error over time, OPT automatically chooses the
optimal transfer and process batch sizes. Additionally,
OPT's managerial parameters allow criterion to be set in
the model which emphasize managements' scheme of
objectives: short or long range throughput, inventory
reduction, clearing the backlog, schedule disruption
protection, as well as a number of other considerations.

In short, OPT can direct the manufacturing facility
toward Just-In-Time production faster and more precisely.
With OPT, there is no need to gradually lower the water
to identify the rocks one at a time. We can find out
where the rocks are, remove them and lower the water all
at once.

UNIFORM PLANT LOADING

All of the Just-In-Time elements interact to produce
a synergistic effect - a result that is greater than the
sum of the parts. Uniform plant loading is achieved by
the Japanese by deriving a firm monthly production plan.
The output rate of the plan is frozen. The same mix of
products to be produced every month is built every day.
If possible, the same mix is produced _every hour_. This
approach, together with queue and wait time reductions,
moderates the impact of schedule changes. This assures
that there is always a total mix of product under
production to respond to variations in demand. The
impact is much smaller than, for example, the impact with
MRP where lot sizing from the Master Production Schedule
down through the bill of materials can telescope a minor
schedule change into a major impact on the shop floor.

The Japanese success with uniform plant loading
depends on manual effort and experience through trial and
error. OPT can -through simulation - achieve the same
effect automatically in a fraction of the time.

KANBAN PRODUCTION CONTROL SYSTEM

The Japanese use a simple card system - called Kanban
- for production control.

The production Kanban authorizes production, while
the conveyance Kanban pulls raw material into a work
center. When a work center prepares to produce a
container of parts, it pulls a container of raw material
from its inventory. In the container is a conveyance
Kanban (CK). The CK is removed and sent back to the
feeding work center. The feeding work center uses the CK
as its authorization to remove one container of its
finished goods to the downstream work center. Before the
container is sent, a production Kanban is removed and
used to authorize production of material to replace the
material being sent. The process ripples through the
factory's work centers like a domino effect. The Kanban
cards are used to pull material through the system one
container at a time.

The key to Kanban is not the cards themselves, but
the _discipline_ and concepts in play here. Material is
not moved or produced without Kanbans. Together with
Just-In-Time production, the emphasis is not to balance
capacity, but to balance flow. The objective is not to
activate work centers 100%, but to utilize them only to
the extent necessary to support the flow of containers
through the factory. The schedule for a given work
center is not dependent upon its production potential,
but is based upon the number of production Kanbans
received. In effect, the same concepts which drive the
Japanese Just-In-Time application are evident in OPT.
The difference is that the OPT Rules - the thoughtware -
is supported by the OPT software. The power of the
computer is used to facilitate the concepts. As a result
of the computer assist, the thoughtware becomes reality
in a fraction of the time necessary for the Japanese
approach.

MINIMIZED SETUP TIME

Just-In-Time demands an increased number of setups.
Increasing setup frequency can be unwieldly where setup
times are excessive. This is why the Japanese target for
setup times of less than 10 minutes everywhere in the
plant.

While the approach works, it is very costly to reduce
setup times everywhere in the plant. With OPT we can
zero in on reducing setups by starting where the
reduction will do us the most good. In the bottlenecks
setup time reductions increase the process time
available. In the non-bottlenecks setup time reductions
increase idle time and do nothing for productivity. OPT
identifies the bottlenecks for our consideration. OPT
simulations show the effect of specific setup time
reductions. Iterative simulations show us where the
setup reductions provide the greatest return on
investment. Avoiding time consuming manual analysis as
well as trial and error, OPT shows us where 90% of the
benefit can be achieved at 10% of the cost of reducing
setup times throughout the plant. The focused approach
through OPT is faster and more cost effective.

RESPECT FOR PEOPLE

Much has been written concerning the Japanese
emphasis upon respect for people. In contrast, the
American approach has been termed a "respect for hope" -
hope that the forecast is correct, the schedule is valid
and Murphy won't strike the plant. Many of the
Just-In-Time elements related to a respect for people
listed in Exhibit C have been attributed to cultural
differences. This is certainly one factor. But the
elimination of waste efforts actually facilitate a
respect for people. Building Focused Factory Networks,
easier to manage than highly vertically integrated
plants, makes it possible for Bottom Round Management -
decision making at the lowest possible level in the
organization.

There is another major element to the respect for
people. A change in the way workers are viewed. The
American approach has been to use Cost Accounting systems
to monitor work center activation. The emphasis has been
to activate the work center 100%. This approach looks
upon idle time as an unnecessary evil. The worker who is
not working becomes the target of our attempts to
"improve efficiency". But what happens when a work
center is activated beyond the point of its effective
utilization? Consider an example where a non-bottleneck
work center supports a bottleneck:

	Bottleneck Resource	Non-Bottleneck Resource
	X ⟵――――― Y	
Utilization	100%	50%
Total Demand	300 hrs./month	150 hrs./month
Capacity	300 hrs./month	300 hrs./month

While Y is only 50% activated, it is utilized to the
maximum extent necessary to support X. Activating Y in
excess of the 50% level will not increase X's output.
The only result will be to build an inventory in front of
X waiting to be processed. As we have seen, activating Y
beyond the 50% level would violate a number of the
Just-In-Time concepts as well as OPT Rule 3 -
"Utilization and activation of a resource are not
synonymous". Maybe instead of using our cost accounting
system to drive Y's activation to 100% in the interest of
"efficiencies", we should crosstrain the Y workers to
help with the X workload. Maybe we would be better off
reassigning the Y workers to Quality Circles when their
work is done. Maybe our attitude toward the workers
stressing an end to idle time only to build unnecessary
inventory should change. Maybe we would build trust and
a respect for people instead of inventories and poor
quality. As evidenced by the Japanese, Just-In-Time
companies are in a much better position to offer their
workers lifetime employment and their subcontractors a
stable workload than companies who do not use this
approach.

The use of OPT software and thoughtware can allow us to focus on the Just-In-Time approaches to the elimination of waste. It took the best Japanese companies 30 years to achieve Just-In-Time production. We don't have the time to merely equal the Japanese accomplishment. Using OPT, we can achieve Just-In-Time production in a fraction of the time and effort. In a short time, we can go further than the Japanese have gone in 30 years.

The weakness of the Japanese approach to implementing Just-In-Time is its failure to recognize the Pareto principle and to focus upon those areas that have the greatest impact upon the company's profitability. This weakness forces the Japanese to try to improve production operations by attacking many areas within the plant rather than the few areas that have the greatest impact upon their profits. Using OPT to identify where and how to proceed will enable U.S. companies to capitalize on the Just-In-Time techniques much more quickly, obtaining a much better return on the effort than the Japanese were able to derive. We _can_ leapfrog the Japanese - not by taking 30 years to copy their effort but by taking advantage of their Just-In-Time approach along with the new technology of OPT. The new technology holds the promise of enabling us to reverse the unfavorable trends we have seen in our manufacturing plants, and to insure our survival as a major industrial power.

BIOGRAPHY

Mr. Fox is the Executive Vice President of Consulting for Creative Output, Inc. - the developer of OPT (Optimized Production Technology). He has over twenty-five years of line and consulting experience in the United States, Europe and Japan. He has worked for or directly assisted some of the major corporations in the Western World in solving materials and manufacturing problems.

Mr. Fox began his career as a foreman and has held most line and staff manufacturing positions, including Vice President of Manufacturing and General Manager. He has published a number of articles on the OPT Concepts and their implications for manufacturing companies. He was among the first to document the techniques of Japanese Manufacturing and identify the reasons for their enormous success. In addition, his work on managing materials in a business downturn is also frequently cited in professional journals and management publications. Mr. Fox is a frequent speaker at professional and industry societies, seminars and forums.

Prior to joining Creative Output, Mr. Fox was a Vice President with the management consulting firm of Booz, Allen & Hamilton. He received a B.S. degree in Engineering from Notre Dame and an M.S. in Industrial Administration from Carnegie - Mellon University. He is active in APICS and has served as the President of the New York City Chapter.

L.I.F.E.: LOWERING INVENTORIES FOR EXCELLENCE

Ken Stork, CPIM*
Motorola, Inc.

In recent years, the American press has made a major discovery--JAPAN. We continue to be bombarded with success stories on: Just-In-Time, Kanban, Quality Circles, Robotics, etc. APICS, not to be outdone, has launched a Zero Inventory Crusade. Many Americans are reluctant to embrace these "new" concepts for a multitude of reasons. This is most unfortunate, as American industry pioneered most of these "new" concepts decades ago.

INVENTORY

The Japanese concept that inventory is evil and conceals problems appears radical to many practitioners. Only once in 20 years of liNe experience was I ever under <u>real</u> and <u>continuing</u> pressure to <u>reduce inventory!</u> My employer was in a sales boom growing 100% per year and achieving a large profit/return on net assets in excess of 100% per year. The only reason for the pressure to reduce inventory was that other large portions of the same corporation were losing money at an equal rate, and bankers insist that you pay your notes when they come due. My normal experience was pressure from my boss, typically a manufacturing director, to grow inventory even faster when business was good.

During economic slowdowns, it also was permissable for inventory to grow as it was a better alternative than cutting schedules, laying off or reassigning employees, reducing delivery schedules with suppliers, etc.

Inventory only goes down when MANAGEMENT insists upon it and tracks performance. Unfortunately, these same managers soon lose interest as their attention is diverted to other priorities, and the organization returns to its historical methods of "managing" inventories.

ARE YOU TURNED OFF OR TURNED ON?

A subtle but significant problem are the current terms: Just-In-Time, Zero Inventories, Stockless Production, etc.

- They imply perfeection, and we may be far from perfect today. Frequently, there is a backlash to the continuing barrage on Japan.
- These labels, terms imply an ultimate goal, e.g., <u>Zero</u> inventory.
- Reasonable, attainable, reach out, short term goals are more credible and acceptable--e.g., Half the Distance To The Wall.
- I developed a more accurate descriptive label--L.I.F.E.: Lowering Inventories For Excellence.

<u>HOW FAR HAVE WE STRAYED?</u>

FORD MOTOR COMPANY

- 1903 HAD 203 DAYS OF INVENTORY
- BUILT RIVER ROUGE FACILITIES
- INCREDIBLE VERTICAL INTEGRATION
- 1922 HAD 17 DAYS OF INVENTORY
- THRUPUT TIME FROM BOAT LOAD OF IRON ORE

  BEING UNLOADED TO CAR DRIVEN OFF END OF LINE

  WAS

  48 HOURS

- THIS FEAT IS UNEQUALED TODAY IN JAPAN

PROBLEMS AND SOLUTIONS IN THE WESTERN WORKPLACE

PROBLEMS IN THE WORKPLACE:
- MACHINE BREAKDOWN
- HIGH SCRAP
- BAD RAW MATERIALS
- NO REPAIR PARTS FOR MACHINE
- WORN TOOLS
- WORKER ABSENCE OR TARDINESS
- LATE ARRIVAL OF PARTS
- MATERIAL HANDLING NOT AVAILABLE
- WORKER LACKS TRAINING
- WAIT FOR INSPECTOR OR SETUP PERSON

TYPICAL SOLUTIONS:
- BUFFER STOCK BEFORE AND AFTER THE WORK STATION
- BACKUP MACHINES, OR SUPERMACHINES
- BACKUP MATERIAL HANDLING EQUIPMENT, OR SUPEREQUIPMENT
- EXTRA TOOLS
- EXTRA REPAIR PARTS
- EXTRA WORKERS
- ELABORATE INFORMATION SYSTEMS

JAPANESE CASE HISTORIES

o THE CHAIRMAN OF MITSUBISHI ASKED HIS STAFF - "WHY DO WE HAVE STOCKROOMS?"

o THREE MONTHS LATER HIS STAFF REPORTED TO HIM - "THERE ARE TWO MAIN REASONS"

1. A PLACE TO PHYSICALLY STORE INVENTORY ACCUMULATED FROM USING ECONOMIC ORDER QUANTITIES.

2. A PLACE TO STAGE MATERIALS PRIOR TO THE START OF ASSEMBLY.

o THE CHAIRMAN DECIDED - "MAKE THE STOCKROOMS GO AWAY".

o TODAY MITSUBISHI HAS VERY FEW STOCKROOMS LEFT IN THEIR PLANTS.

MELCO EXAMPLE
(JAPANESE LICENSEE OF WESTINGHOUSE)

o   ONE PLANT'S WIP & RAW MATERIALS INVENTORIES TURNED 12
    TURNS A YEAR.

o   MANAGEMENT - DO BETTER - NOT GOOD ENOUGH

o   4 MONTHS LATER AT 20 TURNS

o   2 YEARS LATER AT 40 TURNS

o   CURRENTLY AT 55 TURNS

o   1985 GOAL IS 100 TURNS

IMPACT OF JUST IN TIME SYSTEM
ON A JAPANESE DIESEL ENGINE MANUFACTURER

	1975	1980/81
DAYS OF INVENTORY	81	29
REAL OUTPUT PER WORKER (INDEX)	100	191
CHANGE IN CURRENT MACHINING COSTS (INDEX)		
ENGINE A	100	72
ENGINE B	100	44
DECREASE IN DEFECT RATES (INDEX)		
ENGINE A	100	56
ENGINE B	100	18
PRODUCT LINE VARIETY (MODELS)		
ENGINE A	190	441
ENGINE B	15	208

SOURCE: BOSTON CONSULTING GROUP

TOKYO SANYO ELECTRIC: HOUSEHOLD REFRIGERATORS

1. DIRECTION SET BY TOP MANAGEMENT (1975)
    "INVENTORY COVERS MANY SINS--INVENTORY LEVELS
    MUST BE REDUCED SIGNIFICANTLY"

2. ACTIONS TAKEN
    • STANDARDIZATION OF PARTS AND COMPONENTS
      BY MARKETING AND ENGINEERING
    • VENDOR DELIVERIES 1-4 TIMES/DAY (PREVIOUSLY
      1-4 TIMES/MONTH)
    • DEVELOPMENT OF MIXED MODEL ASSEMBLY LINE
      FOR LOWER VOLUME MODELS
    • REDUCTION OF SETUP/CHANGEOVER TIMES THROUGH
      EQUIPMENT AND PROCEDURE MODIFICATIONS
    • SMALLER LOT SIZES/MORE FREQUENT RUNS
      (DAILY OR EVERY OTHER DAY)
    • DISCIPLINE AND COMMITMENT TO THE POLICY
      THROUGHOUT OPERATIONS AND OVER TIME

3. RESULTS ACHIEVED

	1975	1980
PRODUCTION QUANTITIES (INDEX)	100	300
PRODUCTION MODELS	120	350
LOT SIZES	2-3 DAYS	1 DAY
INVENTORY LEVELS (WIP)	10 DAYS	1.5 DAYS
WAREHOUSE SPACE	80,000 FT^2	20,000 FT^2

• PRODUCTIVITY UP 126.4%

    • 1975 = 19.3 VEHICLES PER EMPLOYEE

    • 1982 = 43.7 VEHICLES PER EMPLOYEE

• OPERATION 50 PROGRAM

    • 3 YEAR EFFORT TO REDUCE WIP 50%

    • 6.8 DAYS SUPPLY IN 1975

    • 1.8 DAYS SUPPLY IN 1982

• INVENTORY REDUCTION REVEALED PRODUCTION SNAGS

• ALL SUPPLIERS NOW DELIVER DIRECT TO THE LINES

• PEOPLE PROVIDED THE SOLUTION

    • 6 MILLION SUGGESTIONS SINCE 1975

    • 50% ADOPTION RATE

    • 2.6 MILLION SUGGESTIONS IN 1982

• THE PEOPLE AT MAZDA ARE COMMITTED TO PRODUCING THE HIGHEST
  QUALITY PRODUCTS AT THE LOWEST POSSIBLE COST, AND IN THE
  SHORTEST POSSIBLE TIME.
  AND OUR 126.4% SOLUTION TO THE PROBLEM OF CONTROLLING
  PRODUCTION COSTS IS POWWERFUL EVIDENCE THAT THIS COMMITMENT
  IS BEING FULFILLED.

SUCCESS FROM A SYSTEMS APPROACH

    An important and frequently overlooked principle
is to design systems to concentrate on the process.
The following graphic shows two possible situations.

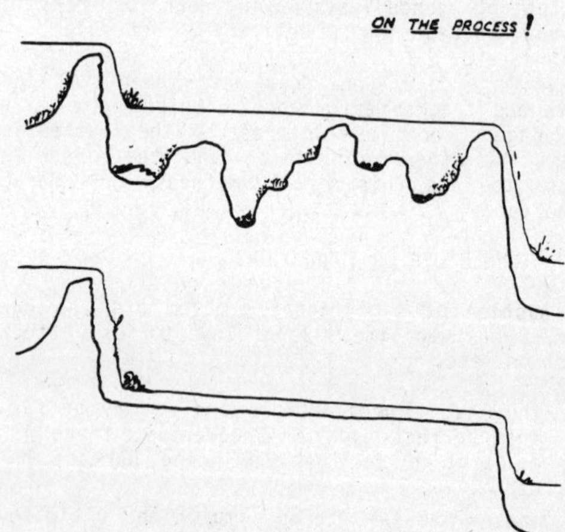

    The top half of the graphic portrays a
manufacturing process like a river with many rocks and
obstructions that reduce and slow the flow of the
river. Following this analogy, a traveler (product)
on this river (manufacturing process) will take a long
time to complete the journey from one end of the river
to their destination (manufacturing cycle time). A
frequent result is the selection of overly complex
manufacturing control systems to cope with our slow
moving river.

    The bottom half of the analogy presents a more
effective solution. Work on cleaning up the river by
solving problems in the factory, e.g., poor quality,
machine downtime, etc. If you work on the process
successfully, systems can be simpler as they will be
used to manage a simpler and more controllable

manufacturing environment. The previously cited Ford Motor - River Rouge example attests to the payback from this strategy. The common problem of poor payback from MRP II in many companies also attests to the difficulty of being successful when our people are using complex systems primarily to cope with every day problems in their working environment.

A MAJOR GOAL: MAKE PROBLEMS VISIBLE

Ed Heard has developed some excellent food for thought and how to proceed.

VISIBILITY PRINCIPLES

* IF YOU CAN'T SEE IT, YOU CAN'T CONTROL IT

* IF YOU CAN'T SEE IT, YOU CAN'T FIX IT

* IF YOU CAN'T REACT QUICKLY, IT WILL BE TOO LATE

THE IMPROVEMENT PROCESS

* OBSERVE SYMPTOMS
* FIND CAUSE
* FIX PROBLEMS

PRE-REQUISITES

* FAST
* ACCURATE
* SIMPLE
* COMMUNICATION SYSTEM

WHAT TO WATCH

* WORK-IN-PROCESS LEVELS
* MATERIAL FLOWS
* TOOL ROOM OPERATIONS
* SCRAP/REJECT RATES
* MACHINE DOWNTIMES
* WORK STOPPAGES
* MATERIALS HANDLING
* TOOL USAGE/FAILURE
* SETUP DURATION/FREQUENCY
* BATCH SIZES
* PRODUCT VARIETY
* DESIGN ENGINEERING CHANGES
* ALL OTHER DISRUPTIONS

Taking this a step further, I have developed what I call looking out the window.

LOOKING OUT THE WINDOW

* EVERY 20 MINUTES:

    * A <u>FULL</u> TRUCKLOAD OF STEEL ARRIVES
    * SAME TRUCK THEN LEAVES--<u>EMPTY</u>

* EVERY 60 MINUTES:

    * AN <u>EMPTY</u> TRUCK ARRIVES
    * SAME TRUCK THEN LEAVES--<u>FULL</u>

* WHERE DO THESE TRUCKS COME FROM?

* WHERE DO THESE TRUCKS GO?

* WHY NOT . . . . ?

Doctor Robert Hall has made a thorough study of this subject and he makes the following major points.

"TO DRAIN THE SWAMP" --

SIMPLICITY IS BEST

AVOID COMPLEXITY

OBJECTIVES OF MANUFACTURING CONTROL SYSTEMS

1. TO MAKE PROBLEMS (IMPEDIMENTS TO FLOW) <u>VISIBLE</u>

2. TO SIGNAL ALL OPERATIONS WHAT TO MAKE WITH MINIMUM FEEDBACK TIME.

3. TO PROVIDE LOW LEVEL CONTROL AND LOW LEVEL RESPONSIBILITY FOR IMPROVING THE PROCESS.

ALL ARE SUPPORTED BY MINIMIZING INVENTORY

Pyramid of Objectives

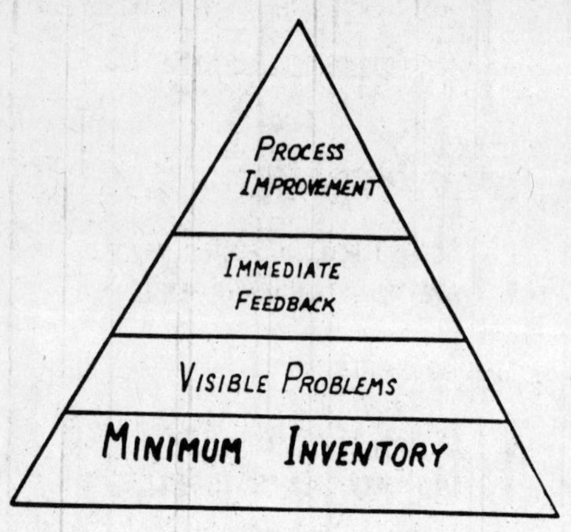

DESIGN THE SYSTEM TO CONCENTRATE ---

ON THE PROCESS!

FROM THIS:

TO THIS:

At this point, we need to reflect on the difference in inventory systems between Japan and America.

INVENTORY SYSTEMS - HOW THEY STACK UP

Inventory Control In Japan Tends To Start With:	Inventory Control in The U.S. Tends To Start With:
Small incremental improvements evolving into large systems as needed.	The implementation of a large computer based system to effectively manage inventory.
The line worker, who initiates many ideas leading to improved inventory control.	Upper management does all the initiating.
An overall point of view, recognizing that inventory control is inseparable from quality control, productivity, etc.	The isolation of the material handling problem or inventory control problem from other plant operations.
Personnel transfers across functional lines.	Little cross-fertilization of job functions.
Long-term stable relationships with suppliers.	Switching suppliers every so often to get the best price.

Operating closely with supplier. Looking for ways to make suppliers more effective.	Altering operations to accommodate supplier inefficiencies.
Frequent supplier deliveries.	Less frequent deliveries.
A long-term overview of policy.	Shorter term policies.
Feedback through the manufacturing system for just-in-time inventory which is ready when needed.	Accurate scheduling which determines what inventory should be used but results in stockpiling when "what is" differs from "what should be."
Desire for lean warehouse and in-process inventory, minuscule safety stock. Computers often used to reach these goals.	Desire for automated and computerized inventory control to improve efficiency. However, safety stocks remain fairly large.

Taken from _Iron Age,_ June 1, 1984 issue.

Particularly disquieting is the marriage of MRP and EOQ.

To illustrate, the following instructions are from Doctor Orlicky's book, Material Requirements Planning, Page 28.

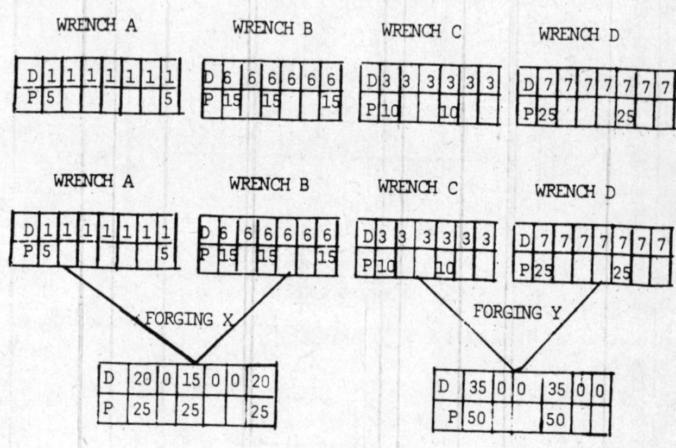

DEMAND PRODUCTION

(LOT SIZING)

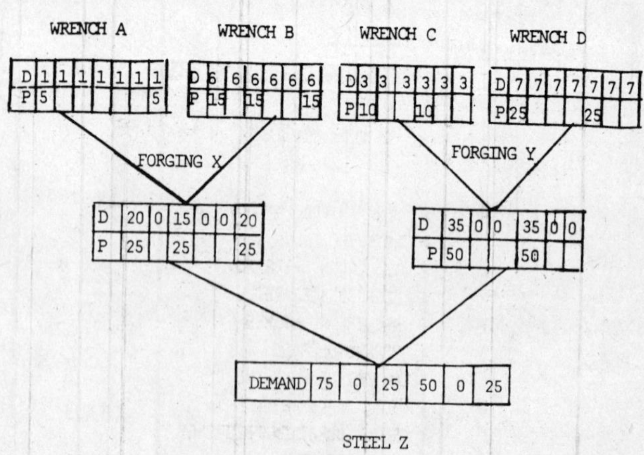

MORAL: PERFECT/LINEAR DEMAND BECOMES LUMPY DUE TO "ECONOMIC" LOT SIZES. IS EOQ REALLY "ECONOMIC"?

CONCLUSION

I am _not_ opposed to MRP as a valid management systems tool.

Early in my career, I was personally involved in several successful early installations in the 1960's. In the 1970's and 1980's I have heard of many examples of unsuccessful system installations. I speculate this is due to a failure to follow this three step process:

1. _Paradigm_ - This is a fancy word for a model of a business. The CEO must develop an overall plan or series of goals and objectives for his business. Some examples are:

   - Achieve sales growth of a minimum of 10% per year.
   - Achieve a return on assets of a minimum of 15% per year.
   - Concentrate the thrust of the business into products and markets where the firm has a distinctive competence.
   - Etc., etc., etc.

2. _Strategies:_ A wider array of functional strategies must be developed by the Vice Presidents of the major functions, e.g., Sales and Marketing, Engineering, Manufacturing, and Finance to execute the CEO's Paradigm and objectives. Some examples are:

   - _Sales and Marketing:_
     - Narrow the product line to concentrate on products and markets where the firm is a strong competitor.
     - Develop an ability to better respond to the requirements of major customers.
   - _Engineering:_
     - Reduce product costs and improve quality due to modular designs utilizing standardized designs and components.
     - Pursue new technologies to develop product leadership.
   - _Manufacturing:_
     - Use a high volume, low cost manufacturing strategy to: reduce costs, improve quality and provide excellent customer service.
     - Minimize manufacturing cycle time to ensure rapid response to customer requirements.
     - Develop improved relationships with suppliers to improve: quality, delivery and cost to support our other strategies.
     - Increased use of automation.

   - _Finance:_
     - Develop strategies to improve return on investment, e.g., improved inventory turnover, faster collection of receivables, etc., etc.

3. _Tools and Techniques:_

   - This becomes an exceptionally long list of supporting systems, tools and techniques to support the functional strategies and the CEO's Paradigm.
   - MRP II may be needed to support our strategies.
   - L.I.F.E./J-I-T/Zero Inventory is an even more likely candidate to support the Paradigm and Strategy examples we have shown. A marriage of these two approaches is an excellent choice, _if_ it is not a software driven process. The key to real success is solving permanently the typical problems we all face on the factory floor. Software alone hasn't and can't do it! It also detracts our view from the problems.

Today I see far too many "experts," including hardware and software vendors, consultants, educators, etc., running around selling the solution -MRP II without any knowledge of the Paradigm and Strategies of the customer. This fails my usual common sense test.

The barrage of stories on Japan has been very good for America. John Welty, an Executive Vice President of Motorola sums it up very well.

"If the Japanese didn't exist, we should have invented them also."

ABOUT THE AUTHOR

Ken Stork is Corporate Director, Materials and Purchasing for Motorola, Inc., in Schaumburg, Illinois. His career in Materials Management began as a part time Inventory Control Clerk while working his way through college. He has twenty years of line operations experience in industry with GULF & WESTERN, MARTIN MARIETTA, MCC POWERS and ADMIRAL Corporation.

Ken is one of the first 30 people certified as an APICS Fellow and is a Past President of the Cincinnati Chapter of APICS. He previously served as an officer and member of the Board of Directors of the American Materials Management Society, and is a member of George Plossl's Corporate Manufacturing Council. Ken recently became Director of Technical Development for the Repetitive Manufacturing Group within APICS special interest programs.

He has a BSC degree from DePaul University and an MBA degree from the University of Chicago, Graduate School of Business. Ken has taught courses in production and inventory control at the University of Cincinnati and at William Rainey Harper College. He has been a frequent speaker at APICS Annual Conferences and local chapter seminars.

BASIC INVENTORY REDUCTION

Jack B. Harrison, CPIM*
Martin Marietta Aerospace

INTRODUCTION

Inventory reduction is by far the area of greatest potential for productivity improvement available today.

This paper will address both the "why" and the "how" of inventory reduction. It is intended to provide the incentive for inventory reduction, to identify typical areas of opportunity for inventory reduction, and to suggest a methodology for systematic inventory reduction.

As the title implies, this paper will deal with basic concepts, principles, and techniques. No "hairy" algorithms or "secret black box" solutions are required. An entrepreneural instinct and some common sense are all that's necessary.

THE IMPACT OF INVENTORY

Traditional accounting principles and practices have contributed, to some extent, to a historic lack of emphasis on inventories. The separation of the income statement from the balance sheet, and the emphasis on profits, has allowed much of American management to lose sight of a few fundamental truths:

1) We are in business to MAKE MONEY, not necessarily profits.
2) MONEY IS MONEY, no matter what we call it (assets, income, expenses, liabilities, etc.).
3) The real bottom-line objective is to bring in more money than we send out!

Profits are the basis for corporate taxes. It is, therefore, often in the best interests of the company to take actions which reduce profits in order to increase cash flow. The variety of inventory valuation techniques (FIFO, LIFO, average), depreciation policies (straight line, accelerated, estimated life), and overhead proration methods are but a few of the myriad of games that can be played to manipulate profits. We may wish to lower profits in order to reduce taxes, or raise profits in order to enhance the sale of additional shares of corporate stock.

The point is this. Profits do not accurately reflect company well-being. Maximizing profits is not, nor should it be, the goal of the corporation. Profits are used as just one more tool to achieve the real objective of any free-enterprise organization: to maximize net cash flow. Dividends, vendors, and employees are all paid with cash, not profits. More than one company has shown a profit right up to th day they filed for bankruptcy. Yet other extremely lucrative enterprises, such as are commonplace in real estate, may never show a profit.

Once a person recognizes the above truths, inventory reduction takes on a new perspective. Reduction of inventory has an immediate and direct impact on cash flow. A $1,000,000 inventory reduction doesn't represent a savings of $140,000 per year (the traditional cost-of-capital approach). It represents a $1,000,000 cash savings right NOW!

The typical American electronics firm turns its inventory about three times per year. Let's take a closer look.

Sales Revenues	$100 Mil
Cost of Goods Sold	$ 80 Mil
Gross Profits	$ 20 Mil
Taxes	$ 10 Mil
Net Profits	$ 10 Mil

Average inventory @ 3 turns/yr. = $27 Mil.

This means that the average amount of money tied up in inventory is equivalent to 2.7 YEARS WORTH OF PROFITS! To put it in more practical terms, the average American electronics firm could double its profits for one full year and not generate as much cash as a fifty percent reduction of inventory. A twenty percent reduction of inventory will generate as much cash as six full months of operation!

Inventory reduction produces cash.

HOW MUCH INVENTORY SHOULD I HAVE?

This question ranks right up there with "Do you still beat your wife?" Everyone knows how much inventory they should have. They should have less than they've got! How much less? Pick a number. I personally like 15% and three months - drop the inventory by 15% in three months with no degradation in quality or shipping performance. It could be 25% in six months; 30% in nine months. Take your pick. Or better yet, ask the people who impact the level of inventory what percent reduction they would feel is a reasonable goal. Once a goal has been reached, set another goal!

The point is this. Spending time and effort on determining the "correct" level of inventory is, at best, a poor use of resources. Too often a target level of inventory is calculated based on the current operating parameters; safety stock policies, existing lot size rules, standard lead times, etc.

These parameters become the "givens." People are expected to reach the target level inventory without changing the underlying parameters. Yet safety stocks, lot sizes, and lead times are the very parameters that must be changed if significant inventory reductions are to be achieved.

Setting inventory reduction targets is an excellent means of producing results. However, never tie the objective to the existing method of operation. It is by changing the way we do business that the major improvements are accomplished.

HOW MUCH INVENTORY DO I HAVE?

This question of how much inventory you've got is not as obvious as it sounds. The inventory level represents a snapshot taken at some instant in time. The actual level of inventory varies over time and, therefore, the value obtained is a function of when we choose to take the snapshot.

TYPICAL SALES AND INVENTORY PATTERN

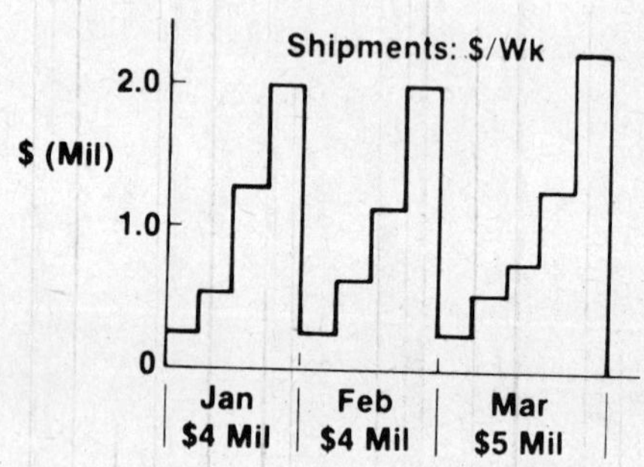

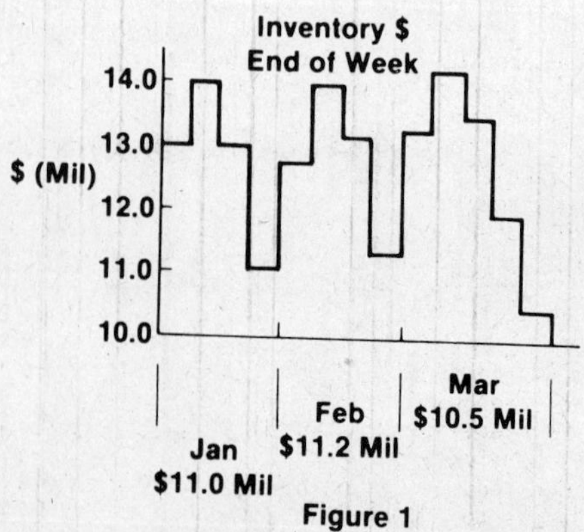

Figure 1

Figure 1 illustrates an all too typical sales and inventory pattern. Using the generally accepted approach of considering only end-of-month inventory levels we would conclude that our average inventory investment is $10.9 mil. However, when you consider the swings that occur within each month (by measuring end-of-week inventory levels) the average investment changes to $12.7 million; a difference of 17% or $1,800,000! Which figure do you feel more accurately reflects the amount of cash actually tied up in inventories?

What do you think causes this typical saw-tooth curve of shipments and the resulting wide swings in inventory levels?

One thing you can bet on when you see this pattern of shipments: Top management responsible for plant operations is being measured on a <u>month ending</u> performance basis. What do you think would happen if we tightened up our measurement to a strictly week-ending basis?

The answer to these questions is obvious, yet it is almost universally overlooked. There is no natural business cycle that causes the month-end spike in shipments. It is 100% self-imposed. It is purely the result of our measurement technique.

The inefficiencies associated with operating as in Figure 1 can be sizable indeed. In addition to an increased average inventory investment, the uneven workload takes its toll in overtime, product quality, and morale problems related to the end-of-month panic.

Let's take a closer look at the current way we measure operations management, and suggest an alternate method aimed at smoothing the saw-tooth curve.

On a month-ending basis, the shipping goal for January was $4 mil. Actual shipments also were $4 mil. Shipping performance was 100%! The operations manager is a hero.

A simple way to emphasize weekly shipping performance without taking the "heat" off of month-ending results is to measure operations on a weekly cum basis. The results for January are shown below.

	January			
Week	1	2	3	4
Cum Shipping Goal	1.0	2.0	3.0	4.0
Cum Actual Shipments	0.25	0.75	2.0	4.0
% Performance	25%	38%	67%	100%
Average Shipping Performance:	58%			

Operations management is measured on <u>average</u> weekly shipping performance, or 58%. This simple change in emphasis has produced dramatic productivity gains in companies incorporating the concept.

SPECIFIC TECHNIQUES

Time and space do not allow thorough discussion of all of the various areas of opportunity for inventory reduction. We will, therefore, concentrate on those opportunities which have, to date, received little exposure in the literature.

First, it is important to understand the distinction between active inventory and inactive inventory. Active inventory is that inventory for which we anticipate a customer demand within the foreseeable future. Conversely, inactive, or obsolete, inventory consists of material currently on the books for which there is <u>no</u> reasonable expectation of a customer requirement.

As we talked about earlier, the reduction of a dollar's worth of active inventory is worth one dollar in positive cash flow. The impact on profits and taxes, however, is small.

On the other hand, a reduction of inactive inventory has a major impact on profits and taxes. The <u>only</u> impact on cash flow is that which is caused by the tax savings.

Let's use an example to illustrate. Joe is a distributor. He has 10 units of product A and 10 units of product B in stock. He sells one unit of product A every week and buys a replacement unit every week. Product B, however, hasn't sold in years and Joe doesn't anticipate any change in the future.

If Joe reduces his on-hand inventory of product A from 10 units to 5 units, what happens to cash flow during the inventory reduction period? For five weeks Joe continues to sell product A and receive cash income.

His cash outflow for replacement units during those five weeks is zero! There is a change to his balance sheet (inventory is reduced, cash is increased) but no change to profits or taxes. In other words, Joe increased his net cash flow by the total cost of five units of product A, the total value of the inventory reduction - tax free!

Joe now decides to get rid of his inactive (obsolete) inventory, product B. He can't find a buyer for product B and decides to scrap all ten units. The inventory write-down reduces profits by the full inventory value of product B. Since Joe's company pays approximately 50% of profits to Uncle Sam, every dollar of inactive inventory written off produces a cash tax savings of about $.50.

Active Inventory:

$1.00 Inv. Reduction = $1.00 Additional Cash.

Inactive Inventory:

$1.00 Inv. Reduction = Approx. $.50 Additional Cash.

The moral of the story? Inventory reduction pays! And, in the case of inactive inventory, disposing of the material can transform a worthless paper asset into valuable cold hard cash.

Dispose of Inactive Inventory

The first simple way to reduce inventory and generate cash, then, is to identify and dispose of all inactive inventory. There are many techniques to identify such material, some sophisticated and some not. The important points to recall are these: 1) Data bases, no matter how good, are seldom 100% accurate. Prior to disposal, always send a complete listing of all proposed items to anyone and everyone who might possible have a need for the material in question. 2) Try to find a buyer for the obsolete inventory. Any loss taken from selling at a price below book value is still tax deductible, and any cash received simply increases the "yield" above 50%. For example, if we sold a $1.00 item to a scrap dealer for $.40, we'd show a $.60 loss per items and save approximately $.30 in taxes. The net result is a 70% yield: $.40 in cash, $.30 in reduced taxes.

Maintain Credible Schedules

Perhaps the most common cause of excess active inventory is the overloaded master schedule. The master schedule drives material requirements planning. An overloaded MPS simply requests more material than the company has the capability to utilize. The solution, however, is generally of an educational/philosophical nature. The mechanics of Resource Requirements Planning (RRP), Rough Cut Capacity Requirements Planning, and detailed CRP are well understood and documented in the APICS literature.

There is no substitute for realistic schedules and commitment to their execution.

Simplify Your Product Structure

Bill of Material structure has a significant, and often overlooked, impact on the level of inventory as well as general productivity. In the traditional MRP approach, each level in the BOM when completed is closed to stores, then kitted with other components and re-issued to the production floor to build the next higher level assembly. The impact of excess levels on total product lead times, material handling, and record keeping is obvious.

Be particularly cautious of the lead time trap. All too often an additional level is added to the BOM to avoid reducing the manufacturing lead time. The logic goes something like this. "Since we don't actually use these parts until three weeks after issue, why not create a separate level of the BOM? That way we can use our MRP to order the parts for use when we actually need them and avoid having them sit idle in WIP all that time."

I've seen this logic applied on numerous occasions. In every case the problem was not in the BOM structure. <u>The lead times were too long!</u>

How much lead time should you have? LESS THAN YOU'VE GOT!

The Japanese successes in reducing all lead times have clearly illustrated both the magnitude of lead time improvement available, and the tremendous productivity potential in so doing.

There is already an excellent body of knowledge available on this subject, and more is being written every day. Take the time to read the literature and start applying it in your company today.

One often overlooked opportunity for lead time reduction occurs when the factory increases its capacity through the implementation of additional work shifts: i.e., goes from a one-shift operation to two or more shifts. Whenever the number of shifts increases, the amount of hours available for work increases. Adding a full second shift doubles the amount of time a product is available for work. This is equivalent to doubling the lead time!

Suppose we've reduced the lead time of a product down to what we feel is a reasonable ratio of process time to available hours. Our product requires twenty hours of processing and the lead time is two weeks (one shift). Available hours = (2 week lead time) x (40 hours/week) or 80 hours. Thus our product lead time currently has: 80 hours available minus 20 hours of process time, or 60 hours of planned slack time.

What happens if we add a second shift? We still require twenty hours of process time but now our available hours have doubled: (2 weeks) (40 hours/shift) (2 shifts) = 160 hours available for work. Slack time is now 140 hours, not 60 hours as before.

Any permanent addition to available hours should be accompanied by a similar reduction in product lead times.

What if your company does not require the additional capacity of a second shift? You might want to consider moving some of the current work force to the second shift. This obviously has no impact on total capacity but it does impact hours available for work. Products are manufactured through a series of operations which must be performed sequentially (nine women can't produce a baby in one month!).

Let's use an example product to illustrate. Our product goes through four operations. Each operation requires eight hours of process time. We're currently on a one-shift operation and produce one unit per day. The minimum lead time is four days (see Figure 2). What happens if we move steps two and four to the second shift? Our capacity is still one unit per day. Our manpower is still four people: two on first shift, two on second. But our minimum lead time and work-in-process level can be cut in half! Operation steps one and two still require eight hours each, but now they can be accomplished in one day.

4 OPERATIONS, 8 HR/OPERATION
BUILD REQUIREMENTS: 1 PER DAY

	1 Shift				
	Day 1	Day 2	Day 3	Day 4	
4 Steps 4 Operators	1 人	2 人	3 人	4 人	Output: 1 per day Lead Time: 4 days WIP: 4 units
	2 Shifts				
4 Steps 4 Operators (2 Per Shift)	2 1 人 人	4 3 人 人			Output: 1 per day Lead Time: 2 days WIP: 2 units

Figure 2

If your company is currently on a one-shift operation, take a hard look at moving some of the work-force to second shift - not for capacity, but for lead time reduction. Remember, cash is cash. Would you trade a $100,000 per year shift premium for a $2,000,000 active inventory reduction this year?

Once you've recognized the facts that: 1) our objective is to maximize net cash flow, and 2) inventory reduction has a significant positive impact on cash flow; then new possibilities abound.

Spend tooling money for quick set-up and changeover in order to reduce lot sizes and lead times.

Implement source inspection to reduce safety stocks.

Pay a premium for vendor stocking.

Reserve vendor capacity to provide specific product flexibility.

Spend money on "building in" quality to reduce the rework loops.

Move toward point-of-use delivery. Eliminate raw material stocking.

Implement a pull through WIP control system. Build only what you need, when you need it.

Provide realistic schedules and allow safety capacity. Then demand performance to the schedule; first on a weekly basis, then daily, then hourly.

THE M O R E APPROACH TO LESS INVENTORY

The M O R E method of productivity improvement combines aspects of MBO (management by objectives) and quality circles.

A valid Measurement of some productivity parameter is established. A consensus Objective is agreed upon and graphically displayed in a highly visible location. How the objective is to be achieved is left entirely to the M O R E team participants. Recognition is provided for results. On-going Education and cross-training programs provide employees with the skills for continued improvements and a knowledge of fundamental productivity goals.

Choose a measurement that affects the level of inventory. It should be noted that the chosen measurement does not have to be all-inclusive. In fact, for best results segment your target to a workable size. For example, instead of measuring total safety stocks, choose the top five or ten part numbers. Instead of attacking all lead times, pick the top few products. Go after lot size reductions on a specific few items, i.e., stick with "bite size" chunks. Any measurement chosen must be quantifiable and best results are obtained with weekly measurement.

Objectives must be established by consensus among all key individuals impacting the measurement. This forces individuals to approach a common objective from a team perspective. It is one of the major benefits of the M O R E technique.

Success breeds success. Choose initial M O R E projects which have a high probability of attainment and can be accomplished in a short period of time (four to six weeks).

Plot actual measurement data weekly and establish a baseline, i.e., determine where you're at today.

Once a consensus objective has been set, plot the target curve: a straight line from the current baseline to the objective. Each week the actual measurement is compared to the target as defined by the target curve, thus providing the M O R E team with an ongoing progress report (see Figure 3).

Recognition is extremely important. Keep the progress graph prominently displayed. Recognition by management, in person, during and following completion of a project is a powerful motivator and good for employee morale.

Education is a key ingredient in M O R E program success. The M O R E process itself provides employees new insight into the roles and responsibilities of other departments, and functional interrelationships. This can and should be enhanced through formal in-house training, cross training, and job rotation programs. Of even greater importance, however, is the establishment of basic productivity philosophies, e.g.: (1) There is no "best" way - what we want to encourage is a continuous striving for a "better" way. Constant improvement is the objective. (2) Inventory is evil. Employees should be formally introduced to the costs and consequences of excess inventories. Inventory reduction should be seen as a primary company goal. (3) Zero defects. Quality is everyone's responsibility.

Let's recap M O R E:
M: Establish a productivity Measurement
O: Set a consensus Objective
R: Provide Recognition for achievement
E: Build upon continuing employee Education

Figure 3 illustrates the results of a M O R E program implemented at Singer Business Machines. The Measurement established was weekly total work-center payroll dollars divided by the quantity of good printed circuit board assemblies (PCB's) produced. No credit was given for rework units.

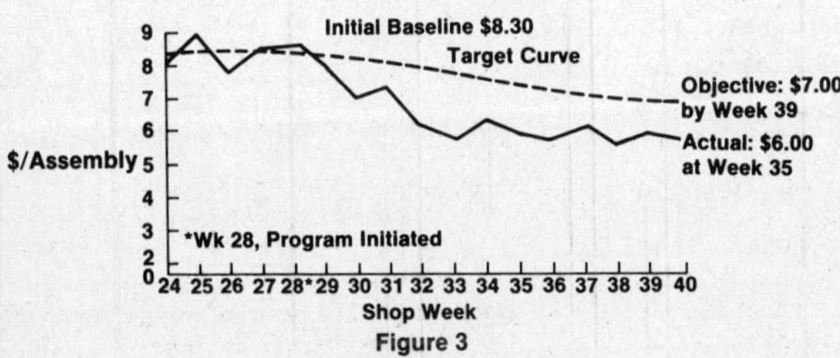

Figure 3

Each of my process engineers was provided the historical data for his/her work center and asked to determine a target cost Objective. The only constraint was that any such objective had to be a consensus between himself/herself and the other key players: quality, manufacturing, design, etc.

Once an objective was established, large posters graphically displaying historical cost per board as well as th target cost curve, were prominently displayed in their respective work centers.

Recognition was abundant. The large graphs posted on the shop floor stimulated interest throughout the plant. Little prodding was required to get the plant manager and his staff to make personal visits to the work centers at various stages of the program. And, the final achievement was acknowledged at a plant-wide informal company-paid luncheon.

The composite results are shown in Figure 3. Every work center exceeded its objective. The labor cost per board through all six work centers was reduced by more than 25% - in seven weeks! With No Capital Spending!

The Educational aspects of the team project were quite significant. Participants gained new insight into the inter-relationships of their various functions. One excellent educational vehicle involved the holding of informal meetings in which a M O R E team would explain their experiences to other interested groups. Longer range educational programs included cross-training, in-house courses (both formal and informal), and tuition refund.

The M O R E productivity approach is simple to implement and can provide dramatic results. It puts responsibility and recognition back into the hands of the "Doers." It promotes teamwork and a common objective. It requires little or no capital spending - in fact, it is typically a significant cash generator! And, it can be applied at any organizational level, i.e., no waiting for corporate approval.

Now it's up to you.

"Basic Inventory Reduction" was first presented at the American Production and Inventory Control Society (APICS) national conference held in New Orleans, November, 1983. Permission has been granted for this reprint.

ABOUT THE AUTHOR

Mr. Jack B. Harrison's sixteen years in industry split equally between Production/Inventory Control and Manufacturing/Industrial Engineering. Positions held include: Materials Manager, Inventory Control Manager, Manager of Master Planning, Process Engineering Manager, Manager of Industrial Engineering and Internal Consultant. He was the implementation team leader of a highly successful Manufacturing Resource Planning (MRP II) system and developed the industry proven M O R E Productivity Improvement technique.

Mr. Harrison is a frequent speaker at professional society conferences, seminars, and dinner meetings and has authored numerous articles on Productivity and Production/Inventory Control. He is listed in the Marquis publication, "Who's Who in Industry and Finance."

He was the founding president of the Albuquerque Chapter of APICS and past vice-president of the Mid-Florida APICS Chapter.

Academic background consists of a Bachelors Degree in Industrial Engineering from Ohio State, MBA in Finance from North Texas State, and CPIM*.

STATISTICAL QUALITY CONTROL START-UP WITH VENDORS

William J. Stoner, CPIM
Hewlett-Packard

OBJECTIVE

A case study reporting our approach to moving all of our (Hewlett Packard's Colorado Springs Division) sheet metal fabrication operation to outside fabricators. The challenges we faced with our documentation for finished assemblies, our local vendors innocence but eagerness to produce defect free parts.

Getting vendors interested in statistical quality control is the easy part; getting them to the point where they are controlling their processes and they can prove it is a whole different ball game.

FIVE YEAR PLAN

In preparing our five year plan, we identified a need for qualified local vendors to provide quality finished sheet metal parts for our Just-In-Time production process. Our sheet metal fab shop needed a major capital equipment expenditure to replace old equipment and improve it's productivity. For our high-tech company to spend big dollars to bend metal didn't fit the plan. The plan called for a complete JIT factory by the end of 1988, and to improve our product introduction cycle by a factor of three. Translated to dollars meant more computer aided engineering and design hardware and software.

The capital dollars needed for a flexale manufacturing sheet metal system would not produce the leverage for our companies future that other items would. This meant we were not going to be in the sheet metal business. We must shift our sheet metal part source from inside to outside suppliers who can provide quality parts JIT; suppliers who already build sheet metal parts, suppliers that have already made the investments and are now working on the leading edge of their technology. Quality vendors.

DEFINE THE QUALITY VENDOR

First, what did we mean by quality. Define quality and apply the general meaning to our customer vendor relationship.

QUALITY: Conformance to the requirement.

REQUIREMENT: $<$ 100 ppm for all parts for:

1. On time delivery
2. Defects

Our goal was to go from having two percent per month of the orders late to less than 100 parts per million late in any one month, and have these parts arrive with less than 100 defects per million.

Quality is what you define it to be. Just remember if you are asking for something that is not doable you will not succeed. You must accept ownership for your part of the agreement. If the parts are late or bad because you didn't perform, the vendor can not be dinged.
For example:

1. Orders to vendor late.
2. Specifications that cannot be obtained.
3. Drawings that do not have enough information (finish or paint instructions).

All vendors are not mind readers - believe it or not. You know what you want. You must be able to define it in such a way others can make the part without a phone call two days prior to planned delivery.

Once the requirements have been defined you must be able to measure the conformance to requirement. If you agree on one of the standard AQL sampling plans, you have just told your vendor, "I expect you to send me bad parts, and I am willing to pay for them." You have also said, "make all of bad parts you have to, just send me the good ones, and some of the bad ones." If this is what you want and you and your vendor have reached an understanding, fine. But, if this is not what you want, state what you want and pay for it.

Inspection programs produce some or all of the following:

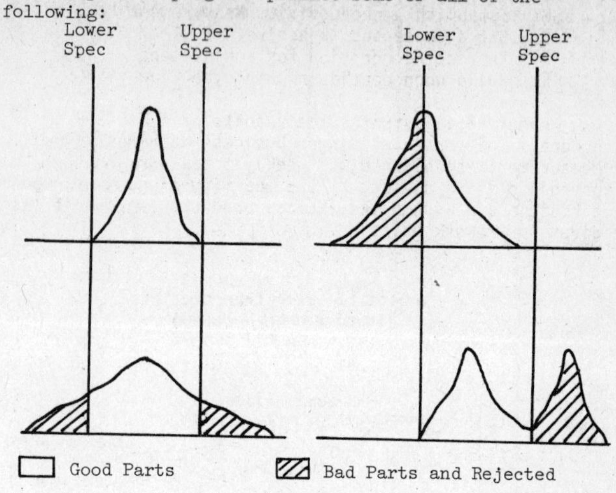

Lower Spec   Upper Spec   Lower Spec   Upper Spec

Good Parts   Bad Parts and Rejected

Figure 1

What we all want is a vendor that will produce all of the parts defect free and deliver them just-in-time. However, the dream vendor is still being searched for by many of us. Others say it can be done, and the professional magazines are full of articles reporting how our competition is dealing with their dream vendors.

What kind of vendors can do this magic? Well, those using statistical quality control (SQC). Notice how hard I have tried to avoid referring to the Japanese, and for good reason. Many make the correlation that the Japanese companies ability to produce defect free parts is because they are better or more dedicated workers. NOT SO. The best Sony plant in the world is in San Diego, California. Then what? Oh yes, the only other factor left - management. Quality parts produced by a company are a direct result of that company's commitment to excellence and meeting the customer's expectation. Very simply, a quality vendor is committed to meet the requirement and has the tools to measure the deviations, if any.

SURVEY THE LOCAL AREA FOR THE QUALITY VENDORS

Surveying the local vendors produced too few candidates. We expended our search to a two hundred and fifty mile radius from Colorado Springs, Colorado. We were looking for quality vendors that would provide parts from their production line to our production line with zero defects.

We believed this objective could be obtained through the use of control charts prepared by the vendor while producing the parts. By controlling the process to produce parts that meet the requirement, you produce quality parts every time.

Three levels of understanding were found when vendors were asked to provide control charts with their parts; 1. they were already providing control charts; 2. they had read about it and were willing to learn how; 3. they didn't know what we were talking about. There were only one or two providing charts to other customers and they weren't sheet metal vendors.

How then to bridge the gap for those who were at levels 2 and 3? Share our expectations with these vendors and be willing to educate and work with them, develop those that were willing.

INVITE THE VENDORS TO SQC TRAINING

In theory you would like all of your vendors to be able to provide defect free parts on time. From an academic standpoint it doesn't take any more effort to educate four vendors than it does forty. Many of our vendors were in need of SQC education, understanding and motivation. Why not provide SQC training to all that will come. Focusing the invitations on those vendors that we have the most problems with, but offering it to all takers.

Now that we had identified in general terms who, what would the training consist of? We were teaching a two-day basic SQC course to all of our employees. After close review we decided that it contained the basic information necessary to produce understanding and create motivation for future action. The course provided practical exercises to show the student how to prepare charts and how to interpret the information once charted.

STATISTICAL QUALITY CONTROL

SEMINAR FOR VENDORS

1ST DAY

8:00	INTRODUCTION TO SQC	DIVISION MGR
8:30	QUALITY PHILOSOPHY	DIV QA MGR
9:00	MANAGE THRU QUALITY (VIDEO)	PHIL CROSBY
10:00	COFFEE BREAK	
10:15	FUNDAMENTAL STATISTICAL CONCEPTS	
12:00	LUNCH	
1:00	CONTROL CHARTS FOR VARIABLES (X, R)	
2:00	BREAK	
2:15	CONTROL CHARTS FOR VARIABLES (X, R)	
	MOVING RANGE CONTROL CHARTS	
4:00	BREAK FOR DAY	

2ND DAY

8:00	WELCOME	SHOPS MGR
8:30	REVIEW PREVIOUS DAY'S ASSIGNMENT	
9:00	CONTROL CHARTS FOR ATTRIBUTES (P, C)	
10:00	COFFEE BREAK	
10:15	CONTROL CHARTS FOR ATTRIBUTES (P, C)	
12:00	LUNCH	
1:00	INTERNAL SHOP APPLICATION AND TOUR	SHOP SUPR
2:00	DATA GATHERING AND SPECIAL TOPICS	
3:00	VIDEO TAPE OF BILL CONWAY	
4:00	BREAK FOR DAY	

Figure 2

A letter, figure 3, signed by the Division Manager which included the two-day schedule was prepared as an invitation. This invitation was addressed to presidents of companies with copies to the local sales contact.

May 12, 1983

Dear . . . . . .

> "People and poor workmanship are really
> not the cause of poor quality; 85 percent
> of all quality problems originate in the
> system, the process or in the materials
> being used."
>
> Paul Ely, Computer Group Vice President
> Hewlett Packard Company

You are an extremely important supplier of parts used in our manufacturing process.

You are a vital part of our manufacturing effort, and I invite you to attend a Statistical Quality Control Seminar at the Colorado Springs Division. The objective of the seminar is to provide tools for improving our communicating link with respect to quality, as well as tools for:

Disclosing natural capabilities of production processes.

Preventing defects through control of production processes.

Separating assignable causes of quality variation.

The seminar will be June 21 and 22 from 8:00 a.m. to 4:00 p.m. Please bring a calculator.

I have reserved two seats for you and look forward to having you as guests at our facility. Please R.S.V.P. to Linda Rowe, 303-590-2301, by Wednesday, June 1.

Best regards,

Tom Vos
General Manager

Figure 3

We have put this seminar on five times for more than 140 representatives of some 80 different companies. Each time we invited 40 companies reserving two seats and limited the attendance to 30 on a first come basis. There was always a waiting list.

Many of the first attendees were sales people. The motivation was to find out, "What does HP want now?" They went away with a new perspective of SQC, its power, and a saying my grandmother used on me many times, "Do it right the first time, you don't have time to do it over." It is so basic I refer to it as "DIRT."

GETTING THE VENDOR STARTED

A seminar is a very emotional thing. You hear, see and do things in a sterile environment. You watch TV presentations and follow professional instructors through in-class exercises. You say, "It's not magic, I can do this stuff, I know what I'm doing." You rush back to the factory about ten feet off of the ground and become surrounded by the uninformed. The "same ol wayers" with questions you don't have the answers for. The instructor is back in Colorado and there is "fire" that needs your immediate attention. It has been burning since the day you left for the SQC seminar. The heart of the problem seems to be, some vendor delivered material that didn't meet spec and Incoming Inspection had rejected it; but the production manager felt the slight deviation wouldn't cause any problem, and besides he needed the material to make shipments for the month. The slight deviation caused an equipment problem, now the whole damn plant is on fire!!!

SQC seems so far away, and the line of least resistance is still the "same ol way." When the vendor orders parts and requests charts, just take the order and hope they don't ask for the charts.

There are at least two ways to move from the "same ol way" to SQC:

1. Managements consistent pressure to insist on charts that concentrate on a total commitment for excellence. DIRT.

2. Customers demanding quality at lower cost, which is another way of saying, DIRT, no time or money for rework.

We have experience with both methods, which ultimately wind up with the same results. The workers controlling the quality of their work using control charts to monitor their process.

CASE #1

A raw material vendor came to our seminar and got excited about the process. The messenger didn't get shot, but sent others from his company to the seminar. They got excited, but realized the seminar didn't give them enough to get started on their own. They asked us if we would train their people. Answer, No. There are many consulting firms that will lay out an education and training program that will be designed to fit your specific needs.

The vendor qualified a firm and contracted them to begin a program to bring them up to a point of excellence. This vendor is not only providing raw material JIT on a weekly delivery schedule with < 100 ppm defects, but is working with their raw material supplier toward a set of similar defect and delivery goals.

The president of the company, in his letter inviting all of his regional managers and staff to the first five-day training session, stated in part, if you don't find a

need for this training and its application, you may be
working for the wrong company. DIRT.

CASE #2

A local sheet metal vendor came to our seminar and
got excited, but was overwhelmed. They were having trouble
producing good parts, and were certain that SQC was the
answer, but didn't have enough understanding of the process
and its application to get started. This caused us to look
at the course content; a motivating overview. We suggested
they collect data and use precontrol as a start. Reviewing
their data told them their processes were not in control.
The more they used the precontrol method to monitor the
production of their parts, the more they saw the value of
the data. They became excited again and ask for more help.
One of our Process Engineers and our Statistion began to
work with the vendor and suggested sampling methods that
would lead them to controlling their processes through SQC.

MAKE THE VENDOR AN EXTENSION OF YOUR BUSINESS

Just getting your vendors to produce defect free parts
using SQC is only part of the $<$ 100 ppm goal. The next
step is that JIT delivery schedule we have been talking
about. After that comes reduced lead time and improved
new product start-up times, and linking the customer and
vendor together.

A long term contract goes a long way toward solving
many of the previous problems. Most of us ask for far
more from our vendors than we are willing to give.
Contract purchasing of capacity and vendor capacity
planning make the vendor an extension of your business.
Gary Landis' article in APICS' 1983 Conference
Proceedings, "Vendor Capacity Planning; A New Frontier for
the 80s" provides us with a Vendor Capacity Planning (VCP)
Checklist. The ANIS (American National Standard Institute)
X12 Sub-committees, which define standard formats for
electronic business transactions, is working on a national
standard for the following data flow:

ANSI X.12 DOCUMENT FLOWS

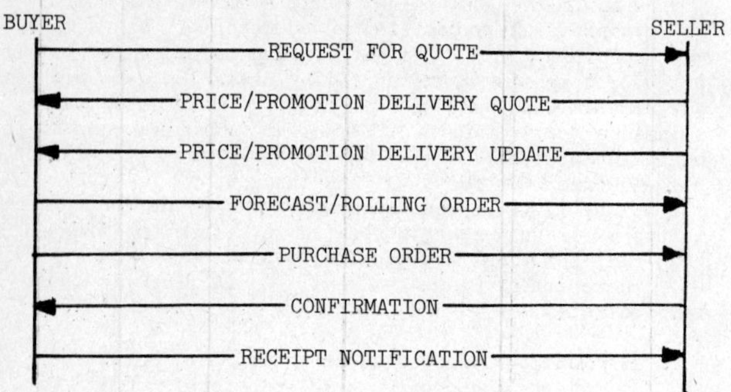

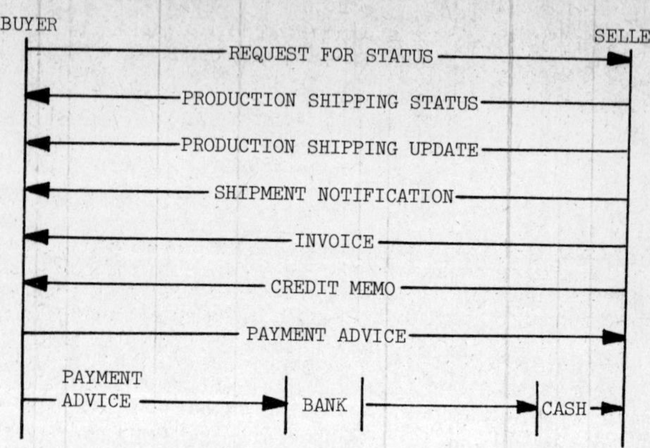

Many of the graphics systems are within the reach of
most customers and vendors. Placing a terminal at a
vendor and transmitting drawings and updates are real and
will happen in the next year for many of our vendors.
With the use of HPMAIL we will be in constant contact with
each vendor. This will be a positive information exchange
based on schedule, capacity, and all of the information
you would give freely to one of your own profit centers.

SUMMARY

Every American business regardless of their product,
don't forget Service is a product, must embrace the SQC
concept and commit to doing it right the first time, DIRT.

American vendors are as eager to perform as those
off shore. Ask for what you need, define the requirement.
Don't over spec to make sure it will fit once it gets to
the production line, spec it right and expect it to be
right when it arrives. If you make your vendors an
extension of your business, they are as interested in
your success as you are, maybe more.

Americans have always prided ourselves on our
innovativeness, but it does little good to be technical
leaders if our competitors can produce the same products
at a lower price. Let's apply some of our innovativeness
to the pursuit of quality.

Your customers expect perfection, give it to them.
Your vendors will give you perfection, ask for it.

IS MY COMPANY READY FOR JIT?

W. A. Wheeler, III
Rath & Strong, Inc.

At the outset, we should make a clear distinction between the appropriateness of the application of certain JIT elements and JIT Production. The author has never encountered a company (service or manufacturing) that would not realize significant benefits from certain JIT elements; e.g., TQC, changeover reduction, improved preventive maintenance, etc. JIT Production is much more holistic; it is a philosophy that completely and aggressively adopts a habit of continuous improvement for all operational activities or disciplines. Its goal conforms to Ed Hay's definition of the elimination of waste: "Anything other than the minimum amount of equipment, materials, parts, space, and workers' time, which are absolutely essential to add value to the product."

A first cut at answering the question "Is my company ready for JIT?" can be a series of simply answered questions:

1. Do you call the leader of your JIT effort the "project manager?"

2. Does a beeper still summon your operations manager for problem resolution?

3. Do your buyers currently visit the shop floor less than once a day?

4. Does accounting still advocate more "discipline" on the shop floor?

5. Are bowling trophies more prominently displayed than problem lists?

6. Do blueprints have more red lines than blue?

7. and so on...

While some of the questions above may seem superficial, they strike at the heart of JIT philosophy. If the answer to all questions is "yes," then you may not be ready for JIT. These are, however, merely clues to a deeper set of readiness issues or questions:

- Does management realize and agree with the total savings potential of JIT implementation?

- Does everyone in the company have a common vision of what the operating process will look like in 5-7 years?

- Do you have, at the minimum, a 6-10 month plan that details the tasks to be acted upon, and is it consistent with the 5-7 year vision?

- Do you have an organization that is guiding the effort and resolving jurisdictional questions?

- Do you know if you have the requisite skills inventory to assure that the plan is achievable?

- And finally, are the climate and the politics of the company conducive to the JIT philosophies of bottom-up problem identification/resolution, acceptance of challenge from errors, and continuous improvement?

When the leading Japanese firms embarked upon KANBAN 15 or more years ago, they probably would have answered "No" to most of the questions above. Even 7 years into the journey, they may not have been able to answer in the affirmative because they were (and are) still developing JIT. In the U.S., we have the advantage of their wisdom. Therefore, with some pre-work, we can focus our efforts on the objective of improvement through JIT and not dilute our efforts by trying to discover where we are headed. It is the pre-work (Readiness Assessment) that should enable U.S. companies to get a 7-10 year jump on the implementation process that this presentation specifically addresses.

OPPORTUNITIES AND FUTURE OPERATING PROCESS

Developing a vision of future operations (5-7 years) and the opportunities (cost reduction potential) to be realized is a "chicken & egg" activity. One cannot do one without the other, and they cannot be done completely sequentially. Both are essential, however, since it Americanizes the JIT process. We must have a base line to track our performance toward a goal. Additionally, we usually need to justify the cost of achieving that goal. All too often, a specific task or program cannot be cost justified on its own, but when incorporated into JIT Production it can be assessed for its contribution. (The ultimate has already occurred at one company--they were able to justify a new piece of capital equipment so that they could run at a slower speed for synchronous flow).

In order for a total opportunities figure to be developed, operating data should be collected. In our experience, many companies have the base data, so it becomes a matter of re-distributing the numbers into a format that facilitates analysis. The data required includes;

- Inventory levels by commodity or family group
  - Raw materials
  - Work-in-process
  - Finished goods

- Work sampling at a level of detail that can be re-analyzed for the exclusion of "non-value adding" elements (labor standards are usually inappropriate for this element)

- Demand Variance

- Inventory by operation (see Figures 1 & 2)

- Costs of Quality and a Pareto analysis of scrap/rework categories

- Lead times (planned and actual)

- Equipment index speeds/demonstrated output/demand rates/utilization

- Routing categorization (if job shop)

- Direct and indirect labor by operation/work center

- Purchased materials by commodity
  - dollar volume
  - number of vendors
  - inventory turns

- Machine downtime by cause/symptom

- Accounting systems' requirements

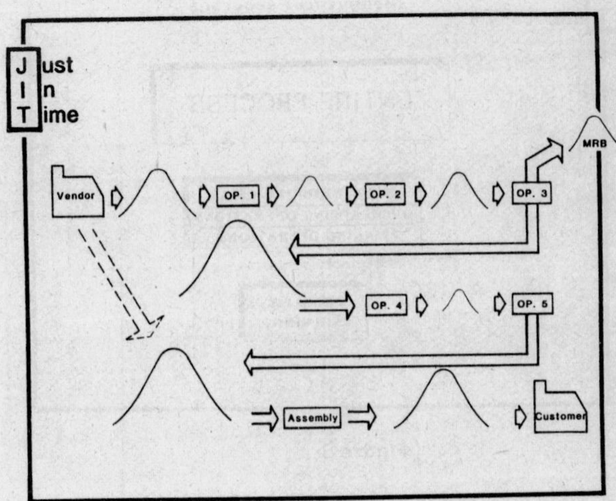

Figure 1

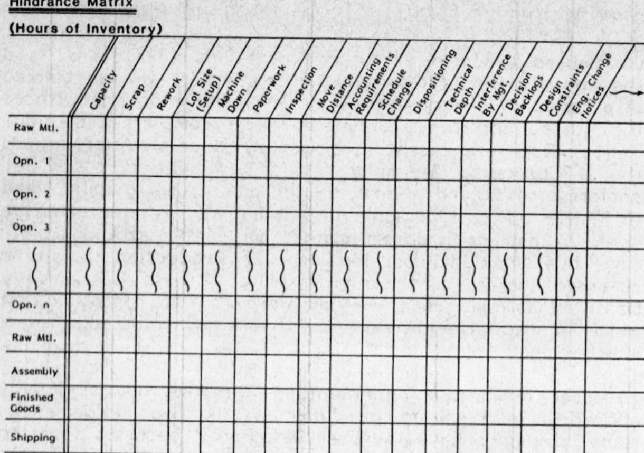

Figure 2

A few comments are required to define the detail of data gathering:

1. The data need not be accurate to the level of decimal equivalents. The purpose of the analysis is to gather data in sufficient orders of magnitude so that the major problems/opportunities can be identified. For the purposes of cost reduction potential, it matters not that the aggregate data is subject to ± 20% variance. The potential is so large that most managers will be thrilled to achieve 80% of the goal. Parenthetically, most estimates err to the low side.

2. The object of this task is not to solve the problems; it is merely to array them for the subsequent planning activity. It is usually sufficient to take the detail to the first level of Paretoization.

3. The Hindrance Matrix (Figure 2) is especially critical to the development of the operating vision. Figure 3 indicates the sequence of improvement thought processes. Once the major bottlenecks or reasons for inventory have been identified, the first activity is to figure out a way to change the entire process so that the operation or reason is eliminated. If impossible, then the next element in the sequence (overlapping) is investigated, and so on.

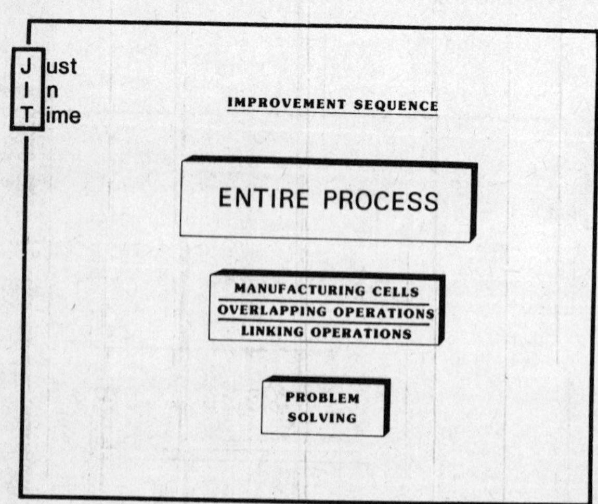

Figure 3

During the data gathering phase, the team should be thinking about the future layout and operations. Once the preliminary operating data has been analyzed, it is usually most effective for each team member to develop, independently, his or her vision of the future. Then the ideas should be compared, discussed, and meshed. Obviously, a high degree of knowledge about JIT technologies is required for this activity. Furthermore, this is not an approximate time for problem solving. It is, rather, the last time the team members will have an opportunity to think in a manner that is totally unencumbered by past practices. It should go without saying that the thought processes should be rooted in data and in pragmatism. This visionary activity will probably take a few iterations as indicated in Figure 4.

Once the operating layout of the future has been agreed upon, then the cost reduction opportunities can be calculated. Again, the operating data collected earlier serves as input. Figure 5 indicates the results from five companies (1 job shop, 1 process, and 3 repetitive manufacturers).

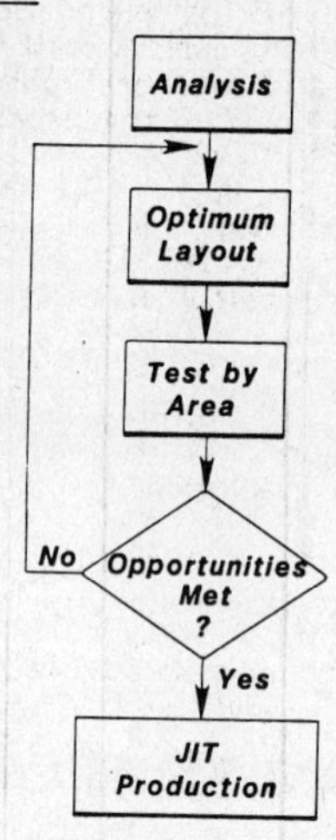

Figure 4

OPPORTUNITIES
(% IMPROVEMENT)

	Repet. Mfg. 1	Process	Repet. Mfg. 2	Job Shop	Repet. Mfg. 3	Range
Manufacturing Lead Time	89	86	92	83	85	83-92
Inventory						
Raw	35	70	70	73	50	35-73
WIP	89	82	85	70	85	70-89
Finished Goods	61	71	70	-	100	0-100
Changeover	75	75	91	75	94	75-94
Labor						
Direct	19	50	}29	5	-	0-50
Indirect	60	50		21	38	21-60
Exempt	?	?	22	?	?	?-22
Space	53	n/a	39	?	80(est.)	39-80
Cost of Quality	50	63	61	33	26	26-63
Purchased Material	?	7	11	6	n/a	6-11
Additional Capacity	n/a	36	42	n/a	-	0-42

Figure 5

SKILLS AND CLIMATE ASSESSMENT

Studies have shown that one of the three leading reasons Japanese companies failed in the implementation of JIT was the lack of qualified industrial/manufacturing engineers. Experience in U.S. companies has led us to question whether some companies have enough qualified quality assurance and maintenance personnel as well as manufacturing engineers. Additionally, some companies have a dearth of people with demonstrable problem solving skills. These observations present an interesting paradox to the JIT philosophy. While we expect to push the problem resolution down the organizational structure, who is going to instruct and support the skill development at all levels? If the few qualified persons are dedicated to everyday activities, who will do the training? At the risk of over-simplification, if each discipline cannot dedicate at least 25-40% of its time to instruction and support of JIT implementation, then it had better figure on hiring more technicians. Again, oversimplifying, we often find that purchasing, training department, and floor supervisors realize a change in job content, but not in numbers. There is often a pool of planners, dispatchers, and quality inspectors who can be retrained to fill the additional resource requirements.

The point is that a skills inventory and resource analysis should be performed during this planning stage. Otherwise, a company will realize a slower implementation schedule and may not achieve the full benefit of the cost reduction potential. A plan for re-allocation of resources should be developed and published soon after the implementation kick-off. This usually goes a long way in allaying the uncertainties in some constituents' minds. Furthermore, it invites their active participation by challenging them with something new and purposeful.

Climate surveys come in all shapes and sizes. The degree of formalization of the survey is not as critical as the areas to be addressed. Key considerations should include:

- Systems & Structures
  - Early warning signals

- Management Practices

- Clarity of purpose and objectives

- Support/Departmental Relationships

- Planning, Innovation, and Communications

- Rewards

If the climate within the company or even within a few key departments is not conducive to team work, multilevel communication, mutual trust, self-motivation, and recognition, the team should investigate remedial activity before undertaking JIT Production.

If the climate survey is carefully constructed and a few major hindering factors are identified, it is usually possible to zero in on the few causes. For instance, if a few departments' attitudes vary to the negative of the norm, those few supervisors or one manager needed to be reviewed or coached or both. If, however, the inhibitory factor pervades the organization as part of its culture, then it would probably be wise to reduce the goals and develop a program with more staff participation in the problem solving/implementation.

[Note: We have seen one instance where the chief executive was so autocratic and involved that significant savings were realized in spite of themselves. One observer noted; "QWL = 0%, JIT = 80%."...So much for the text book!]

The key point of this section is that if the skills are missing or the climate is not conducive to effective implementation, don't do it until the deficiencies have been corrected. Some of the early JIT successes will be realized, but frustration and disappointment (even a hostile strike, in one case) will prevent the full realization of JIT Production.

ORGANIZATION/PLAN

Figure 6 indicates an example of a successful organization for the management of JIT implementation. This structure assures that the process is managed and is not episodic. The duties of the Steering Committee include:

- Set clear goals/expectations for JIT/SGIA

- Appoint SGIA members

- Identify priorities/tasks

- Resolve "conflicts"
  - interdepartmental
  - existing policies/procedures

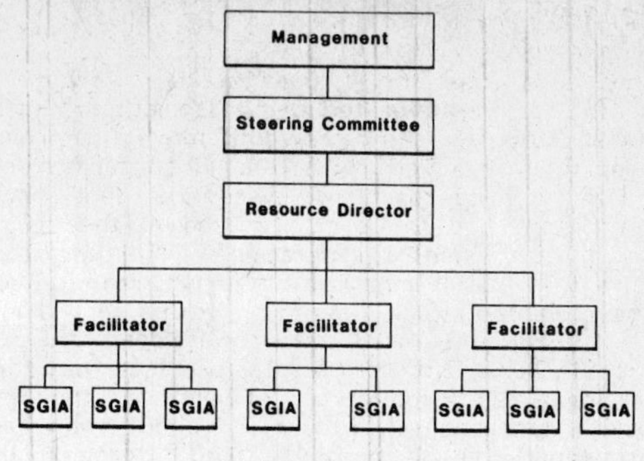

Figure 6

- Track SGIA progress and remedial implementation

- Develop and support the manufacturing mission

- Provide aggregate leadership/"champion"

- Promulgate progress to all

- Amend plan/policies as appropriate

- Cause appropriate training to occur

The members of the Steering Committee are often the management staff, plus the Resource Director and, sometimes, key support personnel such as Quality Director, Purchasing, and Shop Steward. Our experience indicates that the top ranking member of the committee should not be the Chairman, since the decision making process should be collaborative and flexible.

The final step in the Readiness activity is the plan. The steering committee should be instrumental in the development of the plan:

1. Prework

   - Steering Committee formation and definition of its mission.

   - Acceptance of the opportunities, goals, and vision

   - Facilitator training (if necessary)

2. Plan Guidelines

   - Assure that every discipline is involved
   - Tackle the biggest problems or greatest opportunities first
   - Divide the problems into discrete tasks
   - Identify tasks that have the greatest chance of success and high visibility
   - Assure that every element of JIT is tasked up-front
   - After first task successes, expose all to JIT
   - Initial plan should go no more than one year but should focus on the ultimate vision of the operations 5-7 years out.

Figure 7 depicts a macro-level plan adopted by one company.

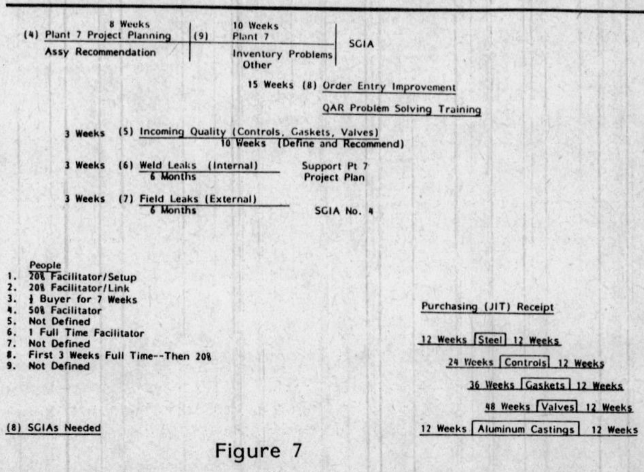

Figure 7

CONCLUSION

When my colleagues and I first started working on JIT implementation, we advocated doing "something" to see how it worked. Sort of a "try it, you'll like it" approach. As the companies involved with the first forays into JIT matured in their approach, we discovered that some of the early successes had to be re-assessed in the light of the emerging final vision of operations. Furthermore, some managements became impatient with the "mini successes," and they wanted more tangible results on the income sheet. In one instance, they questioned the need to continue the implementation despite the fact that they were nowhere near JIT production. Therefore, the Readiness Assessment approach was introduced about two years ago. The preliminary results indicate the latter approach has already surpassed the "shotgun" approach in goal achievement. As a result, the 2 month review/readiness planning is the recommended starting point toward achievement of JIT Production.

LESSONS TO BE LEARNED FROM THE KANBAN SYSTEM

Chaiho Kim
University of Santa Clara

INTRODUCTION

Recently there has been a great deal of interest among American manufacturing companies about Japanese manufacturing practices, particularly the kanban system. A great deal has been written about the mechanics of the kanban system. But recently those who have studied the workings of the kanban system have begun to point out that the kanban system would not work without the other activities that the Japanese manufacturers practice in addition to the mechanics of the kanban system. In fact, Professor Richard Schonberger who is one of the foremost authorities on the kanban system in America points out in his celebrated book "Japanese Manufacturing Techniques," that western industry is not really ready for kanban. He argues that western companies do not have the prerequisite conditions for kanban to be useful. The purpose of this article is to describe what this author considers to be some essential prerequisite conditions for the kanban system to work and to argue that, in the absence of these prerequisite conditions, a manufacturing system would be worse off having a kanban system than not having it.

We list below five prerequisite conditions which we believe to be essential for successfully implementing a kanban system. They are:

1. Stable Master Production Scheduling
2. Automatic Setup
3. Reliability of the Productive Resources
4. High Manufacturing Process Yields
5. Multi Function Workers and Flexible Work Rules.

One does not have to be a manufacturing expert to recognize that many of the prerequisite conditions listed above are desirable conditions for any type of manufacturing system whether it uses kanban or MRP to handle materials. But this article is perhaps one of the few articles written about the kanban system that explicitly argues that a manufacturing system would be worse off with kanban if the prerequisite conditions are not present.

KANBAN SYSTEM

The mechanics of the kanban system are described in detail in a number of articles cited in the references. We will therefore describe here only those features of the system which bear upon our subsequent discussion.

There are essentially two types of kanbans in a typical kanban system: a conveyor kanban and a production kanban. A layout of the physical configuration of these types of kanbans is provided in Figure 1.

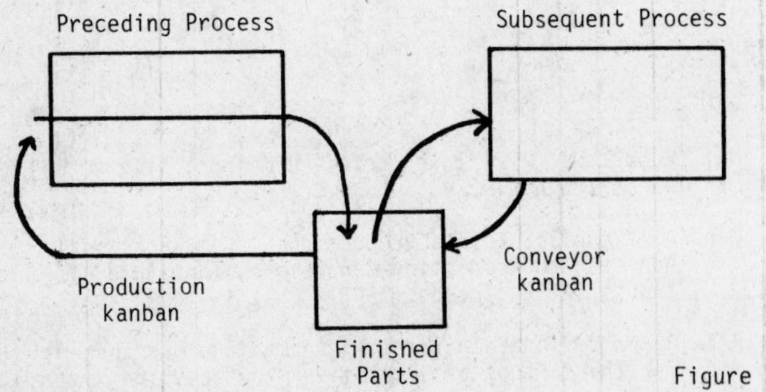

Figure 1

A conveyor kanban is essentially an information processing system. It is designed so that a process in a manufacturing system uses a conveyor kanban to inform its preceding processes of the rate at which it is consuming the parts produced by them. This information conveyance is done through the following features of a conveyor kanban: A process cannot withdraw a container from its preceding processes without a kanban card and such a withdrawal should occur only Just-in-Time for the subsequent process to use the parts. It would seem that the parts finished at the preceding processes should be transported as soon as convenient to the subsequent processes since the finished part should be stored, if anywhere, at the locations where they will be subsequently used. However, if parts finished by the preceding processes are transported to the subsequent processes without some defined rules, then, the preceding processes would have a difficult time figuring out the real consumption rates of the parts they produce by the subsequent process. The conveyor kanban provides such rules.

While the conveyor kanban performs an information processing service, a production kanban is a production control device. A manufacturing system uses a production kanban to control preceding processes from producing at rates faster than can be consumed by the subsequent process. This is done through the following feature of the production kanban. Each time a container is transported to a subsequent process, a production kanban is freed. A production system cannot proceed to produce a new item without such a freed production kanban.

NOT JUST IN TIME BUT WITH JUST ENOUGH CAPACITIES

Japanese manufacturing companies are known to believe that inventories are the cause of all evils in manufacturing and make an utmost effort to reduce the inventory levels to zero. They believe that this objective can be accomplished if all things are produced just in time to be either sold or used to support subsequent assembly operations.

The most important purpose of keeping inventories is, however, to meet the unforseen demand whether it is for final sales or for subsequent production processes. Such unforseen demand can perhaps be met adequately even without having inventories if the production processes possess enough excess capacities. However, a Just-in-Time system that assures zero inventories which can be accomplished only through having excess capacities is not likely to be a desirable system. Any gain to be realized by having zero inventories is likely to be dissipated through excess capacities.

What is desirable for a manufacturing system is, then, not just to produce Just-in-Time, but to produce with Just-Enough-Capacities. For our subsequent discussion, we will call these JIT/JEC, the dual desirable goals of manufacturing systems in general.

MASTER PRODUCTION SCHEDULING

One desirable feature of a manufacturing system with the JIT/JEC goals is the ability of the preceding processes to forecast the demands which will be made of them in the somewhat distant future. However, this is the very feature that the kanban system does not provide. Since the master production schedule is given only to the final assembly process under the kanban system, the different levels of the preceding processes are oblivious to the demands which will be made of them beyond the very immediate future. In a sense, then, this feature of the kanban system is incompatible with the espoused goals of the system, which are to produce just in time with just enough capacities.

Why then does the kanban system at Toyota work? It turns out that the kanban system at Toyota works in spite of the lack of forecasting abilities of the preceding processes and not because of it. Toyota has done something to its manufacturing planning process so that it works in spite of the fact that the preceding processes do not have abilities to see far ahead. The company pursues a level production plan over a relatively long period and the master production schedule is frozen for a month. With this type of production planning and scheduling, the preceding processes do not have to be concerned about having to adjust their capacities because they can reasonably expect that the demands which will be made of them will not change for some time. Of course, when a manufacturing process operates in an environment where the demand for its product is stable, the process can eliminate the necessity for the buffer stocks and, in turn, reduce its over all inventory level.

Suppose now an American manufacturing company decides to institute a kanban system but without stabilizing the production levels or freezing the master production schedule. Then the kanban system is likely to bring about drastically worse results than that of the MRP variety because of the kanban system's nearsightedness. Thus, instead of producing Just-in-Time with Just-Enough-Capaci-

ties, things are produced Not-in-Time because of Not-
Enough-Capacities (that is, we have NIT/NEC instead of
JIT/JEC).

AUTOMATIC SETUP

The usual production scheduling practice among the
American manufacturing companies is to estimate the total
setup times required to carry out the required number of
setups called by the master production schedule, and load
the work centers accordingly. However, one thing which is
difficult to do even with sophisticated computerized MRP is
that of scheduling the precise times of setup changes. In
the kanban system, scheduling the setup changes would be
even more difficult because of the system's inability to
project the needs for setup changes far ahead.

In an MRP environment, the uncertainties pertaining to
the timing of setup changes are resolved through inventory.
In theory, then, a manufacturing process that relies on the
kanban system should have even higher levels of inventory
to deal with the problem of uncertainties pertaining to the
timing of setup changes.

The interesting question is, then, how do the Japanese
manufacturing companies which rely on the kanban system get
away with zero inventory. The answer has to be obvious.
They must not have high setup times. In fact, the ostensible goal of many Japanese manufacturers is to reduce the
setup times to zero. It is a well publicized fact that the
setup time which took 2 to 3 hours at Toyota in 1950 was
reduced to about 2 to 3 minutes after 1970. What we wish
to emphasize here is that unless the setup times can be
drastically reduced, the kanban system with zero inventory
is likely to be disruptive to the manufacturing process.

RELIABILITY OF THE PRODUCTIVE RESOURCES

If a manufacturing system is fine tuned to the extent
of operating with zero inventory under the Just-in-Time
system and at the same time have Just-Enough-Capacities,
such a system does not have much tolerance in the sense
that something can go wrong at one part of the system
without seriously affecting the operations at other parts
of the system. After all, as we have pointed out above,
one important function of inventory is to decouple the
manufacturing processes from each other.

What is the implication of this observation for the
JIT/JEC system? Obviously, equipment, machines, and workers must be reliable; that is, breakdowns should not occur
in any part of the manufacturing process. What would be
some likely outcomes if a breakdown does in fact occur? It
would depend on where such a breakdown occurred. Suppose a
breakdown occurred at a preceding process. Then, the subsequent process would not get the part it needs to maintain
its production. Suppose a breakdown occurs at a subsequent
process. Then, the preceding process will be prevented
from producing anything and, in turn, the machines and
equipment for the process will remain idle and the workers
will perhaps twiddle their thumbs while the broken down
subsequent process is being fixed.

HIGH MANUFACTURING PROCESS YIELDS

The JIT/JEC system obviously cannot operate well in an
environment where the yields of the preceding processes
vary. This is because the subsequent process is allowed to
withdraw items from the preceding process only just in
time. If an item withdrawn from a preceding process just
in time to be used by the subsequent process turns out to
be defective, then the subsequent process will have to go
back to the preceding process to withdraw another item.
But the previous item was withdrawn just in time, which
means theoretically that the subsequent process will have
to stop until the next item arrives. One can see how
disruptive this can be to a manufacturing system.

Clearly, then, a kanban system with JIT/JEC goals
cannot operate in an environment where the manufacturing
process yields are not extremely high. But then Toyota is
well known for its total Quality Control program whose
ostensible goal is to have zero defects.

MULTI FUNCTION WORKERS AND FLEXIBLE WORK RULES

The above listed four prerequisite conditions will go
a long way toward preventing different processes in a
manufacturing system from going out of balance with each
other. However, even highly maintained machines and equipment will break down. A well trained and seasoned worker
does make mistakes. A JIT/JEC system must have a way to
correct the situation immediately when the process in the
manufacturing system goes out of balance with each other
because the system does not have in process inventory to
weather the situation.

How does Toyota, for example, handle this problem. It
does it by what they call ANDON. Suppose a worker spots
trouble in the manufacturing process which would put some
part of the process out of balance with respect to some
other parts. Then, a worker is allowed to push a button
which, in turn, flashes either a yellow or red light
depending on the seriousness of the trouble spotted. In
the event that the red light is flashed, the entire process
would come to a halt. In any event, the workers are
allowed to be shifted to wherever they are needed to
rectify the problem which caused the manufacturing process
to go out of balance.

Being able to shift the workers to wherever they are
needed is then, in a sense, the last trump card of the
kanban system to insure that materials, parts, and semi-
finished items move smoothly in the manufacturing process.
However, shifting of workers is possible only if the
workers are trained to handle several different jobs and
the rules governing the workers are flexible enough to
allow such shifting of workers from one job to another.

CONCLUSIONS

In this article we have argued that (1) stable master
production scheduling, (2) automatic setup, (3) high reliability of productive resources, (4) high manufacturing
process yields, and (5) multi function workers and flexible work rules are essential for a successful kanban
system whose goal is to produce Just-in-Time with Just-
Enough-Capacity (JIT/JEC). We have also provided some
reasons why we believe that a manufacturing process may be
worse off having a kanban system with the JIT/JEC goal if
the prescribed prerequisite conditions are not present.

Unquestionably many Japanese manufacturing companies
have demonstrated that they can produce goods more efficiently than their American counterparts. One very important question that we raise is this: Is it the mechanics
of the kanban system which principally account for their
efficiency, or is it the Japanese manufacturers' ability to
meet the above stated prerequisite conditions which contributes toward their efficiency. The question is relevant
because even a manufacturing system which utilizes MRP
instead of kanban should be able to reduce its in process
inventory by satisfying each of the stated prerequisite
conditions. The question is important because if it is, in
fact, the five stated conditions which principally
contribute toward the efficiency of the Japanese manufacturers, then, American manufacturers perhaps can increase
their productivities without actually kanbanizing their
factories by focusing their efforts on these stated conditions instead of exchanging their MRP terminals for kanban
cards. Perhaps these may be the real lessons that the
American manufacturers can learn from their Japanese
counterparts.

This is not to take any credit away from the kanban
system, however. It is an amazingly simple and yet truly
elegant manufacturing information and control system.

REFERENCES

Hall, Robert W. Zero Inventories, Homewood, Ill., Down
    Jones Irwin, 1983.

Monden, Yasuhiro, Toyota Production System, Practical
    Approach to Production Management, Institute of
    Industrial Engineers, 1983.

Rice, James W., "A Comparison of Kanban and MRP Concepts
    for the Control of Repetitive Manufacturing Systems",
    Production and Inventory Management, First Quarter,
    1982, pp. 1-15.

Schonberger, Richard J., Japanese Manufacturing Techniques,
    New York, Free Press, 1982.

Suginori, Y., Kusunoki, K., Cho, F., and Uchikawa, S.,
    "Toyota Production System and Kanban System,
    Materialization of Just in Time and Respect for Human
    System", International Journal of Production Research,
    15(6), 1977, pp. 553-564.

ZERO INVENTORY (JUST-IN-TIME) EDUCATION: INTEGRATING WHAT ALREADY EXISTS

Karin Kolodziejski
Tektronics, Inc.

INTRODUCTION

In the rush to implement the simple yet seemingly revolutionary concepts of Just In Time or Stockless Production, it's apparent that many companies have forgotten to step back and perform an essential task: the articulation of a coherent training and development strategy that is consistent with the overall strategic direction for manufacturing. That's the cornerstone from which all change efforts should emanate.

The objective of this paper is to provide some focus and direction for training and development strategy formulation for manufacturing. Specifically this paper will examine ways of integrating a variety of education and training programs so that maximum organizational impact is achieved.

A SCENARIO

Consider the harried plant manager who learns enough about Just In Time to know he wants to implement it. In addition to an implementation strategy, he realizes that a training program on Just In Time concepts is needed as well. He commissions someone (e.g., a key administrative person, the materials manager, a training specialist) to implement a Just In Time Training Program. The appointed one researches Just In Time concepts and discovers that Just In Time is an amalgam of many interwoven philosophies and practices, each hotly debated regarding the feasibility of their implementation given prevailing American business culture.

Just In Time (or Stockless Production if you are well read) (Hall, 1983) is attitudinal, a management style and set of practices, a belief, and a set of techniques. Underlying successful Just In Time implementations are a variety of both "hard" and "soft" technologies such as: effective group problem solving techniques; worker participation (quality circles or small group involvement activities); managers skilled in participative management techniques; climates that reward the speedy surfacing and resolution of problems; zero defects or parts per million; process control charting and methodology; supportive supplier management practices; team building; floor layout; etc., etc., etc.....

By now the individual entrusted with the task of developing a Just In Time Training Program is wondering how the bits and pieces fit together and where to begin. Well, the work has already begun.

A REVIEW OF CURRENT COMPLEMENTARY EDUCATION EFFORTS

Five major training and development topics will be discussed here, each containing elements of what the Just In Time (JIT) experts say makes for successful JIT implementations. As each program is dicussed, more than likely you will recognize that you have either attended such a program, sponsored such a program, developed/acquired such a program for your company, or are peripherally aware of such programs being run in or for your company, or that a similar program is being planned for your company. If you experience a shred of recognition as you read these program descriptions, these are the programs that can easily be and must be integrated into a coherent JIT training strategy.

QUALITY CIRCLES TRAINING PROGRAMS

If you were to peruse the membership directory of the International Association of Quality Circles, you would find thousands of names of individuals and companies who clearly have some interest in the Quality Circles effort. It's well publicized (by Quality Circle consultants) that Quality Circles cannot be implemented without appropriate training and development. Let's examine a typical outline for a training program for Quality Circles members:

Q. C. MEMBER TRAINING

° Problem identification techniques
  - pareto

° Cause analysis techniques
  - fishbone diagrams
  - structure tree analysis
  - pareto

° Data collection techniques
  - control charts
  - run charts

° Brainstorming techniques

° Solution generation & selection techniques

° Cost-benefit analysis

° Presentation techniques

Wouldn't having all levels of employees skilled in such techniques make the speedy surfacing and resolution of production related problems a "fait accompli"? The Japanese seem to know this, hence small group involvement activities are considered to be an integral part of their manufacturing strategy (as we have rushed over to dissect and ingest it).

Quality Circles programs were seeing widespread implementation in the United States before the U. S. became enamoured with the beauty and simplicity of JIT. Quality Circles programs for the most part were not viewed as an element of the overall business strategy. It wasn't until we really started studying Japanese Production Systems under a microscope that small group involvement activities or worker involvement emerged as a key element of JIT. Many a trained and experienced Quality Circles Program facilitator in this country has moved on to other employment opportunities, after watching the initial burst of enthusiasm for the Circles program die a slow "unintegrated into the strategic direction of the company" death.

Clearly, for a good training and development strategist, the connections are there for the making. One absolute of training design is that the points of integration from concept to concept, program to program must be built, drawn out in the context of discussion, and internalized by the training program participant. Sending a first level manager to a Quality Circles leader program one year and to a JIT techniques program the next without building on the relationships between the two is like giving our training dollars to the Japanese to fund advanced manufacturing research!

QUALITY AWARENESS/ZERO DEFECTS PROGRAMS

What American company hasn't or isn't rushing to press with the latest quality awareness campaign? As the U. S. world market share of televisions, stereo equipment, automobiles, and electronic equipment has been penetrated by the Japanese and our leadership threatened if not extinguished in some of those categories, quality improvment, in many companies, has been placed at the top of the list of key corporate objectives.
(Does this ring true for your company?) If the management of your firm wasn't fortunate enough to mainline the "Crosby Quality Vaccine" (Crosby, 1984), then you probably have or are planning a home grown quality awareness program, as well you should. The secret has been out for awhile, that near zero defects (defects per million) is integral to a successful JIT system (Schonberger, 1982).

Once the defect prevention mindset has been developed, some of the skills needed to put that goal into operation are effective problem identification and resolution techniques. Guess who already learned how to do that in Quality Circles training? Also, management must provide a climate that supports the surfacing of problems. Didn't they learn about that in last year's Effective Management Program? These concepts are not new nor are they revolutionary, yet for these concepts to stick and for people to change behavior the training strategist has to ensure that the relationships are clear to help people make the connections. Discrete skill building without a context or a driving, well-integrated set of purposes seldom causes lasting behavior changes.

<u>STATISTICAL QUALITY MANAGEMENT PROGRAMS</u>

Probably one of the high ranking accomplishments of the Japanese has been the application of Statistical Quality Control (SQC) techniques in their manufacturing processes. Statistical techniques are used by workers and management alike to control processes and ultimately manage the business of manufacturing. The United States with all of our emphasis on quantitative methods and sophisticated financial analysis has not yet uniformly adopted the core value of empiricism (Miller, 1984).

The proliferation of SQC training programs on the market is an indication that the trend is moving in the right direction. Often SQC training programs are front ended with quality awareness and zero defects programs so the relationship between zero defects accomplishment and process control can be solidified. With the implementation of SQC techniques follows greater worker control, better, faster problem identification and resolution, and an increased demand upon participative management skills. You begin to see the complexity created by the action-reaction cycle. The skill set required by managers and workers alike is almost poetically inter-related.

<u>SUPPLIER MANAGEMENT PROGRAMS</u>

Another element of the Japanese manufacturing strategy is the relationships Japanese manufacturers have built with their suppliers. The relationship is collaborative, supportive and characterized by a good deal of information exchange. American industry, especially auto manufacturers are making great strides here also. Many companies have established supplier excellence awards to recognize reliable and high quality suppliers. Supplier education programs are mushrooming as well.

Education about supplier management practices thus takes a variety of forms. They are:

° Buyer and procurement professional educational programs;

° Engineering/Procurement/Supplier interface programs;

° Supplier education programs on Material Requirements Planning (MRP), process control theory and application, JIT principle and practice.

There are a number of companies that are footing the bill to educate their key suppliers in how to control their processes to achieve zero defects (or parts per million). The ratio of investment payback on such programs is extraordinary. Some sources indicate that an expenditure of .003 cents to prevent a defect at the source (suppliers shop) would have had a corresponding $300.00 expenditure to catch the defect in the final stages of assembling the product. Hence investing in supplier education programs yields high quality paybacks over time.

In supplier management programs the principles of participative management extends outside of the factory. Managers and professionals skilled in collaboration and team oriented problem solving are required if a closeness to key suppliers is the business goal. So often in generic management skill building programs (e.g., communication skills, conflict resolution skills, problem solving skills), participants have a hard time transferring the discrete skills they learned in the program back to the job. That occurs for a variety of reasons, however some of why that problem occurs has to do with fact that often the training program objectives are not related to the overall business strategy. JIT and related strategies are wonderfully integrated and complimentary. To educate people by compartmentalizing JIT concepts is to destroy some of the beauty.

<u>MATERIAL REQUIREMENTS PLANNING PROGRAMS (MRP)</u>

A great deal of credit and thanks should be (or should have been) extended to Joseph Orlicky and Oliver Wight whose education efforts and writing enabled us to make the shift (both in mindset and practice) from the economic order quantity (EOQ) to planning quantities over time based upon actual need. Hence the evolution of JIT in this country is and or will probably will be smoother. Imagine trying to change from EOQ to a lot size of one?

Those who proselytize "out with MRP and in with JIT" are neglecting to consider how people learn and change. Think about a stock room clerk who attended forty hours of MRP education two years ago. Now he goes to a class and finds out that the stockroom will go away now that the plant is implemeting JIT. Think about how that stockroom clerk's attitude toward the management of the company will be impacted. Some old timers know that all they have to do is wait it out and most everything comes full circle again.

Just like any of the other programs discussed previously, if you trained on MRP you need to build points of integration in your JIT education program. People can make lots of transitions to new things if they understand why, how it fits, and if it seems to make good sense.

<u>TOWARD AN INTEGRATED STRATEGY</u>

Let us return to the plight of the plant manager's designate who by now has put together some objectives and an outline for the proposed JIT training program. The plant manager nods approval and asks: "How soon can we have everyone trained?" Hopefully this training program designer responds "Well, we really have already begun!"

In fact, for a whole host of American companies, that oversimplified scenario has lots of truth. One need only examine the growth records of firms that develop and market custom and packaged training programs, materials and media carrying any of the titles discussed earlier in this paper. Fortunes were made overnight by companies that went into the market with the latest trendy training product in the arena we have been discussing. Clearly, lots of training has taken place.

The program designer should investigate all the education and training programs that his target audience(s) have attended over the last few years. These would include both internal and external seminars and workshops. He should examine content outlines closely looking for content overlap and compatibility. He should also investigate all planned programs. The corporate training and development function may be planning to launch a new team building program or a problem solving skills course that would enhance a manager's skill set and be a supportive "soft technology" of Just In Time.

Some companies have done so much education and training in the areas previously discussed that all that is needed now is an integration course to show how all the programs they have attended fit together. Nonetheless, some research and the development of an integrated strategy for Just In Time Education is required prior to launching such a program.

To summarize, Just In Time is an amalgam of both soft and hard technologies. Lots of work has already begun to build skills in this arena. A coherent training and development strategy needs to be formulated prior to launching into a Just In Time program. It is essential that this training strategy take into account other company-wide training and development efforts as well as the strategic directions of the business.

<u>REFERENCES</u>

Crosby, Phillip B.; <u>Quality Without Tears</u>
New York: McGraw - Hill Book Co., 1984.

Hall, Robert W.; <u>Zero Inventories</u>
Illinois: Dow Jones - Irwin, 1983.

Miller, Lawrence M.; <u>American Spirit</u>
New York: William Morrow, 1984.

Schonberger, Richard J.; <u>Japanese Manufacturing Techniques</u>. New York: The Free Press, 1982.

Karin Kolodziejski is a program manager in Corporate
Planning and Development for Tektronix Incorporated. In
this capacity she is responsible for a series of middle
management programs addressing a broad range of middle
management knowledge and skill areas. Prior to this
position, Karin spent a number of years with Burroughs
Corporation in a variety of manufacturing, quality and
management education positions. Karin holds a Masters
degree in Industrial/Organizational Psychology from Purdue
University and a Bachelors degree from Montclair State
College in New Jersey. Karin has delivered numerous presentations on Manufacturing Education and related topics
including presenting at the 1983 APICS National Conference.

JIT AND QUALITY CONTROL
D. Albert
J. Gaylord, CPIM
TRW Bearings Division

OVERVIEW

Moving toward Just-In-Time has been a slow and evolutionary process. Building blocks had to be completed on a step by step basis over a three year period to establish the basic requirements and provide the necessary employee involvement. Each step required achieving a quality product before the next step could be started. In the end, quality and JIT went hand in hand.

First, our scheduling systems had to be improved to utilize MRP state-of-the-arts so that valid priorities could be established. Our MCS project of Manufacturing Control System addressed the systems issue.

Next, our ability to meet schedules had to improve significantly. This required not only action items but an awareness of the need to meet schedules throughout the entire organization. A program called MUST or Make Your Schedule Today was developed which was really more than just a program of process changes; changes in the way the business was run were required. The program was launched using buttons which people wore as reminders. Making schedules became a major annual goal and all department goals and objectives were in support of MUST.

Now that schedules were being met, inventory reductions were required so that a pull inventory system could be supported. Lead times had to be reduced to react quickly to shortages and schedule changes. TRIM or Target Reduce Inventory More was the next building block program which was implemented. Buttons once again were used to raise to level of awareness with people. The result was a 21% inventory reduction over a one year period.

Variability of schedules was another area which had to be addressed. The scrap rate was high, causing shortages and reschedules. Many parts were required without adequate lead time causing problems with both manufacturing and our vendors. QUEST or Quality Every Single Time was implemented to address the scrap issue. This program extended into the hourly work force and evaluated everything from machinery and methods to paperwork. Where problems were identified corrective action was taken. The result was a 67% reduction in scrap.

Finally, it was time to extend our scheduling and execution systems into the vendors' shops so that we could work as a team. The GET SMART program or Schedule Material And Release Today was launched with our vendors. This is the culmination of our three year effort to establish Just-In-Time inventory.

Five building blocks had to be completed for JIT. These are a good scheduling system, good performance to the schedule, minimum inventory levels, a stable schedule, and worker participation. With these building blocks we have moved forward into JIT.

ENVIRONMENT

The TRW Jamestown Bearing Plant manufactures commercial ball bearings. We also provide all turning and heat treat for two sister plants. Our bills are only three to four levels deep but the product requires a high level of machining. In some cases, tolerances are measured in one-millionth of an inch. We are currently working with our forging vendors on a pilot JIT program.

SYSTEMS

We had a home grown MRP system which was comprised of many disjointed segments and did not integrate all areas. For example, our component planning was run separately from raw material planning and discrepancies between the two could cause either shortages or surplus material. As a result, we have implemented the MSA MRP software package to bring the different areas under the same umbrella. The other fundamental system change that was realized was the home grown system was primarily automatic transaction generated while maintaining card files, the new software was event driven requiring people to maintain one data base and have record accuracy responsibility. The change was painful in terms of manpower and resistance to change but necessary to establish system involvement and ownership. With this item we now had an effective scheduling system.

MAKE YOUR SCHEDULE TODAY (MUST)

Our first employee involvement was MUST. This program addressed the execution phase of scheduling. The first area addressed was master scheduling. Reports were developed to match customer demand with production schedules so that valid due dates could be established at the assembly level. The schedules then drove back through the shop providing valid priorities to all areas. Once the priorities were valid, component shortage reports were developed and worked daily. Measurement controls were developed to track current status and maintain an ongoing track record. By establishing credibility and controls in schedules we were able to create an awareness of the need to meet schedules and of the impact of missing schedules. Our commitment to meeting schedules had dramatic impact to our customer service levels almost immediately and set the stage for JIT.

TARGET REDUCE INVENTORY MORE (TRIM)

The next area addressed was to reduce inventory. In the beginning we had long lead times and long queues. Component orders were released as soon as material was available so that manufacturing could run as efficiently as possible even though conflicts were arising based upon the schedules (MUST). An ABC approach was developed to see where combined setups were warranted and where existing volumes supported multiple setups for efficiency. Lead times were reduced and queues were reduced, lowering work-in-process inventory. Substitution increased in the short term and the increased manufacturing costs were more than offset with inventory reduction cost savings. A raw material consolidation program was developed so that inventory costs were reduced, actual inventory was reduced, inventory was more flexible, and setup costs were reduced. Once again, the materials and manufacturing areas were able to establish common goals and achieve beneficial results. With less inventory and small queues, parts could flow quickly through the shop providing pull scheduling and setting another building block for JIT.

QUALITY EVERY SINGLE TIME (QUEST)

With the programs already implemented, we had made significant improvements toward JIT but one problem still plagued us which was a large amount of unexpected schedule changes which was due to product quality or scrap. This program included both a technical project called Manufacturing Variability Control (MVC) and an employee involvement program.

The MVC project provided the data necessary to review machine capabilities and respond by taking corrective action when needed. A macro study was conducted without regard to operator intervention. The results of this study were evaluated to determine if the machine appeared to have adequate capabilities. If not, corrective action was pursued and the macro study redone. If the machine appeared to be capable, a detailed and controlled micro study was conducted to determine specific machine capability. Once again, if the machine did not hold tolerances,

corrective action was pursued and the study redone. If machine capability was adequate, periodic in-process inspection is done so that tolerances are maintained and scrap is minimized.

The remaining portion of QUEST was an employee involvement program using five teams targeted to specific areas. Each team has implemented changes covering process changes to paperwork changes.

Scrap has been reduced by 67% by the QUEST project. All employees have been involved and a participation attitude has been established. Along with this attitude the variability of our schedules has been reduced which has stabilized our vendors' schedules.

SCHEDULE MATERIAL AND RELEASE TODAY (GET SMART)

At this point we had completed the internal building blocks required for JIT and it was time to reach out to our vendors. Monroe Forging was the pilot program we began with. Up to this point our performance measurement was monthly and our objective was to measure weekly.

The vendor participation relationship was started three years ago and just recently formalized using the GET SMART program. We provide Monroe

visibility of requirements out over a 4-6 month period while their lead times are 4-6 weeks. In conjunction with this, our purchasing department is working with Monroe's vendors to reserve capacity and material to minimize the lead time for forging raw material. These two items have allowed Monroe to establish a stocking program so that efficiencies and delivery performance have improved. We have been able to release 98-99% of all Monroe forgings directly to the floor for production as a result of this program.

SUMMARY

In order to provide Just-In-Time inventory, the basic building blocks must be established:

1) You must have a good scheduling system to provide valid priorities.
2) You must execute the schedule your system provides.
3) You must minimize inventory to reduce queue and lead time so that pull inventory scheduling gives you the parts needed.
4) You must eliminate as much variability as possible in your scheduling so that change and confusion are minimized.
5) You must involve employees because it is their knowledge, expertise, and performance which provides the ultimate success.
6) You must work with your vendors so that you both have ownership in the success of your program.

With these steps, JIT is the realization of the benefits of a quality MRP system.

David J. Albert

Dave joined the TRW Bearings Division in 1980, as plant manager of the Jamestown Plant, where he has been the spearhead of the Just-In-Time program.

Prior to this assignment, he worked for White Motor Corporation as operations manager from 1977 to 1980 and spent 10 years as a General Electric "gypsy," entering their manufacturing training program in 1967, and subsequently holding six positions of increasing responsibility in manufacturing operations.

He is active in the Jamestown Rotary Club and is a member of the American Production and Inventory Control Society of Manufacturing Engineers.

Born in New York City, Dave was graduated from Hofstra University with a B.S. in mathematics and industrial engineering, and he has pursued graduate studies in finance at Marist College, Poughkeepsie, New York.

John Gaylord, CPIM

Currently, John is the manager of advanced materials at TRW Bearings Plant in Jamestown, New York. His responsibilities are designing and implementing both computer and manual manufacturing related systems. In the past three years, since he began at TRW, they have implemented MRP and a dispatch system as well as many smaller programs establishing daily controls.

Previously, he worked for NCR Corporation as a technical consultant with the MISSION manufacturing software package. He worked both with customers and the manufacturing plants within NCR.

He holds both a Bachelors and a Masters degree in mathematics from Stetson University.

THE ZERO INVENTORY QUALITY CONNECTION

Lawrence J. Utzig
General Electric Company

INTRODUCTION

In 1980, General Electric established management exchange agreements with several Japanese companies including Toyota, Toshiba and Hitachi. This paper is based on what was learned from those agreements and provides an introduction to concepts, procedures and techniques for achieving the high in-process quality levels needed to operate with a "Zero Inventory" production system. Workers and line management are the focal point for pursuing quality perfection and actually achieving "parts per million" defect levels. Small lot production is a reinforcing concept in both process "cause" control and fast defect detection and root cause correction.

The objective of ZIPS is to flow material through the plant with a minimum of intervening queues. In-process quality must be at very high levels because of reduced protective stocks. High quality is obtained through implementing a continuous never-ending program to eliminate defects in pursuit of perfection.

Specific techniques for preventing defects through process approval, surveillance and confirmation, along with low cost approaches for detecting defects, when they occur, and "real-time" root cause analysis are the major elements of the program. Important aids are innovative ways to "mistake proof" machines and processes, implement self-stop and quality management by sight procedures and place responsibility for "control" of in-process quality in the shop.

ZERO INVENTORY/QUALITY CONNECTION

There are three key factors that describe the relationship between a Just-In-Time production system and parts (or in-process) quality.

1. JIT requires near perfect parts/process quality levels.

2. JIT small lots enhance early detection of quality problems.

3. Substantial cost benefits accrue directly from reduction of in-process scrap and rework.

None of us are strangers to the third factor. We have based our quality programs on reducing both in-house and field failures because they waste money. "Make it right the first time" has been our theme. In too many quality programs, however, meeting an annual bogey or target for scrap/rework reduction has usually been good enough. The motivation to achieve perfection (zero defects) was missing because the incremental cost reduction from elimination of scrap and rework beyond a low level already achieved versus the incremental cost increase to achieve the reduced defect levels was not significant. With JIT the pursuit of quality perfection is not only necessary but worthwhile, because the overall benefits to the business are substantial.

A way to pictorially link quality and small lot production is shown in Figure 1.

If we trace the arrows on the right we see the reduction in WIP (or running small lots) exposing quality problems that heretofore may have been hidden or considered acceptable. With JIT we can't live with these problems, we must eliminate them, which results in improved quality. Improving in-process yields allows further reduction in lot sizes, exposing further unacceptable situations.

If we follow arrows to the left we see how small lots make it easier to more quickly detect quality problems allowing quicker corrections and thus "preventing" defects in subsequent parts. With larger lots, defects that could have been detected in the first few pieces may go undetected until the entire lot is checked.

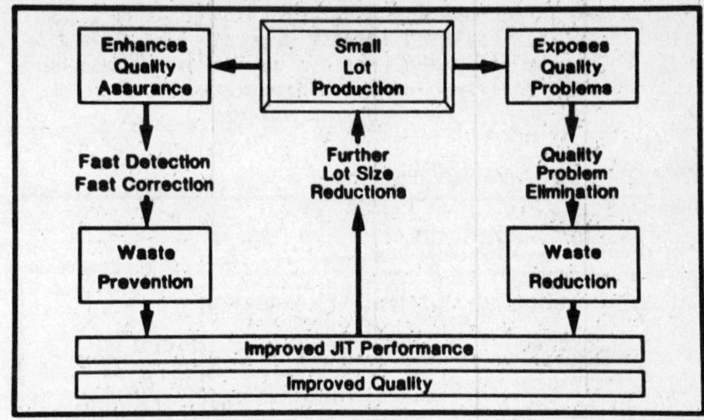

FIGURE 1

JIT quality objectives are never achieved. A JIT quality program is a continuous, never-ending pursuit of perfect in-process quality and this will naturally lead to low defect levels in the field as well. If we didn't continuously set our quality sights higher each time we reach a higher plateau, we would not be able to achieve the full benefits of JIT production.

JIT QUALITY CONCEPTS

There are two major concepts that we must accept if we are going to continually reduce defects in order to operate in the JIT mode. This is true no matter what the defect level we are starting from. They are not "either"/"or". Both must be addressed if we are serious about achieving quality perfection.

1. We must do everything necessary to prevent defects from occurring in the first place because very few processes are perfect

2. Failing to do 1. with 100% certainty, we must discover defects when they occur (or as quickly thereafter as possible) and make immediate corrections. (Theoretically, no parts should have been or be produced with defects that are not known).

It follows then that defect levels should never go up. They should always go down, or at the worst, stay level. If a defect is known to exist, that is generally enough information to eliminate its occurrence in future parts that are produced.

DISCOVER DEFECTS WHEN THEY OCCUR

Let's look at the second concept first.
"How can we discover defects when they occur?"
Toyota and Hitachi say, "Build it into the process or have each worker check 100%." (Of course the best way to check parts 100% is to build it into the process, but this may not always be possible). When a defect does occur, the worker makes an immediate correction or asks for help. In many of our plants this approach requires a new mind-set.

Normally inspectors sort out the defects, summarize the results and someone in Q.C. goes after the corrective action. This is a long cycle and doesn't always get at the root cause.

It's important to recognize that merely eliminating the inspector and having the operator do the sorting isn't much different than having the inspector check on the operator. OPERATORS SHOULD CHECK THEIR WORK AT THE MOST MEANINGFUL TIME IN THE CYCLE, NOT TO SORT THE BAD FROM THE GOOD, BUT TO CONFIRM THAT THEY ARE DOING EVERYTHING CORRECTLY, AND WHEN THEY ARE NOT, TO KNOW IT QUICKLY AND TO MAKE A FAST CORRECTION.

Shigeo Shingo calls it "information" or "prevention" inspection as opposed to "judgment" or "sorting" inspection. Kind of like comparing the "health examination" by a physician to the "death certification" by a coroner.

Figures 2 and 3 compare the Coroner (or Inspector)

approach with the Doctor (or Operator) approach. As can
be seen in Figure 3, the inspector makes a post mortem
inquiry into parts quality to "find" defects, whereas the
operator makes frequent checks of parts or process to
prevent defects, resulting in fast correction of defect
causes. This approach requires a mind-set and a procedure
change by both quality planners and workers.

Prevention Inspection

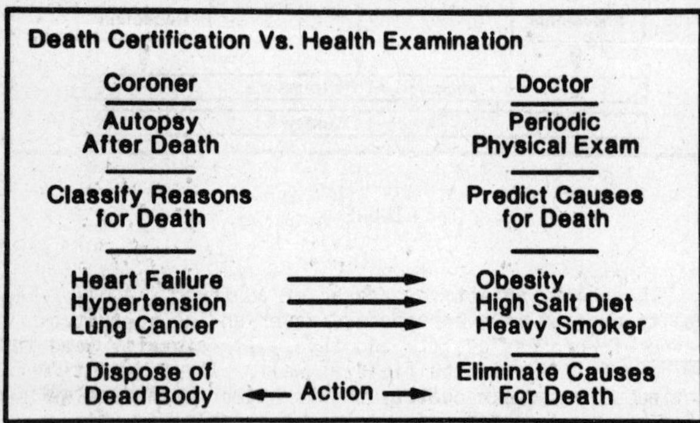

FIGURE 2

Prevention Inspection

FIGURE 3

Why are parts checked? To make visible what is being
done wrong in order that defective parts are not produced.
When self check (or operator checking) is prescribed,
there are certain rules that our Japanese management
exchange partners said must be followed. First and
foremost this kind of parts checking should always be
viewed as information, "health exam" inspection. And it
goes without saying that insistence on 100% compliance
with the standards is an absolute necessity. Other rules
are listed below:

o Simple gauges, simple training, simple methods
  should be used, and no more than 2-3 checking
  operations should be included.

o Operators should have all the gauges, tools and
  written instructions needed.

o Visual standards are needed if "sensual"
  characteristics are to be appraised.

o Consider mistake proofing where human error or
  compromise may be a factor.

MISTAKE PROOFING

Why do workers make mistakes? Typically we find three
major reasons.

1. They lack the knowledge or skill.

   This is controllable through proper selection and
   training of the particular person for the job.

2. Management has not established consistent quality
   standards and workers are confused.

   What is a reject today should be a reject tomorrow
   and should have no relationship to delivery
   requirements. The familiar exhortation; "that's
   ok, we'll fix it in the field", or "that's only
   cosmetic, we'll reduce the price and sell it as a
   second" have no place in a JIT quality program.

3. They make careless mistakes because of boredom,
   fatigue, distraction, carelessness, etc.

   While we have accepted some level of "operator
   error" as impossible to eliminate, the Japanese
   companies that practice "Pokayoke" or mistake
   proofing have accepted the fact that because humans
   will make errors it is for that reason that we must
   adopt ways to prevent these errors. Their goal is
   perfection.

   Pokayoke is the elimination of careless mistakes
   through mistake proofing.

Typically there are three levels of mistake proofing.

1. Build it into the product design or process (jig or
   adaptor system). This is the most effective method.

2. Sound an alarm when a mistake is made.

3. Develop a precaution check list to alert operators
   to potential mistakes and where extra care is
   required.

The first method is the most positive way, because the
operation is aborted if a mistake is made. Figure 4 is an
example of how fixturing can prevent mistakes by aborting
the process.
With the old fixture, the part was held by a spring
and it was possible to insert the wrong end into the
fixture. With the new fixture, the spring is replaced by
an "O" ring. If the chamfered end of the part is
inserted, the part will not be held in the fixture. This
is a simple, low cost example of Pokayoke. Many more were
observed in Japanese companies. What better way to do
100% "inspection" to prevent defects?

Mistake Proofing By Fixturing

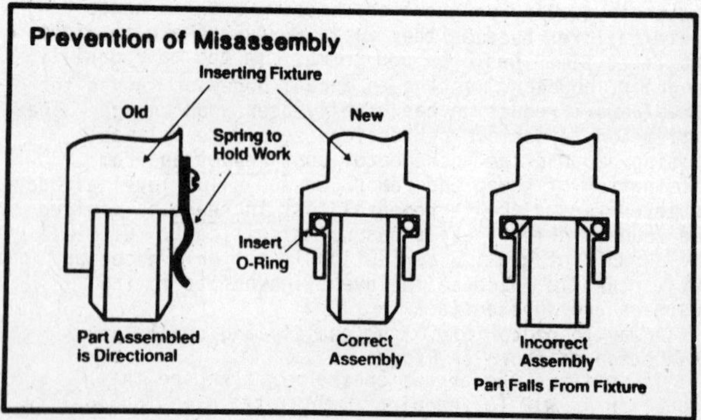

FIGURE 4

ROOT CAUSE CORRECTION

Discovering defects quickly has little value if fast
feedback and fast correction is not a part of the "new"
approach. Real-time problem solving is the goal of JIT
quality programs. As in so many other JIT concepts, this
requires a new mind-set. Help should be immediately

forthcoming if the shop cannot correct the cause of
defects when they are discovered. This means that
supporting functions should be on the shop floor where the
action is (maybe even a part of the shop manager's
organization) rather than "on call" in a remotely located
office.

Correction of cause means that defect analysis should
uncover the "root" cause not the symptom. These Japanese
companies continually stressed the need to ask "why?"
until a root cause is found. Typically at least 5 whys
are needed. (see Figure 5)

JIT Quality

<table>
<tr><td colspan="2">Getting to Root Causes
--Attempts to Answer "Why" Type Questions
--Ask "Why" Five Times
Example: Machine Stopped</td></tr>
<tr><td>1. Why Stopped?</td><td>-Fuse Blown</td></tr>
<tr><td>2. Why Overloaded?</td><td>-Lubrication of Bearing
Not Adequate</td></tr>
<tr><td>3. Why Lubrication
Not Adequate?</td><td>-Lubrication Pump
Failed</td></tr>
<tr><td>4. Why Pump Failed?</td><td>-Shaft Worn and Rickety</td></tr>
<tr><td>5. Why Shaft Worn?</td><td>-Chips Entered Inlet Port
Because No Strainer</td></tr>
<tr><td colspan="2" align="center">Why Did the Problem Occur?</td></tr>
</table>

FIGURE 5

PROCESS CAUSE CONTROL

Now let's look at the first concept. Prevent defects
from occurring in the first place by putting the controls
on the "cause" of defects rather than on the parts or
assemblies produced. (Even with quick detection and quick
correction it's not as good to find the defect as it is to
prevent the defect.)

Every process has parameters "within the process
itself" or "upstream" that determine the quality of the
parts produced. Proper planning and development of the
process to produce 100% good parts requires the
identification, not only of the parameters that need to be
controlled, but also the acceptance standards for the
parameter control plan. Proper control of these "inputs",
eliminates the need to check "output" of the parts
themselves.

Easy to say, not always easy to do! Figure 6
illustrates the proper approach to process cause control.

Process Cause Control

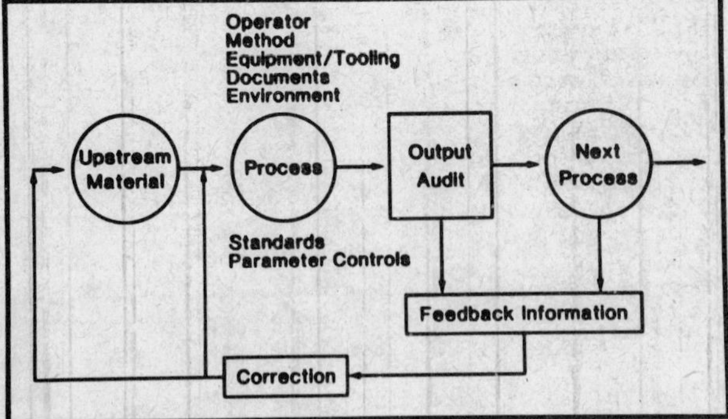

FIGURE 6

The process itself is described as the operator, the
method, equipment and tooling, drawings, instructions,

specifications, the shop environment and so forth.
Establishing the standard for each of the foregoing and
the method of their control is an integral and necessary
part of approving the process in the first place.

Upstream of the process, we have preceding operations,
vendors, handling, etc. These must also be controlled if
the output of the process is to be perfect. In many shop
situations, the only way to achieve a high quality level
of process output is to include positive control of
upstream operations/materials e.g. plastic molding, die
casting, porcelainizing, etc.

Downstream of the process under study are subsequent
operations (in effect, the next operation in line can be
looked upon as the customer). Although the process should
be controlled by "surveillance" of upstream material
inputs and parameters within the process, it is not unwise
to temporarily conduct a minor parts audit at the output
of the process and to permanently implement a
"confirmation" that the process stays within the
prescribed limits by checking parts at the next
operation. (These checks should be simple and easy to
perform and always built into the process if at all
possible).

At all of the surveillance and confirmation points
described above, discovery of a single defect should
result in a fast feedback to the source and a correction
made at that time or within a reasonable period of time to
eliminate the problem. Naturally, in starting a JIT
quality program, the time to implement correction will not
approach real time without practice and experience. In
many situations, age-old problems such as poorly
maintained machines, inadequate methods and fixturing,
poorly calibrated instrumentation or poorly trained
operators will have to be corrected before the "process
cause control" system described earlier will work
effectively. In effect, processes such as these have
never gotten out of the process approval stage. Results
from implementing Surveillance plan results can be
predicted merely by revisiting existing problems that are
well-known but were never corrected.

SUMMATION

A JIT quality program is a continuous, never ending
pursuit of perfection. Defect levels will be reduced,
aiming at the "zero defect" level, if processes are (1)
controlled at the source to detect and eliminate the
"cause" of defects and (2) when defects do occur, they are
discovered quickly and corrections are made immediately
(ideal).

Each and every operation, no matter how simple, should
be viewed as a process with parameters that must be
analyzed and prepared for control; e.g., operators
trained, methods debugged, drawing tolerances and quality
standards established, designs modified, etc.

Once the "process" is approved, input material is
under control and the process controls have been
established, then a process/product surveillance plan
should be implemented to detect "out of control"
conditions so that corrections can be made.

The surveillance plan should include monitoring of the
input material, the process parameters themselves and an
audit of the product coming out of the process with heavy
reliance on sequential inspection by the next operator.
The surveillance plan is aimed at confirming that the
process is in control and when abnormalities are
discovered that corrections are made quickly. Root cause
analysis is a vital part of the entire scheme to assure
that corrections eliminate the <u>cause</u> of the defects and
not just the symptoms.

The process is never-ending and will result in
continuous reduction of defect levels over time with zero
defects as the target and parts per million levels an
achievable goal. Thus the JIT Quality admonition becomes
a reality; DEFECT LEVELS SHOULD NEVER GO UP!

Figure 7 is a model for a parts per million control
system. There is no mystery in what needs to be done.
Companies in the U.S., years ago, prescribed the
fundamentals; Japanese companies in subsequent years
provided the disciplined approach; and JIT (or Zero
Inventories) now and in recent years is providing the
motivation.

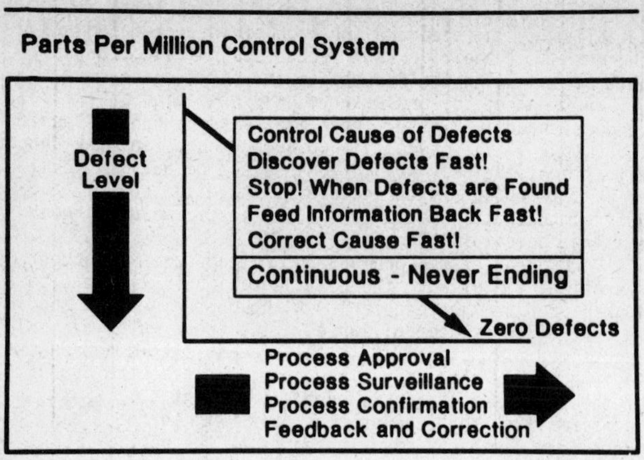

FIGURE 7

Larry Utzig has been with the General Electric Company since he graduated from Carnegie Institute of Technology in 1951. He has held various managerial and professional positions in Quality Control and Manufacturing in Utility, Industrial and Defense businesses. Since January, 1982 he has been active as a production management consultant with assignments both within General Electric and with outside companies that are either suppliers or customers of G.E.. Since his meetings with Toyota and other Japanese companies in four trips to Japan, he has concentrated his efforts primarily on JIT production systems and new approaches to controlling manufacturing quality.
He is the author of several papers published by the American Society of Quality Control on corporate quality strategies and customer-based measurements of quality and is an active presenter with ASQC.

AN ASSESSMENT OF JUST-IN-TIME IMPLEMENTATION

Richard J. Schonberger
University of Nebraska

FOREWORD

Just-in-time production is rapidly becoming the new way of life in the world's better manufacturing companies. Almost all industries are included. There are still some serious misunderstandings of JIT's objectives. Most notably, there is too much spending on equipment without regard for the flexibility of the plant.

IMPLEMENTATION OF JIT

Just-in-time or zero-inventory production is being implemented in most of the better known industrial firms in the world, and, along with total quality control, may become Japan's most valuable exports. A rough estimate is that several thousand companies and tens of thousand plants (besides those in Japan) now have just-in-time (JIT) efforts under way. These include many, or most, of the Japanese-owned subsidiary plants scattered around the world. They also include most of the Fortune-1000 largest industrial corporations in the United States.

In a small number of companies the accomplishments are in the order of ten-fold reductions in throughput time. For example, several of Hewlett-Packard's and Omark Industries' plants have achieved these levels of improvement.

Just-in-time has been commonplace in Japan for 15 years or more, but its beginnings elsewhere date back only to about 1980. General Electric was the first or among the first to mount a JIT campaign: 2 projects (or plants) in 1980, 10 in 1981, 20 in 1982, and 40 in 1983. GE's JIT efforts are notable in that they are in a variety of types of manufacturing: locomotives, dishwashers, huge vacuum circuit breakers, jet engines, generators, lamps (light bulbs), coffee makers, and more. These products are high and low volume, high and low variety, discrete and process, make-to-order and make-to-stock, smokestack and light assembly.

FAILURES/SUCCESSES

Are there any JIT failures to report? Any cases of "large expenditures on JIT with little or no return?

None that I know of. There are some potential disasters in the making that are referred to as JIT projects but which really are in violation of JIT's spirit of keeping things simple and flexible. More on that subject later.

Real JIT efforts have some built-in anti-failure attributes. For example, if a producing work station is moved 1,000 feet closer to a using work station, thereby reducing throughput time and inventory by several hours, how could it be anything but successful?

This example, moving work stations close together, is the foundation of JIT. It eliminates several forms of waste and cost in one fell swoop:

* Transit time
* Queue time
* Transit inventory
* Queuing inventory--resulting from unsynchronized operations
* Space
* Time between occurrence and discovery of defects (part of the great quality dividend of JIT)
* Uncoupled processes and resulting poor environment for problem solving (other part of the quality dividend: get stations linked together in time and distance so that operators will have reason to embroil themselves in problem solving)

The most successful JIT campaigns are those that put their main emphasis on moving work stations. At one GE plant their JIT effort features "moving a machine a day." At Omark's Guelph, Ontario, plant, which makes saw chain, their old flow distance, as of November, 1982, was 2,620 feet; in their new layout metal forming machines have been moved together to reduce the distance to 173 feet. The throughput time was cut from 21 days to 3 days, with 1 day as a target for the near future. When the time drops to one day, they get rid of the rest of their finished goods inventories; they become strictly make-to-order with service approaching the pure just-in-time ideal.

The "Buick City" project in Buick's Flint, Michigan, manufacturing center, is the same kind of effort: relocating virtually every machine and work center for quick throughput and no space for materials to stop and accumulate.

Rockwell's telecommunications division has a high-variety, low-volume plant with standard metal forming equipment near Dallas. For over two years they have been tearing apart their machine centers--sheet metal, spot weld, shear, saw, grind, NC lathe, and so forth. The machines are moved into cells making families of parts that follow similar flow paths. This concept, called group technology or cellular manufacturing, is the basis for just-in-time production where there are many part numbers and small production runs.

Any small job shop already uses group technology, simply because they have never become so large as to have multiple machines of the same general type. When small companies ask me how to implement JIT, the answer, therefore, is not to re-layout their equipment but to make the most of their fortunate situation of short flow paths. They must build on their flexibility by reducing setup times, become fanatical about machine maintenance, perfect a system to guarantee quality to their customers, and develop a competitive analysis capability as a cornerstone of product and process development.

ROLE OF AUTOMATION

Some companies are calling their JIT effort "continuous flow manufacturing." This term, perhaps coined at IBM, is as good as any, since it nicely captures the JIT vision of products not stopping. Some people infer that this means a plant full of conveyors or automated materials handling. But automated handling--and automated processing as well--costs money and may make the system less flexible. A cardinal principle of JIT is to become more and more flexible.

No machines, including robots and gravity-feed conveyors, are as flexible as people are. Therefore, the world's leading JIT companies, especially Toyota and its key suppliers, have been introducing automation piecemeal, as solutions to problems. The automation is mostly small home-made devices to measure, hold, index, push forward, receive, orient, align, and so forth. The devices make it easier for humans to work efficiently, safely, and without error. They also pave the way for further automation and perhaps robots.

Robots begin to replace people, typically to achieve greater quality than people are capable of; for example, robot welding and painting for greater uniformity.

In electrical and electronic assembly the same principle applies. Hitachi, NEC, Sharp, Canon, Matsushita, and many others have been automating incrementally with cheap, flexible

pick-and-place robots and simple home-made
automatic pieces of equipment.

Western companies involved in light
assembly have not yet learned the keep-it-
simple formula. We hear too much about big-
spash automation projects, such as IBM's PC
plant in Boca Raton, Florida, and Apple's
MacIntosh plant in Hayward, California. These
plants surely are enormous financial successes
even though the investment in equipment is very
high. What is too often overlooked is the
simplicity of the products themselves. The up-
front design engineering seems to have been
done masterfully to yield products that are
quite easy for robots to make (our leading
electronic "box" companies have learned to
design products with virtually no screws). It
also would be quite easy for humans to make.

As more companies learn to design products
for quality and manufacturability (design's
role in JIT), the threshold of high performance
will be raised. The leaders, such as IBM and
Apple, will by then have learned how to lower
the cost by using problem-push rather than
technology-pull automation. The byproduct will
be the preservation and enhancement of
flexibility. In the ideal, part of the
equipment in the plant is simple, dedicated,
home-made devices that cost so little that they
may be discarded when sales of the product
bottom out. The more costly equipment, and the
labor, will be flexible and adaptable to the
next generation of products.

If I seem, in this assessment of JIT, to
be spending a lot of time on equipment, it is
because that is the aspect of JIT that is least
understood.

PURCHASING AND QUALITY

The aspect of JIT that is best known is
JIT purchasing: getting frequent deliveries in
small amounts from suppliers. JIT buying
dovetails with the now vigorous movement in
good companies to get supplier-assured quality.
Just-in-time deliveries must be of good
quality, or the customer plant will be plagued
by severe stoppages.

Most of what we read in the business press
about JIT concerns purchasing. How misleading
the stories are. Most of our top companies are
working on supplier development, but this takes
years. The reductions in raw material
inventories are coming slowly, as one supplier
at a time is covered by a long-term contract
instead of sporadic purchase orders and bids.

In Western industry the quality movement
began before the JIT movement. Quality has
taken an independent course. Now the quality
and JIT movements are merging. They should
become indistinguishable in the West as they
are in Japan, and this is beginning to be the
case in some companies like IBM, GE, H-P, and
the auto companies. Nothing lowers the cost of
quality so fast as cutting inventories and
thereby the number of units to be reworked or
scrapped when a lot is bad. And the best
grease for a JIT system is defect-free
materials so that extras are not needed. (Have
you noticed that our APICS dictionary does not
include the word quality or other related
words? This is not an oversight by the
dictionary's author and editors but rather an
accurate reflection of our narrow vision.)

DATA GENERATION AND PROBLEM-SOLVING

Thus far, Western JIT plants have been
slow to take advantage of the opportunity to
record all of the events that slow or stop
production. Such data generation is basic to
JIT, but it means giving shop floor operators
some new responsibilities. Many companies are
now having operators record quality levels on
process control charts. That smooths the way
for adding some type of red light/yellow light
system: The operator turns on the red light

when there is a line stoppage for bad quality,
machine trouble, lack of parts, etc.; the
operator turns on the yellow light when there
is a slowdown but no need to stop the whole
line. These trouble-light systems are
everywhere in the Japanese auto industry, and
in many other industries as well.

Some plants in the West have had lights
for years, unrelated to a JIT campaign; for
example, lights on press-cure machines in a
tire plant and on final test equipment in a
printed circuit board shop; and call lights to
summon the "utility person" when someone wants
to go to the rest room.

The JIT lights are different. They not
only summon help (at least in the case of the
red light); they also require that a record be
made of the reason why. The record should be
on a blackboard or clipboard or both.
Periodically the different types of problems
are tallied. The supervisor uses the data to
prioritize problems and to assign project teams
to solve the problems. If there are
quality control circles, the circles can
perform some of the data analysis,
prioritization, and so forth.

As a rough guess, there may be 50 to 100
plants in North America that have installed red
and yellow light systems as a part of a JIT
campaign. But most have not added the tally
boards and therefore are losing the most
valuable benefits. One well-publicized case in
which the lights are used correctly is at the
Greeley, Colorado, division of Hewlett-Packard.

KANBAN

Kanban is a Japanese word meaning card--
the user's signal of a need to pull another
container of parts from the source of the
parts. Very few companies in the world use the
dual-card kanban system that Toyota employs for
many of its part numbers (Renault in France
does use it). Simpler one-card systems, or
better yet, visual signal systems (both also
perfected and widely used by the Toyota family
of companies) are more common. Perhaps several
hundred Western JIT companies now use such
signal systems. At H-P, Ft. Collins, there is
one operation where the signal for more parts
is removal of a plastic tub of parts from a
sensing platform. At H-P, Greeley, an empty
"kanban square"--outlined in yellow tape--is
the visual signal for another disc drive box.
At GE's lamp division, truck drivers collect
kanban cards when they unload, and the cards
signal which components should be delivered
next time. At one integrated circuit
fabrication plant in France, the JIT group
devised a more generalized signal system, which
enabled throughput time and inventories to be
cut in half: a daily meeting of all the fab
center supervisors to make sure that lot
movements are synchronized; no more making and
pushing lots forward unless the next stage is
ready to process.

In conveyor-paced production, kanban is
present in disguise. It is the chain pulling
the parts forward, one unit at a time. Of
course, Western industry has long had many such
systems. Now these lines are being outfitted
with warning and stop lights and with charts to
record hourly production and problems. Our
challenge is to back this concept into prior
stages of production and to extend it into
high-variety, low-volume production.

JIT ACROSS INDUSTRIES

Whatever the auto industry does receives a
lot of press. Thus, the auto industry's JIT
efforts are best known. Many other industries
are equally involved in JIT--and quality--as
their new manufacturing concept. There are
enlightened companies in weaving, tires,
sandpaper, paper and packaging materials,
bottling, wire, semiconductors, canning, and

plastics, to name a few. Products in these
industries tend to follow standard flow paths
and to be made in large enough quantities that
they are sometimes thought of a part of the
process industry. But they produce many
different sizes, colors, grades, and
formulations, and generally have large
inventories between changes and between
production stages.

These "process" companies are moving
toward shorter production runs (opposite to
traditional beliefs!) and fast changeovers.
Tight process control, total preventive
maintenance, frequent small deliveries of raw
materials, and synchronized scheduling are also
part of the formula. In most cases the
greatest needs are somehow to evolve toward
smaller, more flexible equipment and, often, to
move equipment so as to shorten the flow path.

For example, Western tire plants currently
have first-stage tire-building machines grouped
together, second-stage together, and so forth.
The first tire plant that moves its machines
into flow lines--not so difficult or expensive
to do for some of these machines--will surely
gain immediate competitive advantages; sharp
reductions in cost of quality will be the most
immediate and notable of the advantages.

In semiconductors the situation is the
same, except that the equipment is far more
complex, immobile, and costly to move into flow
lines. It appears that not even the Japanese
semiconductor plants have rationalized their
layouts. The door is open for semiconductor
plants to figure out how to do so; a few flow
line modules of the most mobile and flexible
machines would be the place to start.

Opposite to the process industry are the
low-volume, high-variety producers. Most are
very small--machine shops, foundries, and other
general-purpose job shops. These companies are
less likely to know about JIT at this point.

Some are large, however: plants making
locomotives, aircraft, ships, some large
mainframe computers. A few of our aircraft
companies (e.g., Hughes) are quite involved in
JIT. The contracts may call for only one
airplane per week or per month, but even that
offers the possibility for sychronized
regularity in scheduling the thousands of
production steps. In shipbuilding a revolution
of sorts (begun in Japan) has been taking
place. It features synchronized scheduling of
standard work packages, standard flow paths,
and cellular grouping of processes or machines.
By these techniques the time to build ships has
been reduced from months to days for some
shipbuilders. This is just-in-time production
applied to the most complex of production and
inventory control environments.

Finally, there are the large-volume makers
of consumer and industrial tools, appliances,
furnishings, and so forth: cameras, cassette
recorders, toys, shoes, luggage, washing
machines, generators, motors, desks, power
supplies, and thousands more. This is the
manufacturing sector that seems to absorb JIT
most easily, because much of the production is
labor intensive. Since labor is flexible, the
cost of JIT in these industries may be modest.
Often the bulk of the cost is for education,
training, and coordination. In advanced cases,
involving automation, robotics, computer-aided
engineering and processing, the costs are much
higher. The winners in the automation and
conputer-integrated manufacturing wars on the
horizon will be those that preserve flexibility
so that features, models, and even whole
product lines may be changed at low cost. A
tall order, to be sure, but many competitors in
Japan already know how to do it.

BIOGRAPHICAL SKETCH

Richard Schonberger is a professor in
production management at the University of
Nebraska-Lincoln. He is author of <u>Japanese
Manufacturing Techniques: Nine Hidden Lesson
in Simplicity</u> (New York: The Free Press,
1982). Dick and his associates provide
seminars and consulting for manufacturing
companies worldwide.

VARIABLE QUEUING—A MEANS TO REACH JIT
Richard Adden Wagner, CPIM
TRW

The goal to reach just-in-time-production has been established by many companies, however the results have ranged from excellent to disastrous. The view of many American companies is the Japanese have discovered a secret to maintaining low inventories and great performance. Has the competition found the secret of "control?" Maximizing resources: inventories, machines, facilities, personnel, and therefore money is the key. The approach of this paper is directed toward work-in-process inventories but should be considered as a rough model that can be applied to other areas as well.

DEFINING QUEUES

The definition of queue from the APICS dictionary is "a waiting line. In manufacturing, the jobs at a given work center waiting to be processed. As queues increase, so do average queue time and work-in-process inventory." By redefining and expanding the definition of queue as "any item requiring additional value, and that value is required for completion of the product it is in queue. As the average queues increase so do inventories." This will include a variety of value items. Orders that have been received by customers and that have not been shipped and invoiced, and collected should be considered value items.

The Just-In-Time production concept requires production of the exact quantity at the required time with a plus or minus factor to schedule of zero. The ideal lot size is one; the ideal set-up is zero; and the ideal queue is zero. Value is added from start to finish and no portion of the value is in queue. These items or areas where value items might be in queue are, but not limited to: order entry processing, engineering design, material ordering, material delivery, move or transfer times, inspection, waiting, and repairs.

The goals to reduce inventories or value items at any level from receipt of order to receipt of cash should be analyzed for the desired results. The analysis should include a detailed approach to include problem areas that might surface, but not too detailed to cause undo time loss in finishing the analysis. For this analysis we will use the work-in-process inventory as the value item. We will first assume that there is excessive inventory, the factory will not be reorganized into a focus factory concept, turns on inventory are too low, lead times are too long, large amounts of capital are not available for new equipment, and quality will remain constant.

SETTING A TENTATIVE GOAL

At this point a tentative goal is set to define the depth of the analysis. A twenty percent decrease in leadtimes is the targeted goal. The tentative goal has been defined, the analysis is beginning, and we must check our current procedures to determine if the starting point we currrently think we are at is the true starting point. If leadtimes are currently ten weeks, we need to define all increments of the ten-week period. We will start by redefining the period as fifty days. If time and resources are available you may desire to redefine the period in shifts or hours. During the fifty-day period our product is:

1. Running on a machine.

2. Being set up on a machine.

3. Being inspected.

4. Being moved to another location.

5. In a process cycle (i.e. baking, annealing, etc.)

6. Waiting for material.

7. Being repaired/reworked.

8. In queue waiting (both before and after any of the above).

Each of these are analysed from a typical product. The comparison should also be made from what our industrial engineers think is happening in the facility to what is really happening

The total waiting time can be divided by the total leadtimes to find an overall queue as a percent of manufacturing time. This percent should also be compared to run, set up and process time at each operation or process. This analysis should be performed on as large a sample and product mix that can be completed with the resources available.

The large sample is beneficial to reduce the potential error caused by different product flows as depicted in Figure 1. The product mix may vary by 20% or

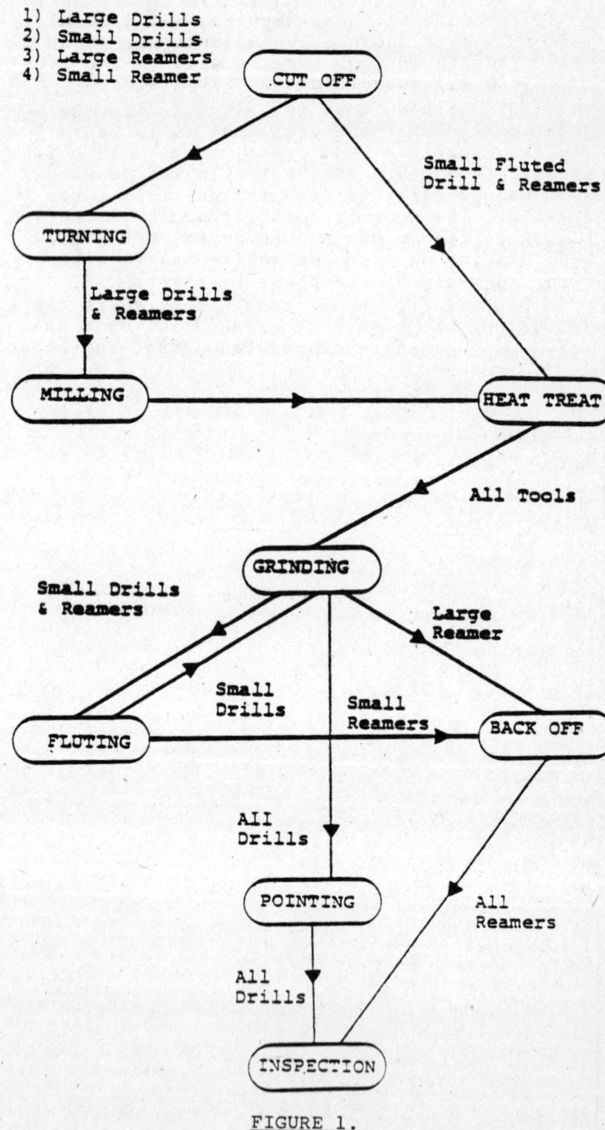

<u>FIGURE 1.</u>

30%. Knowing that the results of average queues compared to the mix can have an impact on the sample we may wish to increase our sample. The sampling techique should be in accordance with proven sampling methods. If the sample is not representitive of the total, resources available maybe misdirected and the target that is established may be unobtainable. Many texts are available on sampling techniques and should be reviewed for proper sampling procedures. A computer can greatly enhance the process by making the total data available for consideration in calculating averages and deviations.

Time at Standard

	Description	Days
1.	Run	7.2
2.	Set Up	.8
3.	Process	2.0
4.	Inspection	1.3
5.	Waiting on material	.1
6.	Being repaired/reworked (# repairs)	.1
7.	Being moved (25 x .1 = 2.5 hrs.) (#moves * average move)	.3
	Subtotal (1-7)	11.8
	Leadtime 50 days	50.0
8.	Waiting - In queue	38.2

FIGURE 2

The example listed in Figure 2 shows the projected time the order is worked on compared to lead time is 80% (items 1-3 Direct labor/Total leadtimes) If items 1-7 are considered the queue time falls to 76% or 38 days. A twenty percent reduction in leadtime when looking at the sample would seem to be an easy target. If considering this data alone, the target should be increased for a greater reduction in leadtimes. At this point, other considerations should be evaluated keeping in mind a target that is reached is a step that allows people to feel good about themselves and continue to strive for greater improvements.

Comparing the quoted or planned process flow to the actual process is the next step. The actual process might take more or less time than is planned in the leadtime. A comparision of planned to actual at each step of the leadtime process may determine that the failure is in schedule adherence, or the lack of good scheduling techniques. If this is the situation scheduling adherence and techniques should be reviewed. A review of the actual performance may determine that the product is not moving after it is completed at a given operation or process. If this is the case, a review of your material handling procedures should be made. The solution may be to add material handlers, material movement equipment, improve shipping methods, or revise the factory layout. If the problem is in fact determined to be actual waiting time before an operation, the following situations should be analyzed.

If a work station has too much work all or most of the time, the centers in question should be considered for additional planning and scheduling. This center should be considered a controlling work station. If work is waiting in all areas of the factory, we should consider what will happen as the waiting time is reduced.

If an area has no work, it will in fact have idle time and money will be lost due to poor utilization of equipment and/or personnel. Also, if the queue is uncontrolled, periods of large queues to almost no queues, the planning and scheduling techniques should be addressed. If the queue is high throughout the factory, queues can be researched in greater detail, and at this point a determination of current queueing methods should be made. The current queuing methods might be established by:

1. The current method of scheduling.

2. "That's the way we've always done it."

3. Default.

A study of current queues in each area will probably determine that queues have to be established on a perception of the work remaining. Two days work in one area may be viewed as excessive by one individual and "I'm sending everyone home at noon if I don't get more work" by another. Education is now an important step in the process. The team approach is a good place to start. The discussion of the benefits of reduced queue will assist you in making the future changes. Allocation of the queues and queuing methods should be solicited from all participants to reach the desired goal for the "whole" organization. Some of the proposals might include:

1. Five days of queue at each operation (direct and indirect)

2. Allow one, two, or three days for each sequence on the routing.

3. A fixed queue time at each direct labor or process operation.

Although some proposals would require that leadtimes be doubled or tripled, all were evaluated as a possible alternative. A tentitive allocation of queues should be established.

THE FIXED QUEUE

The "fair share" queue system is hard for an individual or group to pass up, although most feel their situation requires special consideration. But a fair share system will usually be well received because everyone is sharing the load, and the benefits. By sharing the queues evenly a "fixed queue" is established by everyone. The method of allocation of this "fixed queue" is generally harder to establish because of the scheduling system or scheduling problems that are currently in use. The fixed queueing method of scheduling should be reviewed before installation to insure compatibilty for future goals of leadtime reductions and Just-in-Time production, especially if the system uses computer generation of leadtimes and scheduling.

VARIABLE QUEUE

The application of these queue reductions could be planned with a "variable queue" approach. This is having the scheduling technique use the fixed queue as the default condition for the variable queue of today. As the new queuing target is reached, the default can be changed to a lower queue. This allows for a step-by-step reduction in leadtimes and will allow bottle necks to surface slowly, so that each can be fixed in a timely manner. They may reveal shortage or overage of equipment, manpower, or scheduling and planning methods. A shift in the product mix will also appear sooner as the queues are reduced. This shift in product mix can cause problems. Individuals from all areas should be aware of this and be advised to watch for this problem in advance. The variable queue can also be used to schedule hot jobs. By uniformly reducing the queues, all work centers will have the same amount of queue time to plan production for a given order, and therefore the automatic reduction in leadtimes to establish the plan delivery for the hot job.

OTHER CONSIDERATIONS

Queue time is usually the major component of leadtime. Leadtimes can also be improved by improved material handling, new equipment, shorter set up times, improve purchasing methods, better forecast, and factory reorganization. Some methods are available to the production control group without large expenditures of time and resources, they include but are not limited to:

1. If overlapping scheduling (performing work at more than one operation simultaneously is used) queues will be lower, however, queue times can still be used to reduce overall leadtimes.

2. A daily, AM/PM or hourly scheduling/planning method will assist in shorter queues. If ten hours work is scheduled for weekly periods the

change to hourly scheduling will reduce the scheduling period to 1.25 days (based on an eight hour day) plus queue compared to a 5 day period with a built in queue of 3.75 days

The variable queuing techniques will slowly and systematically allow you to reduce your leadtimes until work only arrrives at the next station just-in-time, so you will possess the secret of control.

ABOUT THE AUTHOR

Richard Adden Wagner is the Production Control Manager at TRW, Cutting Tools Division located in Augusta, Georgia. Adden has ten years experience in various production and inventory control assignments, including system development and implementation of MRP/CRP/SFC systems for electronics and basic metals industries.

He has a B.S. degree in Business Adminstration and an A.S. degree in Data Processing. He is recognized by APICS as a CPIM. Adden is a charter member and past president of the Augusta APICS Chapter.

IMPLEMENTING ZERO INVENTORY PRODUCTION IN A JOB SHOP MANUFACTURING ENVIRONMENT

Jack G. Youngkin, CPIM
Price Waterhouse

Production and inventory control practitioners in the United States now have a basic working knowledge of the concepts, principles and techniques generally associated with Just-In-Time (JIT) manufacturing. Several U.S. companies are now implementing a number of these techniques achieving results similar to Japanese manufacturers: 85% reductions in manufacturing lead times, 50-75% reductions in WIP inventories and set-up times, lower costs for direct labor, rework and inspection and increased utilization of factory floorspace. Furthermore, not all of these companies are engaged in what can be characterized as repetitive manufacturing. Some are traditional job shop producers involved in batch manufacturing of customized products to customer order.

In repetitive manufacturing, JIT can be adopted quickly generating substantial benefits over a short period of time. Job shop manufacturing, however, presents a more difficult implementation challenge but with potentially much larger benefits. The goal is clear: to achieve the simplist, least costly means for every possible aspect of manufacturing practice. This article describes specific approaches for installing JIT production in a job shop manufacturing environment. The use of group technology, flexible manufacturing centers and factory automation will also be examined as they relate to Just-In-Time implementation.

There are several fundamental differences between job shop manufacturing and repetitive manufacturing. A job shop is usually characterized by discrete unit fabrication and/or assembly which is planned and controlled by lot sizes. In addition, the use of alternative routings and high cost general purpose equipment is common. The goal of JIT production is to achieve continuous, or repetitive, production. It is characterized by a fixed flow path of material and utilizes specialized lower cost equipment, which is planned and scheduled by rate. JIT lies at the opposite end of the spectrum from the job shop concept. This presentation describes an approach for implementing JIT manufacturing or Zero Inventory Production (ZIP) in a job shop environment. The terms JIT and ZIP are synonymous and will be used interchangeably throughout.

Set-Up Reduction

Reducing machine set-up times may be the single most important technique utilized when transforming a job shop into a more flow-oriented manufacturer. More advanced methods such as group technology and dedicated production lines require minimal set-up times. In a job shop, lot sizes are generally determined by applying the EOQ model. Lengthy set-ups for attachments such as dies, necessitate large lot sizes. Because a majority of the lot may not be used immediately and must therefore be stored, EOQ lot sizing invariably leads to high WIP inventories. Reducing set-up times allows smaller lot sizes which will give the job shop manufacturer lower WIP carrying costs and increased flexibility.

Like JIT in general, set-up time reduction should be approached as a team effort. Ideally the team might include members from manufacturing engineering, tool and die maintenance, production control and manufacturing who are thoroughly familiar with the equipment and its functions. Full support from top management is essential to ensure set-up reduction does not become a "one time fix".

Total machine set-up usually includes the following tasks: assembly of tools, material and manpower; removal and storage of current attachments; installation of desired attachments; adjustment of attachments for proper performance; and testing and inspection. The tasks may be performed while the machine is still running (external set-up) or while the machine is down (internal set-up).

When attempting to reduce total set-up time, each individual task must be considered.

The set-up reduction team should first concentrate on those changes which can be affected at minimal or no out-of-pocket costs. Generally, set-up procedures and reduction of internal set-up times fall into this category. A methods analysis should first be conducted to evaluate current practices and procedures paying particular attention to the "why's". All movement by the set-up team must be essential. Good procedures may in fact already exist but may not be uniformly applied. The trick is to document the procedures, train all set-up crews/operators in their proper execution and ensure that the procedures are uniformly enforced. Attention must also be paid to performing as much of the procedure as possible when the machine is running (external set-up). This requires all attachments, tools and workers to be waiting when the machine stops. Immediately after use, attachments and tools should be cleaned and prepared for their next set-up. Set-up times may be reduced 50% or more by applying these simple and low cost methods.

After new procedures have been put in place the set-up reduction team can focus on moderate cost items. Minor modifications of dies, tools or fixtures may reduce attachment installation and removal times. These costs should be handled out of departmental budgets. Hinged bolts, quick disconnects, clamps, roller platforms, and tooling carousels have all been used to generate set-up reductions. For example, AP Parts developed a quick release snap-on pilot which reduced pilot changeover by 95%. Minor modifications are relatively easy to implement and can lead to a further 15-25% reduction in set-up times.

Only when the team has achieved the easier low cost reductions should attention be paid to higher cost alternatives. Reducing or eliminating adjustments and standardization of dies, tools and parts may involve design changes requiring capital expenditures. At Mercury's Fond du Lac plant, die standardization cost an average $2000 per die but reduced set-up times for its 450 ton die cast machines over 75%. These higher cost items should be justified on an individual basis and may lead to an additional 15% reduction.

If the majority of set-up time reduction can be accomplished relatively easily, why are lengthy set-up times so prevalant? Simply, the task has not become a priority until now. Reduced set-up times can be accomplished by setting lofty goals and taking a long term perspective. A continual examination of the entire set-up process is required. Start with the easy changes so that visible results will encourage further effort. Finally, as reduced set-up times lead to smaller lot sizes and greater flexibility, more absolute set-ups will be required. Therefore, efficiency may be gained by having machine operators do their own set-ups where feasible.

Total Quality Control

Total Quality Control (TQC) is essential for successful implementation of JIT. Remember, JIT requires fabricating or assembling only as many units as is necessary. Without large batches there will no longer be a large pool of parts to pull from when a defective part is found. With elimination of the inventory "safety valve" and emphasis on quality over production, quality problems must be corrected immediately to avoid delays in the production schedule. TQC also emphasizes quality at the source. In other words, it requires shifting the burden for quality from quality control to production and ultimately to the machine operator. It employs the principles of process control, linestop, defect prevention and visable measures of performance to achieve its goal of continual improvement in quality.

To get started, a statistical capability study should be conducted. By comparing output to part print tolerances, ratings can be established for priority purposes. Quality problems identified must then be attacked as a joint effort between production, engineering, quality control and other affected parties. Operators must also check quality on a continuous basis using statistical methods such as checking the first and last parts of every run against critical tolerences to catch machine variances before they become a problem.

By transferring the burden for quality from quality control to production and with smaller lot sizes, quality problems may be identified and corrected as they arise. There is also an increased responsibility for engineering to design quality into the process. TQC is a state of mind and is essential to ensure the success of your zero inventory program.

Housekeeping and Preventative Maintenance

Housekeeping and preventative maintenance are not new to U.S. manufacturers but they do take on special significance when implementing a ZIP program. Housekeeping not only means keeping work areas clean but also that all attachments, tools and materials should be kept in specified locations. Everything used for one operation should be kept together and cleaned or refurbished and returned to its storage location immediately after use. Housekeeping is critical to enable fast frequent set-ups, preventative maintenance and attention to quality.

Preventative Maintenance (PM) is required to ensure a high quality product is produced when needed. Remember ZIP will reduce WIP inventory which prevents using the stockroom as a safety valve. Variation in a machine's performance caused by inattention will have an adverse effect on the TQC program. PM begins by including time in the production schedule and making operators responsible for performing checks. The payout for PM comes not only from prolonging equipment life but in enabling production to reduce defects, rework and downtime leading to successful JIT implementation.

Dedicated Production Lines (DPL)

Once set-up reduction, quality, and maintenance programs have been established, the project team must attempt to create a more continuous work flow through the job shop. It may be possible to break-up part of the job shop by rearranging work centers into production lines. Each line would be dedicated to the manufacture of a group of similiar parts (or an individual part if warranted by sufficient volume). This can usually be accomplished by stationing machines or assembly operations sequentially according to the required routing (Figure 1). When used for multiple parts, the line will require quick changeover from one part number to the next. Therefore, it is critical that set-up times be minimal, enabling smaller lot sizes. To achieve JIT benefits, the lots can be further reduced by using overlapped production. For instance given a lot size of 20, Station A may make two parts and pass them to Station B before starting work on parts three and four. Buffer stock is normally required at the end of the line to account for output unpredictability.

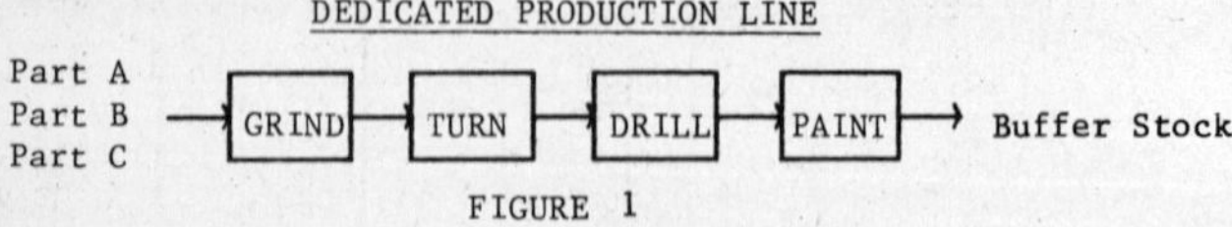

DEDICATED PRODUCTION LINE

FIGURE 1

In order to gain maximal benefits it is desirable to locate the DPL output adjacent to its point of use. In this way output may be geared to the production rate of the next work center thereby minimizing buffer stock. The line must also be balanced to equalize the workload of operators on the line. If necessary, Kanban should be implemented to pull production based on the demand of upstream work centers. Normally production is pushed by the daily schedule. By definition a push system, such as MRP, will require a certain level of WIP inventory which is contrary to the strict interpretation of Zero Inventory Production.

There are several advantages to DPL's. First, the lead time to complete a part number may be reduced up to 90%, greatly enhancing flexibility. Secondly, paper work required to track items through work centers will be greatly reduced and finally WIP inventory may receive another round of reductions. More importantly through the use of DPL's, job shops may begin evolving into JIT manufacturers.

Group Technology

Group Technology (GT) is another technique which can be used to generate work flow in the job shop. Under GT a group of 3-30 dissimilar machines are combined into a U-shaped cell which will process a family of parts. In order to develop families, parts must be classified based on key design and manufacturing characteristics and then be grouped according to commonality. Although large scale grouping of parts may become a major effort, flexibility may be gained by utilizing a computer-based parts coding and classification system. As optimal parameters fluctuate, the capability would then exist to conduct a new analysis and to possibly restructure the cellular system.

Once established, part families must be grouped together into proposed cells for routing evaluation. Cells may be set up to produce a completed product or subassembly. Alternatively cells may process part families with similar geometric features or with the same process sequencing (Figure 2). The only requirement is that the cell must be designed to handle all machining, or assembly capabilities, required by its family and contain the proper attachments, tools and operators. Substantial effort is required for the detailed design. Once set, only the proposed cells with sufficient machine utilization would be implemented.

GROUP TECHNOLOGY CELL

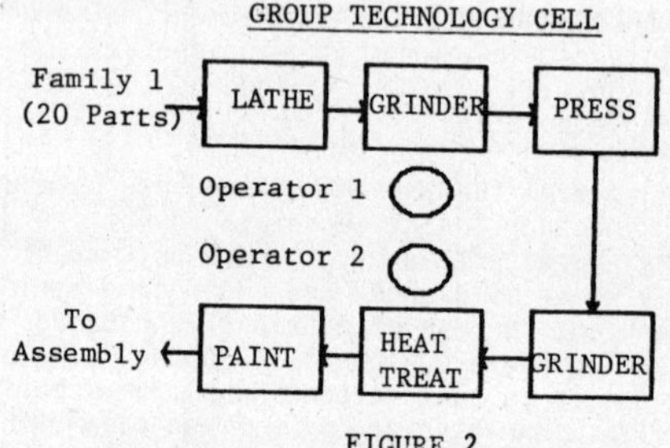

FIGURE 2

As with DPL's quick set-ups and small lot sizes are essential in order for GT cells to achieve Zero Inventory Production benefits. Productivity can be increased by training a skilled operator to set-up and run all machines within the cell. Also if space permits, cells should be located adjacent to their point of use to allow reduced buffer stocks. Output from the cell must also be balanced according to the production rate of the next operation. The cells cycle rate is determined by the operators who must tour the cell, manually moving parts from machine to machine, and can be roughly controlled by adding or subtracting workers.

When set-ups, machine operation and material handling are automated by robots, programable controls and transfer devices, cells are referred to as Flexible Manufacturing Centers (FMC). The advantages of FMC's will be discussed in the next section.

Finally, in designing GT cells, preference should be given to smaller specialized equipment over more costly general purpose equipment. Additional machines may always be purchased to gain required capacities. Specialized equipment is easier to set up and fits nicely into the concept of dedicating machines to each GT cell. For example Omark Industries must heat treat most of the chain saw teeth that it forms. Instead of utilizing a large heat treat oven in a central area, each cell may have its own small laser heat treater. Remember with GT, flexibility and quick set-ups are the name of the game.

Flexible Manufacturing Centers

As mentioned previously fully automated group technology cells are commonly referred to as Flexible Manufacturing Centers (FMC). A typical FMC would consist of a group of numerically controlled processing centers clust-

ered around a robot and connected together by an automated
material handling system to transfer the workpieces. The
system is normally integrated under the computer control.

In addition FMC's often include Automated Storage and
Retrieval Systems (AS/RS). These systems are intended to
centrally store and retrieve workpieces as needed by the
cell. Because these AS/RS's imply storage of WIP inventory, they are not compatible with a zero inventories
program. Once production is streamlined and WIP reduced,
there is little need or economic justification for its
installation.

Some FMC's have the capability to handle alternative
routings which allow several different parts to be processed within the system at one time. Because of the
buffer inventories required for random operations, this
flow pattern is not suitable for zero inventories. Instead the FMC should be set up for sequential flow in
which multiple routings are not allowed. With small lot
sizes and quick changeovers, sequential flow can still
allow processing of multiple part numbers at the same
time. For example, parts A and B could be processed on
machines 3 and 1 respectively, with machine 2 shut down
for tool changes.

FMC's make it possible to cope with changing mixes of
parts and product designs providing more customized production capabilities. Reductions in direct labor involvement will reduce rework and scrap. In general, FMC's will
result in another round of improved quality, reduced
inventory and shorter manufacturing lead times. More
importantly, the flexibility gained will make it feasible
for a job shop to obtain continuous customized production.

Factory Automation and Computer Integrated Manufacturing

Factory Automation is regarded by some to be the only
route to survival in today's increasingly competitive
environment. Customers are increasingly demanding high
quality, low cost, custom products built on short notice.
At the same time increasing labor costs and growing overhead have squeezed profit margins. Computer Integrated
Manufacturing (CIM) has the potential to achieve total
factory automation through integrated plant computer and
automated manufacturing systems. These systems include
computer aided design (CAD), computer aided manufacturing
(CAM), numerically controlled machines and robotics. CIM
will allow on board machine diagnostics, automatic process
monitoring and shutdown, robotic control of FMC's and
simulation of customer orders. The benefits to be gained
also include improved quality, reduced inventories, flexibility, automation of small batch production and the
reduction of new product development cycles.

Zero inventory production and CIM are separate but
compatible goals. In fact, the implementation of a ZIP's
program is essential if the automated factory is to become
a reality. For example, using robots to increase work
center production is self defeating if downstream processing cannot handle the increased product flow. To succeed
an evaluation must first be directed towards the underlying products, procedures and processes. JIT provides the
focus for this effort.

To date CIM has not become a reality because of
problems in sharing common data essential to integration.
Solving these problems is only a matter of time. By
beginning a ZIP program today your plant will be taking a
giant step towards the computer integrated factory of
tomorrow.

JIT Purchasing

For many manufacturers purchased material costs may
exceed 50% of the final product sales price. Because of
the resulting large investments required for purchased
inventories, Just-in-Time concepts must be extended to
suppliers in the form of JIT Purchasing. JIT purchasing
requires orders to be released and delivered on a more
frequent basis, which will allow substantial reductions in
purchased inventories. The effort should be continual
with a goal of daily deliveries of the exact amount of
materials to be used.

This implies that close coordination with the supplier is essential. Long-term order requirements, such as
MRP output, must be made available so that the supplier
can plan production. JIT purchasing is a two-way street
built on trust. The elimination of price buying and
establishment of long-term business relationships are also
important to ensure success.

Their is another equally important reason for implementing JIT purchasing. The quality of purchased materials used must be controlled in order to achieve total
product quality. The goal is zero defects for all materials so that elimination of purchased inventories is
feasible.

Like all JIT concepts and principles JIT Purchasing
should initially be applied on a small scale. Negotiations with a few local or regional suppliers should be
conducted stressing the win-win advantages. For instance
Hewlett-Packard held a vendor day to include JIT and
invited 25 top vendors, representing $30 million worth of
1983 purchases. Companies such as Kawasaki, Black &
Decker, Hewlett Packard and Harley Davison have found that
an overwhelming majority of suppliers will be receptive.
As experience and benefits are gained, JIT purchasing can
be expanded to a larger number of suppliers. Increased
inventory turns, stockroom space savings and reduced lead
time are all benefits which can be achieved relatively
quickly. In time it will become evident that the long-
term advantages of JIT purchasing far outweigh the short
term benefits of the low bid philosophy.

GETTING STARTED

Education

Educating the organization in the concepts, benefits
and techniques of ZIP is essential to create enough interest to get the program off the ground. Once started,
continual interest will be generated by results. This
effort must start at the top. It is essential that top
management realize that JIT will affect the entire organization. Success will be determined by how well the
various departments pull together as a team. Therefore
contradictory corporate and departmental policies must be
identified and eliminated. Just as important is for
executives to gain enough knowledge to judge the performance of the implementation team. Often plant trips and
lectures can be used to serve the purpose.

Once upper level management has been indoctrinated,
training sessions and seminars can be held for the rest of
the organization. Attention should be paid to the whats,
whys and hows of JIT implementation. All personnel must
be prepared for the possibility that job assignments may
be unpredictably changed. It is especially important for
line management and operating employees to accept responsibility for making improvements and to not feel their
jobs are threatened. This may become an issue in the
future as at least one company has been forced to make
layoffs due to efficiencies gained through JIT. Therefore, the program should emphasize the long-term benefits
ZIP would give to the company. Education is a continuing
effort and can not be overdone. It must be conducted both
formally and informally in order to ensure success.

Analysis

Once top management has been "sold" on the concepts
of JIT and have pledged their commitment, a thorough
analysis must be conducted to identify "areas of opportunity". At this point a full-time project leader should
be chosen to direct the efforts. A project team must be
created to initially include members from production,
engineering, and quality control. Additional members from
affected departments should be added prior to implementation. A sub-team should also be established to specifically address set-up reduction.

The study document must specify which areas of the
job shop have the potential to be transformed into continuous flow manufacturing. Once project areas are identified, priorities must be established. Also at this stage
a pilot project should be identified and company-wide
programs such as preventive maintenance, housekeeping and
total quality control must be planned. A time phased
implementation schedule must then be developed and approved by top management.

Pilot Program

ZIP implementation should begin with a pilot program
in order to reduce risk during the initial trial and error
stages. The objective is to provide a moral booster and
to dispel the doubt that will invariably arise. Real
benefits must be shown. To ensure success the pilot
project should be limited to a single product or product
line and must encourage the involvement of foremen and
operators on the shop floor. Normally, the pilot project
is identified during the analysis state.

Implementation

Once the pilot project has been successfully completed, ZIP programs throughout the plant should begin
immediately. As discussed earlier, set-up times will have
to be drastically reduced before the job shop can achieve
continuous flow manufacturing. Therefore, set-up time
reduction must be the first priority. JIT implies production only as required to meet daily requirements. This
means it is not enough to achieve a flow oriented shop.
High product quality, flexibility and reliable equipment
are also essential to reduce the need to hold inventory.
Once the program has begun, improvements must be made
visable to everyone. Results must speak for themselves if
the organization is to gain confidence that JIT is in fact
the proper way to go.

Initially it may only be possible to convert a small
portion of the job shop to continuous flow production.
Even so, it is important to note that reduced inventories,
improved quality and increased flexibility can be achieved
without reaching the goal of continuous flow. JIT really
means discarding old "truths" by continually reviewing
products, processes and procedures in order to achieve
manufacturing excellence. Implementing ZIP is essential
to compete in today's competitive environment in which low
cost, quality products must be produced on short notice.
The job shop must not be left behind.

Jack G. Youngkin, CPIM, is a Senior Manager in the
Management Consulting Services department in the Dallas
office of Price Waterhouse. He has extensive experience
in helping clients solve business problems in the electronics, defense, aerospace and process industries.

Mr. Youngkin's experience includes assisting clients
in the evaluation, planning and implementation of manufacturing systems in the aerospace, electronics and process
industries. He also has directed manufacturing improvement programs, inventory reduction studies and profit
improvement programs for a wide range of industrial concerns. Mr. Youngkin previously held a number of manufacturing positions during eight years at Texas Instruments.

Mr. Youngkin holds a BBA in Production and Operations
Management from North Texas State University. He is a
Past President of the North Texas Chapter of APICS and has
served as Region VI Director of Membership and Chapter
Development. Mr. Youngkin is a frequent speaker at APICS
dinner meetings and seminars.

LOADING AND UNLOADING THE SHOP FLOOR IN DISCRETE AND REPETITIVE ENVIRONMENTS

John F. Proud, CPIM*
Xerox Computer Services

ROLE OF MATERIAL PLANNING AND CONTROL

Balance -- That's the secret! The path to operating or working in a successful manufacturing company is to properly balance the elements of the production triangle --schedule, cost, and quality (Figure 1). As you might suspect, this is not an easy task. It's no secret that objectives exist in manufacturing which are in direct conflict with each other.

Production and Inventory Management text books have long described three (3) basic objectives we all work hard to attain. These objectives are to satisfy the customer's needs using a reasonable amount of inventory which permits economical use of the factory resources. As we look at these objectives, it can quickly be seen that inventory is a common denominator. This is a very important point to recognize!

FIGURE 1

Inventory is defined as the quantity of goods or material on-hand. Now, taking a closer look at inventory, we should realize that inventory exists for two (2) reasons:

1) To support production
2) As a result of production.

Here, production is the common denominator. It then follows that if we plan to get control of our inventories, we first must get control of production.

The ultimate company objective is to optimize profits. Optimize means to make as **perfect, effective,** or **functional** as possible. Those are three very powerful words we just used - - **perfect, effective,** and **functional**. How many of us really work hard to optimize (make as perfect as possible) the profit picture. Well, that's where it's at today! If companies want to stay competitive, they need to answer the question --"How good are we?"

Many questions have been asked Production and Inventory Management personnel over the last few years. Some of these questions are: Is inventory necessary or evil? How much inventory is necessary? Why is inventory needed? Is the production environment discrete or repetitive? What should it be? All these questions should and need to be answered.

Once the above questions have at least been acknowledged as legitimate inquiries, we are ready to address a whole new set. Does the Zero Inventory Crusade make sense? Is it realistic to have inventory anywhere that is not actively in process? What has to be done to our systems for Zero Inventory concepts to work? Do these philosophies apply to your business?

DISCRETE ENVIRONMENTS

Production is the process or method of machining, assembling, fabricating or combining resources into finished goods or sub-assemblies. The production environment, which is often referred to as manufacturing, can be divided into two categories: (1) discrete and (2) repetitive. The major characteristics of the discrete environment are listed below:

- Work order oriented
- Random job movement
- Smooth output is difficult to get
- Large queues
- Heavy transaction based
- Paper orientation
- Scheduling by available resources
- Significant work-in-process (WIP) inventory investment

The discrete manufacturing environment presents many problems for the professional in material planning and control. First of all, work orders (manufacturing authorizations) are generally created to communicate the production plan to the floor. These work orders create a need for detail tracking and expediting. Second, material is often staged at work centers which creates queues and excessive WIP inventories. This excessive WIP often must be expedited to maintain priorities.

Due to the large volume of work on the floor, accurate order status is difficult to secure. Besides not having a good handle on each job's location, many releases to the floor are often late causing additional problems. The whole process generally is very costly.

To assist the material planner in getting the job done, a tool known as the Closed Loop Manufacturing System can be used effectively to properly plan and control the material movement on the floor (See Figure 2).

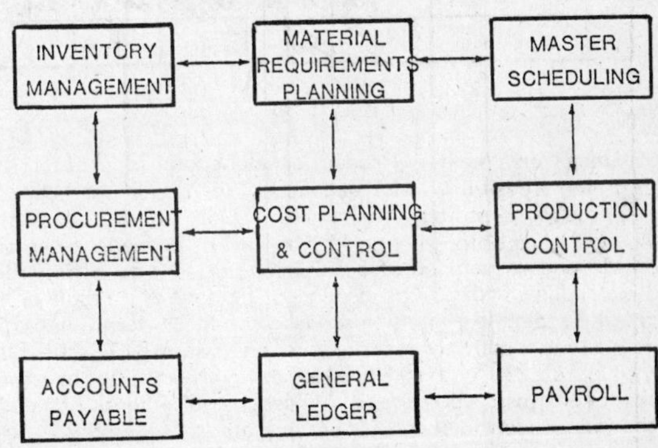

CLOSED LOOP CONFIGURATION

FIGURE 2

The Closed Loop system in the discrete environment is driven by the Master Production Schedule (MPS). The objective of MPS is to plan for and control the impact of independent demand on material and capacity. Simply, what MPS is intended to do is balance the delivery schedule with the cost and quality of the product (See Figure 3a).

MASTER PRODUCTION SCHEDULE

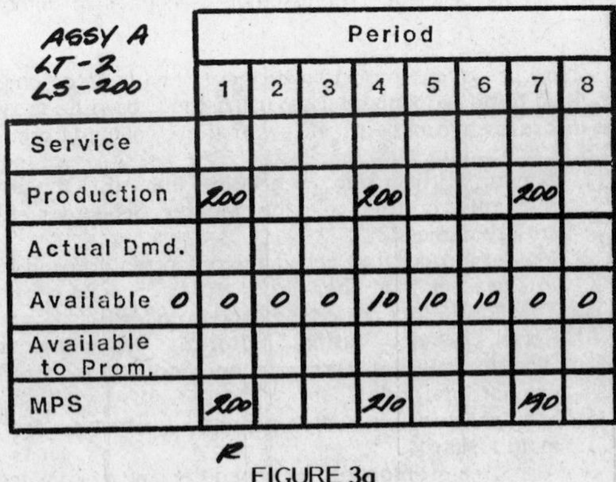

ASSY A LT-2 LS-200	1	2	3	4	5	6	7	8
Service								
Production	200			200			200	
Actual Dmd.								
Available	0	0	0	0	10	10	10	0	0
Available to Prom.								
MPS	200			210			190	

FIGURE 3a

The figure shows assembly A has a demand of 200 units in periods 1, 4, and 7. The Master Scheduler has responded to this demand by placing replenishment orders (work orders and firm planned orders) in the periods which correspond to these requirements. The MPS line displays orders by their due dates.

The recommended lot size for assembly A is 200 units. The Master Scheduler has elected to override the recommended lot size by placing orders of 210 in period 4 and 190 in period 7. In the aggregate the three orders average 200 as defined by the lot sizing policy. When the requirements and replenishments are identified by date and quantity, the MPS system can calculate the projected available balance for all future periods.

MATERIAL REQUIREMENTS PLAN

PART NUMBER ASSY B
LEAD TIME 1
LOT SIZE 250
SAFETY STOCK —
SERVICE REQUIREMENTS 5/PER100

		PERIODS							
		1	2	3	4	5	6	7	8
PROJECTED GROSS REQUIREMENTS		5	215	5	5	195	5	5	5
SCHEDULED RECEIPTS			250						
PROJECTED AVAILABLE BALANCE	30	25	60	55	50	-145	-150	-155	-160
PLANNED ORDER RELEASE					250				

PART NUMBER COMP X
LEAD TIME 3
LOT SIZE 500
SAFETY STOCK 100
SERVICE REQUIREMENTS —

		PERIODS							
		1	2	3	4	5	6	7	8
PROJECTED GROSS REQUIREMENTS					500				
SCHEDULED RECEIPTS		150							
PROJECTED AVAILABLE BALANCE	100	300	300	300	50	50	50	50	50
PLANNED ORDER RELEASE		500							

FIGURE 3b

Once the Master Production Schedule is created and tested for feasibility, it becomes the driver to Material Requirements Planning (Figure 3b). Our figure shows that assembly B has both independent as well as dependent demand. The independent demand of 5 units per period is to satisfy field service requirements. The dependent demand is a result of the MPS build schedule exploding down to the MRP item. Assuming it takes one assembly B to make an assembly A, the build quantities of 210 and 190 are offset by lead time to create lower level gross requirements. These requirements are added to the independent demand for service parts. Assembly A has a work order for 200 units which is scheduled to be completed in the current period. The figure assumes all assembly B's required to build assembly A have been issued and therefore no additional demand is generated.

As we look at the MRP format, we notice a work order for 250 units is scheduled to be received in period 2. Since our example shows assembly B has 30 units in stock, MRP can project future inventory balances. A positive net balance has been projected thru period 4. In period 5 a potential shortage of 145 units is sensed by the system. This projected shortage has generated a computer planned order (CPO) to be released in period 4 (offset by lead time for assembly B). The CPO for assembly B becomes input to the next lower level component X. The MRP logic described for assembly B applies to component X.

There are many important concepts and logic assumptions which need to be recognized when using the Closed Loop system in the discrete environment. A few of these concepts are:

1) Master Production Schedule lots (FPO) are manually created by the Master Scheduler to satisfy demand.
2) Master Production Schedules are often created in lots greater than one.
3) These MPS lots act as the drivers to MRP.
4) Parts planned using Material Requirements Planning use lot sizing techniques, which often are not lot-for-lot.
5) Safety stock is very popular in many MRP installations.
6) A material planner or scheduler must convert computer planned orders manually to scheduled receipts (work orders and purchase orders).
7) MRP systems assume infinite capacity is available to handle the demand (lot size has a great impact).

Lets keep these in mind as we analyze the Zero Inventory concepts and define what must be done to implement these concepts into the classical Closed Loop approach.

ZERO INVENTORY CONCEPTS

According to Robert W. Hall, author of Zero Inventories, the goal of ZERO INVENTORY (STOCKLESS PRODUCTION) is to find practical ways to create the effect of an automated industry which will come as close as possible to this concept of ideal production. Stockless production implies an even flow of materials and promotes repetitive manufacturing. This means that automation may well displace manual labor. We probably all have seen the effect of automating many functions the manufacturer does daily. As a company moves towards automation, no person should be assigned to do a task which a machine can do more economically.

Many companies through history have converted from discrete to repetitive environments, ie. the automobile industry. To make it easier to understand this and how it all relates to the Zero Inventory Crusade, let's review the characteristics of repetitive manufacturing:

- Capacity is dedicated
- Tooling is specialized
- Routings are fixed
- Balance between work centers
- Processing time is short
- Queues are very short
- Production is driven by daily schedules
- Paperwork is held to a minimum
- Product sequence is efficient
- Set-ups and changeover are rapid.

An analysis of the supporting system's objectives in the repetitive and discrete environments show the following differences:

REPETITIVE - - levelize the production flow
DISCRETE (MRP) - - reduce the material wait time.

To implement Zero Inventory concepts, the manufacturer should produce the products the customer wants only at the rate the customer wants them. What the manufacturing system should do is support this environment which requires speed and minimal manual intervention.

PUSH vs PULL SYSTEM

The system described to support discrete environments is often referred to or takes on the characteristics of a PUSH system. A PUSH system is one where orders are launched and "pushed" through the factory to meet some established due date. Lot sizes have great impact on the PUSH type system. The MPS is critical to the PUSH system, but not nearly as much as to the PULL system. A PULL system is one where orders are placed at the end item level and work is "pulled" through the factory to satisfy the demand for the end item. A better name for MPS in the PULL System is just Master Schedule.

A company driving production by using a PULL system must do a few things to their classical material planning and control systems. Four key interfacing systems need to be enhanced:

1) INVENTORY CONTROL must accurately record work-in-process (WIP) balances and define the part/work center relationship.

2) MASTER PRODUCTION SCHEDULE AND MATERIAL REQUIREMENTS PLANNING must recognize flow orders and support allocation functions.

3) PROCUREMENT MANAGEMENT must have the capability to receive directly to work-in-process and support automatic releases of purchase orders.

4) SHOP FLOOR CONTROL (WIP CONTROL) must support the issue/completion cycles as well as backflushing/backfilling techniques.

Now, so we don't get too nervous and feel this is an overwhelming task, let's understand that expeditors have run PULL systems for years. When the expeditor concentrates only on the "hot" order, he is running a PULL system. The problem is that when the expeditor is done, generally a mess is left behind.

PREPARING THE PRODUCTION PLAN

What needs to be done? First of all, a Production Plan which establishes the overall rate of production and an appropriate model mix is created. This is done so that everyone can prepare in advance. Remember, in the Zero Inventory philosophy, the Production Plan only communicates information so people can prepare for what is expected to occur.

This Production Plan will become the constraint in which adjustments to the model mix will be made. The other thing we want to remember at the production planning level is that a level schedule is one that requires material to be <u>pulled into final assembly</u>. This needs to be done in a pattern uniform enough to allow the various elements of production to respond to the pull signals. Look at Figure 4.

SPREADING LOGIC EXAMPLE

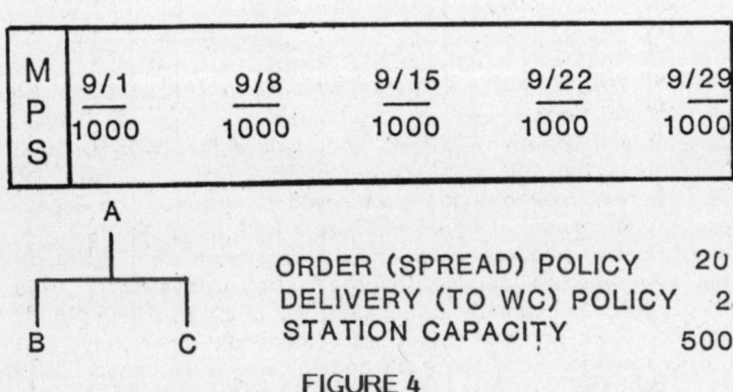

FIGURE 4

A demand exists for 4,000 units over the first twenty (20) days. To apply spreading logic the system uses a delivery policy table as well as the line station capacity. If 4,000 units are required and the delivery policy is every 2 days, the system can see there needs to be 10 deliveries of 400 units every other day. Next, the station capacity is checked. If the capacity at the station is 500 units, the calculated release amount (400 units) is less and okay to schedule. If the station capacity is 300 units, the releases to the floor could only be for 300 units and deliveries would have to be scheduled in different increments (eg. lots of 300 on Monday, Tuesday, Thursday, or 200 in the morning and 200 in the afternoon).

Again, this spread logic is used at the production plan level to project the anticipated schedule. The Final Assembly Schedule (FAS) will be the actual pull schedule which will trigger the rest of the system to respond. That's the key to Zero Inventory!

COMMUNICATING TO LOWER LEVELS

The Production Plan plays a very important part in the whole process. Decisions made at the production planning level are translated into discrete part numbers, quantities and due dates. These results are then loaded into the Master Schedule. This is done by creating manual or automatic firm planned orders (FPO).

Firm planned orders are orders which can be frozen in quantity and time. Once these orders have been placed in the Master Schedule, the computer does <u>not</u> automatically change quantity or due dates. Recommendations for changes will be generated on the exception report, but no actual changes will take place. Planning and control time zones covering the Master Schedule horizon are very important in this process (Refer to Figure 5).

PLANNING & CONTROL TIME ZONES

1	2	3
FIRM	FIRM/FORECAST	FORECAST
ORDERS	F.P.O.	C.P.O.

FIGURE 5

Zone one is called the FIRM zone and only has committed customer orders. Zone three is the FORECAST zone and is used only to communicate what is expected to happen -- no action is required by anyone. The intermediate zone is a combination of forecast and firm orders. This is the zone where firm planned orders are used. What the Master Scheduler wants to do is create a level schedule satisfying the booked customer demand as well as the expected customer demand.

Once the schedule is put into place, it needs to be input to Material Requirements Planning. Let's take another look at the MPS format (See Figure 6).

MASTER SCHEDULE

ASSY A
LT - 2
LS - 200

	Period							
	1	2	3	4	5	6	7	8
Service								
Production	10			160			200	
Actual Dmd.	100	65	25	30		10		
Available	0	90	25	0	20	20	10	0	0
Available to Prom.	10			170			190	
MPS	200			210			190	

FIGURE 6

As customer orders are received against items in the Master Schedule, they are loaded into the actual demand line. This triggers a couple of things to happen:

1) The forecast or production plan quantities are reduced in the appropriate period by the actual demand booked (eg. the 30 and 10 units booked in periods 4 and 6 have reduced the remaining production plan quantity of 200 in period 4 to 160).

2) The available-to-promise is calculated for each MPS lot using the formula (MPS - actual demand or 210 - 30 - 10 = 170).

3) The MPS lots remains unchanged.

To communicate these requirements to MRP, the system must know which type of environment it is supporting. If the environment is discrete make-to-stock, the MPS line (build schedule) is used as the MRP driver. In the discrete made-to-order or repetitive environments, a combination of the actual demand and available-to-promise is used as the driver.

For example, look at periods 1 thru 3. Customer orders have been loaded into the system at the rate of 100 in period 1, 65 in period 2, and 25 in period 3. These demands have been subtracted from the MPS lot of 200 leaving an ATP equal to 10. Therefore, the gross requirements input to MRP (assuming a zero lead time for simplicity) would be 110 in period 1 (100 actual demand + 10 ATP), 65 in period 2 (65 actual demand + 0 ATP), and 25 in period 3 (25 actual demand + 0 ATP). Period 4 would send 200 units to MRP using the same logic. If final assembly lead time is associated with the part, the demand is offset by that lead time before passing it to MRP.

Now, let's review a key Zero Inventory guideline. Except for final assembly, actual production is executed in response to a <u>pull order</u>, not a schedule. The planning schedules are provided so production can prepare for what is expected to happen.

CREATING DETAIL REPLENISHMENTS

Material Requirements Planning plays a key role in leveling the plan for all product structure components required to satisfy the final assembly schedule. When requirements are generated for a part under MRP control, the replenishments necessary to satisfy this demand are automatically created using flow orders. Once MRP has determined the total quantity needed to satisfy a particular demand, the order policy (generally discrete), delivery policy, and station capacity are reviewed to determine the flow order quantities and dates. At this point in the process, the flow orders are automatically loaded into the MRP logic. These orders will in turn explode down to the next level to create additional demand. This process continues level-by-level until the system is instructed to stop the explosion (done by part coding).

The process just described can be totally automated. It is certainly conceivable that flow orders could be created for all the assemblies and manufactured parts required to satisfy the final assembly schedule. Not only could flow orders be generated for all make parts, but releases to suppliers also could be automatic. If Purchasing has negotiated vendor contracts, MRP can generate the releases against those contracts. This would inform the supplier of the exact date and quantity the material is needed. If you want to look at zero inventory concepts --that's it!

Now we are ready to generate the shop load report. This load report should cover a short horizon so the Shop Scheduler can evaluate any potential capacity problems in the near future. Periodically, Capacity Requirements Planning should be run to look out over a greater horizon taking into account suggested firm planned orders and computer planned orders. But, when we are getting ready to execute the plan to meet the Final Assembly Schedule, we need only to review the short-term plan.

If the load needs leveling, it is generally done using a simulation model. Once a balanced load has been determined, it is evaluated to see if the Final Assembly Schedule can be achieved. Remember, the spreading logic should have created a fairly level load. Of course, it is possible some work centers may have had uneven workloads created. The challenge is to level those areas without jeopardizing the final objective which is to deliver the product as defined in the FAS without carrying excessive inventory. When the plan has been completed, execution becomes the next task at hand.

EXECUTION OF THE MASTER PLAN

When the time arrives to issue material to the floor, the parts are picked as detailed on the picking report. The material is forwarded to the production station where it will be used (Inventory Control has the
part/work center relationship). The part inventory balances at the work center are incremented by the issued quantity while the stores inventory balances are decremented.

As the production process takes place, the status of the order becomes very important. Not only is this information important, it is sometimes very difficult to get. To operate a successful system, there needs to be some type of feedback mechanism. This mechanism can report every operation as it is completed, or only at selected checkpoints in the process. Generally the latter way is preferred in a pull environment.

The checkpoint can be established at various major operations along the production path or could be limited to the final operation step. With the checkpoints in place, the system can use backfilling and backflushing techniques to update the shop status. When a checkpoint operation is reported to have produced "X" quantity of product, the system then backfills all the proceeding operation quantities making the assumption those operations also had to be completed. Of course, this is only true in a serial processing mode. The backfilling method allows the system to unload the capacity requirements for all work centers affected by the part being reported.

Backflushing is used to relieve the work center inventories. If the completed part uses materials which have been issued to its own work center, the following logic takes place. The inventory of the part being reported complete is incremented by the quantity reported. The system then explodes the reported part through its bill-of-material to identify the components necessary to build the completed part. Each of the component's inventory balances at the work center are reduced by the appropriate quantity. The explosion process described can be done for one level or multiple levels. If the process is truly repetitive, the multiple level is desired.

If the reported completed part is built from parts which are produced in other work centers, the process is slightly different (See Figure 7).

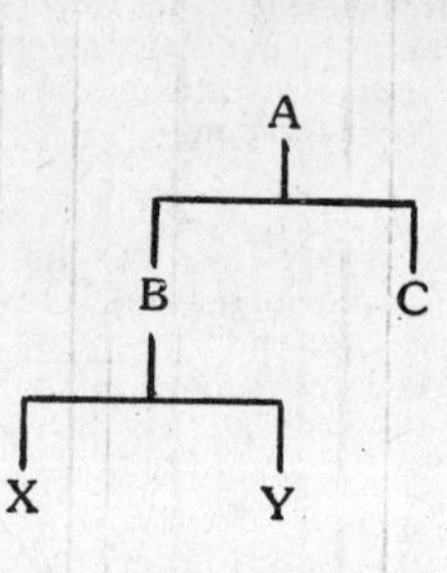

PN	OH	WC
A	+	200
C	−	200
B	±	200
	±	100
X	−	100
Y	−	100

FIGURE 7

Assembly A is being reported as complete thru the checkpoint. Therefore, the inventory for assembly A in work center 200 is incremented by the quantity reported complete. The explosion process then begins which identifies that components B and C were needed to build assembly A. The work center inventory for these parts is reduced by the appropriate quantity. Next, the system recognizes component B is an assembly built in another work center. So, in order for assembly A to have been built, it needed B's. These B's had to be in work center 200 and therefore the inventory quantity for B's in work center 200 is incremented by the appropriate quantity. Assembly B is then exploded to identify the components necessary to build it. This process would identify components X and Y.

In order to have moved assembly B to work center 200, it would have had to have been built. Therefore, the inventory balance for assembly B in work center 100 is both incremented (reflecting the producing of the assembly) and decremented (reflecting the movement of assembly B to work center 200). Finally, the work center inventory quantities for parts X and Y are decremented. The work-in-process inventory is now in balance as of the described transaction.

TYING IT BACK TO THE PULL SYSTEM

The existance of a PULL system does not reveal problems by itself. It is the reduction of inventory which does it. That is what the user of Zero Inventory concepts is intending to do -- reduce inventory to highlight production problems. Once the problems are identified, various alternative solutions can be analyzed until a solution is selected. The chosen solution is then implemented to solve the problem. Once the identified problem has been solved, the inventory is further reduced to uncover other problems.

Hall states in his book the PULL system should be capable of controlling the inventory level of any part number at any point of use on the plant floor. Each part should be made at only one work center, but it may be used at several. Ideal stockless production (Zero Inventory) drives people to examine operations in detail for the purpose of eliminating waste of time, waste of energy, waste of material, and waste from errors.

Once these concepts are understood, analyzed, and accepted, management must carefully plan and control at the Final Assembly Schedule. A management summary, known as the Production Sales Inventory report, displays actual production against plan. The same calculations are performed for sales (actual sales against plan). Using this data, inventory balances are projected and compared to company policies.

Management can analyze the inventory plan to see if in fact an inventory reduction plan is in place. As production is completed and shipments made, the resultant inventory is displayed. This inventory is compared to plan to identify any deviations.

POTENTIAL BENEFITS

Zero Inventory suggest the inventory investment will be lower. By reducing the work-in-process inventory, the production cycle times will be reduced. These reductions can lead to improved quality, lower rework, and reduced scrap. Part shortages, often a problem in the manufacturing environment, can be reduced which will result in less expediting. Additionally, the material handling problems may also be reduced.

What will it take? Well, five things are needed.

1) A quality product needs to be produced.

2) Ideas for improvement should be solicited.

3) Good communication channels need to be set up.

4) People need to get a perfectionist attitude. **(Remember, _optimize_ means to _make_ a _perfect_, _effective_ and _functional_ as possible.)**

5) A system to support the environment needs to be in place.

Automation may well displace many manual tasks. The planning of a levelize flow of material, the direction to issue material to support that plan, and the updating of the product movement can now be done using the closed loop system. The message is clear! We all must start to work a little smarter using systems which support Zero Inventory as well as the traditional material planning and control concepts.

BIOGRAPHY OF JOHN F. PROUD, CPIM*

John is currently the National Education Manager for Xerox Computer Services, a division of Xerox Corporation. Xerox Computer Services is a recognized leader in providing industry with manufacturing, distribution and financial systems. Its success is based on proven software, state-of-the-art concepts, consulting, implementation, and education.

Prior to his present education assignment, John spent several years with three other Xerox divisions where he functioned as a Manufacturing Control Analyst and Consultant. In addition to these Xerox assignments, he has been a Systems Analyst as well as the Manager, Systems and Programming.

John has a Bachelor of Science degree in mathematics and a Master of Science degree in Management Sciences. He has been involved in a variety of APICS seminars, had numerous articles published, lectured at California State University, Fullerton, and served as Vice-President Programs for the Orange County Chapter. Currently, he is a member of the Master Planning sub-committee for the Certification Council.

THE KEY TO THE LEAD TIME CONTROL: JIT AND GT

Philip Y. Huang, Ph.D., CPIM*
Virginia Polytechnic Institute and State University

FOREWORD

Batch manufacturing has long been known for its lack of efficiency. Long production lead time, inability to meet due date, and excessive work-in-process are just a few examples of batch manufacturing problems. The purpose of this presentation is to address the potential solution to these problems by integrating just-in-time production philosophy and group technology.

Facilities in a batch manufacturing environment are usually arranged according to their function. Milacron's survey indicated that typical jobs spend 95 percent of their time either in moving between machines or waiting for available machines. Priority sequencing rules were suggested to resolve this problem, however, the real problem is caused by the wide range of products processed and the dissimilar routings. Unless the true problem can be studied and solved, lead time control cannot be effectively achieved.

Just-in-time production emphasizes the reduction of lot size by reducing setup time. The work flow analysis of the group technology suggests logical facility layout. The combination of these two, which to some extent has been done in Japan, would contribute greatly toward efficient management of batch manufacturing. Simulation experiments will be used to illustrate this point.

LEAD TIME

Batch manufacturing which constitutes between 60 and 80 percent of all manufacturing has traditionally been characterized as a production process which handles large variety of jobs with small to medium batch size and dissimilar routings. General purpose machines and skilled labor are consequently required to be able to work on various types of job batches. Since skilled machine operators are paid at a higher wage rate, it has been a common practice to maintain certain level of backlog. On the other hand, machines performing similar functions are grouped together and form a work center. Job batches are moved from work center to work center according to their individual routings.

The ability of batch manufacturing to meet due date is primarily determined by how fast can the system complete jobs, or the length of manufacturing lead time. As Wight pointed out, the lead time can be broken into the following elements: set-up time, running time, move time, wait time, and queue time. With the exception of running time, which is the length of time machines actually work on job batches, the remaining four elements are created either by the specific facility layout or the unique sequencing and routing problems in batch manufacturing. A survey conducted by Cincinnati Milacron [5] have found that a typical job batch spends 95 percent of the lead time either waiting for available machines, moving between work centers, or waiting for a forklift truck. Moreover, 3.5 out of the remaining 5 percent of the lead time are devoted to setting up machine tools which leaves only 1.5 percent devoting to actual machining. Consequently, batch manufacturing has been known for its long manufacturing lead time, high work-in-process, inability to meet due date, and lack of efficiency.

The lead time problem in batch manufacturing may be further compounded by a phenomenon which has been labeled as "lead time inflation", [9]. When actual lead time is longer than the planned lead time for some reasons, the person who places the order would naturally respond the situation by increasing the planned lead time which in turn would trigger an earlier release of job orders, and thus increasing the backlog in the shop. The actual lead time may become even longer due to the larger backlog. As a consequence, it is not uncommon for a shop to be quoting lead times of 36 to 48 weeks while the actual manufacturing lead time can be as short as five working days [9].

THE SOURCE OF THE PROBLEM

The literature of job shop scheduling has traditionally focused on the impact of using various priority sequencing rules such as the shortest processing time, the minimum slack, the critical ratio, etc. By prioritizing job batches waiting in line, these studies tried to identify better sequencing rules for a specific performance criterion such as the average throughput time or the average lateness. While there is no doubt about the significant contributions made by these studies, the original source of the efficiency problems in batch manufacturing seems remained unattacked.

As pointed out earlier, a typical job batch spends about 95 percent of its lead time in waiting or being moved. The source of the problem is actually originated from the noticeable backlog on the shop floor, as well as the functional facility layout. Unfortunately, priority sequencing studies offered very little help to reduce either the work load in work centers or job transit times. Moreover, most job shop scheduling studies assumed that setup time is either a constant and thus can be included as a portion of machine processing time or so small that it can be neglected. However, as indicated in Cincinnati Milacron's survey job batches spend more time on setting up machine tools than on machining itself. It seems inappropriate to assume that setup time is negligible. The significance of setup time in batch manufacturing may be attributed to the fact that job shops typically process a large variety of job batches. The need for frequent changeovers has made setup time a significant portion of the manufacturing lead time. Priority sequencing studies once again made simplified assumptions and did not attempt to reduce setup time. On the other hand, setup time has been typically assumed to be sequence independent. Few studies actually attempted to reduce the amount of setup time required by exploring the dependence relationships among the setups for different job batches.

In short, the problems in batch manufacturing can be attributed to the large variety of jobs, the function layout, and the massive backlogs in many machine centers. Job shop scheduling studies failed to attack the source of the problem directly. It is no surprise that the suggested priority sequencing rules were abundent while the successful implementation of these rules were few. However, the lead time control problem in batch manufacturing may be resolved, at least partially, by integreting the just-in-time production philosophy and group technology since they offer hopes to alleviate the source of the lead time problem.

JUST-IN-TIME PRODUCTION

Among all the manufacturing systems, continuous production such as oil refinery and automobile assembly are perhaps the most efficient in terms of the equipment utilization, the throughput time, and the work-in-process inventory. The ultimate goal of JIT production, which may never be achieved, is to operate job shop just like a flow shop. Working toward this goal, JIT production first requires a drastic reduction in lot sizes. In fact, only if the lot sizes can be reduced to a single unit, the ultimate goal of JIT can be achieved. From economic standpoint, too small a lot size may not be able to justify a full setup. The only possible way to reduce the lot size while still considering the balance between setup costs and inventory carrying costs seems to be the reduction of time required for a setup. In recent years, numerous Japanese as well as American firms have made successful attempts to significantly reduce setup time. Illustrative examples of setup time reduction techniques are provided in [4,6, and 8].

The control of manufacturing lead time can be a lot easier if setup times can be reduced to their lowest possible level. On one hand, the reduction of setup time can contribute directly to the reduction of the set-up portion of the manufacturing lead time. On the other hand, smaller setup times can justify smaller lot sizes. In this case, an item can be produced just-in-time to meet its demand, rather than to build up to its inventory level. Moreover, since the shop receives smaller job orders, the work load in terms of machine hours now becomes smaller. This in turn can help to reduce the queueing, perhaps the largest portion of the manufacturing lead time.

GROUP TECHNOLOGY

Quick setup and small batch size of the JIT production obviously can reduce the setup and queueing portion of the lead time. With the existing functional layout, however, they offer little, if any, help in alleviating the 'move' time. On the contrary, they may even create traffic problems for the shop floor due to the frequent request for delivering small batches. In order to successfully implement just-in-time production, it may be necessary to rearrange the layout of production facilities. The group layout of group technology seems to be able to provide some helps in reducing the 'move' time.

Although GT concept has been available for quite a while [2,3], the actual implementation of such a system in this country is rather scanty. Essentially, GT applied flow line concept to the production of 'families' of similar products or parts. Machines on the shop floor are arranged into groups, each capable of completing the entire process necessary for the production of a 'family' of products. Figure 1 displays a typical functional layout for batch manufacturing. Machines performing

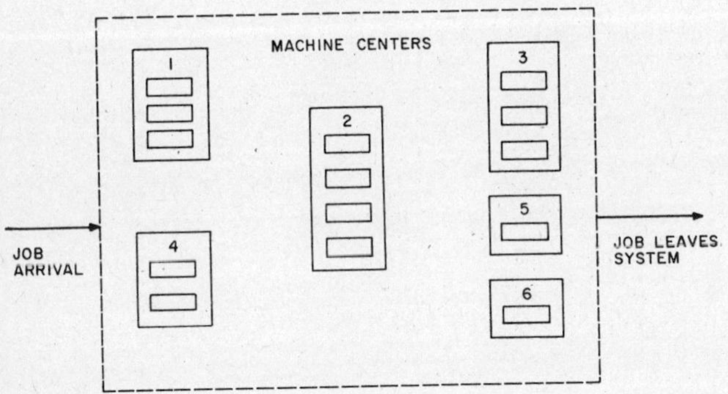

Figure 1. The Job Shop Configuration

similar functions are grouped into a work center. Job batches are carried from work center to work center according to their individual routing sequences. As a contrast, Figure 2 depicts a typical group layout with four machine groups, each capable of processing a specific product 'family'.

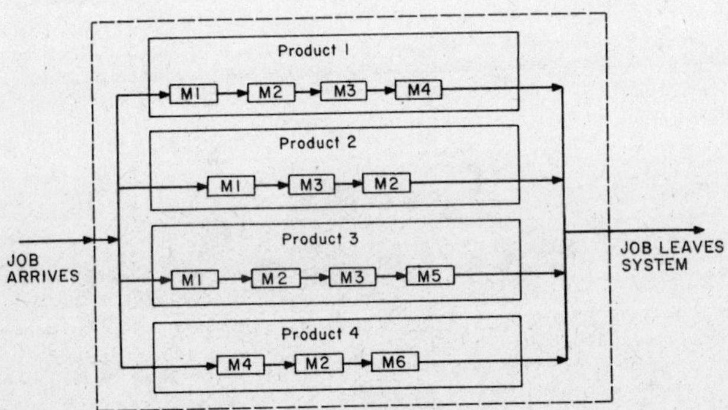

Figure 2. Group Technology Configuration

This family-group approach of group technology can significantly reduce the transit time, since all the machines required to complete the process of a product

'family' are physically located adjacent to each other. Moreover, there usually exists a dependence relationship between the setup time and the job requiring the setup. Setup time required for a new job similar to the one just completed should be smaller than that for a completely different job. The product 'family' of GT contains mostly similar products, and hence there is a good opportunity to further reduce the total setup time [1].

LEAD TIME CONTROL: JIT & GT

The lead time control in batch manufacturing has been a persistent problem. JIT and GT provide us with a potential key to gain control of the manufacturing lead time. The quick setup, multiple and timely vendor delivery per day, small lot production, and stable master production schedule of JIT are all effective tools to reduce the setup and queueing portion of the lead time. The group machine layout and product families of the group technology are helpful in reducing the setup and transit portion of the lead time. Consequently, the combination of JIT and GT should be a powerful and effective tool for lead time control in batch manufacturing.

In fact, Toyota's production management system is a good example of interpreting JIT and GT. The 'U' shape layout which allows operators to handle multiple machines actually is a unique form of GT group layout. The quick setup, small lot size, and U shape layout are all contributing significantly toward the success of Toyota in gaining high productivity as well as impressive quality.

To provide further evidence, computer models programmed in SLAM [7] will be constructed to simulate the operation of a batch manufacturing using the concept of JIT and GT. A similar model for a traditional job shop with functional layout will also be developed for the purpose of comparison. The results of this simulation study will be presented at the meeting.

REFERENCES

[1] Black, J. T. "Cellular Manufacturing Systems Reduce Setup Time, Make Small Lot Production Economical." Industrial Engineering, Nov. 1983, pp. 36-48.

[2] Burbidge, John L. The Introduction of Group Technology, John Wiley & Sons, New York, 1975.

[3] DeVries, Marvin F., Susan M. Harvey, and Vijay A. Tipnes. Group Technology: An Overview and Bibliography, Metcut Research Associates, Inc., Cincinnati, Ohio, 1976.

[4] Hall, Robert W. Zero Inventories, Dow Jones-Irwin, Homewood, Illinois, 1983.

[5] Houtzeel, Alex. "Computer Integrated Manufacturing," Proceedings of the 1982 Academic-Practitioners Liaison Operations Management Workshop, pp. 23-37. American Production and Inventory Control Society.

[6] Monden, Yasuhiro. Toyota Production System, Institute of Industrial Engineers, Atlanta, GA, 1983.

[7] Pritsker, A. Alan B. and Claude Dennis Pegden. Introduction to Simulation and SLAM, John Wiley & Sons, New York, 1979.

[8] Shingo, Shigeo. Study of 'Toyota' Production System from Industrial Engineering Viewpoint, Japan Management Association, Tokyo, Japan, 1981.

[9] Wight, Oliver W. "Input/Output Control: A Real Handle of Lead Time," Production and Inventory Management, 3rd Quarter, 1970, pp. 9-31.

Philip Y. Huang is Associate Professor of Management Science in the College of Business at Virginia Polytechnic Institute and State University. He received his Ph.D. in Business Administration and M.A. in Economics from the Pennsylvania State University; and B.A. in Economics from the National Taiwan University. He is a certified Fellow (CPIM*) of the American Production and Inventory Control Society (APICS).

He has presented professional papers at such meetings as American Institute for Decision Sciences (AIDS), the Institute of Management Science (TIMS), Academy of Management, Winter Simulation Conference, the American Statistical Association, the Atlantic Economic Conference, S.E. AIDS, and S.E. TIMS. Moreover, he has been invited as guest speaker to address various groups of managers at chapter meetings of the American Society for Personnel Administration and APICS.

He has published articles in Decision Sciences, International Journal of Production Research, Computers and Operations Research, Journal of Systems Management, Industrial Engineering, Business Accounting (Kiggyokaikei, in Japanese), Review of Business and Economic Research, and others. His article on Japanese Just-in-Time production published in Decision Sciences has won the 1983 Stanley T. Hardy Best Paper Award. He is a member of AIDS, TIMS, and APICS. He is also the founder and faculty advisor to the Virginia Tech Student Affiliate Chapter of APICS.

JOB SHOP MRP AND JUST-IN-TIME AT THE DAMROW COMPANY

Mike Hatch, CPIM*
DEC International, Inc.

The objective of this article is to clear up some misconceptions about the meaning of MRP and the meaning of Just-In-Time Production and their working relationship. Also to describe some of my recent experiences with each in our job shop (Damrow Company), where we manufacture make-to-order equipment for the food and dairy industry.

APPLIED SINCE THE MASTODON HUNTS

The definition of MRP in the APICS dictionary states in part: "A system which uses bills of material, inventory and open order data and master schedule information to calculate requirements for materials." This is a sufficient definition for the dictionary, but it does not describe what the MRP logic is in the broad sense. The formal though process of planning the start and completion of interrelated future events with lead time offsets has been practiced by humankind since the first organized mastodon hunt and probably much longer.

This logic was used to build pyramids and churches and to set military strategies throughout history. This technique became more structured mathematically and graphically during the late 1940s as Engineers grappled with the complexities of planning and building nuclear submarines. At this time, the technique was named Program Evaluation and Review Technique (PERT) and Critical Path Method and was still manual. With the advent of inexpensive computing power in the early 1960s, the technique was placed on the computer.

This automated planning logic was applied to manufacturing a wide variety of products as well as other types of projects. In the manufacturing setting, the technique came to be known as Material Requirements Planning or MRP. While the computer allows us to replan more frequently and accurately to accommodate more changes than was possible during our mastodon hunting days, the logic has not changed.

In manufacturing, prior to formal requirements planning systems, someone had to think through the MRP logic to get the product out the door. It was usually the Shop Foreman to whom this task fell since no one else was doing it and the ultimate responsibility for product completion was his. We can be certain that in manufacturing companies, where management has decided "MRP won't work," some lower level employees are frantically working through MRP logic to ship products. Unfortunately this neglects other important responsibilities, as in the Foreman's case.

The many companies that have had successful experience with MRP understand the technique for what it is, a powerful and essential planning and plan monitoring tool. Equally important, they understand what it is not. It is not a production control technique or an inventory reduction system. It is not in any way competitive with, or exclusive of execution techniques such as just-in-time production, shop floor control or KANBAN (A Japanese card system for Shop Floor Control). In fact, MRP is very much, mutually, complimentary with those techniques. We must set our goals within our manufacturing business and use our formal MRP system as a tool to attain them. Zero inventory or just-in-time production may or may not be one of those goals. If it is, then our company policies, disciplines and inputs to MRP must conform to that objective.

THE BATTLE TO ACHIEVE

Just-in-time production is a not-too-early, not-too-late delivery of both purchased and manufactured items to manufacturing processes and operations. It means keeping parts storage areas between operations as clean as possible. It means feeding purchased items directly to production. It requires a significant quality assurance effort from suppliers and employees to move as closely as possible to zero defects. Just-in-time means new efforts to reduce manufacturing setup times and parts processing times. In short, the objective is to reduce inventory at all points between receipt of material and shipment of product.

There are some major benefits to be gained from moving toward just-in-time production. The most important are improved customer service through shorter lead times, reduced inventory investment and ultimately reduced plant construction costs since less space will be required for given production levels.

Battles to achieve just-in-time production will be fought on three major fronts; Purchasing, Shop Floor Management and Manufacturing Engineering.

SELECT TEST CASES

On the purchasing front, an important first step is to select perhaps two suppliers as just-in-time delivery test cases. Select suppliers that you have a good working relationship with and purchase enough volume from them to make the test meaningful. Meet with the suppliers and map out a plan with their full knowledge and cooperation. You will probably be discussing such items as more deliveries, small quantities, leadtime reduction, quality and your projected requirements; sensitive subjects for each of you. Once you have agreed on a test plant, put it into effect and measure the performance. Your MRP system will help plan and monitor just-in-time deliveries and most important, your MRP projected requirements will help your supplier plan his production.

PURCHASED COMMODITY EXAMPLE

During the past two years, we have put into effect a just-in-time agreement with our major steel vendor. The vendor provides more deliveries and lower quantities than in the past. We provide requirements forecasts from our MRP system. During the test period, both quality and delivery problems surfaced that caused late starts of jobs and disrupted production in general. These problems had been hidden by excess inventory in the past. The first step was to meet with the vendor and outline our just-in-time plan. This was in conjunction with our purchasing contract which had a maximum five day lead time clause and price protection as well. We had previously purchased sheet steel by the pound and usually by minimum skid loads of twenty to fifty sheets. We were now going to order by number of individual sheets per our daily MRP recommended release requirements. Orders would be phoned in daily and accumulated for two to three days by the vendor for the next truckload. We ordinarily receive two truckloads per week. We would cut the shop order one to two days prior to receipt of the steel and immediately issue it to the job when received.

QUALITY/DELIVERY PROBLEMS EXPERIENCED

This was agreed to by the vendor and established as our company policy for this commodity. The only planned inventory would be one to four sheets in the most used item numbers versus the ten to twenty-five safety stocks we had carried in the past. At first the new program seemed to work very well, that is, while we were still working down the $125,000 inventory we had been carrying for many years. Over a couple of months this dropped to the $20,000 to $30,000 range and we began to experience some problems. The first was quality. If a job needed five sheets, that's all that were ordered. If two were rejected due to surface marking or other quality problems, we could not start the job. Prior to just-in-time we could nearly always find five good sheets out of an inventory of twenty-five. Poor quality sheets in the inventory could either be used in a few places where standard quality was not important, or more likely, sit in inventory for an extended period of time. Job starts were delayed, causing problems for foremen and employees and affecting customer deliveries as well.

We visited with the vendor and reviewed their inspection procedures and requested that they be tightened up. They agreed to this. Meanwhile, delivery problems surfaced. I surveyed our actual lead time history and found that the five day lead time was being exceeded in thirty percent of the cases. This also began to cause production problems, it also had been hidden by excess inventory in the past. The quality, while improved, still was not acceptable either so another meeting was scheduled with the vendor. We made requests for improved lead time, reviewed delivery and paperwork procedures and further efforts in inspection of the product. This was agreed to and the problems were solved. After our inventory had reached low levels, it took about three months to straighten out the quality and delivery problems that surfaced.

PURCHASED COMMODITY RESULTS

It has been two years since we began these procedures and it has been working well since. Our lead time is averaging three days with five maximum and rejects to the vendor have been minimal. Our average inventory in this commodity has been permanently reduced from about $120,000 to $130,000 to the $10,000 to $20,000 range and our zero inventory policy was upheld. With considerable credit to a very cooperative vendor, we have reduced our inventory in this commodity by 90 percent. Other commodities have been selected for similar action.

IN-PLANT JUST-IN-TIME

On the shop floor, particularly in a job shop like ours, inventory has traditionally been considered a positive thing by plant personnel. Like billowing smokestacks, piles of inventory between workcenters was traditionally believed to indicate prosperity. Of course, the opposite is true. In a repetitive manufacturing shop, it is possible to program out some inventory through line rates and material handling systems. As we move toward the low quantity job shop, operations personnel have more influence over work-in-process inventory levels. This is a problem of psychology and re-education of employees. We have worked with our foremen and employees formally and informally to instill a recognition that idle inventory has a negative impact.

It is common in a job shop that slowdowns occur when input area inventory begins to drop. It appears that layoffs or reduction of hours are coming and efforts are made on the part of workers and even sometimes foremen to "stretch" the available work. This attitude is ingrained after many years. The result of this is decreased labor efficiency and utilization. For our just-in-time policy we want to always keep the input area inventory (queue) at the lowest level possible. There are several things that need to be done in the job shop before this inventory can be reduced. One prerequisite is that purchased items be supplied on time. This is to avoid the need to keep several jobs available so that if parts are short for one another can be substituted. Some of the aspects of just-in-time purchasing such as single source longer term vendor agreements can be useful in the job shop as well as in the production shop. Insuring a good level of availability of purchased parts is an important step toward reduced work-in process inventory levels in the job shop.

SETUP, LOT SIZING AND QUALITY

Looking at the shop itself, setup times, past lot sizes and quality need to be considered. Manufacturing engineering and shop personnel should have a program for setup reduction. Setup is a significant part of total production time in a job shop and such a program by itself can provide substantial savings. A body of knowledge on this is coming to be available. Also, it has come to be known that smaller, just as needed, lot sizes force quality into manufactured parts. This has been well documented in the United States and Europe, as well as in Japan. The benefits of improved quality, which can carry a substantial cost reduction coupled with decreased setup times where possible indicate that smaller lots increase overall productivity.

As in my steel purchasing example above, to attain smaller, more frequent lots, necessitates near-zero defects. If quality problems arise, production stops and action must be taken. If we adhere to our just-in-time policy, then the only alternative is to take steps to assure quality parts will be produced throughout all workcenters. We have formed a management committee for quality and also have a quality circle group of shop personnel looking at ways to improve quality. Our first efforts have been in engineering to insure that dimensions and tolerances are proper and

reasonable. Now we are studying the gateway workcenters to determine if quality levels are acceptable there. We will continue this process through the feeder, sub-assembly and final assembly workcenters. The solution to quality problems will be operator training, new methods and, in some cases, new tooling and equipment.

EMPLOYEE EDUCATION IN JUST-IN-TIME

Training of foremen and workers is the key to reducing work-in-process inventory in the job shop. The projected schedules and workloads generated by the MRP system must be fully understood and used by the foremen and plant manager. We are not going to keep all of the backlog physically on the shop floor. Our results in this area have been slow, but measurable. During the past two years, our work-in-process inventory value has decreased 25 percent with increased production.

THE ROLE OF MRP

Material requirements planning provides a planning base for our manufacturing operation. It is a formal way to translate the master schedule, which represents top management's sales and production objective, into tactical plans for labor needs and materials procurement. It provides a plan against which to measure our progress. We know that if we stray too far from the plan we are not meeting the objectives of the company.
Each company must define what "too far" is and what corrective actions need to be taken when this occurs.

An MRP system requires a number of input parameters, one that gets a large amount of attention is the lot-sizing parameter. Most MRP software allows the selection of several of those including variations on the traditional EOQ formula, variable buckets and lot-for-lot. Lot-for-lot is basically the just-in-time approach. We have used the option extensively anyway for one time, infrequently used or very costly items. As we implement our just-in-time policies, we will use it for more items. There is no reason to manufacture or purchase more than needed if the overall cost advantage can be gained this way. Another key parameter is safety stock. Our policy, since we have been using MRP the last several years, has been to move toward limiting the use of safety stock to independent demand items. Mainly, this is for service parts and the safety stock is used to maintain a desired level of customer service and not for production. For dependent demand items, we have eliminated safety stocks in most cases and we rely on MRP for planning needs for these items. There are other parameters such as planned lead times, maximums, minimums, etc. that must be used to meet just-in-time objectives. The execution systems in purchasing and on the shop floor must support the plan and feed back information so that performance can be monitored.

OVERALL COMPANY PLANNING

The extension of MRP logic across a broader spectrum of company activities such as marketing, distribution and finance, has been called MRP II. This is gaining wide acceptance among more sophisticated companies as they tie these various planning systems together to provide a comprehensive formal planning system. These efforts represent a giant step forward in improving the management of manufacturing businesses. A key point here is that the traditional material requirements planning system provides the vital link between these top-level management systems and the execution systems.

CONCLUSION

Just-in-time production can be accomplished, to some degree, in a job shop as well as in repetitive manufacturing. MRP is designed to be a planning, replanning and plan monitoring system. Just-in-time is an approach to reducing inventory throughout the manufacturing operation and a philosophy that is a part of the plan execution systems. MRP and Just-In-Time Production should each be a part of the overall company strategy if zero inventory is a goal.

ABOUT THE AUTHOR:

Mike Hatch is Vice-President, Manufacturing at
Damrow Company, Division of DEC International, Inc. He
has directed the successful installation of a complete
manufacturing system and has been involved in other
installations in the US and Europe. His experience
includes both job shop and repetative manufacturing. He
holds a B.S. in Industrial Engineering and an M.B.A.
from the University of Wisconsin and is a member of the
adjunct facility there. Mike is CPIM* and a past
president of the Fox Valley APICS Chapter.

MPS/CRP IN TRANSITION FROM MAKE-TO-ORDER TO JUST-IN-TIME

Gerald A. Rewa, CPIM*
Haworth, Inc.

INTRODUCTION

Like many companies, Haworth is evolving from a Make-To-Order job shop environment toward a more repetitive Just-In-Time manufacturing operation. Many changes had to be made in our philosophies, our attitudes, and our practices. This presentation addresses some of the changes made to the Master Production Scheduling and Capacity Requirements Planning systems during this transition.

PAST ENVIRONMENT AND SYSTEMS

Haworth manufactures and distributes office interior systems. We have three manufacturing facilities in or near Holland, Michigan, and have distribution centers in Holland, Los Angeles, and Toronto. We have enjoyed a rapid growth rate throughout the life of the company.

The MPS and CRP techniques used were essentially standard, traditional ones. Each product line was broken down into the options available to the customer. These options had specific part numbers, which were MPS controlled.

A Planning Bill of Material was created for each product line, using a forecasted usage percentage for each option. The Production Plan, expressed as weekly quantities of each product line, was loaded into the system and exploded through the planning bills, creating Production Forecasts for the MPS controlled items. The material planner manually input supply orders for all MPS controlled items, based on these demands.

The CRP system took the supply orders for all items and extended them against the routing file. The output was a detailed report of production hours, by day, for each Work Center in the system. It also compared the requirements to the stated Work Center capacity, in both weekly and cumulative quantities.

The Order Entry system loaded each individual customer order into both the distribution system and the manufacturing system. The demands for MPS controlled items were pegged to the proper product line planning bill as customer demands. These demands reduced the Available to Promise (ATP) during the weekly MPS run. The new ATP was then exploded through the planning bill to produce revised Production Forecasts at the MPS item level.

PROBLEMS

The MPS and CRP systems described above were satisfactory when Haworth had fewer product offerings and a lower volume of business. By 1983, however, our list of available product options had grown to the point that there were literally millions of possible end configurations.

The number of MPS controlled items was getting out of hand, and the option usage percentages were getting too small to forecast with any degree of accuracy. Small errors on individual planning bills often added up to large errors in total.

We began to experience excessive system run times as our order volume increased. It was determined that the major cause was the size of the customer demand file in the manufacturing system. Since we were loading each customer order individually, we were entering thousands of demand records each day.

Our projections of continued rapid growth and expanding product offerings clearly indicated that changes had to be made quickly. Keeping in mind the company's commitment to adopting JIT techniques, the solutions to the above problems had to meet the following criteria:

- The system must provide a schedule that is relatively stable in the short term. This would aid us in scheduling frequent deliveries of smaller lots of material.

- The system should allow master scheduling at the most flexible stage of completion, in support of corporate objectives of shorter lead times and maximum customer service.

- The system should reduce computer run times as much as possible. This was necessary to offset the increased run times from more supply orders of lesser lot size.

CHANGES TO MPS SYSTEM

A two person team representing Material Planning and Purchasing was formed to review Haworth's entire product offering, and determine the appropriate items for MPS control. The team found that although the option usages varied greatly by product line, certain items which were used in multiple product lines (such as particle board, fabric and sheet steel) had quite constant usage, based on total shipment volume. Likewise, the team found that as incoming orders fluctuated monthly, the production/shipment level showed a steady rate of increase.

The third major finding of the team was that there was not a single manufactured item with more than 15 days cumulative lead time, which was significantly less than the current customer order lead time.

These findings indicated that a major restructuring of the Planning Bills was in order. Some of the planning bills were for products with very few options; these bills were left as they were. The other product line planning bills were either eliminated entirely, or reduced to contain only the critical, unique, or long-lead time purchased parts.

The remainder of the MPS controlled items were grouped into "Common Usage" Planning Bills. The commonality is based on common usage across various product lines, rather than 100% usage on all variations within the same product line.

An example of a "Common Usage" Planning Bill is the planning bill for fabric. It contains the most popular color/texture offerings, expressed as a percentage of the total fabric usage. We then correlate total fabric usage to shipping volume and extend it by planned production to arrive at planned fabric usage. This number is then exploded through the fabric planning bill to get Production Forecast for each fabric color. No attempt is made to predict whether the fabric will be used on panels, tackboards, or other accessories. (In the past, the same fabric color number appeared on the planning bill of every fabric-covered product. Keeping the option forecasts consistent was very difficult indeed.)

CHANGES TO CRP SYSTEM

The previously explained changes to the Planning Bill/MPS system created a problem in our Capacity Planning system. Under the new MPS approach, most of the manufacturing supply orders would be driven entirely by customer order demand. Supply orders would be sparse or nonexistent outside of customer order lead time, and therefore, the capacity requirements for those periods would not be reliable. (Information for periods inside the customer order lead time would be sufficient for short range capacity planning.)

Capacity requirements visibility is now provided through the use of Load Profiles, or Bills of Labor, and a Resource Requirements Planning system.

A Load Profile performs the same function in Resource Requirements Planning as a routing performs in standard CRP. It contains all the "Load Centers" that an item utilizes, and the amount of the resource used at that Load Center.

The Load Centers used at Haworth are all the critical resources for which we wish to plan capacity requirements. In some instances the Load Centers are actual Work Centers:

some Load Centers are whole departments; some are Key
Suppliers.

Load Profiles are set up for the Product Line Planning
Bills or the Common Usage Planning Bills. During the
Resource Requirements run, the Production Plan for each
planning bill is exploded through the Load Profiles,
summarized by Load Center by time period, and compared to
the stated capacity for each Load Center.

There are some drawbacks to using Resource Requirements Planning instead of Capacity Requirements Planning.
You do not get part number level detail, so you may miss
some specific capacity information. Secondly, the
capacity projections are based on the Production Plan,
and have not been netted against available inventory.

Three conditions exist at Haworth which mitigate
these drawbacks.

- Most capacity requirements are unaffected by color,
  so much of the forecast variations are of little
  effect.

- If an item has unusual capacity requirements it
  would probably be critical enough to be on a
  Product Line Planning Bill, and would have
  sufficient capacity requirements visibility
  through standard CRP.

- As JIT techniques are implemented and fine-tuned,
  inventories will be reduced, lessening the
  overstatement of capacity requirements.

An additional benefit of using Resource Requirements
Planning is that it allows you to do simulations and
"what if" analysis. The system can be run independently
from the MPS and MRP systems, so actual production and
purchasing schedules will not be affected. Different
product mixes or capacity constraints can be tried, and
their results evaluated.

The Load Centers need not be capacity related. A
Load Center for "Dollars In" could be set up, with each
product's average selling price entered in the Load
Profile. Rough revenue projections could then be made,
using varying product mixes or pricing structures.

CHANGES TO ORDER ENTRY SYSTEM

In addition to the aforementioned MPS team, a project
team was assembled to redesign the interface between the
Order Entry system and the MPS system.

The approach that the Order Entry Interface team took
was to remove the individual customer orders from the
manufacturing system. Manufacturing was to have one
customer: Distribution. Manufacturing no longer needed
to know who the final customer was. All Manufacturing had
to do was to produce X units of product A on day 3, or
Distribution would be late on a shipment.

The Order Entry Interface now receives customer order
information from the Order Entry system and separates it
into shipping information and manufacturing information.
The shipping information is sent to the Distribution
system. It includes the items ordered and quantities,
the scheduled ship date, and the shipping address.

The manufacturing information includes the ship-level
items and quantities and the date Distribution needs the
product to meet the individual customer order shipment
promise. The interface totals the quantities for all
orders for the same product and date, and enters a single
customer order record into the manufacturing system. If
an order for that item is already present for that day,
the quantity will be changed, rather than a new order
created.

The material planners now see only one demand record
per shop day, rather than numerous entries. Reports are
much smaller and easier to use. Response time for on-
line inquires is much quicker. And more importantly, run
times have been reduced from the greatly reduced customer
demand file.

RELATIONSHIP TO JIT

The changes to MPS and CRP are not classic Just-In-
Time techniques. They are really the results of
applying JIT philosophies to specific problems.

JIT is not a set of programs to code into a computer.
JIT is a fundamental approach to any manufacturing
problem. Let's look at some of the basic JIT concepts and
how they apply to the MPS/CRP changes at Haworth.

- Concept: Reduce inventory to expose problems.

In trying to reduce inventory, we discovered that
our MPS methods were causing us to produce unneeded
inventory. We consequently reexamined our entire MPS
philosophy.

- Concept: Question everything you do, and
           search for a better way to do it.

Our planning bills were constructed the way they
were because an "expert" told us it was the "right"
way. After we examined them in light of what we wanted
them to do for us, we arrived at a new approach. We now
get the information we need, more accurately, with less
manual effort.

- Concept: Do not commit a flexible resource until
           the last possible moment.

Under the old methods, we placed manufacturing
orders for final assemblies six months before we needed
them. When actual customer orders came in, we had to
rely on manual reschedules to prevent unneeded inventory.
These reschedules sometimes weren't made.

Now, we hold inventory at its most flexible state -
raw material and purchased parts. Raw material now
represents a larger proportion of total inventory, but
the actual level of raw material is steadily declining.

- Concept: Eliminate waste.

This concept is usually thought to mean eliminate
excess or obsolete material. It also means eliminate
unneeded information from your systems. Our new order
entry interface eliminated excess information from our
Manufacturing system. The information still exists in
our Distribution system for those who need it. Meanwhile, the Manufacturing system's customer demand file
is 70% smaller, and the whole system runs better without
the excess weight.

RESULTS/BENEFITS REALIZED

There have been very real, positive effects on
Haworth's performance since the Just-In-Time transition
began. Some have been the direct results of specific
program changes. Others have come from the overall
improvement in the way we approach manufacturing
problems. Each improvement seems to generate additional
improvements in other areas.

In addition to the intangible benefits, the
following measurable benefits have been realized.

- Total Inventory Reduction approaching 30%

- Total Inventory Turns doubled in one year

- Finished Goods Inventory Turns near 35

- Customer Order Delivery Performance
  increased nearly 40%

- Supplier Delivery and Manufacturing Schedule
  Completion, measured daily, are at record highs.

These results are only the beginning. They all
have strong trends of improvement. As set up times and
lot sizes are reduced, we will continue to get new
records of performance.

CONCLUSION

Haworth did three things to change its MPS and CRP approaches to facilitate its movement to JIT practices.

- We examined our product lines, and drove our MPS control to the most flexible and controllable level.

- We began using a Resource Requirements system that was available all along, but we didn't realize it was needed.

- We put customer order information back into the Distribution and Customer Order Management systems, and gave Manufacturing only the information it needed to perform its function.

The "new" approaches we implemented are not really new. They've all been done before. What is important is that we were commited to closely examine our methods, and we did not hesitate to change what needed changing.

ABOUT THE AUTHOR

Jake Rewa is now Inventory Control Manager at Haworth, Inc. in Holland, Michigan. He joined Haworth in 1982 as Manufacturing Data Base Manager. He spent one year on corporate project teams, dealing with the Sales Forecast System and the MPS/Order Entry Interface System.

Prior to joining Haworth, Jake held various Materials Management positions, including Master Scheduler, MRP Project Manager, Lead Production Planner and Buyer. He has served APICS as a Board of Director member at the Chapter and Regional levels. He was certified at the Fellow level in 1981.

Jake has a BBA degree from Western Michigan University, and is pursuing an MBA at the same institution.

OVERLAPPING OPERATIONS—A STEP TOWARD JUST-IN-TIME PRODUCTION

Dennis J. Kulonda, CPIM*
James Madison University

Like many of the concepts included under the just-in-time umbrella, the concept of overlapping operation start dates as a way to shorten processing times is not new. In theory, it is easy to show that this technique can reduce in-process time dramatically, simultaneously reducing inventory and improving customer service. Despite these apparent advantages, the method has not received widespread attention as a tool for performance improvement. This paper explores the potential applications of overlapping and the factors affecting the decision to use or not to use this technique.

The presentation begins with an exposition of the overlapping technique. The benefits, costs, and parameters related to overlapping are examined in detail. Both planning and control aspects of overlapping are considered.

With this conceptual framework in hand, the paper describes a survey to determine the extent of usage of overlapping as compared to other planning and control tools. Preliminary results of the survey are presented in this paper. Additional findings will be presented at the conference. These would relate to specific factors influencing the decision to use overlapping. Factors to be considered include, for example, type of product, type of process, layout, operation duration, extent of centralized control, capital intensity, and top management measurement approaches.

THE THEORY OF OVERLAPPING OPERATIONS

The concepts underlying the use of overlapping operations are best illustrated by an example. The basic data for all illustrative examples is shown in Figure 1.

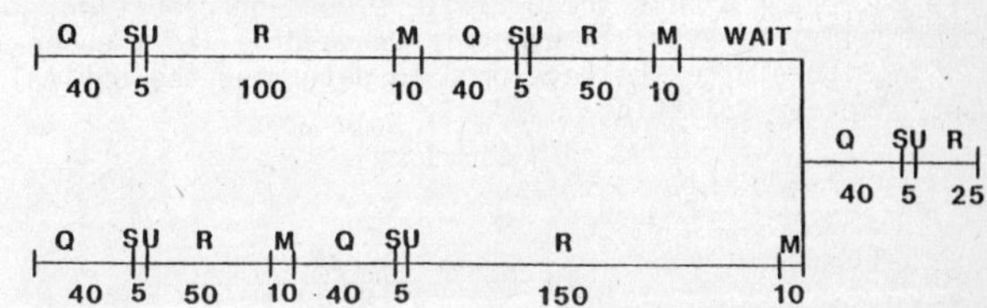

FIGURE 1 EXAMPLE PRODUCT/PROCESS DATA

Using the product and process data in Figure 1 and conservatively assuming ten hour movement time allowances for movement of work between operations and forty hours of queue time at each operation, we can easily estimate the completion time for a specific order. For an order of 100 pieces, the completion time would be 380 hours. These calculations are shown in Figure 2. They assume standard logic for routine job shop processing. That is, orders to produce B and C are released at the same time, and an order for A is released when B and C are completed and moved to stores. Futher, it is presumed that jobs queue up in front of each operation center.

Now let us examine this same scenario using overlapped operation start dates and dividing the work into two batches. Here we are assuming typical logic for overlapping to be effective:

- batches of work are moved to the succeeding operation as soon as they are completed

	QUEUE	SU TIME	RUN TIME	MOVE TIME	TOTAL
ASSEMBLY A	40	5	25		70
TURN B	40	5	100	10	
DRILL B	40	5	50	10	260
MOLD C	40	5	50	10	
INSP C	40	5	150	10	310

TOTAL HRS 310 + 70 = 380

FIGURE 2 CALCULATION OF ORDER COMPLETION TIME

- upstream operations are set up and ready for incoming batches
- move and queue times between operations are eliminated
- overlapping is done in a way that eliminates the possibility of gaps or idle time

Figure 3 shows the resulting schedule. Note that the elapsed time is decreased from 380 hours to 192.5 hours. Part of this reduction (140 hours) is due to the elimination of move and queue times and the remainder (47.5 hours) is due to the overlapping itself.

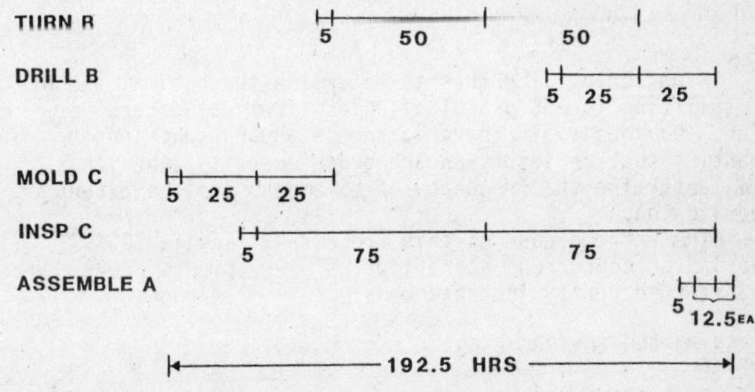

FIGURE 3 OVERLAPPING WITH TWO EQUAL BATCHES

Further compression of order completion time can be achieved in either of two ways. One way is simply to continue with two batches but to arrange the quantities so that total completion time is minimized. If this is done, the completion time is further reduced from 192.5 hours to 171.25 hours. This is shown in Figure 4.

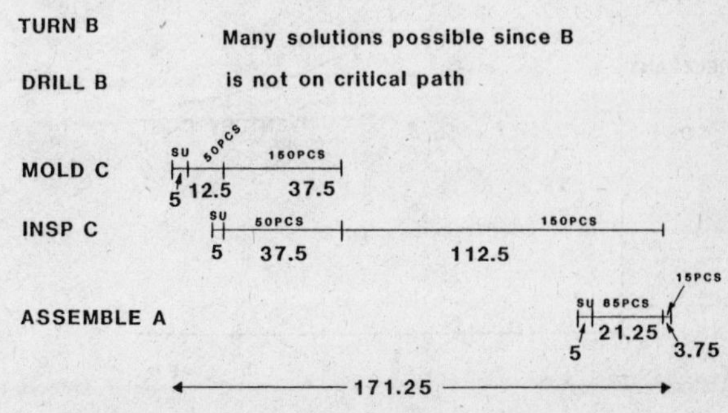

FIGURE 4 OVERLAPPING WITH TWO VARIABLE SIZED LOTS

An alternative way to reduce completion time is to divide the order into more than two batches. This permits additional overlapping but requires additional stock handling to accomplish more frequent moves. For example, Figure 5 illustrates the case where the order is split into four batches. There, job completion time is reduced from 192.5 hours to 173.5 hours. Notice that the 19.0 hours reduction is not as dramatic as the initial 47.5 hour reduction that resulted from the first overlapping step going from one to two batches. Subsequent division into smaller lots will have a correspondingly smaller impact. This is because the longest operation time governs the entire cycle and limits the ultimate amount of reduction. Theoretically, however, an economic trade-off like the one shown in Figure 6 can be developed to determine the optimal amount of order splitting.

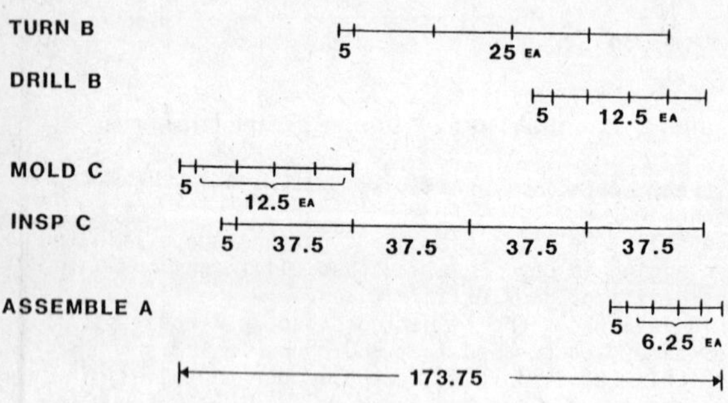

FIGURE 5 OVERLAPPING WITH FOUR EQUAL LOTS

Fine tuning like this to determine the optimal amount of splitting is not practical unless item values are very high. Obviously, if there is some standard container quantity that is less than the order quantity, then this will determine the frequency of movements and the extent of overlapping.

The extreme case of this order splitting is 100% overlap or concurrent operations. There, pieces are transferred nearly instantaneously.

PLANNING AND CONTROL USES

The illustrative example above describes the impact of overlapping operations as a means to shorten throughout time and reduce inventory as well. There are two ways in which the overlapping technique can be viewed:

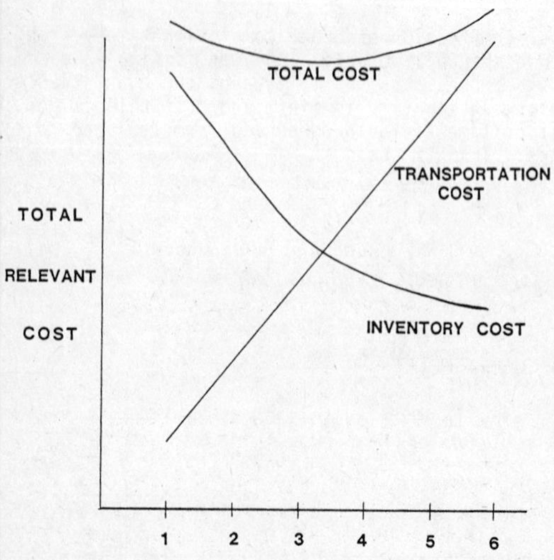

FIGURE 6 CONCEPT OF OPTIMAL ORDER SPLITTING

-   in reactive mode, as one of several control tools at management's disposal to shorten throughput times to meet a critical delivery date
-   in proactive mode, as a basis for planning so that quoted delivery times are shortened and work-in-process reduced by the amount of overlapping as a matter of normal operation.

In either mode, communication to accomplish the precise timing of events is critical. In the reactive mode, this may often be accomplished informally simply because the action is outside the normal way of operating. One would expect to see frequent use of a dispatcher negotiating with sending and receiving foremen to accomplish the coordination of split lots.

In the planning mode, overlapped operations are a normal event, and the communication to accomplish them must be built into the formal information system. Where formal computerized systems are involved, overlapping requires both additional information in the routing file and additional logic in the operation scheduling programs. One proven software system provides for overlapping via a code that specifies whether an operation is normally overlapped with its predecessor. This system permits overlaps to be specified in hours or pieces and permits specification of concurrent operations. The user need only determine the extent of overlap using the methods described in the first part of the paper and indicate this in the code. The backward scheduling logic in the system takes this into account so that Shop Floor Control load data and Capacity Requirements Planning projections accurately reflect the overlapping start dates. It is important that this timing be considered or else the CRP information will be unuseable.

Where operations involve the assembly of several components, a further extension of the overlapped concept is the staggered delivery of components to the point of usage in the parent assembly routing. In contrast to the usual job shop logic of issuing all components upon release of the parent, this arrangement allows the user to defer issue of specified components until the exact time of need.

Here again a distinction between the planning and control aspects can be drawn. Use of the formal system to plan material for staggered delivery of components represents a planning use of the technique. Releasing an assembly order with component shortages to meet a critical due date is a reactive or control use of the same idea.

In isolating these planning and control distinctions, we can better assess how companies use these techniques to accomplish delivery and inventory objectives.

CURRENT APPLICATION OF THE THEORY

In order to understand how companies typically apply overlapping operations, a survey was sent to a selected group of companies. Each of these companies operates with a formal manufacturing system. Further, each employs a software package that supports both the planning and control aspects of overlapping. The survey explores both uses.

The survey of planning uses of overlapping operations was designed to isolate the extent to which companies plan for overlapping. This group of questions is shown in Exhibit I below. The first three questions focus on the overlapping techniques applied to operations. Remaining questions focus on alternative approaches to work-in-process reductions. Questions 4 and 5 focus on the use of parent lead time reductions either by item (question 4) or across the board (question 5). Such lead time reductions in planning would delay the release of materials and reduce in-process levels.

Questions 6 and 7 refer to reductions in move time and queue time allowances which would reduce work-in-process by shortening shop cycles. Question 8 refers to the use of staggered delivery of components to reduce in-process by delaying the arrival of specific components.

In contrast, the second group of questions, shown in Exhibit II, focuses on the use of overlapping as compared to other options for compressing job completion times in an expedite situation. These questions relate to the frequency of use of each of the potential actions. The options include informal expediting, automatic rescheduling, selective rescheduling, overlapping, provision of additional capacity, and revision of the master schedule.

This group of questions asks you to indicate how you use the software when you want to reduce lead times in general. Please note that this refers to planned reductions affecting a group of items, work centers, or operations. Questions in the <u>next</u> section refer to the actions you might take to reduce the completion time in an <u>individual</u> order. When you want to reduce levels of work in process, you can choose among several system features. Which features do you use?

FEATURE	DO YOU USE NOW? YES NO	DO YOU EXPECT TO USE IN THE FUTURE? YES NO UNDECIDED
1. Overlapping Operations by Pieces (Actually indicated on routing)		
2. Overlapping Operations by Hours (Actually indicated on routing)		
3. Concurrent Operations (Actually indicated on routing)		
4. Item Lead Time Reduction (Actually reduce lead time on the item master)		
5. General Lead Time Reduction (Actually reduce system lead time in MRP)		
6. Work Center Move Time Reduction (Actually change move time allowance)		
7. Work Center Queue Time Reduction (Actually change queue time allowance)		
8. Component Lead Time Offset Adjustment (to delay the requirements for selected components in an assembly)		

EXHIBIT I: SURVEY QUESTIONS ON PLANNING USE

Changes in customer needs or changes in due dates of related dependent demand items can cause you to reschedule operations and take action to meet the new date. When this happens, you may use several approaches to meet the new requirements. In some instances you might use more than one approach. When you must make changes in an already scheduled item, how often do you use the following options?

	WHEN WE MUST CHANGE, WE USE THIS			
	OFTEN	OCCA-SION-ALLY	SELDOM	NEVER
1. Reschedule Order Using System (Change Due Date and let SFC reschedule)				
2. Use Informal Expediting (Tags, word of mouth hot lists)				
3. Change Operation Dates in SFC (to effectively reduce move and queue time allowances on this order only)				
4. Setup Overlapping Operations (on this order only)				
5. Setup Concurrent Operations (on this order only)				
6. Setup Additional Machines (to shorten run times)				
7. Break Setups				
8. Provide Additional Capacity (by running overtime, or subcontracting out a competing item)				
9. Change the Master Schedule				

EXHIBIT II: SURVEY QUESTIONS ON CONTROL USE

FEATURE	DO YOU EXPECT TO USE IN THE FUTURE? YES	NO	UNDECIDED
1. Overlapping Operations by Pieces (Actually indicated on routing)	6	7	6
2. Overlapping Operations by Hours (Actually indicated on routing)	2	9	8
3. Concurrent Operations (Actually indicated on routing)	10	5	4
4. Item Lead Time Reduction (Actually reduce lead time on the item master)	15	-	4
5. General Lead Time Reduction (Actually reduce system lead time in MRP)	12	2	5
6. Work Center Move Time Reduction (Actually change move time allowance)	8	7	4
7. Work Center Queue Time Reduction (Actually change queue time allowance)	11	2	6
8. Component Lead Time Offset Adjustment (to delay the requirements for selected components in an assembly)	14	2	5

EXHIBIT III: SURVEY RESULTS IN PLANNING SITUATIONS

	WHEN WE MUST CHANGE, WE	
	USE THIS	DON'T USE THIS
1. Reschedule Order Using System (Change Due Date and let SFC reschedule)	16	3
2. Use Informal Expediting (Tags, word of mouth hot lists)	7	12
3. Change Operation Dates in SFC (to effectively reduce move and queue time allowances on this order only)	5	13
4. Setup Overlapping Operations (on this order only)	1	18
5. Setup Concurrent Operations (on this order only)	2	17
6. Setup Additional Machines (to shorten run times)	5	12
7. Break Setups	10	9
8. Provide Additional Capacity (by running overtime, or subcontracting out a competing item)	17	2
9. Change the Master Schedule	13	5

EXHIBIT IV: SURVEY RESULTS IN CONTROL SITUATIONS

PRELIMINARY SURVEY RESULTS

Preliminary survey results regarding approaches to planned reduction of work-in-process are summarized in Exhibit III. There it can be observed that item lead time reduction, across the board reductions in lead time, and component lead time offset adjustment are the most frequently used approaches. Interestingly, each of these are centered on timing of material delivery and stockroom issue.

Closely behind are actions that are focused at the work center level, namely, move time reduction and queue time

reduction. Queue time reduction is the more commonly used
of the two. This is to be expected because queue times are
more arbitrarily determined than move times. The operation
oriented techniques, overlapping and concurrent operations,
are generally less commonly used. However, concurrent
operations is more popular than overlapping, suggesting an
all or none situation. The reasons for this are unclear and
need to be further investigated.

Preliminary results regarding the alternative
approaches to meeting an order due date are shown in Exhibit
IV. Interestingly, the most frequently cited approach is
item 8, provision of additional capacity. This suggests
that it is often necessary to change resource levels rather
than reallocate resources to resolve a conflicting schedule.
However, the next most frequently cited approach is to let
the system reschedule orders. Taken together these facts
could indicate an over-reliance on the system by its users.
That is, they permit the system to realign shop loads by
resheduling and then adjust resources to resolve critical
load situations. A more optimistic interpretation is that
automatic rescheduling is permitted on future orders and
that resource adjustments are used in the critical short
term situations where options are limited.

Other interesting observations include the relatively
frequent mentions of broken setups and changes in the master
schedule. In theory, both of these actions should be last
resort solutions to critical situations. Yet their frequent
mention suggests otherwise. The least frequently used
expediting tools are selective operation date management
(item 3), the overlapping approaches (items 4 & 5), and the
use of parallel processing (item 6). All items are
fine tuning steps requiring considerable communication to
achieve results in an expedite situation.

What is surprising is that the use of overlapping in an
expediting situation is less frequent than in the planning
situation. This suggests that the factors relating to the
practicality are somehow tied to permanent characteristics
of production. If true, this says that process steps,
product characteristics, type of manufacture, or plant
layout rather than management discretion are major
influences on the decision to use overlapping.

Further research is necessary to identify which factors
are important and what, if any, barriers need to be overcome
to increase the application of overlapping. Certainly,
whatever steps must be taken are the same ones in the
Just-in-Time journey. It is clear that the predominance of
use in the planning mode suggests that overlapping
operations support is important in formal systems.

BIBLIOGRAPHY

Fogarty and Hoffman, Production and Inventory
Management, Southwestern Publishing 1983, pp.387-392.
New, Colin, "MRP and GT: A New Strategy for Component
Production", Production and Inventory Management, Vol. 18,
No.3 (1977), pp. 50-62.

ACKNOWLEDGEMENT

The author wishes to acknowledge the support of Management
Science America, Inc.

BIOGRAPHICAL SKETCH - DENNIS J. KULONDA

Dennis Kulonda is an Associate Professor of Business
at James Madision University in Harrisionburg, Virginia.
Formerly, an industry specialist with the Manufacturing
Systems Division of MSA in Winston-Salem, NC, he has over
fifteen years experience in manufacturing with
responsibilities ranging from industrial engineer,
manufacturing supervisor, and staff engineer with the New
Departure - Hyatt Division of General Motors; senior
manufacturing consultant with Ernst and Whinney; and
Professor of Production Management at the Babcock Graduate
School of Management at Wake Forest University.

Dennis is active both in APICS and IIE where he speaks
frequently at their regional meetings. He is recognized as
a CPIM at the Fellow level.

He holds a B.I.E. from General Motors Institute, an
M.I.E. from Cornell University, and a PH.D. from North
Carolina State University.

JUST-IN-TIME PRODUCTIVITY IMPROVEMENT— CASE EXAMPLES

Leroy D. Peterson, CPIM*
Michael J. Klich, CPIM
Arthur Andersen & Co.

INTRODUCTION

A great deal has been written about the tremendous just-in-time productivity improvements achieved by Japanese companies using a variety of low-cost plant operating policies. Unfortunately, to date, little has been presented on the dramatic improvements made by U.S. companies in this vitally important area. This paper will describe the methods used by some U.S. companies to increase productivity and will discuss the improvements recently achieved by these companies.

PRINCIPLES

Although the companies achieving dramatic productivity improvements have been diverse in terms of applications and levels of manufacturing integration, they have used fairly standard principles in designing and implementing their production improvements. The scope of these improvements usually includes the following:

- o Focused Subplants
- o Flow Operations
- o Space Utilization
- o Transport Methodology
- o Supplier Program

FOCUSED SUBPLANTS

The term "focus" has become familiar to us in the last few years. In simplest terms it is the limiting, or focusing, of processes or technologies within a plant or subplant. A typical out-of-focus plant maintains a large, central stores area where all purchased material and various levels of work-in-process subassemblies are forwarded. A single area is designated for receiving and inspection, and all incoming material flow passes through this point. Shipping docks may also be combined with these receiving docks, or they may be located in a separate location.

The major problem with these out-of-focus plants is the excessive movement of material, which spawns an army of material handlers to convey the product through the process. With this heavy material movement also comes the need to process numerous transactions to record the movement of material from receiving through the manufacturing process and out through shipping.

OUT OF FOCUS

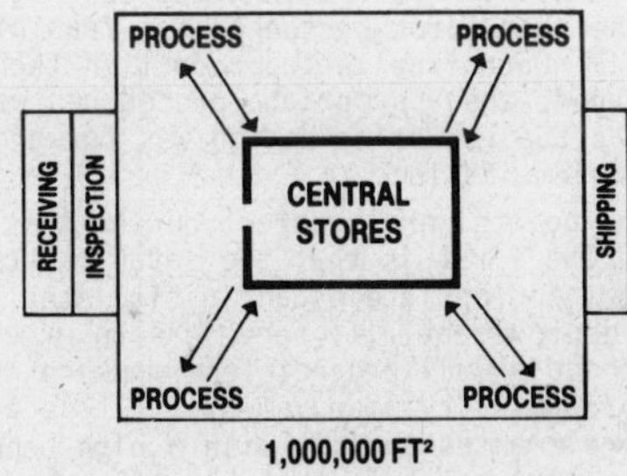

IN FOCUS

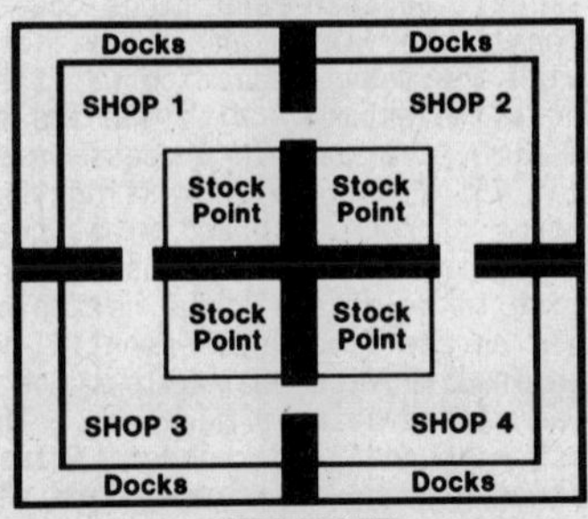

A plant in focus segregates processes or technologies into smaller subplants to limit the span of control. We no longer have a large, centralized storage facility, because the material needed in Shop 1 is stored within Shop 1, the need for a large, centralized storage area is eliminated. The material is received via a dock that is specifically designated for a particular subplant, with material being stored within the subplant. Incoming inspection stations may be needed in the short term and can either be set up at each subplant or maintained centrally if duplication of test equipment is costly. Central inspection, however, usually causes material movement to approach unacceptable levels and should therefore be avoided.

One area of sensitivity that usually arises with regard to focused plants is the perceived high cost of building outside accesses for focused subplant docks. In terms of cost and benefits, the indirect labor savings throught the decrease in material movement more than prove the benefits of establishing the subplants. To realize benefits in the short term, the outside docks may be replaced by a material delivery aisle traveled by automated driverless vehicles.

Once the material produced within the subplant is completed, be it subassembly or finished components, the completed product is placed in an outbound storage area within the subplant. A subassembly is "pulled" to the next subplant. Finished components are packaged and shipped directly from the outbound storage area.

In terms of supervisory control, a subplant allows for easy visual survey of all materials, process flows and finished components within a fairly small area. This proves to be extremely beneficial in allowing production control personnel to assess the status of material levels and production output easily.

FLOW OPERATIONS

The major goal in designing processes within the focused subplant is to develop an in-line flow that reduces work-in-process inventory and throughput times. This applies not only to the assembly process, but to the machining centers as well. Inventory serves as the buffer for unexpected "blips" in the production process. It is easy to see why the typical response to production problems is to maintain exaggerated inventory levels, rather the the minimizing of the inventory via one-time solutions to production problems. We have found, however, that by designing the flow operations with minimal inventory levels defined, many of these vintage production problems are uncovered and resolved. The corresponding reduction in work-in-process inventory and throughput times introduces exciting new flexibility to the shop floor.

IDEALS

LOT SIZE

CONTAINER SIZE

MOVEMENT QUANTITY

In designing for flow operations, several ideals should be kept in mind. First, the ideal production order quantity is one. Only enough of the product is made to satisfy the customer's order. No additional product is manufactured simply to increase the production lot size. Paramount to the order quantity limitations is the reduction of machine setup time. This is usually the initial step in productivity design and can produce large gains in short periods of time with minimal costs.

A second ideal is limiting of part container sizes. Large containers take up substantial cubic and floor space and typically are guilty of very low space utilization. Also, large containers require large material handling devices for transport. In terms of space utilization and ease of movement, the ideal is to limit the number of parts that fit into the container to one. If only one part is in the container, the implication is that no container should be necessary.

A third ideal in flow operations is designing for a part movement quantity of one. This means that only one part is staged between each worker on the line. As soon as the product is completed, it moves on to the next process. Process design innovation is very important in this case to develop the flow for this minimum transit quality. If a single part can be moved between processes, wait time for the remainder of the lot is essentially eliminated.

SPACE UTILIZATION

One principle that is always underestimated in productivity improvement is space utilization. In fact, often the only time the discussion of manufacturing and warehouse space takes place is when an authorization for expenditure is pending for plant brick and mortar additions. This is quite unfortunate, as from our experience a very direct relationship exists between practical space utilization and manufacturing costs.

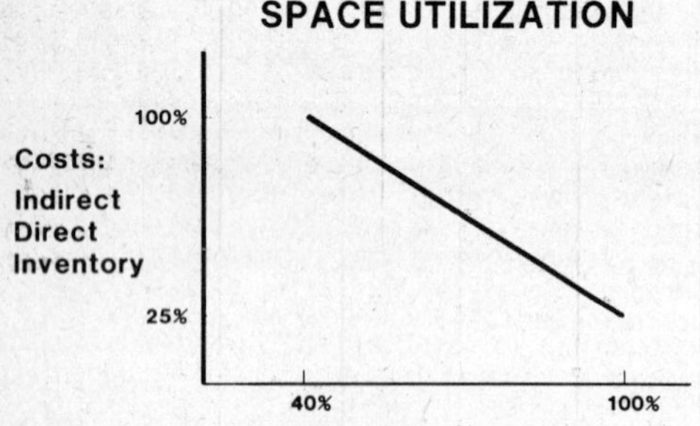

From initial plant tours, we have found that on the average most companies use only about 40% of their floor space effectively. Wide transport aisles, large unused spaces between machines, and open areas designated for work-in-process inventory storage are major causes of the ineffipient space usage. We can use this as a benchmark and consider manufacturing costs at this point to be 100%.

As we improve the manufacturing and warehouse space utilization by compressing the unused space, we see a corresponding drop in direct and indirect labor costs and a reduction in inventory. Indirect labor cost is reduced because workstations on assembly lines or machines in manufacturing cells are located close enough to allow material to be passed from hand to hand or on short conveyors. When large components are to be moved by forklift or cart, they are now being moved shorter distances. Direct labor cost decreases because parts and tools are placed in front of the worker within easy reach. The worker no longer has to move, reach or walk long distances to obtain tools and parts; therefore, the nonproductive movement time within the direct labor content is reduced. Inventory costs are reduced by the improved material flow, which squeezes out buffer inventory pockets. Because the manufacturing space is compressed, inventory has nowhere to be staged and is forced to continue down the process.

In combination, the reduction of these three manufacturing cost components is directly related to the improvement in overall plant space utilization.

TRANSPORT METHODOLOGY

Once the plant has been focused and the processes have been designed to use the manufacturing space effectively, the design of material transport methods is a logical next step in productivity improvement design. Ideally, the large transit distances between receiving and stores have been eliminated, and through the use of in-line flow operations, material movement between processes can be close to a hand-to-hand operation. When material has to be moved a longer distance, smaller containers moved via handcarts or conveyors should replace large, bulky containers requiring heavy material movement vehicles.

In addition, the transport design should maximize the utilization of the transport devices. The outbound area of a process should be in close proximity to the inbound area of the next process in the sequence. In this way, the handcarts or other material handling devices carry full loads from storage point to storage point, thus minimizing the distances covered with empty carts.

SUPPLIER PROGRAM

Another general principle in the productivity improvement design is the development of an appropriate supplier program. A main thrust here is to develop long-term supplier relationships with both the customer and the supplier working toward reduction of costs and improvement of profits for both parties. Among the goals attained in the supplier program are local sourcing, frequent delivery, shop-ready container designs and quality at the source.

Typical supplier programs begin with agreement by the customer management group of specific purchasing goals and then continue with extensive communication with selected suppliers. This communication becomes easier as the supplier base is consolidated. Once the goals have been agreed upon, standard purchase orders may be replaced by customer requirements, which may then update supplier production schedules directly from the customer. The better understanding of customer processes gained from improved communication and agreed upon goals helps the supplier improve product production. This understanding is extremely important in developing the appropriate production and inspection standards at the supplier in order to ensure incoming part quality at the customer.

CASE EXAMPLES

The first productivity improvement case example deals with a large diesel engine manufacturer. The main assembly plan houses both the diesel engine assembly process and the machining centers for the approximately 50 large machined components. The productivity improvement pilot projects deal with three of the machined components, namely, flywheel, flywheel housing and piston.

The scope of the productivity improvement projects was to reduce the machining setup times, reduce work-in-process inventory, compress manufacturing and storage space, and focus inventory at the production lines.

The first task was to develop a machine setup reduction methodology to be applied at all machining centers. An initial setup reduction task list was developed as an aid in the review of setup reduction potential. Such time-consuming activities as attaching threaded fasteners and searching for tools were documented and studied. The setup was then reviewed with production supervisors, engineers, setup personnel and/or machine operators. Machine setup reduction techniques were then developed and the new setup times determined with a target of 75% reduction. These techniques were again reviewed by the shop floor personnel for feasibility and final approval. Once final setup reduction techniques had been designed, the appropriate procedures were outlined and the setup reduction design was forwarded to tooling for implementation.

Two major points were apparent during this phase of the project. The first is that the setup reduction review was very appropriate as an initial step toward productivity improvement. It served as an excellent means of introducing all project team members to the benefits of productivity improvements. It is also a task that can be implemented quickly with a high benefit at low cost. A second point is that the setup reduction percentages achieved were directly proportional to the time spent on the review. Even though a 75% setup reduction was the target, further reductions could be achieved through additional observation and study.

Coupled with the setup reduction was the reduction of work-in-process inventory. With machine setup at 25% of the initial time, the work-in-process inventory could be in effect cut 75% solely by increasing the number of setups by a factor of four. In addition, the machining lines were studied to identify pockets of work-in-process inventory waiting to be moved to the next process. These inventory levels on the line were essentially eliminated by designing an in-line flow that allows for only one piece part to be stored between machines. The original machine centers, with one large inbound storage area and one large outbound storage area each, were eliminated and replaced with machine cells, each processing one specific

product group. The elimination of the inventory pockets,
coupled with the lot size reduction due to the setup
reduction, yielded dramatic reductions in work-in-process
inventory.

Once the machining line had been established and
proper line balancing achieved, the machining department
layout was redesigned to make better use of the manufacturing floor space. This had the effect, as mentioned
earlier, of reducing both the direct and indirect labor
costs. It also freed enough space on the shop floor to
adequately focus the incoming material at the production
line.

In summary, the savings proved to be quite dramatic. The average reductions for various operating costs
for the three machining lines are as follows:

Machine Setup Time	81%
Raw Material Inventory	80%
Work-in-Process Inventory	95%
Finished Component Inventory	61%
Direct Labor	48%
Indirect Labor	60%
Floor Space (Occupancy Cost)	59%
Total Annual Operating Cost	35%

The second case example of productivity improvement
deals with an office product assembly operation. The
assembly process uses components, over 95% of which are
purchased. The major internally fabricated components
are printed circuit boards. In this case, two pilot product lines--one office product assembly line and the
printed circuit board assembly process--were picked for
pilot projects.

The scope of the project was similar to that of the
first--reduce work-in-process inventory, reduce the
throughput time specifically in the printed circuit board
assembly, reduce direct labor content and improve
manufacturing/storage space utilization.

In the office product assembly process, the major
investment in work-in-process inventory was in subassemblies. The main assembly build took place in the
morning, with subassembly build occurring in the afternoon. Without the synchronization of subassembly build
to main assembly build, the inventory level of subassemblies ranged from 5 days' supply to 20 days' supply. The main task here was to review once again the
assembly and subassembly processes and redesign these
processes into an in-line flow. Subassemblies now would
be built in conjunction with the main assemblies. The
line would then be redesigned to allow for the handing of
individual subassemblies across the line to the main
assembly stations, rather than directing large subassembly carts through the aisles. In addition, all
in-line storage areas were eliminated, thus reducing the
opportunity for buffer inventory to accumulate. The goal
of the project was to solve the production problems that
made the buffer inventory necessary, rather than allowing
this inventory to be staged.

A major improvement in the assembly process was the
development of a CONBON (KANBAN) material handling procedure. Through the use of CONBON cards between the
assembly/subassembly process and the focused storage
area, line supply personnel utilization was improved.

In-line flow design was also used in the printed
circuit board assembly process. Lot sizes were decreased
by reducing the setup times for automated printed circuit
board component insertion equipment. CONBON material
handling procedures were also designed for the printed
circuit board process. These procedures applied both to
the picking, kitting and preparation of components, and
to the printed circuit board assembly process itself.
Once the printed circuit board assembly throughput time
was sufficiently reduced, the CONBON procedures could be
implemented between the printed circuit board assembly
and the office product assembly.

The savings for both areas are as impressive as in
the previous case.

OFFICE PRODUCT ASSEMBLY

Work-in-Process Inventory	90%
Direct Labor	20%
Floor Space (Occupancy Cost)	50%

PRINTED CIRCUIT BOARD ASSEMBLY

Work-in-Process Inventory	90%
Finished Assembly Inventory	70%
Throughput Time	90%
Setup Time	67%-93%
Direct Labor	20%
Indirect Labor	50%
Floor Space (Occupancy Cost)	46%

SUMMARY

The dramatic productivity improvements realized
today in the U.S. are being achieved by a diverse group
of manufacturing companies. Although the operating characteristics may be different, these companies do have
specific principles in common. Each of these corporations had a top management that was extremely dedicated
in its pursuit of these productivity improvements. In
addition, the communication between the executive team
and other manufacturing levels was very strong, with the
discussion flow going both ways. These successful companies have instituted these productivity improvements
via pilot projects that pay back on a timely basis.
Pilot projects also offer an excellent training vehicle
for new project team members. With the successes exhib-
ited by the ever-increasing number of forward-thinking
corporations, these manufacturing productivity improvements will be adopted as the standard operating procedure
of the '80s.

BIOGRAPHIES

Mr. Leroy D. Peterson, a partner in the Management
Information Consulting Division of the Chicago office of
Arthur Andersen & Co., is in charge of the firm's world-
wide manufacturing industry program.

Mr. Peterson has been the partner responsible for
innumerable manufacturing client engagements and is
responsible for quality assurance reviews of the most
significant client engagements all over the world. He
has been heavily involved in just-in-time projects for
the past two years. His extensive manufacturing experience puts him in top rank of international consultants,
with hands-on experience in detail design and installation of just-in-time and closed-loop manufacturing control systems.

He has had extensive experience with several automotive manufacturers. He has been in charge of projects to
develop systems for new plants for European, Japanese and
U.S. manufacturers, and thus has had the unique opportunity to observe the technology of each.

Since his graduation from the University of Illinois
(B.S. in engineering, M.S. in business administration) in
1962, Mr. Peterson has been employed as a manufacturing
consultant. He is an active member in a number of manufacturing organizations and a former director of the
Chicago chapter of the American Production and Inventory
Control Society (APICS). He has authored a number of
articles published in the APICS Journal and is a certified CPIM Fellow.

Mr. Michael J. Klich, a manager in the Chicago
office of Arthur Andersen & Co., is a consultant specializing in the design and installation of closed-loop manufacturing systems and productivity improvements. His
clients include some of the largest companies in the
utility, defense and telecommunications industries. Due
to the major profit improvement impact resulting from his
productivity work, he is frequently requested to speak to
professional and company groups on this subject.

Mr. Klich heads the manufacturing productivity
improvement practice in the Chicago office and is one of
the most experienced members of the firm's worldwide productivity team. In this capacity he consults with the
firm's nationwide clients. He is coauthor of the firm's
Manufacturing Productivity Improvement Design Reference
Manual.

Mr. Klich has a bachelor's degree in mechanical
engineering and a master's degree in industrial administration from Purdue University. He is also a member of
the American Production and Inventory Control Society
(APICS) and is certified in production and inventory management.

JUST-IN-TIME IMPLEMENTATION: JOB SHOP VERSUS FLOW SHOP

Edward V. Spurgeon
General Electric Company

INTRODUCTION

This presentation compares Just-in-Time (JIT) implementations at two small General Electric plants. Each plant has less than 1,000 employees. One is a Flow Shop that produces small consumer products such as coffeemakers and toaster ovens at a rate of about 20,000 units/day. The other is a Job Shop that produces custom switchgear apparatus.

Both plants are achieving significant benefits as they move toward JIT production. Although the implementation approach in each plant is similar, the program focus is different. This presentation will discuss the similarities, differences, and lessons learned from these two JIT programs.

BACKGROUND

Inasmuch as the words "Just-in-Time" connote different things to different people, let's first clarify what we mean by Just-in-Time manufacturing. At the G.E. plants being discussed, JIT is seen as a broad manufacturing philosophy focusing on eliminating costs that do not add value to a product or service. Inventory is one of these costs. Inventory is an important focus of Just-in-Time because by lowering inventory we can expose and solve hidden quality problems and productivity problems in a business. As we work to eliminate costs that don't add value, such as inventory, we are challenged to rethink the way our plants are designed and operated. We see opportunities to synchronize and link operations. But we realize that there are prerequisites to making these ideas work. The prerequisites include involving operators in an active role in quality control, preventive maintenance, and problem solving. The prerequisites take time to implement, therefore, Just-in-Time is a long term approach. But it is one which everyone in an organization can understand and rally around.

Just-in-Time requires significant changes in the mindset of an organization. In G.E. implementing JIT concepts is strictly voluntary. As of this writing, over 40 G.E. plants have active JIT programs underway. Some started four years ago.

HIGH VOLUME PLANT - HOUSEWARES, ASHEBORO, NC

The Asheboro Housewares plant manufactures small consumer appliances including: coffeemakers, toaster ovens, irons, hair dryers, make-up mirrors, and heating pads. Total daily production of all models is about 20,000 units. Raw material includes plastic, steel, aluminum and fasteners. There are over 100 different labor operations per product including molding, die casting, stamping, drilling, tapping, assembling, testing, and packing. The plant employs about 500 non-union employees.

PROGRAM DIRECTION - HIGH VOLUME PLANT

As early as 1980, Asheboro's management was learning about JIT through a Management Information Exchange that G.E. had negotiated with the Toyota Motor Company of Japan. In 1982, the plant required additional space for new product lines. The Plant Manager and the Manager-Manufacturing Engineering decided that JIT concepts could free up the space needed.

The JIT work was originally led by the Manufacturing Engineering organization. They decided to create what was called a "Super Line" for the highest volume product -- the coffeemaker. The coffeemaker assembly line was redesigned so that two different models could be produced on the same line at the same time. This would eliminate changing over the line to a different model every two weeks and would facilitate reducing finished goods stock.

Unfortunately, the new mixed model line required more work stations and would have to stock a larger variety of parts. This triggered the first JIT breakthrough. It was decided to set up the line with no more than one day's worth of parts stocked on the line. (Previously one week's worth of material was stocked at the assembly line.) Inasmuch as there was no space available in the stockroom, a plan was developed to flow material directly from contributing areas, such as the mold room, to the assembly line on a daily basis.

In order to control the flow of material to the assembly line, spaces and bins were designated at each work station on the line. The spaces and bins were numbered and outlined with yellow paint. Each space would hold only one day's supply of material. Then a material move plan was developed to indicate to the material handlers the specific routings and material quantities required every day. In the process of developing this plan, they found that the material handling costs were reduced by 30% over past practice!

As the new "Super Line" was put in place, an effort was made to upgrade the appearance of the area. It was cleaned up and painted from floor to ceiling. There were designated spaces for everything that was supposed to be available -- materials, tools, even dustpans and brooms. There was a place for everything and anything out of place stood out like a "sore thumb".

Communications were very important. Management studied the latest books on Just-in-Time and had weekly discussions on its application. Hourly employees were introduced early to JIT via meetings with their supervisors, and in quality circle meetings. The Plant newspaper featured articles on Just-in-Time and interviewed employees on how they felt about it. A library of JIT literature was established for reference and use by all employees.

The "Super Line" concept proved very successful. More and more JIT ideas were introduced. Quality became a key focus. Operators were trained to be able to take responsibility for 100% inspecting their work. Operators posted statistical quality control data on charts. Display cases illustrated appearance standards. Each area was assigned a table where operators could place items that they were concerned about from a quality viewpoint. Every day the Plant Manager and his staff would review the quality tables and take appropriate action. Needless to say, quality took on a new meaning. People walking through the spotless plant observing the quality charts on the walls came away with the feeling that here was an organization that really cared about quality products.

Error proofing ideas were introduced for particularly troublesome operations. Green, yellow and red trouble lights were installed so that an operator could signal immediately for help. A repair work station was set aside toward the end of the assembly line so that any repair work could be performed immediately.

The success achieved on the coffeemaker line encouraged the expansion of the program throughout the entire plant. Additional training was conducted. Key managers traveled to the Kawasaki Plant in Lincoln, Nebraska, to discover additional JIT ideas. Other employees attended G.E. JIT Roundtable meetings. These are semi-annual, two-day meetings where JIT practitioners exchange ideas.

The next round of successes included: vendor deliveries of glass carafes daily instead of every three days; delivery of carafes direct to assembly lines instead of to a stockroom; relocation of contributing operations adjacent to the assembly lines; and reducing set-up times and lot sizes.

The program is seen as never ending, a striving for continued elimination of waste. But, in addition to achieving the original goal of freeing up 50,000 ft^2 of floor space, the results for the first year of the program were:

	Improvement Over Prior Year
Direct Labor Productivity	15%
Indirect Labor Productivity	25%
RIP Inventory	40%
Scrap and Rework	33%

JOB SHOP PLANT - SWITCHGEAR, BURLINGTON, IOWA

The Burlington Switchgear plant manufactures medium voltage circuit breakers incorporating vacuum interrupters and various meters and protective devices to meet customer specifications. Although there are two basic models, the various configurations and options mean that each unit shipped is different.

The plant of about 300,000 ft^2 includes sheet metal fabrication, machine shop, plating and painting, sub assembly, final assembly, test and pack.

This business is known for its innovative product designs and high quality and productivity.

PROGRAM DIRECTION - JOB SHOP

Burlington management first learned about JIT concepts through a presentation by one of G.E.'s Internal Consultants. The Burlington plant JIT program started in early 1982.

The program was led by the plant manager who, as part of G.E.'s Management Information Exchange, studied JIT at Toyota. He felt that JIT would be a good focus for further improvement in productivity, and for inventory reduction. Initially there were some doubts about applying JIT concepts in a Job Shop environment. Up until this time the plant had been trying to increase lot sizes to gain economies of scale. How could you change people's thinking to the advantages of small lot production, and make such a radical change in an already successful business?

The JIT mindset did not happen overnight. It took months to convince people that JIT made sense in a Job Shop. Presentations were made to the entire salaried workforce. Small meetings and plant newspaper articles carried the message to the hourly workforce.

The managers debated where to start. The best area would be one of relatively small size, but yet visible, and representative of other operations. It would be helpful to have a fairly simple area with no major yield problems, and an area where there was a high likelihood of success. The frame stacking area was selected and a cross-functional team was organized to work on JIT.

The first change was from weekly schedules to daily schedules. Instead of putting weekly lots of material out to the assembly area, daily flow was initiated. Two assembly lines were consolidated into one. This cut work in-process in half and saved 7200 ft^2 of space.

A second JIT team was formed to tackle the sheet metal fabrication area. Twenty parts were selected to be produced in daily lot sizes and matched to the assembly line requirements.

Today 167 parts are produced to a daily schedule in weekly lot sizes. WIP has been reduced from about a 10 week's supply to 1-1/2 weeks. This resulted in the cancellation of the lease on a warehouse and saving $130,000/year in rent.

The key to smaller lot sizes in sheet metal fabrication was quick set-up. Burlington became a leader in G.E. in set-up time reduction. By standardizing die heights, modifying and improving clamping devices, reducing transportation time, and using two man change teams, the allowed time of 56 minutes for a die change in a 45 ton press was reduced to 1.5 minutes, a 95% reduction. Similar reductions are now being achieved on larger presses.

The JIT program at Burlington was expanded into the Breaker sub-assembly area. The area was rearranged for better material flow and daily scheduling and daily lot sizes were introduced. A 90% reduction in WIP was realized along with a 10% productivity gain. There are now ten JIT teams at Burlington and the program is still in its early stage.

First year results include:

	Improvement Over Prior Year
Direct Labor Productivity	7%
Indirect Labor Productivity	15%
RIP Inventory	22%
Floor Space	20,000 ft^2

COMPARISON OF APPROACH

In both Asheboro and Burlington, the approach to implementing JIT was similar. First the top manager at each location became committed, and established a priority for the program. Then education about JIT was conducted, eventually reaching the entire organization. A pilot area was selected, a team put together, and work started. There was a minimum of planning, and virtually no economic justification. However, it is interesting that both programs did focus on priority areas in each business and that both plants received immediate benefits from space reductions.

COMPARISON OF JIT CONCEPTS UTILIZED

This is where the programs differed. Asheboro focused on going to mixed model production. Burlington was already scheduling mixed models ("too mixed" they would say!). Both plants went toward daily lot sizes. This concept was a lot easier for Asheboro. Burlington had to first carry out a major program of set-up reduction. At Asheboro, in many cases, it was already economical to run smaller lot sizes.

The plants put emphasis on orderliness, cleanliness, plant layout, and management by sight. Both of them worked on operator involvement. But Asheboro found it beneficial to focus on quality and difficult to make a major improvement on quick set-up of molding machines. Burlington's emphasis was on quick set-up in sheet metal stamping.

Neither plant found Kanbans to be helpful at this early stage in their programs.

COMPARISON OF PROBLEMS ENCOUNTERED

Many of the problems encountered were similar, for example:
- changing people's mindset about economic lot sizes;
- insufficient manpower to make the needed changes and solve the "rocks";
- measurement system focusing on the elements instead of on the total system.

However, there were some major differences. At Burlington it was found that Engineering documentation was an impediment to small lot sizes. In addition at Burlington, because of the business cycle, there was considerable concern about a possible lack of work situation, while at Asheboro the problems were in the area of schedule stability and vendor interfaces.

COMPARISON OF BENEFITS

On the surface, the economic benefits at Asheboro exceeded those at Burlington. This may not actually be the case inasmuch as Asheboro was in a period of increasing order volume and Burlington was in a period of declining volume. A more likely conclusion is that the potential benefits are equally large in a Job Shop, but may take longer to achieve.

LESSONS LEARNED

In reflecting on these two JIT programs, there are several key factors that are thought to be critical to success:
- Consider JIT as a concept, not a project to be scheduled and completed. Therefore, "Don't plan it to death. Start small and build on your successes."
- Make sure that the program focuses on a priority need of the business, otherwise JIT will soon fade from view.
- Early in the program, obtain the involvement of all the operators in the plant so they can help solve the problems that are exposed. Be ready to accept some mistakes.
- Assure the understanding and commitment of the top manager on site before attempting a program like JIT that involves major changes from prior practices.
- Remember that JIT isn't just a manufacturing program. It challenges the total organization. Marketing and Engineering also play vital roles in the scheduling and design decisions that impact on the ability to operate Just-in-Time.

SUMMARY

The Just-in-Time concepts apply equally well in a Job Shop environment as in more repetitive manufacturing operations. The basic approach to implementation is similar in both environments. It involves management commitment followed by education of the entire plant organization.

Once an organization understands the JIT principles and techniques, it will become apparent which JIT concepts can be of most value to particular operations. The focus of each JIT program will be different. But the benefits are available to both Job Shops and Flow Shops alike.

WILL THE *REAL* JUST-IN-TIME PURCHASING PLEASE STAND UP?

Edward J. Hay, CPIM*
Rath & Strong, Inc.

Two of the questions most frequently asked about implementing Just-In-Time programs are:

1. Doesn't JIT simply push inventory back to the supplier? and

2. How do you get your suppliers to go along?

Obviously, there is a widely-held perception that the function of JIT Purchasing is, first, to force suppliers to hold more inventory so that the buying company can hold less, and, second, to convince them to incur and absorb added costs by making daily deliveries in small, uneconomical lots.

Nothing can be further from the truth. In true Just-In-Time Purchasing, the supplier must benefit just as much as the buying company. Just as importantly, neither party will reap the real benefits of Just-In-Time until the supplier, too, is operating under "Zero Inventories."

How could such a misconception come to be so widely held? Unfortunately, there is no shortage of examples of exactly this kind of pressure being brought to bear on suppliers in the name of Just-In-Time. When such examples occur, chances are very high that the buying company is making one of two common mistakes.

The first common mistake is to believe that Just-In-Time is an inventory reduction program. It is not!! The second common mistake is to reverse the proper sequence for implementing Just-In-Time. The proper sequence is for a company to truly learn what Just-In-Time Production is and to clean up its own internal act by implementing JIT within its own four walls before involving its suppliers in anything other than a quality assurance program.

Either of these two mistakes will result in demands for delivery "just in time" before the necessary groundwork can be laid for the supplier to be able to manufacture "just in time." Just-In-Time delivery without Just-In-Time production can only be done by building inventory-- and inventory is the root of all evil.

TRUE JUST-IN-TIME

At the heart of Just-In-Time philosophy is the elimination of waste. Waste is defined as:

> Anything other than the absolute minimum resources of material, machines, and manpower required to add value to the product.

The key is the ultimate elimination of anything which is excess or which does not add value. Waste is not eliminated by trading it for another form of waste, nor is it eliminated by moving it from one part of the process to another part of the process. This is especially true if this type of trade-off benefits that part of the process which accounts for 30% of the cost of the product and penalizes that part of the process (purchased content) which accounts for 70% of the cost of the product.

WASTE IN THE PURCHASING PROCESS

If we take a hard-nosed look at everything that goes on in the purchasing process and apply the test of absolute minimum resources or the test of adding value, most of the process will be identified as waste. Establishing source and price is not waste because it is, in effect, creating the necessary resource. Actual production by the supplier is not waste because it adds value to the product. Everything else in the process, however, is waste.

Once source and price have been determined, what value is added by any of the following?

- Purchase Orders/Releases
- Acknowledgements
- Expediting
- Transportation Costs
- Loading/Unloading
- Counting
- Receiving Reports
- Inspecting
- Sorting
- Scrap
- Rework
- Returns to Supplier
- Moving
- Storing
- Repackaging
- Invoices

What value is added to the product by having inventories, whether they are caused by safety stocks, safety time (early delivery), minimums, or lot sizes (truckloads, price breaks)? In addition, unless there is a capacity problem, establishing multiple sources violates the principle of absolute minimum resources.

Just-In-Time Purchasing is identical to Just-In-Time Production in that it is a collection of old and new techniques for solving problems so that waste can first be minimized and ultimately eliminated throughout the entire process.

QUALITY AT THE SOURCE

Companies committed to implementing JIT recognize that the most important means of eliminating waste is through the principle of Do It Right the First Time, or Quality at the Source. After-the-fact assessment (or sorting the good from the bad by inspection) must give way to, and ultimately be replaced by, process control and pre-control which prevents defects from happening in the first place.

In the purchasing process, this means working with the supplier on his premises to help him establish process capability and process control. Quality at the Source is not an easy process, nor is it quick. It requires the right attitude (toward prevention) to get it started. It requires substantial time and commitment for operator training and problem solving as well as to establish the habit of continuous improvement to get it going. Even after the costs (wastes) of sorting, scrap, rework, and returns have disappeared, it will take a good deal more time to build the confidence that everything will continue to work right. Only then will people be willing to begin to eliminate the other wastes of inspection, safety stocks, safety time, control systems, and backup sources.

These cost reductions should benefit the supplier even more than the buyer. In spite of this, however, such long-term effort and commitment will not be readily forthcoming from a supplier who thinks he might lose the business at the next round of bidding. Conversely, the buyer cannot develop quality assurance programs with high confidence levels with hundreds or thousands of suppliers.

Quality at the Source points to long-term relationships with fewer but better suppliers.

SPECIAL ARRANGEMENTS

Another means of reducing or eliminating waste is through special, mutually beneficial arrangements with suppliers.

Given the determination to eliminate waste, given the time to find mutually beneficial solutions to problems, and given time to develop confidence in one another, buyer and supplier can make special paperwork arrangements. Formal purchase orders or releases can be replaced by automatic revolving signals. Acknowledgements can be eliminated. Individual receiving reports can be simplified or reduced to monthly reports. Individual invoices can be replaced by monthly statements organized specifically for cost accounting entries and complete with proof of delivery. Both the supplier and the buyer benefit equally from reduced and simplified paperwork systems.

Transportation is an especially fertile field for special arrangements aimed at getting smaller, more frequent deliveries while maintaining or even reducing transportation costs. The key, of course, is to establish regular, repetitive transportation patterns. This is the buyer's responsibility and is the direct result of implementing Just-In-Time cycle time and level loading techniques.

Once patterns are established, a number of special arrangements can be made. Commercial carriers can be replaced by contract carriers with fixed routes. Truckloads can be made up of partial loads from several suppliers. Several suppliers can be coordinated to do their own delivery by alternating responsibility. Obviously, the fewer pick-up points (suppliers) there are, the less complicated the transportation patterns will be.

Hand in hand with special transportation arrangements are special material handling arrangements. Special returnable containers can be developed to eliminate the waste of throw-away containers. If designed correctly, they can be used for shipping and at the point of use to eliminate repackaging.

Separators can eliminate counting (inspection for full or not full). Given special containers and repetitive patterns, special loading/unloading arrangements are possible. Given special containers, Quality at the Source, and level loading, purchased material can be delivered directly to point of use, eliminating storing and extra moving.

Special arrangements, whether paperwork, transportation, or handling, tend to be developed one at a time and, therefore, tend to be different from one supplier to another. Like Quality at the Source, special arrangements also point to long-term relationships with fewer but better suppliers.

SINGLE/MULTIPLE SOURCING

Traditionally, single sourcing has been considered bad by definition. Periodic campaigns are mounted, complete with special tooling budgets, to reduce the risk of being single sourced. But Just-In-Time tells us the fewer suppliers the better for eliminating waste, and that single sourcing, if done correctly, is good rather than bad. How can we reconcile these two opposing views?

First, I would suggest that we are really much more single sourced than we might think. We typically buy the majority of non-productive items from single sources. Also, how many cases do we have where Engineering has specified one particular supplier or has certified only one particular supplier? How many proprietary items do we purchase? How many items are single sourced from other company plants? In how many cases have tooling costs prohibited more than one source? Do we have several sources for a commodity, but allow individual items within the commodity to be single sourced?

Secondly, let us examine the most frequent objections to single sourcing.

1. What if the single source should burn down?

    Answer: Use whatever contingency plan you now have if your own plant or any other plant in your company burns down.

2. What if they have a wildcat strike?

    Answer: What plan do you have if your own plant goes on wildcat strike?

3. How do I know I am getting the best price if I cannot test against other sources?

    Answer: Homework, knowledge of the supplier's cost structure, and the habit of continuous improvement.

4. A single source would have too much leverage and could dictate prices and terms.

    Answer: This assumes an adversarial attitude rather than one of common interest and mutual cooperation. Adversarial relationships and single sourcing do not go together.

As the acid test of a company's feeling against single sourcing, I would drop the subject with any company which would refuse to _be_ a single source to its customers.

The potential benefits of dealing with a substantially reduced number of quality suppliers are worth summarizing here:

1. Ability to focus on a few key quality assurance programs.

2. Reduced freight costs.

3. More opportunity for special arrangements in paperwork, transportation, and handling.

4. Economic leverage more concentrated.

5. The demand on the supplier is much more stable, predictable, and repeatable if he supplies an entire commodity rather than selected items. See Figure 1. With this kind of predictability, the supplier can plan his capacity efficiently while waiting until the last minute to make decisions on mix. This reduces lead time drastically.

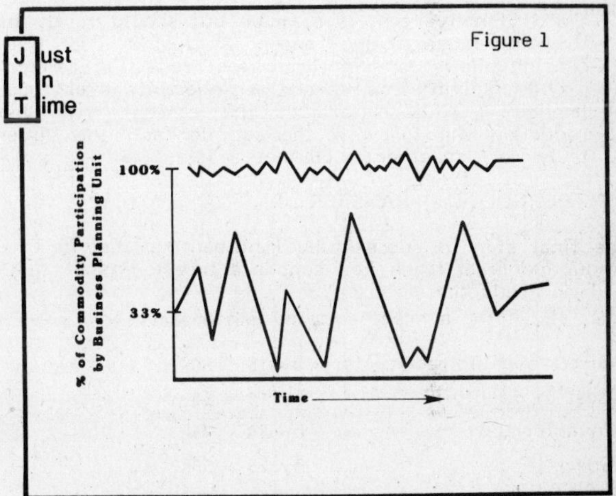

SUPPLIER SELECTION/EVALUATION

Single sourcing is obviously not without risk. Making a logical case in favor of single sourcing does not make these risks go away. In moving toward single sourcing, there are several steps we must take to minimize the risk.

1. Do not go immediately to single sourcing. Start by gradually reducing the number of suppliers.

2. Identify and eliminate past reasons for multiple sourcing (quality problems, poor supplier, unclear specifications, etc.).

3. Take great care with the supplier selection process.

A team approach to supplier selection is usually best, with representatives from Purchasing, Manufacturing, Quality, and Finance almost always involved. Other functions such as Engineering, Maintenance, Toolroom, and Scheduling would be included as required.

The team should be selecting the best supplier rather than simply the best price. There are many important criteria for selecting suppliers, and cost is only one of them.

1. Responsiveness. The key ingredient to a successful relationship is the demonstrated willingness and

ability of the supplier to be responsive to customer needs. In some cases there need not even be a bid selection process, because one supplier is clearly more responsive than all others.

2. Geographic Location. Geographic location is important because the closer the supplier is to the point of use, the less chance there is for disruption of supply. Obviously the lead time is shorter. Additionally, the many working sessions required for a successful contract make it easier for rapid communications if the supplier is geographically near the purchasing department.

3. Size of Supplier. The size of the company should be small enough to assure genuine interest on the part of the supplier. (Obviously it cannot be so small that it is incapable of satisfying all of the anticipated demand). In a very large supplier organization, access to the chief executive officers is limited and the chance of getting to the real decision makers is minimized. However, a "focused factory" within a large corporation is usually acceptable.

4. Financial Stability. Financial stability must be sufficient to assure continued health and enough funds for continued cost improvement efforts.

5. Quality. Quality is critical to the overall success of any relationship. A high rejection rate is at cross purposes with the concept of minimum inventory.

6. Technical Competence. The technical competence of the supplier is critical to continuing cost reductions.

7. Cost. Finally, cost is a factor but should rarely be the only factor. The concept of Just-In-Time purchasing allows for significant cost reduction through problem solving and special arrangements over time. Implicit in this criteria is the concept that cost reduction will follow if the supplier and the buyer truly work together to eliminate waste.

JIT TECHNOLOGY TRANSFER

The final step in successfully implementing Just-In-Time Production is to teach key suppliers how to install Just-In-Time Production themselves.

After all, if the average company can improve:

Direct and indirect costs	by 15 – 50%
Cost of quality	by 15 – 50%
Inventories	by 50 – 75%
Space	by 25 – 50%
Lead time	by 50 – 75%
Setup times	by 50 – 75%

Why can't key suppliers be shown how to use the same techniques for similar results? Due to the magnitude of improvements available from Just-In-Time techniques, this is probably the greatest single opportunity for cost reduction through continuous improvement.

In return for help in implementation, the supplier would be expected to share the benefits in the form of cost reductions passed on to the customer. It is important to note that the supplier's profit should not be targeted as a contributor to cost reduction. Instead, the supplier must be allowed a reasonable margin above cost of sales to reinvest in further productivity improvements. As in Figure 2, the supplier may indeed be making a higher percentage of profit after implementing Just-In-Time, but this is consistent with the objective of mutual benefit.

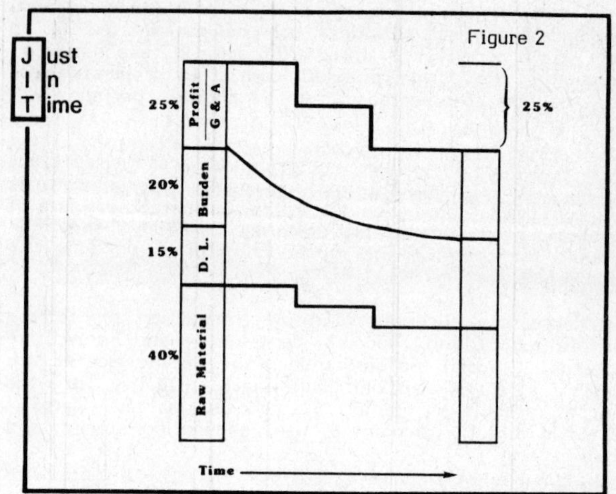

SUMMARY

In industry today, there seems to be a commonly held misconception that Just-In-Time is an inventory reduction program whereby manufactures reduce their own inventory at the expense of their suppliers who are required to keep more inventory to survive. We now know that true Just-In-Time abhors inventory no matter where it finds it, viewing it as proof of the existence of waste.

A true Just-In-Time relationship between buyer and seller is long-term in nature, equally beneficial to both parties, and dedicated to the principle of continuous improvement in the future.

ABOUT THE AUTHOR

Edward J. Hay is a Vice President of Rath & Strong, Inc. and is recognized as one of the leading United States authorities on Japanese techniques for improving productivity and quality.

In addition to in-depth studies in Japan of the most successful companies there, he has researched Japanese companies operating in the U.S. More importantly, he has, himself, been actively engaged in "Americanizing" and implementing those techniques which are readily adaptable to U.S. culture and management style.

He has a professional background of over twenty years of line, staff, and executive experience in Materials Management covering large and small businesses in consumer, industrial, aerospace-electronics, and automotive products.

He is certified at the Fellow level by APICS and is a frequent speaker at such events as the Indiana University Annual Business Conference, the University of Nebraska Japan-U.S. Business Conference, and the APICS National Conference.

JUST-IN-TIME VENDORS ARE COMING

Brian John O'Connor, M.A.
B. J. O'Connor International Ltd.

FOREWORD

This paper deals with the revolution in purchasing being brought about by the introduction of the just in time (JIT) approach.

It covers both vendors of capital equipment and vendors of materials, parts, sub assemblies and assemblies.

Benefits being obtained are described with examples from current practice. It shows that profit improvements are possible by means other than increased sales. In a number of cases the savings being made in purchasing equal the profits of the company.

The case studies show how lead times are being cut by 50%, inventories by 75% and costs by 50% to give increased flexibility and higher profits.

The objective is to assist the reader to select those techniques appropriate to his operations.

INTRODUCTION

The intense interest in this approach on both sides of the Atlantic originates from a growing need to reduce costs to remain competitive.

Some executives see it as a way for big corporations to impose their costs on their suppliers, the so called leverage approach. Yet JIT is universally applicable. It works for big and small corporations. Costs can be reduced substantially by cooperation between customer and supplier.

Foreign competitors now offer finished goods in the home market at prices equivalent to our raw material costs. Reaction to this problem must be fast. But reaction may be too late. Are there any alternatives to a JIT approach now?

The important question is how can this approach be implemented in practice and how should it vary from industry to industry?

In 1982 at the Chicago APICS Conference we described the JIT approach based on experience gained on our first zero inventory projects.

We used the analogy of the river of inventory. The rocks (problems) that appear as the level of water (inventory) is lowered. The importance of passing clean water from supplier to customer was also emphasised - making the supplier responsible for high quality product being sent on to the customer.

At Chicago there was a great debate as to whether JIT should start in the main plant or at suppliers.

Today this discussion is over. The initiative is being taken both by suppliers and customers.

The situation has changed since 1982. Many more companies are implementing as fast as their resources will allow. This paper is based on examples from a number of corporations in different countries.

Figure 1. ARE "BUCKET" SYSTEMS COST EFFECTIVE?

TRADITIONAL PURCHASING

Why is traditional purchasing being questioned?

Has it not served us well?

It is not easy to sum up the many reasons for failure, but traditional purchasing has fostered high costs. Our corporations can no longer afford costs arising from:

- conflict negotiation based on competitive price quotations
- lack of trust between buyer and vendor
- long delivery lead times
- large quantities delivered infrequently
- high administration costs both at suppliers and customers
- complex administration systems
- high investment in inventories
- many suppliers competing annually for the same business
- acceptance of low delivery and quality performance.

Increasingly top executives are no longer convinced that traditional purchasing is bringing in the results required to survive. They recognise that too many dollars are being wasted both at suppliers and in their plants.

JIT PURCHASING

JIT purchasing is very different from traditional purchasing. It takes time to realise what can be achieved. Hardly anyone understands the full implications of introducing JIT on first acquaintance. This is because they are so used to traditional adversarial purchasing. JIT demands a rethink of principles and techniques. In direct contrast to traditional purchasing it is founded on:

- close cooperation supplier/customer based on cost (not price) analyses
- development of trust between supplier and customer
- short delivery times
- small quantities delivered frequently
- low investment in inventories
- simple administration systems
- few suppliers
- a continuing drive for high productivity, quality and delivery performance.

More and more companies are converting to the JIT approach and substantial savings are being achieved. What is of great importance is that it is also fun implementing.

WHY SHOULD WE CHANGE?

The dollars saved in purchasing make a direct contribution to profit. With JIT the cash saved indirectly can also be very substantial in other parts of a corporation. For example, dollars invested in administration, such as accounts, inspection and computing can be diverted into main stream activities such as R & D, production and sales.

Successful implementation is only achieved after detailed analysis of the current situation and of the potential for cost reduction.

Successful projects depend on the involvement of companies' best people united to meet the higher standards of performance set for the buyer's and vendor's companies.

All the companies described in this paper use JIT principles, but each application is tailored to the company's own circumstances.

Industry after industry has learned that to survive in manufacturing they have to become more flexible in production and cut costs.

The emphasis is moving away from systems and the processing of information and returning to making and selling.

Cost savings are being made in and thru design and production.

Computer and associated administrative systems

installed to reduce costs are often increasing
costs.

JIT vendors are an important part of the
fight for survival.

EXAMPLES

The following examples are taken from
different types of manufacture to prove that JIT
can be used in industries other than the
automotive. They show what can be done if
resources are allocated to this approach.

1. BEVERAGES

This is an industry where many "experts"
(systems and process) claim that JIT is not
appropriate.

During an especially hot summer, sales of well
known drinks increase significantly. The company
had to change the production plan based on sales
forecasts to one designed to meet actual customer
demand.

This might appear to be easy in the beverage
industry. But inadequate flexibility, long set
up times and long runs led to critical capacity
being used to produce goods which end up in
finished stock.

The problem is that the equipment was not
designed for fast change over from one beverage to
another. Quick product changes have not been seen
as an important feature of beverage production.
What is perceived as important are: production
per hour, losses within target, hitting the
financial budget and quality.

With the advent of the JIT approach, efforts
were concentrated on increasing flexibility by
reducing change over times and improving
relationships with suppliers to achieve faster
response times to the company's demands.

Prior to implementing JIT, purchasing was not
considered significant. Purchasing was a passive
order placing department. Management believed
that the buyers' annual quantities were too small
to persuade suppliers to reduce costs and deliver
frequently.

This is a common belief. Many buyers do not
believe that they have sufficient power to
influence their suppliers. But this is "three
quotation, adversarial thinking" and definitely
not JIT.

Starting with cans, market factors were
included in the JIT discussions. It was possible
to emphasise the strategic importance of the can
in the market for the can manufacturer. The
result of negotiations on this one 'A' item is an
annual overall profit increase of about 20%.

Label printing is another interesting
example. Technology in the printing industry is
moving in support of JIT. Printing machines are
being designed to facilitate change overs, to
produce smaller production batches and to reduce
inventories.

Here the buyer was purchasing large quantities
of packaging and labels to obtain price
reductions. In practice, these arrived too early
and in excess quantities. Inventories were too
high and labels became obsolete.

JIT for this company now means greater
flexibility in manufacturing and at suppliers and
increased profits. JIT is going to be applied
progressively to all aspects of this business.

2 ELECTRONICS

An essential aspect of JIT purchasing is the
generation of close cooperation between customer
engineers and supplier engineers. Using the
abilities of all concerned in design and
production of the product is a key part of the JIT
philosophy.

In this example, the supplier understood the
approach and joined in the spirit of cooperation
from the beginning. By using his special insider
know how he was able to change his production
process to come up with a <u>50% reduction in cost.</u>

This is a result which the customer would
never have considered on his own. The customer
might well have targeted for only 10% reduction.
In addition the customer could not have achieved
this reduction without the supplier's know how.

Typically one problem solved (one rock
removed) reveals another. The supplier had been
calculating his profit margin as a percentage of
his manufacturing cost. He now found that his
profit had halved along with the manufacturing
cost.

Also by changing the process he had reduced
the work load on his plant and created unexpected
spare capacity. (See Figure 2)

Everyone was concerned that the supplier, in
helping his customer, had harmed his own
business. Apparently he had paid for the benefit
to his customer by reduced profit and insufficient
work for his operators.

However, the supplier should welcome these
problems (rocks) and look upon the challenge in a
positive way.

Reduced costs mean that he is ahead of his
competitors in production techniques. Spare
capacity allows him to take more work from other
parts of the customer's group.

The real benefit of close supplier/customer
cooperation goes to the end customer. Both
supplier and customer have a better chance of
surviving if they work to a common objective.

JIT means using suppliers' special knowledge
to improve productivity and quality and to
reduce costs.

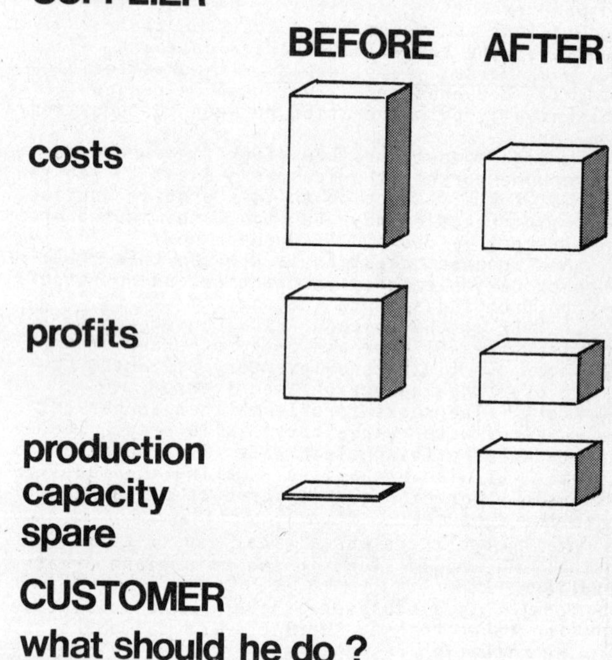

Figure 2

3 SPECIALIST MACHINE MANUFACTURER

In this engineering company a great deal of
basic analysis was carried out at the beginning of
the project to understand the pattern of
purchasing. JIT cannot be implemented on
guesswork and intuition.

This analysis included classifying suppliers
according to their strategic significance.

With over 4,000 suppliers and 60,000 purchase
orders each year it became obvious that profit
potential was being missed. Purchasing resources
were being dissipated across too many suppliers
and by too much administration.

The in depth analysis revealed a more serious
situation:

American Production & Inventory Control Society

- suppliers at risk, financially unsound and
  doubts about their survival
- products at risk, small number of companies
  able to manufacture special products
- a number of sole suppliers taking advantage
  of their unique position.

The buyers, who were trained in the
traditional, three annual quotations approach,
were in touch neither with the home market, nor
the international market, nor with their
suppliers.
They were not carrying out market, financial
and cost analyses all of which are key to the JIT
approach.
JIT requires very close cooperation between
customers and suppliers as in example 2. This
cooperation must go deep and include a joint
analysis of the suppliers' costs in order to
effect cost reduction, higher productivity and
improved quality.
In this case the traditional buyers resisted
the use of the JIT approach. They were very
surprised when their suppliers welcomed the new
approach.
Under JIT a professional supplier will
cooperate to produce the most effective product
for the end customer.
The manufacturer and supplier set ever higher
standards, but also ensure that the supplier
survives. JIT is to the advantage of end
customer, manufacturer and supplier.

4 FURNITURE

This concerns a furniture manufacturer
supplying direct to superstores. It is an example
of the initiative starting with the supplier.
The high cost of financing raw materials, work
in progress and finished goods at the suppliers
and finished goods at the superstores was the
starting point.
These inventories were taking up expensive
space, were being damaged in stores and in
transport and were becoming obsolete.
<u>Both manufacturer and superstores were
planning additional warehouses.</u>
This is one example, amongst many, of companies
who have cancelled/delayed the construction of new
warehouses because of JIT.
Production is built to a plan generated by the
superstores. The customers do not buy according
to this plan with the result that high stocks
exist in both manufacturer's and superstores'
warehouses.
This is a classical dilemma which often
attracts a mathematical/computer solution.
In this case, however, the project started in
the supplier's assembly areas with the objective
of increasing manufacturing flexibility and
reducing inventory costs.
Effort was concentrated on improving
production flow by changing layouts, reducing
change over times from one item of furniture to
another and reducing batch sizes.
As always <u>the workers on the lines</u> came up
with a number of excellent ideas with which to
smooth production flow, for example, removing
girders.
All of the components of JIT were used, in
particular, batch sizes were reduced from 10,000
to 2,500 and the layout improved. With flexible
female labor the number of dedicated assembly
lines were increased from 9 to 27. (See Figure 3)
Success in increasing flexibility in assembly
and reducing inventory levels raised two further
questions.
How early in the manufacturing process can the
smaller batches be identified?
Can the product be assembled and then loaded
directly on to waiting trucks for transport to the
superstores, thereby eliminating all finished
goods stocks?
These possibilities are under active
consideration.
The dollars saved in inventory can now be
reinvested in modern production capacity. The

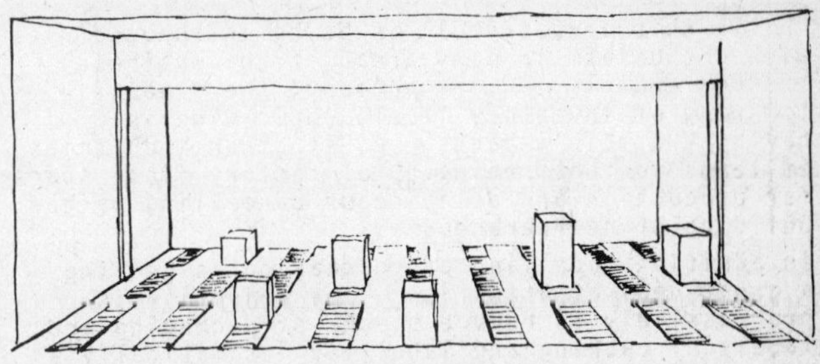

Figure 3

equipment suppliers are in for a shock. They are
now being asked to supply equipment suitable for
the JIT approach with:

- high speed changeover of tools
- low work in process levels
- in line monitoring of quality
- in line packaging and labelling

One of the many benefits of this type of
approach will be the elimination of the dinosaurs
- the fork lift trucks. There will be no need to
truck between processes, in and out of stores and
onto trucks.

5 ENGINEERING

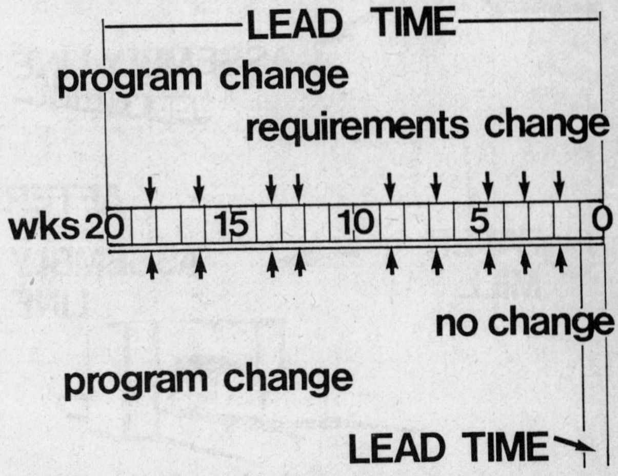

Figure 4

The reduction of lead times brings many direct

benefits. There are so many examples in practice
that it is difficult to select one for this paper.
     Part of the safety stock mentality, associated
with traditional purchasing, is the increase of
lead times in order to cover up for inefficient
suppliers.   The most extreme example encountered
in 1984 was a <u>20 week lead time for a 24 hour
service stockist.</u>
     The result of this "inflated lead time" is
that orders are placed too soon on the stockist.
Those orders then undergo numerous amendments
during the lead time. The buyers are puzzled by
the logic behind this, but somehow the practice
persists because the lead time is <u>trapped</u> in
the computer. Unnecessary costs are incurred
by both companies, although the users know
that the real lead time can be used in practice.
     What is so attractive about short lead times
is that they:

  - eliminate unnecessary ordering activity
  - reduce the need for forecasting (See
    Figure 4)

     Reduce lead times and other expensive problems
will reduce at the same time.

6   PHARMACEUTICALS

     In this industry JIT is being introduced
with enthusiasm in many areas of the business.
     For example, in one company, the gradual
lowering of inventory levels world wide is
having two main impacts. As in other industries
it leads to the freeing up of factory floor space
for production and delaying or cancelling of the
building of new warehouses.

In addition labelling and packaging is getting
a great deal of attention. The objective is
progressively to reduce stocks of packaging and
labels by packing and labelling automatically as
in line production operations.
     The impact on vendors is substantial, not the
least of which is the elimination of certain
processes. In addition batch quantities, lead
times and in process inventories are dramatically
reduced. (See Figures 5 and 6)

BEFORE

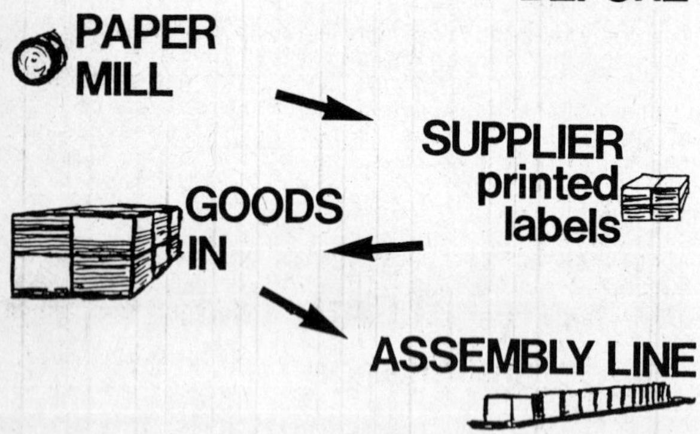

Figure 5

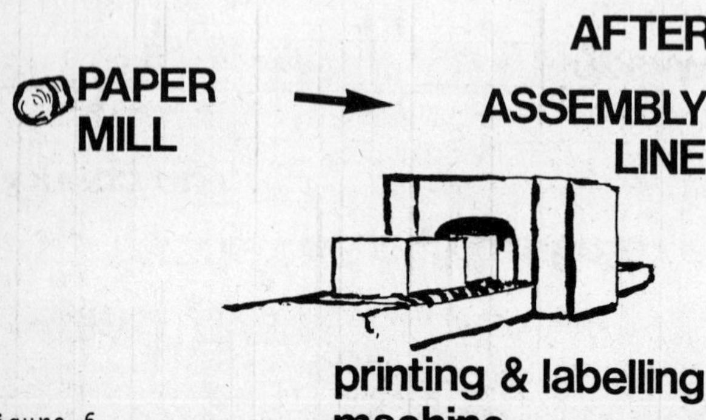

Figure 6

7   AUTOMOTIVE

     JIT vendors are expected to generate
improvements in quality and reduce costs thru
their own initiatives, and to cooperate with
the initiatives of their customers.
     New criteria are being set for suppliers.
Those who are unwilling or unable to meet the new
standards are eliminated. In the case of one
corporation it is expected that after three years
of the JIT approach very few of the current
European suppliers will survive. (See Figure 7)
     The criteria used to vet suppliers are:

  - financial stability
  - technical development, state of the art
    capability
  - management capability
  - growth potential
  - delivery on time plus flexibility
  - high quality
  - competitive costs

     To compete internationally manufacturers can
no longer afford the costs of inefficient
suppliers. Costs which originate with the
supplier enter the manufacturer's business and
multiply like mosquitoes on a pond. These costs
include safety stocks, administrative procedures,

Figure 7

8   TOILETRIES

"Make or buy" is always an important
consideration in manufacturing, but with JIT it
comes into sharper focus and attains a new
importance.
     This example concerns a manufacturer of
consumables with a distant supplier of plastic
parts in a foreign country.
     The "make or buy" investigation triggered by
JIT showed that total costs were higher with a
supplier than by manufacturing in house.
     Bringing the manufacturing in house had the
following beneficial results:

  - elimination of inventories at supplier <u>and</u>
    manufacturer
  - elimination of transport costs
  - elimination of <u>all</u> lead times
  - elimination of <u>supplier</u>'s overheads and
    profits
  - reduction of labour and material costs
  - enhanced quality
  - introduction of kamban on the assembly
    lines.
(See Figure 8)

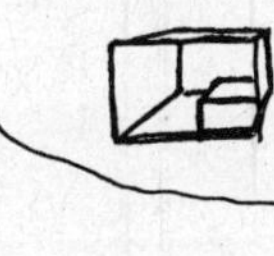

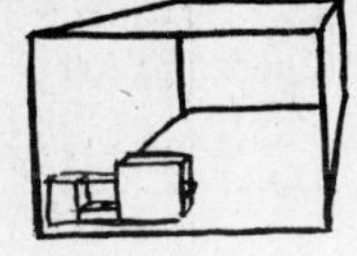

Figure 8

The President's comment:"This is what JIT did for us. We are excited by our success so far and we are carrying on."

CONCLUSIONS

The approach to JIT purchasing described above can be used in all manufacturing companies.

We know the principles work in practice, since many Western companies are using them with great success.

Each company situation is different and requires detailed analysis at the start, and a total management commitment to implementation.

As each improvement is realised other opportunities become apparent.

Cooperation gets results. The vendor has usually a great deal to contribute to his customer's business. The least we should do is to involve him.

Dollars released by this approach are now available for investment in R & D, production and sales.

This is one way to remain in manufacturing in the current competitive climate.

Team work is an essential ingredient at both the manufacturer's and at the supplier's plants. This includes design engineering, quality control, production/industrial engineering in addition to the buying function.

Just in time is just like making love - the more you do it the more you like it. And it is profitable.

Figure 9   "COME ON IN MEN. THEY ARE ONLY ROCKS.

........NOT SHARKS."

BIOGRAPHY

Brian O'Connor is Chief Executive of B. J. O'Connor International Ltd., a company which he founded in 1970. Its offices are in Weybridge, England and Frankfurt am Main, West Germany.

The company has two main functions: manufacturing consulting to multinational companies and training of top executives in manufacturing.

Current projects are in 10 countries and the O'Connor team consults in all the major European languages, such as French, German, Dutch and Italian.

Training workshops are organized in European capital cities on a bi-monthly basis on materials management subjects.

Brian studied at Sheffield and London Universities. In line management he held positions from foreman to managing director in manufacturing corporations.

As a public speaker he has lectured on materials management in Europe and the U.S.A..

Brian presents a paper to the APICS Las Vegas Conference today for the fourth time. Previous presentations have been in Hollywood, Florida, Los Angeles, California and Chicago, Illinois.

The case study material on which this paper is based comes from current multinational projects from Scandinavia to Switzerland.

The approach described in this paper and being implemented by O'Connor customers is revolutionizing their businesses.

The challenge is obvious. Success is based on the millions of dollars being saved....or rather the millions being reinvested in manufacturing's future....just in time?

VENDOR SUPPORT SYSTEMS—PARTNERS IN PROFIT

Thomas E. Arenberg
Arthur Andersen & Co.

OVERVIEW

The objective of this paper is to describe an approach to a new business environment between companies and their vendors. This new relationship does not rely on massive leverage due to the size of the buying company. Instead it builds a "parternship" based upon cooperative efforts to reduce the overall cost of doing business. This paper will discuss the history of the business problem, benefits, elements of the program and approach.

HISTORY

Western manufacturing companies that have reevaluated traditional purchasing methods and procedures have found these practices to be a basic source of productivity and cost issues. The traditional purchasing mission has focused on reducing purchase price through frequent issue of requests for quotation to the market. Although recognized as important, delivery schedule and quality performance have been minor factors in selecting suppliers in practice. It is also common to maintain multiple suppliers as protection against the possible disruption of business due to strike, fire or other "uncontrollable events."

Emphasis on price as a basis for supplier selection has resulted in short-term relationships with suppliers. Suppliers are geared to accept the possibility that the next order for any item may be placed with another company. The emphasis can drive suppliers to sacrifice quality and delivery for lower cost production and result in a void of cooperative productivity improvement efforts between customer and supplier.

Progressive companies are now implementing Supplier Support Programs based on radically new concepts of purchasing. The main thrust of these programs is to establish long-term relationships with fewer suppliers. The specific objectives of long-term supplier relationships are varied, but the basic principle is to establish a partnership in profitability. In this "win-win" partnership, both supplier and user expect to reap the rewards of increased sales of the end items through lower costs.

BENEFITS

In the new world of longer-term supplier relationships, attention is being shifted from just price to total cost. The customer company recognizes that it benefits from the profitability of each supplier. Therefore, the customer is now vitally interested in assisting and encouraging the supplier to reduce costs in order to maintain a satisfactory profit margin, superior levels of quality and delivery performance.

Changes which leading-edge companies are achieving include:

1. Drastic reduction of the number of vendors used by grouping like parts into packages based on like process or commodities.

2. Establishment of long-term contracts or business agreements. Instead of one-year blanket orders, contracts or agreements of up to five years will be common.

3. Increased responsibility at the source for:

   a. Quality at the zero-defect level

   b. Accurate container quantities

   c. Just-In-Time delivery

   d. Continuous improvement in operations and cost

Specific improvement goals are typically very aggressive.

o Supplier productivity/price improvements	30%
o Total inventory and lead time reduction	90%
o Quality _without_ inspection	100%
o Schedule performance	100%
o Packing/unpacking costs	90%
o Freight costs	90%
o Paperwork costs	90%
o Communication improvement	100%

Although many companies are now seeing the benefits of this type of approach, very few are able to understand how to implement this program. It is generally assumed that one needs significant leverage on all vendors in order to implement this program. Several companies, however, are tailoring the supplier partnership approach to their own business.

ELEMENTS OF PROGRAM

Long-term Vendor Support programs will be successful if they are based upon a very open relationship between the buyer and vendor. The buying company must lead the way in operating improvements by having _successful in-house productivity improvement programs_, including:

o Setup Reduction

o Quality Improvement

o Material Handling Productivity

o Storeroom Productivity

o Machine and Process Productivity

o Receiving and Inspection Productivity

Companies must use these in-house success stories to generate enthusiasm with vendors, as well as provide planning and implementation support. The buyers will have to be willing to invest resources in the improvement of their vendors.

The key elements of a vendor support program are:

o _Long-term Contract or Business Agreement_ - This contract or agreement describes the nature of the business arrangement and provides an overall perspective to the goals and objectives of the buyer and vendor. In addition, it describes the package of parts covered under the contract. Finally, the agreement must provide an open channel of communication to resolve all issues while continuing the shipment of high-quality parts.

o _Vendor Delivery Schedule_ - The vendor delivery schedule represents the shipments for all parts in a specific package from a vendor. This delivery schedule shows in daily or weekly detail requirements for parts in that package for the next month. By using the schedule, the purchase orders and change orders are eliminated. Schedules are being implemented manually and through enhancements to existing MRP II systems. The final enhancement for larger companies will be electronic data transfer with electronic fund transfers to close the loop. Schedules will significantly reduce the need for clerical support. Requirements extending out twelve months should also be shown to the vendor for planning purposes. The schedule design builds in ongoing performance measures of delivery timeliness and quality.

o <u>Statement of Objectives</u> - The final element of
the arrangement is a statement of objectives
for operating improvements for the customer and
vendor. This statement may be a specific
percentage of improvement or a general statement,
such as the plan to implement statistical process
control or start a setup reduction program.

PROGRAM OBJECTIVES

Specific objectives for companies involved in these
programs reach most areas of the company.

1. <u>Inspection Elimination</u> - Through process improvement, defects can and should be totally eliminated. As defects decrease, inspection
   requirements also decrease. This does not
   happen all at once and may never happen for
   all parts. The typical transition has been:

   a. Eliminate Incoming Inspection - Vendors
      and parts with a history of zero defects can
      go to source inspection only. On an audit
      basis, the process is reviewed by the
      buying company.

   b. Supplier Inspection Eliminated - Through
      process improvements such as setup reduc-
      tion and material handling simplification,
      the vendors can significantly reduce in-house
      inspection requirements. The objective is
      to have "self-monitoring" manufacturing
      processes.

2. <u>Packaging/Repackaging Improvements</u> - Current
   processing usually requires a significant
   amount of packaging at the vendor and unpack-
   aging at the consuming plant. This handling
   is not value added, and requires significant
   material handling equipment. A typical
   approach is to design a family of standard
   containers that:

   a. Eliminates packaging and repackaging

   b. Provides "free" piece counts

   c. Are delivered and stored in shop issue
      quantities

This packaging is usually shipped in the same bulk as
before, but with smaller containers within an inner
pack. The shipment frequency may remain the same, but
each shipment has a mix of parts that closely matches
the final assembly schedule.

APPROACH

The approach to implementing a Vendor Support program is the same as developing most manufacturing systems.
A thorough review of planning and design is required to
successfully complete the project. Specific products
include:

o A conceptual design of the purchasing strategies,
  objectives and goals. This includes an analysis
  of current and planned purchase volumes and of
  the current vendor base.

o Draft of the contract or agreement to be signed
  by each vendor.

o An implementation plan for approaching key vendors
  and signing agreements.

o Design and implementation of systems to group
  and manage packages or families of parts.

o A training program for all personnel involved
  in the material function of the revised operations.

o A "sales pitch" presentation to vendors, describing the new business relationship and the cost
  reduction programs.

A multi-function project team is required to
complete the typical project. In addition to purchasing
personnel, production planning and control, quality,
design engineering, manufacturing engineering, accounts
payable and the traffic department are involved in the
development process. In addition, several pilot
vendors are selected in order to preview the concepts
and presentation of the material. Vendors have been
very receptive to the cooperative message developed
by these programs.

SUMMARY

Companies attempting to undertake Just-In-Time manufacturing improvements can only obtain a small portion
of the benefits within their own plant. Companies will
have to reach out (not push out) to their vendors in
order to help in implementing operating improvements
throughout their entire supply chain.
There is no canned approach to implementing Vendor
Support programs, so companies must be very creative
to tailor the approach to their business. The key
elements will be in-house productivity success stories
and a commitment throughout the company to a new
operating environment with their vendors.

BIOGRAPHY

Tom Arenberg is a manager in the Management
Information Consulting Division of Arthur Andersen &
Co. - Milwaukee office. He has been the project manager
for Just-In-Time productivity projects for many manufacturers. He has spoken on Just-In-Time manufacturing
topics for APICS, SME, NAPM, NAA and the CPA organization.

"THE RETURN OF THE J. E. D. I."
JUST ENOUGH DESIRABLE INVENTORY
James M. Kozma, CPIM
Motorola, Inc.

Who discovered America? Most history books state
Christoper Columbus in 1492. However, it really appears
to be the Japanese during the 1950's. The Japanese
discovered quality improvement techniques through
Deming and Juran, manufacturing excellence and cycle
time reduction through Henry Ford, while the basic
principles of business management echo Peter Drucker.
These fundamental prescripts have always been buried
deep within a robust American economy. However, times,
economics and the competition have changed.

At Motorola our people have taken a contemporary
approach to these practical principles. Today I would
like to share some of those ideas. Ideas which are a
part of the "American Evolution" to Just-in-time
manufacturing.

THE IDEA?

The Ideal Manufacturing Operation would Operate
with Zero Inventory and Zero Lead times; It would make
products exactly when they're needed. But while the
ideal is not readily doable, anything moving you closer
to that goal is an improvement.

The reason I prefer to call this movement Just-
Enough-Desirable inventory reflects back on the above
statement. Too often people go back to our
manufacturing operations and say look at Toyota and
Kanban. That's where we want to be by the end of the
year. Kanban is really the result of twenty years of
work. (Besides simple accounting methodology - selling
the end product to distribution as soon as it goes out
the door helps your inventory turns look great too.)
Again, what's important is the philosophy - methodology
inventory is evil. It is best stated:
"Inventory is the Graveyard of"
Poor Planning
Poor Manufacturing
Poor Quality
Poor Training
Poor Design
Poor Equipment
Poor Organization
Poor Communications
Poor Staffing
Poor Transportation
Poor Facilities

LOWERING INVENTORIES IS A LONG TERM MANUFACTURING
STRATEGY

Key Elements to this strategy:

(Again Basic Business Principles)
    High Quality
        1.   Raw Materials
        2.   Finished Goods
    Reliable
        1.   Delivery of piece parts
        2.   Delivery of finished goods
    Maximum Asset Utilization
    (Lowest Possible Cycle Time)
        1.   Material
        2.   Labor
        3.   Equipment

THE PHILOSOPHY

Lowering Inventories must be the result of a problem
solving technique, to attack communication flows and
physical material flow. EXPOSE AND ELIMINATE THE ROCKS
IN THE RIVER!!

PREREQUSITES

    1.   CULTURE
         The Motorola culture encourages innovation and
         involvement at all levels -- this has been part
         of the company's philosophy from the begining.
         Quality, delivery and performance are the
         cornerstones to that culture and is emphasized
         by:

         A.   Upper Management Support
              "An Open Door Policy"
         B.   PMP - Participative Management Program
              1.   Regularly scheduled communication
                   meetings with all levels of
                   personnel
              2.   A formal suggestion system
              3.   An internal opportunity system
              4.   Incentive Program
         C.   Inventory Incentive Programs
    2.   ORGANIZATION STRUCTURE
         The organization environment must create a
         conducive organization environment and
         attitude. (The following are the organization
         strategy/structure guidelines established by
         our HFO group for their cycle time program in
         Phoenix.)
         A.   All specialized supporting resources
              structure their activities to enhance
              enhance production quality, delivery and
              cost performance.
         B.   The first and foremost priority should be
              maintain performance levels attained.
         C.   Once goals/objectives are established,
              every person has an opportunity to
              recommend "How to attaine the
              achievement?"
         D.   Hold monthly communications meetings.

MEASURE FOR TOTAL ASSET UTILZATION

Optimium Asset utilization and cycle time go hand in
hand so we should measure the total effectiveness of the
manufacturing organization. Too often the only
measurement for manufacturing is dollars out the door -
no matter what it costs. Key measures should be:
    1.   Cycle Times
    2.   COGS Turns
    3.   Scrap
    4.   Quality
    5.   Downtime
    6.   RONA
    7.   Delivery
    8.   Performance to schedule

TRAINING/EDUCATION NEEDS

To instill confidence in a program to lower
inventories, we should educate everyone to be better
business people.
    1.   Know the competition: Foreign and Domestic
         Make everyone aware.
    2.   Communicate the dollar impact of what's being
         accomplished.
    3.   Make everyone understand thinking differently/
         innovatively is good.
         A.   Visit other manufacturers
         B.   Dissiminate external publications
         C.   Develop a newsletter
         D.   Professional associations

CONTROLLING THE FACTORY

THE MASTER SCHEDULE

    1.   Establish time fence policies which are frozen
         as far out as possible.
    2.   Plan/Schedule in terms of days/hours, not
         weeks. Look at the following chart. 288
         days is more overwhelming than 1.25 or
         even 1.25 or even 41.4

INVENTORY TURNS AND TURNOVER

TURNS	DAYS	WEEKS
1.25	288	41.1
2.50	144	20.5
5.00	72	10.3
10.00	36	5.1
20.00	18	2.6
40.00	9	1.3

    3.   Flexibility in the production process (we
         use the family concept) structure similar
         items for easy cahngeover in the Bill of
         Material/Master Schedule plan unique parts
         separately.

<u>THE PROCESS</u>

1. <u>IMPROVING MANUFACTURING CYCLE TIME</u>

   A. Chose a less complex area/product first,
      with few parts. (We chose our printed
      circuit board operation as one of our key
      areas.)
   B. Review the production process from back to
      front.
         Map production aea observing ques and
         bottlenecks
   C. Slowly/simply lower the W.I.P.
      1. Schedule less
      2. Use plant shut-down
   D. Track your production capacity
      1. Use historical data-standard hours
         produced.
      2. Schedule/resolve bottleneck areas to
         reduce WIP/Cycle Time.

2. Balance your manufacturing resources so
   material flows
   A. Cross train workers
   B. Certify key operators
   C. Review physical line layout
   D. Attack all set-up times
   E. Review equipment, tool, housekeeping
      requirements
   F. Review preventative maintenance needs

<u>PULL VS PUSH   (THE EXECUTION OF THE PLAN)</u>

A pull system uncovers the bottleneck/production you
don't continue to feed material to the floor. There are
various methods to pull material through production.
   1. The Kanban Square is the ultimate pulling
      system.
   2. Tote bins can be the vocal point of pull.
   3. Daily Departmental Production Schedules pull
      material from department to department.
      A. Age the backlog - discover why items were
         not produced. Fix the problem.
      B. Look at items to see why they are normally
         produced smoothly on time versus other
         items
      C. Delta production scheduling - Link
         schedule inputs to outputs adjust the
         Master Schedule. Accordingly, you should
         never build W.I.P.
   4. Plan which parts and assemblies are to be put
      on Just-in-time using Paretos rule. Maybe you
      shouldn't be so concerned about nuts and bolts
      considering quality issues and dollar impact.

<u>THE PRODUCT</u>

   1. Production and materials personnel are involved
      in product design and ECN reviews.
   2. Structuring a product is a decision regarding
      inventory levels. A smooth straight structure
      will eliminate sub assembly levels.

<u>SOFTWARE</u>

Too often many of the large integrated software
packages can become a stumbling block to lowering
inventories. People have to make decisions. A complex
system may become too hard to understand and bury the
information which is necessary therefore:

   1. MRP - Simplify the System
      A. Keep Bill of Materials straight forward.
         Don't structure inventory into the
         product.
      B. Keep bells and whistles to a minimum.
      C. Keep reports to a minimum.
      D. Don't hard wire policy codes into the
         system.
         1. Safety Stocks
         2. Scrap factors
      E. Leadtimes/cycle times must be attacked and
         adjusted downward accordingly.
   2. Personal Computers - (Their time has come) for:
      A. Rough Cut Capacity Planning
      B. Mini MRP Explositions
      C. Business Simulation
      D. Inventory Tracking

<u>SCHEDULING THE OTHER FACTORY</u> - THE SUPPLIER

If your supplier is not benefiting from your
inventory reduction program, something is wrong. Key to
successful inventory management is knowing what you
have, what you want and when you need it? If you are
asking suppliers to give you more frequent delivery by
stocking material for you, then you haven't answered
those key questions.
However, the final step to including the supplier in
inventory management process can be done only by....

REDUCED COMMUNICATIONS CYCLE TIME

   1. Reduce communications cycle time
      A. Internal paperwork (acknowledgements,
         purchase orders, etc.)
      B. External paperwork (supplier delivery,
         acknowledgements, etc.)
      Example:
         The Z.I.P.S. Program (AIEG to SPS)
         1. On time delivery up 15%

         2. Inventory reduced from 5.6 to 2.6
            weeks
      Example:
         Motorola's Partnership for Growth Program
            Have regularly scheduled meetings
         with your suppliers to review the company
         goals and objectives, quality, broadening
         the communications they need.
         1. Develop multi year buys (Purchasing)
         2. On time delivery (P&IC)
         3. New product qualifications programs
            (Engineering)
         4. Quality statistical help (Quality
            Control)

SCHEDULING SHARING PLUS
(A program developed by our Joplin facility)
The objective is to identify similar items and help
the supplier better plan his own production. It's the
family concept revisited.
   1. Select a commodity with several similar custom
      or semicustom parts.
   2. Within the commodity or group, determine which
      finished goods are primarily different because
      of a supplier controlled process change not
      because of a dramatically different bill of
      materials.
   3. Prepare a spread sheet listing all the raw
      materials used and their total cost to build
      the quantity of finished parts on your annual
      forecast.
   4. Analyze the spread sheet to determine which
      B.O.M. items are common.
   5. Based on the cost of the items the buyer can
      calculate the related risks.
   6. Make firm commitments to vendors.

"The American Inventory Evolution"

Clearly we could spend hours touching on a number of
topics relative to the "Zero Inventory Strategy."
Marketing/sales, engineering, quality assurance, finance
-- every facet of the business entity contributes to
this entire process. The same is true of very key
issues such as set up time, housekeeping, standard
container sizes, forecasting and a whole gammit of other
issues.
Most significant are the common threads which link
the "Zero Inventory Strategy."
   1. Each and every individual knowing their
      responsibilities (job).
   2. The discipline required in executing those
      responsibilities.
   3. Teamwork
As we come to grips with this strategy it becomes
clear that "Zero Inventory" and the fundamental
principles it entitles were always a part of American
culture.
For American industry, the 1980's will really mark
the return of the J.E.D.I.: Just Enough Desirable
Inventory.

BIOGRAPHY

Jim Kozma is Senior Administrator of Corporate Materials Management for Motorola, Inc. in Schaumburg, Illinois. At the age of 32, Jim has already acquired over 14 years of operations experience in manufacturing, P&IC Management and Purchasing with both Motorola and Universal Oil Products.

He has a BBA and MBA degree from Loyola University of Chicago, and is a CPIM.

COMPETING AT HOME OR ABROAD
Peter L. Grieco, Jr.
Professionals For Technology Associates, Inc.

Manufacturing companies in the United States have during the last ten years grown stagnant in the quest for productivity. U.S. manufacturers in recent years have started to talk about Productivity, Zero Inventory, Just-In-Time and the Total Quality Control approach. As Richard J. Schonberger states in his book, "The truth is that the west has hardly begun to understand Japanese success factors and much of what is professed in current readings consists of half-truths and misconceptions that stand in the way of rapid progress in catching up with the Japanese."

This paper deals with how Apple Computer, Inc. successfully completed in Fremont, California a highly automated manufacturing facility to build its new product the "MACINTOSH" utilizing the latest techniques in producing this third generation computer every 27 seconds. Apple thought the use of automation, inventory management, repetitive manufacturing, and a total partnership relationship with our vendors that a quality product can be built in the United States and be competitive with the Japanese. We studied the truths and concepts used by both United States and world manufacturers in the design of the plant and systems required.

The major message is simplicity, we started with elaborate plans with a high degree of complexity, and kept adjusting our plan for the simplistic approach. We spent considerable time with all our personnel explaining that Just-In-Time (JIT) and Total Quality Control (TQC) are the way of life at our company. Success can only be achieved by management support and guidance. Most of all a vision with product strategy for the future is a must.

CULTURAL

Apple realized that to be successful in this venture a spirit of cooperation, loyality and people willing to enjoy working together for a cause was important. Like our Japanese counterparts we needed to start a family with our people and bring the vendor base beyond the partnership and part of our family. The Japanese companies are noted for taking care of their people with money, subsidy programs, the management at Apple realized we too must take care of people with creative packages, paying employees when TQC or JIT dictates stopping the production line and living up to being one of the best 100 companies in America. All employees feel pride and making a effort can result in high incentives.

The success of JIT at Apple is due to more than just having the right product at the right time. It is also the result of the homespun, entrepreneurial culture. Thomas J. Peters co-author of the best-selling book In Search of Excellence, states "their is no corporation in the world like Apple Computer."

JUST-IN-TIME PURCHASING

The Purchasing groups responsibility is to continually assess the competitive world procurement environment. It should calibrate the effectiveness of the function, as it interfaces with engineering to define cost effective materials, manage the purchasing cycle and vendor relationship. In addition the group has the overall task to reduce cost and improve the cycle-time of the procurement process.

Purchasing is now required to utilize new techniques such as ship to Work-In-Process rather than stock, paperless purchasing, supplier support and innovation and overall sourcing strategy. The vendor base management role has now taken a leap into the 20th century with techniques such as :

> Partnership Approach (Family)
> Single Sourcing
> Purchase Agreements
> Negotiation
> Vendor Selection Process
> Quality Suppliers
> Fewer Quantity of Suppliers

Most reactions from U.S. purchasing people is that it can only work in Japan, it won't work here. Let me state it does work here, I haven't yet met a supplier who wants to miss delivery dates and ship nonconforming product. The

suppliers are anxious to learn new ideas and techniques to help their business grow. Much to the surprise of people in the U.S. a vendor overseas can meet plus/minus one day delivery in the U.S. as if he was located ten miles away, it requires planning.

Purchasing can help the overall profit picture of the division with low inventory-carrying cost, lower scrap with defects deteched early, lower cost because of learning curves over longer periods of the commitment. Engineering also benefits from fast response to changes, design innovation, and a working hands-on relationship with the supplier. In addition, their are many administrative efficiencies that can be gained:

> Fewer number of Suppliers
> Fewer Quotations
> Minimal Negotiations
> Less Paper Flow
> Standard Containers
> Container Labeling

As a purchasing agent role continues to change, the management must accept the fact of more supplier visits. Management also must be involved with the supplier discussions to exhibit a commitment for the process and the product.

CHANGE, CHALLENGE, OPPORTUNITY

Improving Performance

Todays Materials Manager can apply some of KANBAN better known as Just-In-Time manufacturing control system for the immediate time. Kanban benefits might seem impossible today, but we must start working in that direction. Some of the savings with excellent purchasing involvement that can be obtained:
1. Reduced quality rejects
2. Inventory turnover of 40-60 compared to an average of 6-12 with U.S. competitors.
3. Lower space requirement, thanks to fewer quality rejects and less inventory.
4. High machine uptime rate.
5. A 50-70% higher direct labor productivity showing, resulting from reduced quality rejections, machine downtime, and setup time.
6. A simpler system, with a lot less paperwork

The underlying objectives of "Just-In-Time" is to process with customers and vendors. The idea is to receive material when needed without stocking inventory, expediting or worrying about the quality level. If the materials professional understands the principal of Kanban, and only then, can we start to achieve major savings.

In todays environment the procurement function role must change to provide the material process a competitive edge to compete in the business environment daily with the use of computers. The changing role for these opportunities include:
1. Cost/Quality of the Material
2. Supplier support and innovation
3. The massive paperwork exchange
4. Cycle-time of the procurement process
5. Standardization of purchased material
6. Required inventory levels
7. Vendor selection process
8. Acquisition of material
9. Inspection process

TOTAL QUALITY CONTROL

The Quality Assurance organization should work with purchasing to develop the group of closely-coupled suppliers to provide excellent quality and to minimize the cost of activities required to assure incoming quality. These activities include quality measurement, problem solving, suppliers quality improvement assistance, and suppliers surveys, qualification and certifications.

Quality is the most significant area of improvement in the U.S. that must be addressed in the 80's to compete with the world market. The quality and reliability assurance techniques companies should place emphasis on at present are as follows:
- Emphasis is on prevention throughout the manufacturing cycle, including product design and testing, from procurement to final package.
- No requirements are placed on vendors than those placed on yourself.

- Vendors are encouraged to suggest methods that
  improve piece part quality.
- Establish with all vendors that the only
  acceptable quality goal is zero defects.
- Vendor Quality Engineers (VQE) and Purchasing
  implement joint vendor qualifications.
- Ship to stock program vs. ship to work-in-process.

Each vendor should be told where they rank in your
Quality program. I have illustrated the formula's for
rating vendors.

Vendor Rating

1. Vendor Quality Rating (VQR) is determined in
   incoming inspection.

$$VQR = \frac{LOTS\ ACCEPTED}{LOTS\ INSPECTED} \times \frac{SAMPLES\ ACCEPTED}{SAMPLES\ INSPECTED} \times 100$$

2. Incoming parts per million (IPPM) is an index
   also determined in incoming inspection.

$$IPPM = \frac{DEFECTIVE\ SAMPLES}{SAMPLES\ INSPECTED} \times 1,000,000$$

3. Manufacturing parts per million (MPPM) is
   reported by each manufacturing area.

$$MPPM = \frac{DEFECTIVE\ PARTS}{PARTS\ USED} \times 1,000,000$$

Companies with sound quality programs can obtain
excellent results without any cost. As Phil Crosby states
in his book "Quality is Free", effort is required on an
understanding of what the quality requirements are.

With the Total Quality Control approach and coupled
with JIT an environment with a balance of technical skills
and a attitudinal atmosphere to foster improvements is
required. The goals should be short term and an integral
part of the process. These goals should be armed at making
measureable progress toward conformance to requirements.
The business relationship must be based on clear commitments
to measure programs to obtain zero defects in quality and
delivery.

The development of the quality process to certify
process or ship-to-WIP is a five stage function.

    I.   Comprehension and Commitment
   II.   Competence
  III.   Communication
   IV.   Correction
    V.   Continuance

During stage one we must create awareness and enlight-
ment for the Quality improvement process. This function
causes a recognition for need and a commitment to a total
program. During this stage we also generated a framework
to develop a plan and a organization strategic statement.

Stage two is the planning and development process.
   Establish Goals
   Generate Improvement Measurement
   Training in the Quality Tools
   Establishing Process Review Requirements

The third stage is the process that requires the
longest time element. This step is called the communication
phase and will continue on over the future. During this
time an explanation of process to all levels of the
organization occurs, we have to initiate training and begin
the measurement task.

Stage four is the correction process, it consists of
checks and reviews with progress reporting, determining if
any changes are required and checking the measurements for
validity are part of this phase.

Step five is the continuance process which evaluate
results and improve process or can be stated DO IT OVER
AGAIN.

This five step process is part of the new quality
wisdom:
   Quality Measurement vs. Hoping it will happen
   Prevention vs. Appraisal
   Process Understanding vs. Product Inspection

The definition of cost of quality vQ played a major role
in our process, realizing it may never go to zero was an
important step. The defining of the cost should be used
as a benchmark to measure operation improvements and set

goals to be accomplished with time both in-house and at the
suppliers plants. The three costs most commonly associated
with Quality are Prevention, Appraisal and Failure.

Prevention Cost

The cost of all activities undertaken to prevent
defects in design, development of processes, purchasing,
labor and other aspects of beginning and creating a product
or service.

Appraisal Cost

Costs incurred while conducting inspections, tests
and other planned evaluations used to determine whether
produced hardware, software or services conform to their
requirements.

Failure Cost

Associated costs of products of services that have
been found not to conform or perform to the requirements,
as well as the evaluation, disposition and consumer affairs
related aspects of such failures.

Examples of Cost of Quality are illustrated below:

PREVENTION:

-DESIGN REVIEWS	-OPERATIONAL TRAINING
-PRODUCT QUALIFICATION TESTING	-QUALITY ORIENTATION
-PARTS QUALIFICATION	-ACCEPTANCE PLANNING
-SUPPLIER QUALIFICATION	-ZERO-DEFECTS PROGRAMS
-SUPPLIER QUALITY SEMINARS	-STATISTICAL CONTROL TRAINING
-SPECIFICATION REVIEWS	-QUALITY AUDITS
-PROCESS CONTROL STUDIES	-DRAWING CHECK AND REVIEW
-TOOL CONTROL	-PREVENTATIVE MAINTAINANCE
-ENG'G QUALITY TRAINING	-AUTOMATION

APPRAISAL COSTS

-PROTOTYE INSPECTION	-INCOMING INSPECTION AND TEST
-PRODUCT ACCEPTANCE TESTING	-PROCESS CONTROL ACCEPTANCE TESTS
-SUPPLIER QUALIFICATION	-PACKAGING INSPECTION
-PRODUCT INSPECTION	-INVENTORY AUDIT
-MARKETING SERVICE SURVEY	-MATERIALS REVIEW BOARD
-PRODUCTION SPECIFICATION CONFORMANCE TESTING	

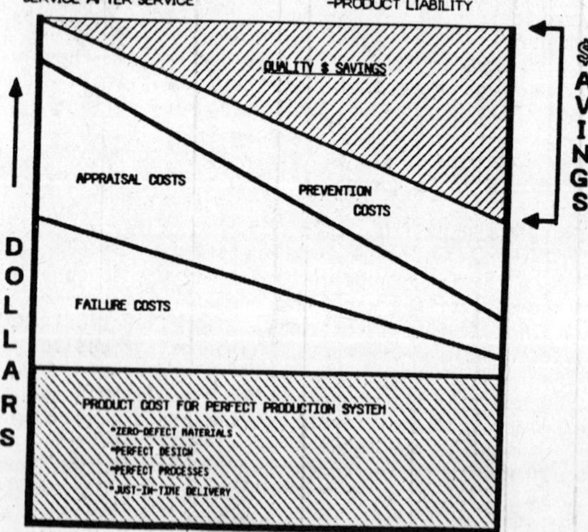

THE MANUFACTURING PROCESS

A key feature of the new factory is the material flow.
The factory has embraced a just-in-time management
philosophy. Components are received daily, with no more
than a ten day Work-In-Process or wall to wall inventory
level, so just enough components are on hand to produce
the daily schedule. In this manner we reduce inventory,
scrap and obsolescence cost.

The majority of our components are qualified prior
to entering the manufacturing process at the suppliers

plants. Our vendors have committed to supply Apple with
100 percent defect-free parts. All vendors are not
shipping zero defect parts today, however the management
commitment is in place. Components are single sourced
where applicable, and when needed second sources are
utilized. Our plan is that a prime supplier on one
component may be the second source on a different
component.

As each component is detrashed and placed into the
handling systems, its identification is entered into the
factory's control computer.

We have categorized MacIntosh into two bulk parts
(A parts) and small parts (C parts). Bulk parts include
video displays, chassis, housings and power supplies.
Small parts are the integrated circuits and discrete
components, like memory devices, microprocessors, capacitors
and resistors. Bar coding is used to simplify part
identification and inventory management controls.

Material arrives and is immediately distributed to the
proper locations at the factory not a typical warehouse.
Large parts are carried by an overhead parts delivery
system to the appropriate work station. Small parts are
handled by an automated storage and retrieval system that
delivers them to the correct stations at the sequencing
and automated component-insertion areas.

Small parts are stored in the factory's two Litton
totestacker automated storage and retrieval systems.
These parts are retrieved from the totestackers by a
computer-controlled crane and sent to each work station in
totes via a conveyer network as employees create a demand.
The system automatically recognizes the empty totes,
retrieves them and sends full totes to the work stations.

Many components and subassemblies are also brought
to work stations by automated guided vehicles. These
battery-powered robots crisscross the factory following
wires embedded in the floor. A worker requests materials
from an automated guided vehicle via a terminal at the
work station. The units are controlled by a microprocessor
based traffic manager.

PRODUCTION DETAILS

Fewer than 300 people are needed to run the factory.
About 170 manufacturing people and about 100 more in
engineering and administrative roles make up the factory
personnel.

Apple will continue to introduce robotics and surface-
mounted device technology into printed-circuit board, final
assembly and packaging areas in the near future. By
constructing the manufacturing plant, Apple management has
reconfirmed its commitment to quality volume manufacturing
utilizing the latest state-of-the-art techniques available.
The production methods used at the factory make it possibly
the most advanced production facility in the world.

SUMMARY

An inventory system based on just-in-time delivery
depends on conditions that seem to make it very different
to implement in the United States. It requires reliable
information about delivery, which implies consistent
behavior on the part of suppliers. Next it requires
superb quality control from suppliers because the quantity
of parts ordered makes no allowance for bad material. With
all said, "IT WORKS". Materials is a place for opportunity,
however, this opportunity cannot be had without change to
accept the challenge. The future is ours.

REFERENCES

Katz, Moskowitz, Levering, The 100 Best Companies To Work
For In America, Addison-Wesly Publishing Company, Reading
Massachusetts 1984

Hall, Robert, Zero Inventories, Dow Jones-Irwin Homewood,
Illinois 1983

Schonberger, Richard, Japanese Manufacturing Techniques,
The Free Press, New York 1982

Grieco, Peter L., A Future Challenge and Opportunity For
Materials Management, CAPICS 22nd Annual Seminar Proceedings
1984

Management Analysis Center, Inc., How Successful Technology
Based Companies Make Purchasing Work 1984

ABOUT THE AUTHOR

Peter L. Grieco is currently Director of Materials
with Applie Computer, MacIntosh Division, Fremont, CA. He
has more than 20 years experience in the industry. Mr.
Grieco has held positions as Senior Management Consultant,
Materials Manager, Production and Inventory Control Manager,
and Financial positions. He has been most recently
associated with Texas Instruments, Digital Equipment Corporation, Coopers & Lybrand and various high-tech companies
during his career.

Mr. Grieco holds a degree from Central Connecticut
State College and a certificate in Accounting from Moody's
School of Commerce. He has served on the APICS Education
and Research Foundation as a Director, National Secretary-
Treasurer, Vice President of Region I, and Past President
of the Hartford Chapter (of the American Production and
Inventory Control Society). He has taught Material
Management courses at Post College, Waterbury, Connecticut,
and has served on the staff of Wayland Baptist University,
Lubbock, Texas. He has lectured for APICS Chapters,
Seminars and spoken at numerous Nation APICS conferences.

ZERO INVENTORY: SECRETS TO SUCCESS IN A START-UP COMPANY

Rufus Crow
Data Management Labs, Inc.

CASH ! CASH ! CASH !

The three most important words in Real Estate are location, location, location. The same three for a start-up company are cash, cash, cash. What differentiates an Apple from an Osborn? Could one answer be that while Osborn people were spending millions in cash for inventory in Hayward, fifteen miles down wonderful Highway 17, the Apple people were planning and building their new just-in-time Macintosh plant in Fremont?

STARTING UP !

Start-up companies are created by people with a new product or service they think will sell. The principals, friends, relatives, venture capitalists and other companies provide funds to get this new company started. From this point on, survival becomes important. Usually, (not always), the reason for failure is financial. Sometimes it is the product, service, market, management or the economy, but usually, with more money, the problems could have been solved. Cash flow is the operative word. Start-up companies have limited cash available. The investors want a return on their investment in a reasonable period of time. Now the new company has to design, build and market the products. This uses up the cash available. Now the new company must sell the products with some profit margin in enough volume to stop cash going out, or face serious problems by using up all the cash they started with. Osborn Computer was clearly a success until sales dropped and there was no cash to help because it had been spent on inventory.

ZERO INVENTORIES

Zero Inventories, A Great American Working Reference, by Robert W. Hall is published by Dow Jones Irwin and sold by APICS chapters everywhere. Mr. Hall gives us his view of the ideal manufacturing system on page two of his book. This system would:

1. Produce products the customers want.
2. Produce products only at the rate customers want them.
3. Produce with perfect quality.
4. Produce instantly--zero unnecessary lead time.
5. Produce with no waste of labor, material, or equipment--every move with a purpose so there is zero idle inventory.
6. Produce by methods which allow for the development of people.

This system has to be the goal of a successful start-up company. It takes close teamwork between Manufacturing, Engineering and Marketing. Obviously, no company will achieve Mr. Hall's goals in todays' world. But what if a company achieves some success? For every product not built that would have ended up obsolete or extra, the company has more cash to spend on other things. For every product built with perfect quality, cash is wasted on scrap. For every day of lead time reduced in the factory, a potential exists to reduce the amount of cash spent on inventory.

O.K., you have convinced me that Zero Inventory is a goal to work towards in an overall way. What specific things can one do in a small company to achieve Zero Inventories?

PLANNING !

Frank Gue, a great Canadian author, said in one of his books that manufacturing consists of two things that happen over and over;

"Plan the work",
"Work the plan"

In small companies, we start with a plan. We review it together and get agreement. Then we start "working the plan". In the first phase, we purchase only enough inventory to build and maintain the prototypes. The preliminary bill of material must be studied for the long lead items that require action to meet the plan.

At DML, we used an Apple II E and a spreadsheet program to develop our original bills of material, inventory listing and production schedule. By varying cost, lead times and schedules, we were able to predict cash flow for inventories. In September 1983, we decided to continue making our first product as customer demand indicated and to concentrate on new products for a word processing division of a major company and for the Digital Equipment Corporation, (DEC), Unibus market place.

RESOURCES AVAILABLE

The spreadsheet programs were not adequate. The manufacturing group consisted of six technicians, one combination rework, shipping, receiving and stockroom person, one combination planner, expeditor, buyer person, and one combination senior planner, master scheduler, industrial engineer, test engineer, production supervisor, quality engineer, and many other job titled persons. That small group of nine people had to do all the jobs. The new products had over one hundred part numbers in each and had aggressive schedules. It was obviously time for an improvement. One more title was added and that was MRP software/hardware selection and implementation person. The APICS magazine, P & M Review, proved to be a very valuable resource. We talked to three companies that had inexpensive, (under $30,000.00), hardware/software solutions. All three had systems in local Silicon Valley companies. The user reactions were solicited. Published articles by APICS members proved very helpful in evaluating the features of each system. One vendor even left his portable Kaypro Computer with his MRP package for us to try out over a weekend ! We didn't buy Dave Brodies' package, but it was an outstanding sales effort !

WORKING !

In August 1983, we purchased the entire MRP package from Micro-MRP Inc., 1065 East Hillsdale Blvd., Foster City, California. They are located about twenty miles from DML. Micro-MRP Inc. has a MRP package called MAX which runs on an IBM PC. The first week we entered our six hundred part masters, their cost each, their location, and quantity on hand. The second week, we entered the bills of material and the open purchase orders. The lead times, vendors, and other key information was entered. In total, about thirty hours were spent over a two week period by two people entering data, running reports, verifying data, rerunning reports, reverifying data, etc. The third week, we entered the latest master schedule and ran the MRP program.

Using the MRP printout, the bills of material and the current inventory, we looked at everyone of the over two hundred active parts and decided on a course of action for purchasing. We created a Lotus Spreadsheet Program to check the Micro-MRP calculations. The only discrepencies we found were the ones we created during the data entry phase. We did discover software problems using MAX, but Micro-MRP solved most of them in a day or two. We had no hardware or software problems that caused any major problems

DISASTER !

After this success, we placed our purchase orders with vendors that would deliver parts on our weekly or biweekly schedule. These were entered in the MAX program and the cash requirements report was run. This told us when we would begin spending the cash we had on hand. Based on this information, we should have renegotiated the deliveries of some of the expensive parts but we did not. Six weeks later, when our major customer cancelled our order and shut down the Word Processing Division, we were left holding too much inventory.

A major cancellation is not something Robert Hall talks about in his book, <u>Zero Inventories</u>. In fact, few speakers or writers ever mention it, but those of us who have gone through it will not forget that painful experience. First, we cancelled all of our purchase orders. Unfortunately, we had too much of the highest cost parts. They are usually the most difficult to get delivery on and one is always tempted to overstock the hard-to-get parts. We used our IBM PC and the Lotus Spreadsheet to create a list of the excess inventories. We also used our word processing package on the IBM PC to create letters attempting to sell off our excess inventory. Isn't it amazing how those parts that you paid three times over list price for suddenly drop in value just as you try to sell them, instead of buying them?

Our other new product, the DML 750 Controller, which runs on DEC Computers, saved us from disaster. The DML 750 uses some of the same parts as our cancelled product. As the DML 750 Controller is gaining favor with DEC users, it is providing the vital cash flow to DML.

Control of DML's inventory was further improved in January 1984 with the acquisition of Micro-MRP's latest release which allows us to dump the data base from our MRP package to DBase II and then on to our Lotus Spreadsheet. This makes special reports like unit cost, "A" item inventory lists, excess inventory on hand and many others very easy to prepare. This helps make a small software package on a PC act like a big package on a minicomputer.

SECRETS

Really, there are no secrets to success in a start-up company that you and I have not read or heard about. The basic principles taught in APICS and Industrial Engineering seminars and classes today are "secrets" to success. Inventories must be matched as closely to actual production and shipping requirements as possible. The potential for obsolesence is higher during the early life of a product. The need for record accuracy in your stockroom, in the bills of material, in the purchase orders, in the shipping and receiving area is vital in a new company. We ended up with a lifetime supply of a certain capacitor because of record inaccuracies. Quality must be important from the first day. The elimination of waste and improvement in product reliability pays more dividends than probably any other single item in helping a new company become successful today. Some companies have estimated that 20% of their product cost could be eliminated if the products were made correctly the first time. A new company is the right place to start implementing ways of reducing the time required to build a product. Things like reducing set-up times, outstanding housekeeping, good manufacturing layouts, a comprehensive maintenance plan and many others help reduce the work-in-process inventory. Perhaps we do not have suppliers in America that will bring parts just-in-time each day, but we can begin strengthening our relationships with our vendors and work towards that goal.

Production and Inventory Control people belong in start-up companies. Knowledgeable P & IC people can help these new companies conserve CASH ! And what is more important, you can help them be SUCCESSFUL.

CREATIVITY AND INNOVATION: THE KEY TO JUST-IN-TIME

Scott A. Levin, CPIM
Arthur Andersen & Co.

THE KEY

A paradigm shift in thinking must take place in the minds of manufacturing managers if they expect to execute Just-in-Time (J.I.T.) manufacturing programs in their plants. By successfully executing J.I.T. programs, manufacturing managers will benefit by achieving increased productivity and profits for their companies. The paradigm shift is the key to unlocking the potential benefits which will be achieved through a J.I.T. program.

This paper will discuss what a paradigm shift is and how to use the creative thinking process to generate ideas in order to achieve a successful J.I.T. manufacturing plant. This paper also will discuss innovation which means the ability to execute these ideas in order to receive the benefits acclaimed by the advocates of J.I.T. manufacturing.

PARADIGM SHIFT

A paradigm is a framework of thought or a model for understanding or explaining certain aspects of reality. A paradigm shift is a distinctly new way of looking at an old problem. This paradigm shift occurs when a new perspective is obtained on an old problem and a new image is immediately visible and clearly in focus. The example in Figure 1 is a classic illustration of a paradigm shift. Looking at this figure from one perspective, you will see an old woman, and if you look at the same picture from a different perspective, you will see a beautiful young woman. If we apply this type of thinking to the manufacturing environment and compare the traditional methods of manufacturing to the new Just-in-Time methods, we begin to make a paradigm shift in thinking.

A NEW PERSPECTIVE ON MANUFACTURING

We must begin looking at manufacturing plants with a new pair of eyes. The traditional perspective on manufacturing is that we must have:

o Just-in-case inventory: 90-120 days.
o Excessive material handling.
o Long manufacturing runs to recover high setup costs.
o Specialty departments performing one manufacturing operation in order to optimize productivity and facilitate scheduling.
o Incoming inspection to check on vendors.
o Three competitive bids from vendors to ensure the lowest cost.

If we make a paradigm shift in thinking and visualize a new Just-in-Time manufacturing plant, we see a plant with the following characteristics:

o One or two days' inventory
o Setup time of no more than 10 minutes
o Short, flexible run sizes
o Supplier partners - sole source vendors
o Focused plant layouts
o Machines grouped sequentially to produce a completed product
o Zero defect programs

Once we understand and visualize how a new J.I.T. manufacturing plant looks, the error of the traditional view of manufacturing is clearly seen. The benefits of a J.I.T. manufacturing plant can only be achieved if manufacturing people really understand the basic concepts behind Just-in-Time manufacturing.

OBJECTIVES OF J.I.T.

According to Bob Hall in his book, Zero Inventories, the goals of stockless production or J.I.T. manufacturing are:

o Produce products that the customer wants.
o Produce products only at the rate the customer wants them.
o Produce products with perfect quality.
o Produce instantly - zero unnecessary lead time.
o Produce with no waste:
   - Labor   - Equipment
   - Material   - Movement
   - Inventory - Space
o Produce products by methods which allow the development of people.

BENEFITS OF J.I.T.

The benefits which have been achieved by the excellent companies which have installed J.I.T. manufacturing programs are:
  o Direct labor productivity increased 25 percent.
  o Manufacturing leadtime reduced 95 percent.
  o Manufacturing space reduced 60 percent.
  o Setup time reduced 80 percent.
  o Scrap and rework (quality) reduced 80 percent.

These benefits can only be achieved if J.I.T. techniques are really understood and if the creative thinking process is applied to solving the traditional manufacturing problems.

CREATIVITY

Once the paradigm shift in thinking has taken place, the process by which managers generate J.I.T. ideas needs to be defined. This process is the creative thinking process. The remainder of this paper will define and describe:

o Creativity.
o Objectives of creative thinking.
o Elements of creative thinking.
o Right-brain thinking.
o The creative thinking process.

Creativity has been defined in different ways such as:

o A new product.
o A new way of looking at something.
o A new way of doing something.

Words which have been used to describe creativity include such words as:

o Imagination.
o Innovation.
o Inspiration.
o Inventiveness.
o Resourcefulness.

The increasing pressure for improved productivity and profitability in organizations has increased the importance of creative solutions to complex problems. A simple working definition used by Mike Vance is that "Creativity is the making of the new and the rearranging of the old in a new way." This definition clearly indicates that not only do we have to come up with new technologies for manufacturing products, but we must improve on the traditional methods of manufacturing by using old methods and principles and applying them in a new way to the existing manufacturing process to improve productivity.

CREATIVE THINKING OBJECTIVES

In order to understand creativity, we must understand the objectives of creative thinking. There are four objectives to creative thinking, and they are:

o The unique factor.
o Show others.
o Romance the idea.
o Plussing.

The most important objective in creative thinking
is to identify the unique factor. The unique factor is
focusing on achieving a unique product or process. In
marketing, this is called the Unique Selling Proposition. The unique selling feature from a marketing perspective might be to develop a new product that will allow you to capture 100 percent of a certain market because no one else has the product. In manufacturing, it
may be a unique process that allows the company to reduce the product cost by 50 percent and therefore compete more effectively with others in the market.

The second objective in creative thinking is to
show others what you have done. By showing others what
has been accomplished, you are able to transfer this
knowledge from one department or plant to another area.
This is how the U.S. manufacturing companies began to
understand the fundamental principles involved in J.I.T.
manufacturing. Executives from U.S. companies visited
Japan and toured Japanese plants to see how they were
manufacturing products with 2-3 days of inventory, 60-70
percent less space, equipment setups of 10 minutes and
small, mixed-model manufacturing runs.

The third objective of creative thinking is to romance the idea. Romancing the idea comes from taking an
old idea, like the time and motion studies, and applying
it to current manufacturing practices in order to improve them. An example of this might be applying time
and motion studies to minimize worker fatigue with a
new, focused assembly-line layout.

The final objective in creative thinking is to keep
plussing the idea, keep improving it through increased
application. For example, if you were working on setup
reduction and the initial reduction took the equipment
setup from six hours to three hours, you would keep
plussing the idea by coming back a few weeks or months
later and reducing the setup from three hours to one
hour and then from one hour to 10 minutes.

ELEMENTS OF CREATIVE THINKING

The first challenge in creative thinking is to generate new ideas. The essential ingredient to generating
new ideas is to have people who think creatively. The
key to developing creative thinking within individuals
in an organization is to increase their perspectives.
Much of creative thinking is figuring out how to gain a
new perspective on an old problem in order to create
something new. There are eight essential elements to
achieving this new perspective. They are as follows:

o The arc concept
o Education
o History
o Insight + outsight = farsightedness
o Neoteny
o Zeroing in
o Ephemeralization
o Five-sensing

The arc concept is illustrated in Figure 2. If we
draw an arc and look at it from Point A, the arc looks
concave; but if you look at the arc from Point B, it
looks convex. The arc has not changed; the only thing
that has changed is the perspective from which you view
the arc.

Figure 2

MANUFACTURING

We have always viewed manufacturing in the traditional way. That is, productivity is achieved by maximizing production runs and optimizing manufacturing efficiency against predetermined standards. J.I.T. manufacturing requires that we produce only what we are going to see each day. This means short, mixed-model manufacturing runs with multiple changeovers. We must,
therefore, have very short setups and flexible equipment. To do this, we need to develop a new perspective
on manufacturing plants.

The second and third elements of creative thinking
are to have the proper educational and historical background on the problem. If a project requires the redesign of a particular product, machine or process, then
the project team members should have an engineering
background. The proper historical background also is
important and can be obtained by studying what has already been achieved so that time is not wasted "rein-
venting the wheel." The proper historical perspective
makes possible major improvements in productivity by devoting time to improving the state of the art in manufacturing rather than developing the process from ground
zero. For example, when the Japanese began to rebuild
their economy after the war, they came over to the U.S.
to see how we were manufacturing our products. They
took the best manufacturing principles back to Japan and
began manufacturing using these techniques. The Japanese spent the next several years perfecting the manufacturing process into what has evolved into J.I.T. manufacturing.

Both insight and outsight are needed if we are to
be farsighted in our thinking. An example of insight is
looking through a microscope and seeing an amoeba and
saying that, next to the amoeba, man is everything. If
we then turn the microscope into a telescope and look
out into the vastness of the universe, we might think
that, next to the universe, man is almost nothing. When
we combine both the insight that we get from a micro-
scopic view and the outsight that we get from a macro-
scopic view, we gain farsightedness and a new perspective on how to solve a problem.

Neoteny is maintaining a childlike perspective.
Neoteny is being open to new stimuli that occur so we
might be able to see things in a new way and not be
biased by our past experience. The childlike perspective means not being judgmental based on past experience. Creativity is based on a willingness to see
things in a new way. Creativity tests have shown that a
person's score in creativity invariably drops about 90
percent between the ages of five and seven. By the time
the average adult has reached forty, he retains only
about two percent of the creativity he had at five.

"Zeroing in" is focusing very intensely on a problem in order to allow the problem to go deep into the
subconscious mind. Typically our best ideas come when
we least expect them, such as when we are driving home
from work or when we are taking a shower or anywhere we
typically do not have a paper and pencil to record an
idea.

It is important to always have paper and pencil or
cassette recorder available in order to record ideas as
they occur. The subconscious mind is always working on
problems, and new ideas may surface at any time. There
is nothing more frustrating than to lose a creative
idea.

Severe time pressures for immediate results often
stifle the creative thinking process and limit risk taking in favor of traditional solutions. It is difficult
to be creative on call. Preparation and incubation, or
letting a good idea sink in and then refining it, takes
time. Working out the problems in fresh new ideas may
be time consuming. Therefore, it is important that a
longer time perspective be taken when evaluating new
ideas.

Ephemeralizing is considering how to make quantum
leaps in productivity, not just gradual changes. Ephemeralization figuratively means productivity. Increasing
productivity is done by thinking how to accomplish the
same objective using different techniques. Telestar
weighs 500 pounds, and it replaced 500,000 tons of
transoceanic cable. MRP II reduced inventory 20 to 30
percent, and J.I.T. manufacturing is reducing inventories 80 to 90 percent.

The final element of creative thinking is five-sensing. Typically we think only visually in our imaginations, creating images by sight. Our perspective can be increased by thinking of problems from the standpoint of touch, taste, smell and sound. By thinking of our products or projects from all the various senses, we increase our perspective.

RIGHT-BRAIN THINKING

Brain researchers have found, through the hemispherical mapping of the brain, that each individual has a left and right side to his brain. The left side is the origin of most analytical thought and speech and is very logical and orderly. The right side of the brain is the source of intuitive and creative thinking. The right side of the brain is the creative side and has tended to be underdeveloped and underutilized.

The formal educational system, as well as many organizations, has stressed rational and analytical approaches to decision making. Most of the rewards and promotions in organizations have come as a result of excellence in left-brain decision making. The left-brain decision-making process is objective, rational and fully documents the steps used in reaching a decision. As a consequence of this left-brain dominance, we have almost completely lost touch with the creative right-side decision-making process or the hunch. There must be a crossover from left- to right-brain thinking if we are to develop organizations where creativity and innovation flourish and grow.

Current researchers are beginning to believe that both sides of the brain must be utilized to originate, develop and execute ideas. The left side of the brain gathers information and analyzes it, while the right brain sees new patterns and can suggest creative solutions. This process is such a rapid, ongoing process that we cannot clearly distinguish between the two processes. We have focused on and rewarded left-brain thinking so extensively that we have minimized the right-brain's intuitive knowing in most mature adults.

THE CREATIVE THINKING PROCESS

The creative thinking process is a five-step process which is illustrated in Figure 3.

Figure 3

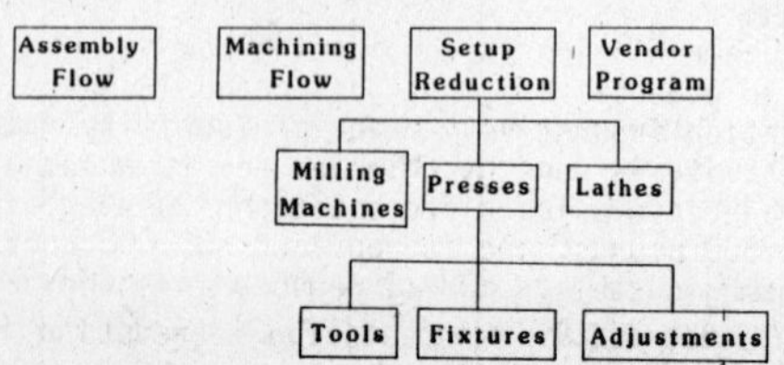

Ideation

The first step in the creative thinking process is ideation or brainstorming. Ideation is the capacity for, or the act of, forming new ideas. The key to a brainstorming session is to have a session with rules which call for no criticism of any ideas. The main purpose of the ideation meeting is to generate as many ideas as possible. The storyboarding technique is effective for improving the ideation process as well as for increasing the number of ideas generated and displayed before the group. A storyboard is made up of a corkboard wall and uses different-sized cards. An example of a simple storyboard is shown in Figure 4.

Figure 4

JUST-IN-TIME PROJECT

If a J.I.T. project is to be worked on, the title of the storyboard or project name would appear at the top. Several topic cards would then be put up under the J.I.T. project. Examples of topic cards might be as follows:

o Assembly process flow design
o Machining process flow design
o Setup reduction
o Vendor program

Under each major topic card, there would be header cards. For instance, in the example under setup reduction, the cards might be the types of machines that are going to be worked on, such as milling machines, presses and lathes. Next, under one of the pieces of equipment, like presses, there would be a list of the types of things that are going to be done to reduce setup time. Examples of this might be locating tools close to the piece of equipment to be setup, developing special fixtures which might help reduce the setup time on the press or making standard adjustments which would eliminate the need for repetitive adjusting of the equipment.

In order to make the ideation process most effective, ideas should be generated from people with many different perspectives. This means that people from different functional disciplines, different ethnic backgrounds, different sexes and cultures, if possible, should be involved with the project. The more diverse the group of people involved in the project, the greater probability that new ideas will be generated.

Critical Thinking Sessions

Once the storyboard has been completed and all the ideas are up on the storyboard, a break is needed to allow the participants to have a chance to think about the ideas that have been generated. A break of four hours is minimum, and a break of a day or two is better.

The second step in the creative thinking process is to reconvene and have a critical thinking session when everyone comes back and evaluates the ideas that have been developed, discards those that are not practical and removes those cards from the storyboard. The critical thinking session is to weed out the poor ideas and, if possible, expand on the more productive ideas. Once the critical thinking session has taken place and all the thoughts are organized along very specific lines, decisions need to be made.

DECISION MAKING AND ACTION PLANNING

Once the critical thinking session has taken place, often difficult decisions need to be made as to what is going to be done, and action plans laid accordingly. One of the major stumbling blocks in the creative thinking process is the inability to make decisions and get management approval to proceed with a new idea. Management has been so dominated by left-brain thinking where every decision has to be logical, orderly and thoroughly documented that often it is impossible to move ahead with radically new ideas which might produce major advances in productivity and profitability. In order to move forward, the new managers must develop a talent for right-brain thinking. Decisive minds of innovative managers and executives must be ones that can make quick and accurate decisions. These managers cannot be constrained by the left-brain mentality which typically bases the decision on near-term practical and financial data. Their decisions should encompass more of the intuitive right-brain thought processes. It is the right-brain influence that can assist the mind in dealing with expressive images, the holistic view of problems and the relational grasping of complex ideas that permit major breakthroughs in productivity.

Many specialists believe management has spent too much time developing its linear left-brain strengths while generally neglecting the enormous creative and intuitive strengths of the right brain. It is the interrelationship and interdependence of the left and right hemispheres that help make a balanced, thinking manager who can deal with today's realities and infinite challenges.

Once the decision is made to go ahead and execute

an idea, detailed action planning needs to take place.
The storyboard can again be used in laying out these
action plans. A planning storyboard can now be created
which considers and plans out the action steps in the
detail that will be necessary to execute the ideas which
have been generated. The same group which generated the
ideas is used to develop and detail the specific steps
that will be used to ensure the accomplishment and execution of the decisions which have been made.

ORGANIZATION

In order to successfully execute any major project,
a project team must be organized. An organizational
storyboard might be used to map out the project team's
organization. The organization storyboard should clearly identify the communication lines that will be necessary to obtain proper approval at each level of management to carry out the plan. Organizational storyboards
must also clearly lay out the lines of communication
that will be necessary to keep all levels of management
informed of the progress of the project as well as the
decision points along the way. Too often organizations
are in the midst of executing a plan without first docu-
menting and organizing the detailed steps required for
implementation.

EXECUTION AND FEEDBACK

Innovation is the key to execution. Theodore
Levitt of Harvard has said, "Creativity is thinking up
new things; innovation is doing new things. Ideas are
useless unless used, and the proof of their value is in
their implementation. There is no shortage of creativity or creative people in American business. The shortage is of innovators." This statement is true, especially in large bureaucratic organizations. One of the
major problems in executing ideas on how to improve the
manufacturing process has been the manufacturing organizations' lack of acceptance or willingness to try new
ideas. Peters and Waterman in their best selling book,
In Search of Excellence, indicate that one thing the
excellent companies do well is innovate. They do not
have paralysis by analysis. Their slogans are, "Do It -
Fix It - Try It" and "Ready - Fire - Aim." Ideas are
executed by trying them. The excellent companies succeed because of effective feedback systems. They learn
from their failures because they understand why a project failed and do not make the same mistake twice.

When successful ideas are executed, the people who
developed the ideas are upheld in the organization with
substantial recognition and rewarded for their efforts.
One of the major sources of new ideas for J.I.T. programs is the workers on the shop floor who are recognized and rewarded in psychological and tangible ways.
This in turn leads to the generation of more ideas and
methods of executing these ideas.

Mental Locks

There are several mental locks which individuals
impose on themselves which prevent them from being creative. Dr. Roger von Oec in his book, A Whack on the
Side of the Head, has said that there are ten mental
locks to being creative. They are as follows:

o That's the right answer.
o That's not logical.
o Follow the rules.
o Be practical.
o Avoid ambiguity.
o To err is wrong.
o Play is frivolous.
o That's not my area.
o Don't be foolish.
o I'm not creative.

The very things that tend to stimulate the creative
thinking process in individuals are looked upon nega-
tively in most organizations. Most organizations throttle creativity by reinforcing these ten mental locks and
not developing a creative climate for their employees to
work in. One of the most important ingredients in developing an organization of creative people is to develop a corporate culture which values and supports creativity. There are several characteristics which describe a working environment where people are free to be
creative. They are as follows:

o Supportive and open to new ideas
o Tolerant of failure
o Participative management style
o Work environment which is beautiful
o Higher-than-average investments in R&D
o Heterogeneous personnel
o Decentralized structure
o Allow risk taking
o Recognize and reward new ideas
o Maintain open channels of communications

Building these factors into the corporate culture
may be a slow process as there must first be a leader
who recognizes a need for these attributes. The key to
executing new ideas in a bureaucratic organization is to
have a person from the ranks who is determined to see
his idea implemented. Peters and Waterman in the book,
In Search of Excellence, call this individual a
product champion. Edward Schon of MIT says, "The new
idea either finds a champion or dies.... No ordinary involvement with a new idea provides the energy required
to cope with the indifference and resistance major technological change provides. Champions of new inventions
display persistence and courage of heroic quality."
Peter and Waterman go on to say that a product champion
or zealot in the ranks is not enough. The product champion needs an executive champion in management who recognizes the importance of the product champion and supports his efforts. Additionally, just having an executive champion does not ensure success; there must be a
godfather or an aging senior executive who is the role
model for championing new ideas. Only with all this
support can a new idea succeed and overcome the threat
posed by the change in the organizational bureaucracy.

PEOPLE - THE ONLY CREATIVE RESOURCE

One of the most important benefits of the creative
thinking process is that it meets the last objective
that was outlined in Bob Hall's goals of stockless production, i.e., the development of people. The process
of generating new ideas is extremely rewarding and motivating to the individuals involved in the process. Reliance must be placed on the individual because individuals, not organizations, create.

There are four levels of learning which man goes
through which must be understood to fully understand the
creative thinking process. They are:

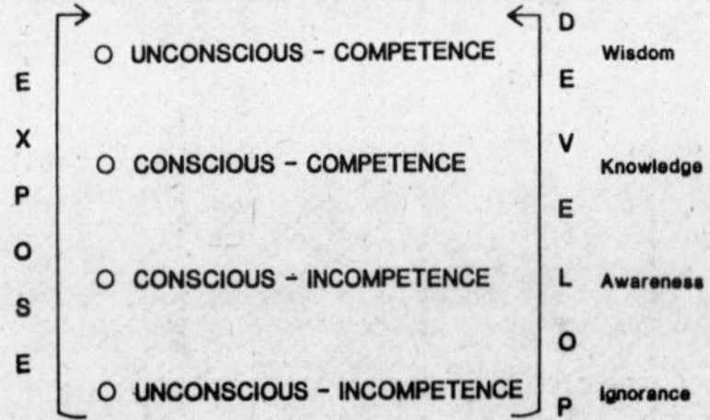

Man develops from a level of unconscious-incompe-
tence, where he doesn't even know that he doesn't know
something, which is called ignorance to a level of unconscious-competence which is called wisdom. A few
years ago we did not know that there was such a thing as
Just-in-Time manufacturing. This is the level called
ignorance. In the late 70s, we developed to the level
of conscious-incompetence where we knew that a J.I.T.
program existed in Japan, but we did not know what to do
about it. This is the level of awareness.

We are now at the level of conscious-competence
where, if we think real hard and apply the new concepts
involved in Just-in-Time manufacturing, we can make a
small department of the plant more productive by applying the J.I.T. techniques. This is the knowledge level.

The Japanese have evolved to a level of conscious-
competence where they don't even think of running a manufacturing plant in any other way. This level is called
wisdom. This developmental process of moving from un-
conscious-incompetence to unconscious-competence is a
step-by-step evolutionary process. The only way we can
take the next quantum leap in our personal development

or productivity is by having a paradigm shift occur in our thinking as a consequence of being exposed to new knowledge.

The essential point is that people love to be exposed to new ideas, especially when they can execute those ideas in practical ways.

KEYS TO CREATIVITY AND INNOVATION

There are ten keys to improving creativity and innovation in people. They are as follows:

o Exposing people to new knowledge
o Developing creative attitudes
o Doing more right-brain thinking
o Getting out of the rut
o Being less judgmental and more artistic
o Trying new things - taking risks
o Being willing to fail
o Playing with problems
o Avoiding falling in love with ideas
o Writing down new ideas immediately

One of the major problems with keeping the creative life cycle alive is that people gradually slide into a routine of doing things the same way. This routine brings along with it a security of always being able to do, quote, "the right thing," end quote. The rut eventually becomes so deep that it becomes more like a grave, and you are unable to climb out of the rut and think and act in totally new ways. The way to break out of the rut is to be exposed to new knowledge which convinces you there is a better and more effective way to accomplish the same objectives.

The only barrier stopping us from breaking out of the rut is the courage to do so. That is why organizations need to tolerate failure in order to minimize the fear of failure within the individuals in the organiza-tion. The organization must be willing to support the courage of the few zealots in the organization. This support is the stepping stone to building a creative organization.

SUMMARY

A paradigm shift in thinking about manufacturing is necessary in order to see manufacturing plants through a new pair of eyes. This new pair of eyes clearly shows us the benefits that we can achieve through Just-in-Time manufacturing. In order to generate the new ideas required to achieve J.I.T. manufacturing, the creative thinking process must be understood. This process is as follows:

o Ideation
o Critical thinking
o Decision making and action planning
o Organization
o Execution and feedback

By applying the creative thinking process, all members of the manufacturing organization are involved and given a sense of meaning, purpose and excitement in their work as they see their ideas executed.

Tom Watson, the former Chairman of IBM has said, "The success of any organization is measured by the extent to which it brings out the <u>great talents and ability of all its people</u>." I believe Mr. Watson was talking about developing a creative climate for all the individuals within the organization so that they could find meaning and purpose in their work. Involved, creative workers are the key to executing J.I.T. programs that really work.

TRACKLESS REQUIREMENTS PLANNING—THE NEXT PHASE

William A. Thurwachter, CPIM*
Arthur Andersen & Co.
(David Storm is presenting the paper at the Conference)

This paper will address the relationship of MRP to J-I-T systems.

BACKGROUND

MRP is a sound approach to manufacturing planning and control. MRP was developed by and for companies with relatively low inventory turns. Success with MRP requires accurate status information. Over the last few years, manufacturing system development and application has concentrated on the material tracking area to support the management of accurate status information.

KANBAN is a sound approach to production control. KANBAN was developed by companies who have achieved relatively high inventory turns. KANBAN is very sensitive to a number of operating practices which need to be in place for it to be effective. KANBAN works for companies that manage their organization using Just-In-Time operating practices. KANBAN is not a material tracking system.

Unfortunately, many companies have dismissed KANBAN and Just-In-Time as only having application in high-volume, repetitive operations. They miss the point and the opportunity. Others look to Just-In-Time as an inventory reduction program. Again, they miss the point. When annual inventory turns fall into the range of twenty or more per year, the inventory financing incentive for further reduction is practically gone. Why then, do companies like Toyota routinely run their operations in the sixty to ninety turns category? For someone attempting to understand the benefits of a Just-In-Time operation, this is a perplexing question. For someone who understands the operating objectives of Just-In-Time, they recognize and admire the superior manufacturing performance consistently demonstrated by Toyota. Ninety turns is world-class performance.

INVENTORY TURNS - A MEASURE OF OPERATIONS EXCELLENCE

We need to look beyond the obvious inventory reduction benefits of a Just-In-Time operation and recognize its broader potential, competitive survival. Product cost comparison studies consistently show a thirty percent gap between many domestic and some Japanese manufacturers. Our higher labor rates are a factor; our lower productivity is a much larger factor. Just-In-Time is a more productive approach to manufacturing. It focuses on the elimination of waste, specifically, the non-value added component of production.

Few good definitions exist for Just-In-Time. The words themselves convey the synchronous production and delivery of component material. Only under extreme conditions is this an appropriate definition. Ninety annual turns represents three to four days to get through a facility. Ninety turns is not synchronous, and yet it represents performance far beyond domestic precedent. Perhaps a better definition for Just-In-Time is to explain what it is not. Most domestic manufacturers continue to run under a practice of Just-In-Case. We manage an operation expecting something to go wrong and provide contingencies to cover all eventualities. The contingency is normally excess inventory. This is an expensive approach. Inventory requires the overhead of management, physical storage/handling and financing. Of course, running under Just-In-Time in a facility with significant operating problems is also expensive. Problems with no contingency mean the operation is continually interrupted. Just-In-Time means removing the needs for running Just-In-Case. This requires durable solutions to operating problems.

A preoccupation with inventory reduction confuses the potential of Just-In-Time. Nevertheless, inventory turns remain a good measurement of company performance. A company capable of twenty to sixty annual turns clearly demonstrates how it has developed its internal operations, as well as its vendor network. High turns are a measure of operations excellence.

FLEXIBLE OPERATIONS

Installation of a Just-In-Time operating philosophy is a commitment to a high-inventory turn operation. High turns mean greater flexibility. High turns require a flexible operation capable of absorbing changes to sales forecasts, product mix and production rates. High turns do not necessarily mean dedicated equipment; dedicating is normally an inflexible approach. Nor do high turns necessarily lead to flexible manufacturing systems (FMS) which typically represent a substantial capital investment. Instead, flexibility can be developed within an organization through the reduction of setup and the application of group technology on existing equipment, along with the application of statistical process control. These practices will lead to a high-turn environment. These practices represent a new frontier for almost all domestic companies. As the processes and operating practices change, so should the systems to manage production.

SYSTEM IMPLICATIONS

MRP II systems have been developed along the line of "plan the work and work the plan." The system logic is based on establishing orders and tracking performance to the order. The "loop" is closed through the system, via open order position. Maintaining accurate status is important to the integrity of the plan. A significant portion of all MRP II software is devoted to material and operation tracking systems.

MRP III, or the integration of MRP and J-I-T is based on a different line of reason. The operating practice of Just-In-Time is "plan the work, but produce what is consumed." MRP II directs the floor and vendor to produce to the plan. MRP III directs the floor and vendor to produce to actual consumption. This is a subtle distinction, but a subtantial difference. Inventory takes on a different role. Under MRP II, inventory was produced to plan in anticipation of demand. "Produce it this week, for I need it in assembly next week," demonstrates the point. Under MRP III, production is authorized through the consumption of previous production. Inventory's role in the production pipeline is to couple production activity. The signal for replenishment is consumption, not anticipated demand.

What does this mean to the systems designer who has a background in MRP II applications? For years we have struggled with developing an accurate dispatch list on the shop floor to coordinate production activity. We have developed real-time, interactive systems capable of dynamically resequencing shop floor priorities. Now with the advent of MRP III, we are replacing the dispatch list with KANBAN cards. Many consider this a step in the wrong direction. However, under the right circumstances (actually the only circumstances), KANBAN is the ultimate in real-time, shop floor control. Production signals are the result of actual consumption. Consumption that exceeds the projected rate sends an earlier signal, no electronics necessary. As long as the increase in demand represents a minor deviation, + ten percent, the ripple can be absorbed. In fact, if the increase in demand for one component against a work center is offset by a decrease for another, the change in the demand pattern will go undetected on the floor. This would not be true under MRP II. The order reschedule or reconciliation would require the intervention of a planner.

System objectives under MRP III should be to support the requirements of a high-turn inventory environment. This means that the predominate use of current systems will be to support operations planning, not control. Closing the loop will no longer be through the system. Rather, the loop will be closed physically on the floor through the exchange of cards (perhaps electronic signals), which are tripped when a container of material is consumed. Feedback to MRP for replanning would be a useless and, therefore, wasted step. In a high-turn environment, the development of a new plan is not based on current status, the production pipeline already contains the prerequisite inventory. Rather, the plan is developed assuming an established set of operating practices which would allow the KANBAN system to function. As companies succeed in converting their operations to KANBAN, the need for traditional inventory and shop floor control systems will diminish.

NEW OPERATING PRACTICES

KANBAN, by itself, has no forward visibility; MRP does. The operation of KANBAN requires setting up the production facility to allow for consumption signals to trigger production activity. A number of practices are necessary:

Model Mix -	establishing a final assembly schedule which allows for a uniform draw of components over a specified time period.
Short Frozen Schedule -	once the model mix has been set, don't change the plan. Why? Because all fabrication operations are staffed based on the production rate specified in the assembly schedule. The frozen period should be from ten to twenty days.
Quick Change -	fabrication must be responsive. Changeover from one job to another should not be a scheduling consideration. If it is, KANBAN will not be an effective priority system.
± Zero Performance to Schedule -	the final assembly operation is pacing the entire network. The network should perform at the same pulse of final assembly. Differing paces will cause surges and render the KANBAN signal ineffective.
Statistical Process Control -	part quality must be improved dramatically. Quality defined as right the first time, coupled with a prevention approach, removes the random nature of an unpredictable process.
Manufacturing Cells -	production activity must be grouped to link sequentially required processes. This will reduce the number of levels in the production network allowing for a more responsive production system.
Flexible Workforce	manufacturing cells will contain numerous processes requiring operators familiar with all the processes in the cell.

These operating practices should not be taken as administrative requirements exclusively for the purpose of installing KANBAN. Rather, they all represent operating techniques which collectively have a dramatic impact on product cost; they reduce it substantially.

SYSTEMS MIGRATION STRATEGY

Becoming cost competitive with overseas competitors is an issue most companies are currently facing. Just-In-Time represents an operating environment for which few of us have any practical experience. Our migration to improved performance will be slow because the work to be done, much less the misunderstanding which needs to be overcome, is substantial. Today, the bulk of manufacturing planning and control systems are order based. They presume central control of inventory and the receipt and issue to an order. Some companies, normally those involved with high-volume production, have developed systems which use schedules in place of orders. Planning and tracking shifts from the lot mentality of an order to the rate mentality of a schedule. Nonetheless, these systems still have a tracking tradition and are designed to accommodate the daily recording of production at key control points in the process. Inventory is still netted in MRP and schedule exception messages are generated. Few people are considering the logical extension to trackless requirements planning. Yet, many people are considering the implementation of KANBAN. The two go hand-in-hand.

Given that most systems are order based, building an MRP III system using an order based package introduces some new problems. Systems should be bucketless (daily) to allow for finer planning. Parts should be identified to allow for capacity plans without requiring netting or offsetting. Without reporting, a new method for removing supply and demand records will be necessary. Backflush won't be necessary because no perpetual inventory is kept. These systems design issues represent a radical departure from our traditions. Yet, they represent the circumstances which define a successful Just-In-Time operation; the goal of the world-class competitors.

FOOTNOTE

This paper addresses operating practices for which few people will feel comfortable. Developing a trackless-based planning system will, undoubtedly, be an evolution for any organization. A complete and successful implementation for a specific company will most likely still require various aspects of their operation to run under a perpetual tracking system. Consequently, systems designers of future systems need to consider the evolution their company will go through as they migrate from order, to schedule, to trackless. Practically speaking, a system capable of supporting a company through this evolution will need all three capabilities. Rather than simplifying future software, this will actually increase its complexity.

MRP & JIT

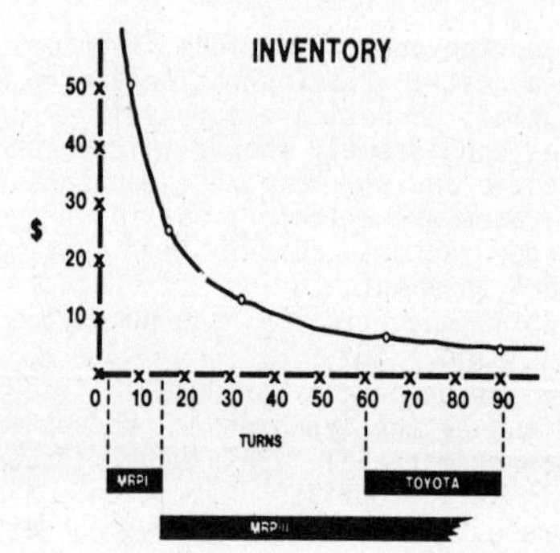

INVENTORY MODEL

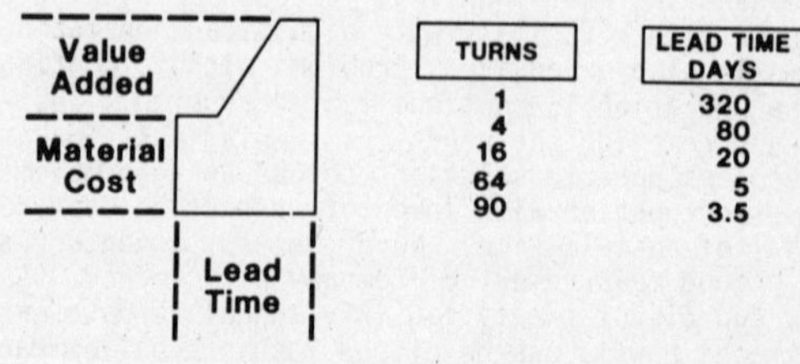

	TURNS	LEAD TIME DAYS
	1	320
	4	80
	16	20
	64	5
	90	3.5

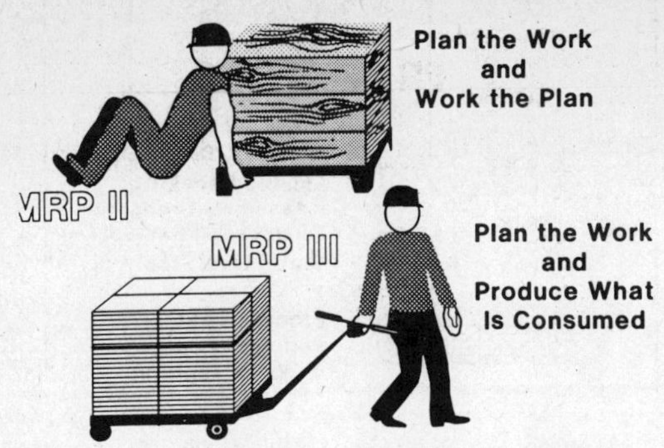
Plan the Work
and
Work the Plan
MRP II
MRP III
Plan the Work
and
Produce What
Is Consumed

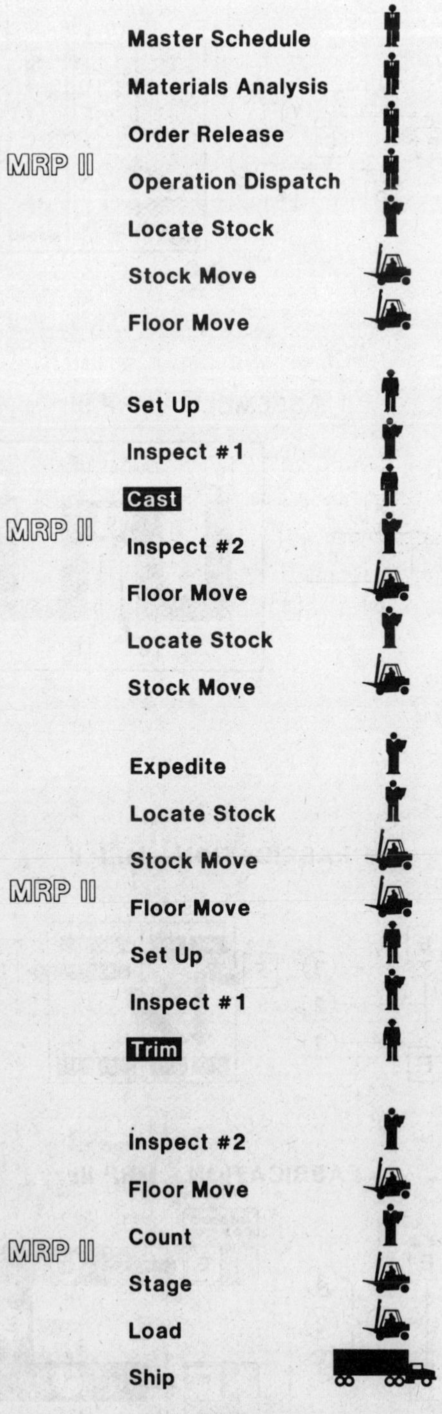

MRP II
Master Schedule
Materials Analysis
Order Release
Operation Dispatch
Locate Stock
Stock Move
Floor Move

Set Up
Inspect #1
Cast
Inspect #2
Floor Move
Locate Stock
Stock Move

Expedite
Locate Stock
Stock Move
Floor Move
Set Up
Inspect #1
Trim

Inspect #2
Floor Move
Count
Stage
Load
Ship

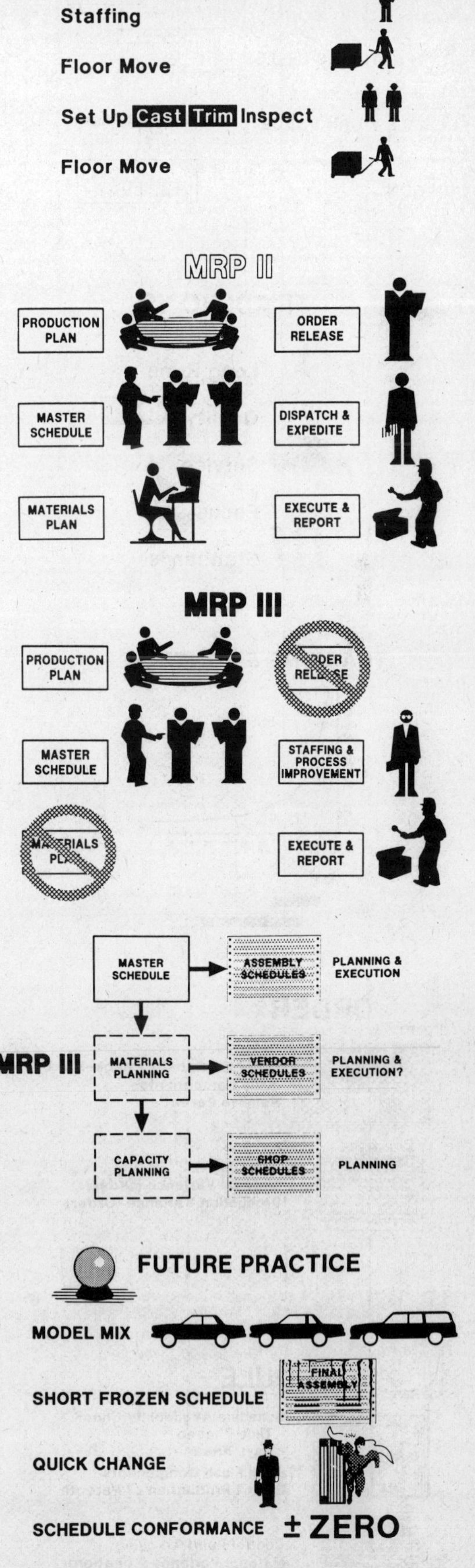
MRP III
Master Schedule
Staffing
Floor Move
Set Up Cast Trim Inspect
Floor Move

MRP II
PRODUCTION PLAN
ORDER RELEASE
MASTER SCHEDULE
DISPATCH & EXPEDITE
MATERIALS PLAN
EXECUTE & REPORT

MRP III
PRODUCTION PLAN
ORDER RELEASE
MASTER SCHEDULE
STAFFING & PROCESS IMPROVEMENT
MATERIALS PLAN
EXECUTE & REPORT

MASTER SCHEDULE
ASSEMBLY SCHEDULES
PLANNING & EXECUTION
MRP III
MATERIALS PLANNING
VENDOR SCHEDULES
PLANNING & EXECUTION?
CAPACITY PLANNING
SHOP SCHEDULES
PLANNING

FUTURE PRACTICE
MODEL MIX
SHORT FROZEN SCHEDULE
FINAL ASSEMBLY
QUICK CHANGE
SCHEDULE CONFORMANCE   ± ZERO

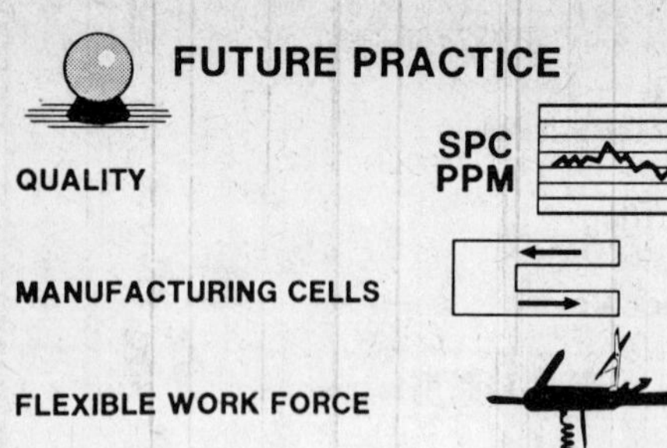

FUTURE PRACTICE

QUALITY — SPC PPM

MANUFACTURING CELLS

FLEXIBLE WORK FORCE

CON BON

TRADITIONS

Long Runs

Quality

Service

Focus

Standards

TRACKING & CONTROL

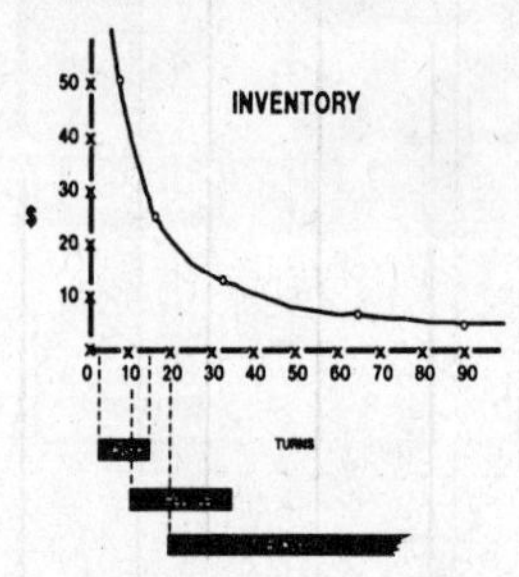

ORDER

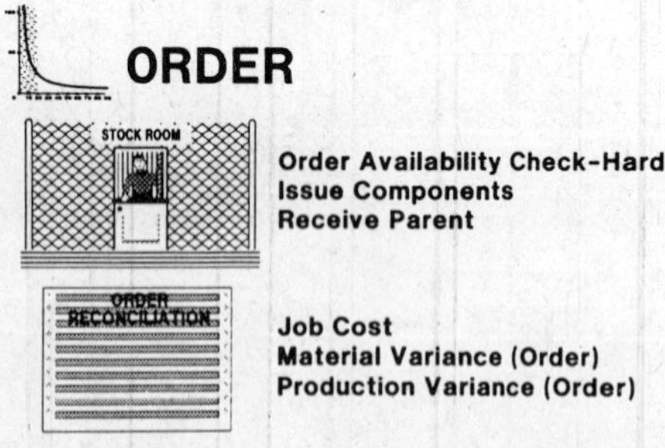

Order Availability Check–Hard
Issue Components
Receive Parent

Job Cost
Material Variance (Order)
Production Variance (Order)

SCHEDULE

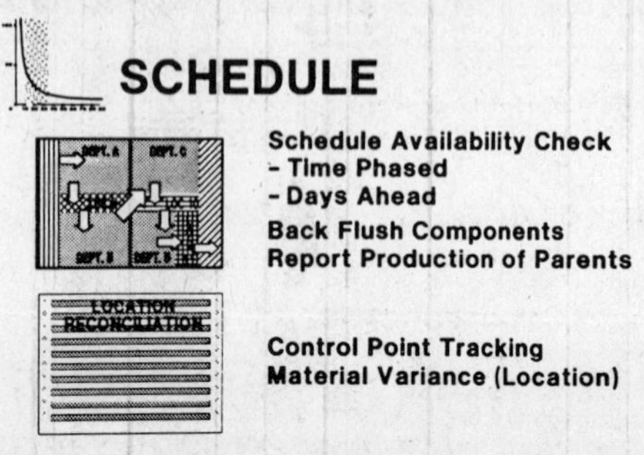

Schedule Availability Check
- Time Phased
- Days Ahead
Back Flush Components
Report Production of Parents

Control Point Tracking
Material Variance (Location)

TRACKLESS

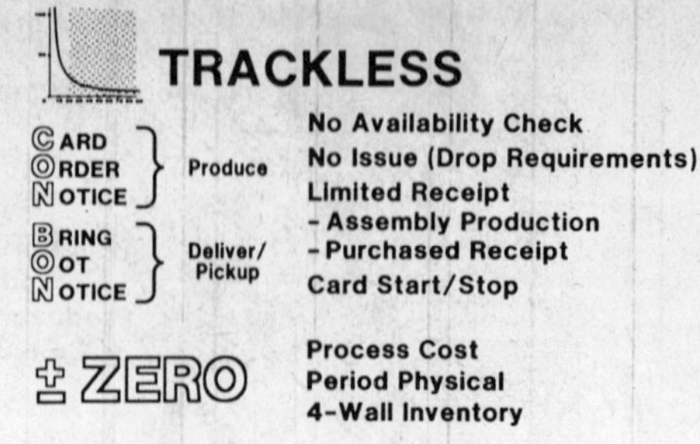

No Availability Check
No Issue (Drop Requirements)
Limited Receipt
 – Assembly Production
 – Purchased Receipt
Card Start/Stop

Process Cost
Period Physical
4–Wall Inventory

ASSEMBLY – MRP II

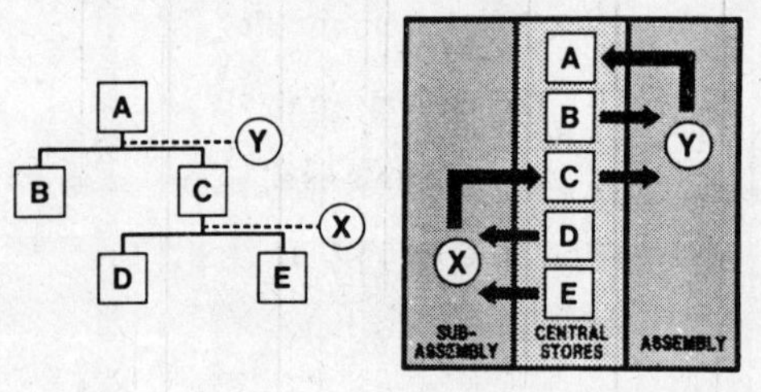

ASSEMBLY – MRP III

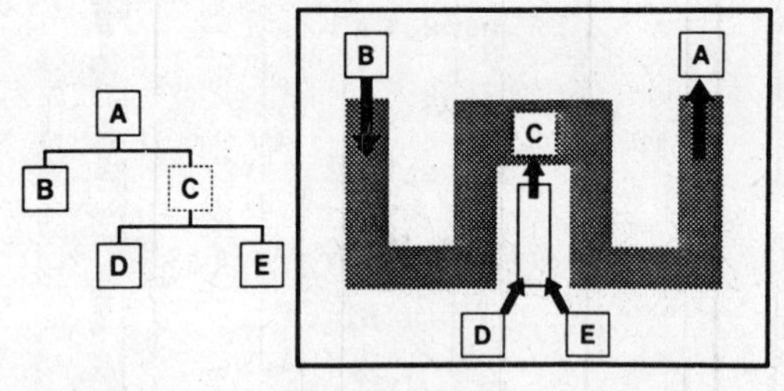

FABRICATION – MRP II

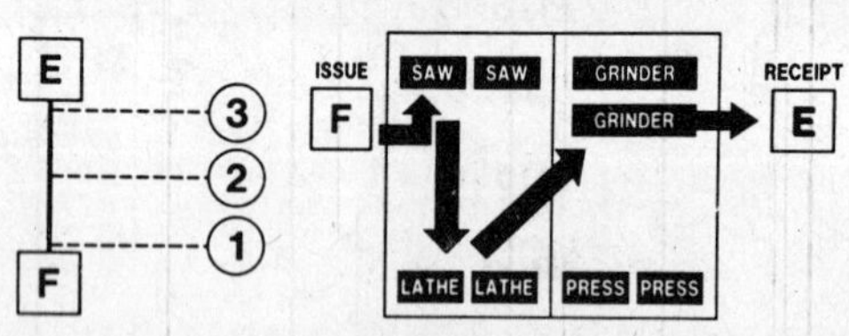

FABRICATION – MRP III

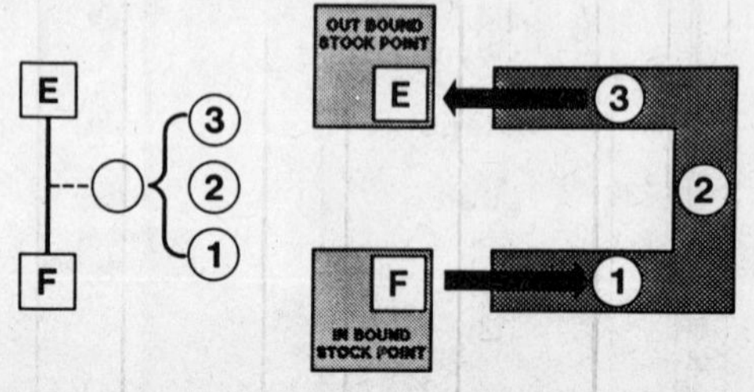

RECEIVING - MRP II

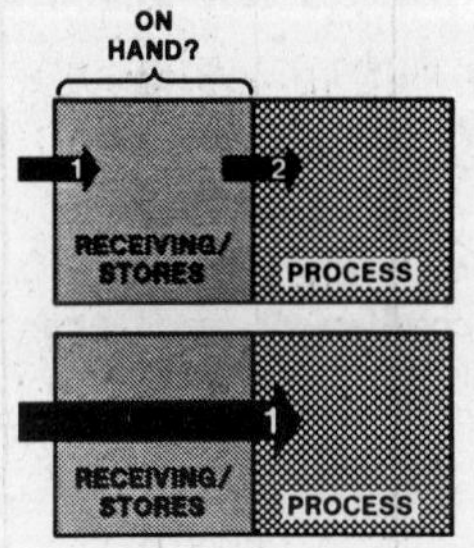

RECEIVING - MRP III

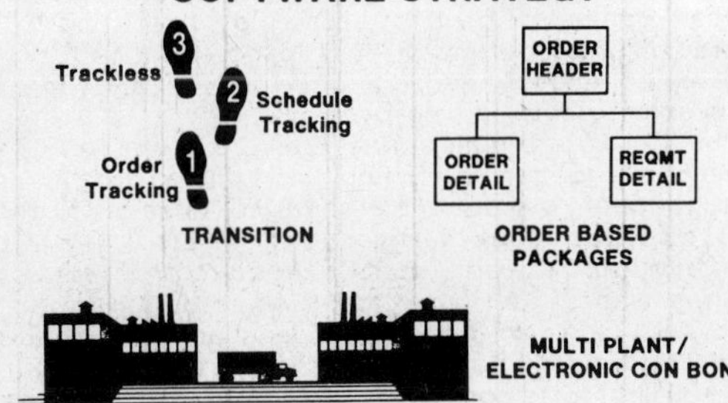

SOFTWARE STRATEGY

DESIGN CONCEPT

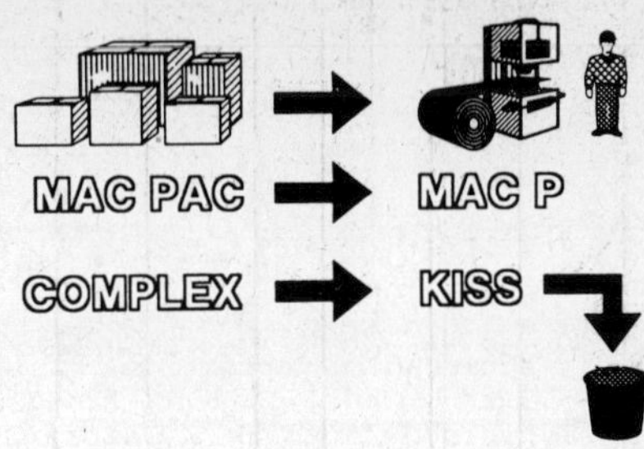

DESIGN ISSUES

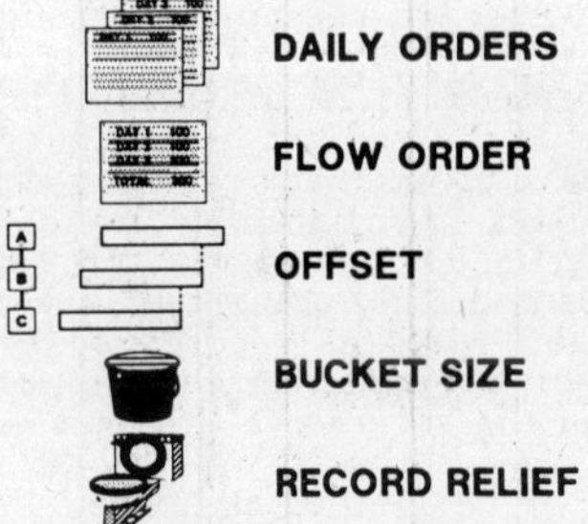

BIOGRAPHY

Mr. Thurwachter is a manufacturing consultant with Arthur Andersen & Co. His engagement experiences range from special studies to the design and installation of integrated manufacturing planning and control systems. Mr. Thurwachter has had exposure and experience in almost all functions of a manufacturing company. He has experience in all manufacturing environments: process - flow and batch; discrete - job shop and repetitive; make-to-stock, assemble-to-order, make-to-order and engineer-to-order.

Mr. Thurwachter is the former chairman for the Milwaukee Chapter of the Institute of Management Science/Operations Research Society of America. He is also a member of the American Production and Inventory Control Society (APICS) and is certified as a Fellow in the field of Production and Inventory Control. As a member of APICS, he is a frequent speaker at the organization's local and national conferences. He is an executive committee member of the Repetitive Manufacturing Group (RMG) within APICS and is currently the Chairman of the Wisconsin/Michigan RMG. He is a member of his firm's manufacturing core group and has responsibility for the repetitive manufacturing segment.

Graduating from the University of Wisconsin-Madison in 1973, Mr. Thurwachter received a degree in Mechanical Engineering and an MBA, specializing in Operations Research and Inventory Control. Mr. Thurwachter is a registered Professional Engineer in the State of Wisconsin.

"PULL" CAN ALMOST ALWAYS USE A "PUSH"
Rich Heard, CPIM*
R. C. Heard & Co.

FOREWORD

The goals set forth in the Zero Inventory philosophy, if achieved to perfection, would create a balanced, continuous flow of product through each firm in the manufacturing community. There would be no idle inventory, only that to which value was being actively added. There are, however, many roadblocks to achieving this ideal. Some of these deterrents are valid, but all of them must be challenged. The majority of this challenge is currently focused on the manufacturing process because it is widely perceived to hold the greatest potential for improvement. Even though this perception is accurate today, it will not remain true as processes are improved. Then our focus will revert back to improved planning and scheduling. In short, "MRP-mania" has been replaced by "JIT-mania". We are accepting the shortcomings of planning and scheduling practices, and looking to JIT as the cure-all, just as we previously accepted the shortcomings of the manufacturing process and looked to MRP for all the solutions. The message of the Zero Inventory Crusade is that we need both, and not one to the detriment or neglect of the other.

The shortcomings of most planning and scheduling systems are rooted in the unpredictability of demand for product, the instability of the output of the manufacturing process, and/or the misapplication (or non-application) of available planning and scheduling tools. All three of these performance degrading characteristics exist in most manufacturing companies. The impact of their uncertainty is very disruptive to the smooth, orderly movement of product. The problem is that we have chosen for years to buffer the impact of the uncertainty instead of eliminating the sources of uncertainty. Zero Inventory focuses on eliminating the sources of uncertainty. The unpredictability of demand and the instability of the manufacturing process are easily recognized problems, but the elimination or reduction of their disruptive impact may not be so easy. By contrast, the identification of needed changes or enhancements to planning and scheduling systems may not be so easy, but implementing these changes can usually be accomplished more readily than changes to customer habits and manufacturing processes.

Dealing with the disruptive impact of uncertain demand and production will not be addressed in any depth in this paper. The primary focus will be on the proper application of planning and scheduling tools, recognizing that those other uncertainties, without treatment, can invalidate the best of schedules. The detailed assumptions of several of the more popular scheduling tools and their impact on smooth product flow will be addressed. Particular attention will also be given to inherent process characteristics which disrupt product flow and how to provide for that disruption in planning and scheduling. A majority of the discussion will also be directed to the clarification of the differences between "pull" and "push" scheduling technologies and their impact on product flow. The key to improved application of scheduling tools in a specific manufacturing process is understanding the details of both the tools and the process, and not accepting the shortcomings of either in the pursuit of excellence in schedule execution.

THE ZERO INVENTORY IDEAL

The Zero Inventory philosophy (shown in Figure 1.) contains a number of goals and implications for improved planning and scheduling systems. The most important message is that we must plan and schedule well before we can execute and control well. The inverse is also implied from our past experiences. That is, we must execute and contol well before we can plan and schedule well. The implication IS NOT that one must precede the other and the dilemma is unsolvable. The implication IS that the two are

ZERO INVENTORY PHILOSOPHY

Strive to find and use the simplest and least costly ways to plan, schedule and control the flow of material through the manufacturing process to :

- *Produce products the customer wants*

- *Produce products only at the rate customers want them*

- *Produce with perfect quality*

- *Produce instantly (zero unnecessary lead time)*

- *Produce with no waste of labor, material, energy or equipment, every move with a purpose so there is zero idle inventory*

- *Produce by methods which allow for the development of people*

FIGURE 1.

compatible and complement each other. Better planning and scheduling will lead to better execution and control, and better execution and control will lead to better planning and scheduling. A second major implication is that our methods must be simple and cost effective. The complexity of the scheduling system will match the complexity of the manufacturing process. Therefore, efforts should be made to simplify the manufacturing process. A complex process or system can also be simplified by breaking it down into smaller, more fundamental pieces. Complexity is a barrier to understanding, and understanding is the basic prerequisite to improvement.

The detailed goals set forth in the philosophy statement all begin with the word "Produce". Before we can produce we must be able to create plans and schedules that meet those same goals. The ideal schedule must reflect what the customer wants, how much they want, and when they want it. It assumes perfect knowledge of customer needs and the ability to produce to meet those needs. It assumes perfect quality with no provision necessary for rework or defect related catch-up. It assumes no delay for setups or changeovers, leadtime is the same as run time. It assumes 100% productivity of labor, no scrap, and 100% equipment uptime and utilization. It is simple enough that all who use it can understand it, execute it with confidence, and contribute to its improvement.

It is these assumptions and their lack of resemblance to reality that have hindered the development of easily understood scheduling technology. Simple technology "won't work here", it "assumes away the problem" and solves the useless residue. Complex technology "won't work here", it "takes a Masters Degree or a PhD to understand" how to apply it. Embellishing simple techniques to allow for realities soon made them too complex to be easily understood. There appeared to be no workable solution but to buffer the uncertainties. The main concern of scheduling technology became one of maintaining the buffers instead of smoothing the flow of product.

Then came the "logic of manufacturing", MRP, and its cousin DRP. The basic logic was sound for scheduling the smooth flow of product to arrive "just-in-time" to be consumed. Then the embellishment began again, because the schedules could not be executed as planned. The realities of manufacturing seemed to defy the simple logic of manufacturing. Then came the realization that until the realities were changed, instead of accepted, smooth flow could not be achieved. The "pull" schedules of MRP and DRP, instead of requiring "push" execution which opposed the smooth flow of the "pull" logic, could be executed with a new "pull" tool called Kanban, if the long-accepted realities were changed.

The Zero Inventory ideal was established, only to be denied by many whose environmental realities "can't ever be changed" significantly enough to achieve the perfection of the ideal. The message that is being missed is that excellence is not perfection, excellence is steady progress toward the ideal. In terms of scheduling technology it is making the schedule reflect the realities that can't be changed today. It is understanding when to "push" and when to "pull", and when to do both, to create executable schedules that flow product as smoothly and reliably as the current manufacturing environment allows. It is utilizing this understanding to continually gain and apply new insight to reduce the barriers to the smooth flow of product.

"PULL" VS. "PUSH"

The key to successfully applying scheduling technology is understanding its impact on product flow well enough to custom fit it to the manufacturing process that is to be scheduled. One of the most misunderstood, and misapplied, principles inherent in the more popular scheduling tools is "pull" vs. "push". The APICS Dictionary defines Pull System and Push System in the context of their application in distribution, production and material control. Later sections will attempt to clarify what appear to be ambiguities in these definitions. First, however, it is necessary to define the basic principles of "pull" and "push" in terms of the flow of product, relative to scheduling and execution. The structure tree, which defines the material flow in the manufacture of Product "A" (see Figure 2.), will be used to define and illustrate these principles.

PRODUCT STRUCTURE TREE

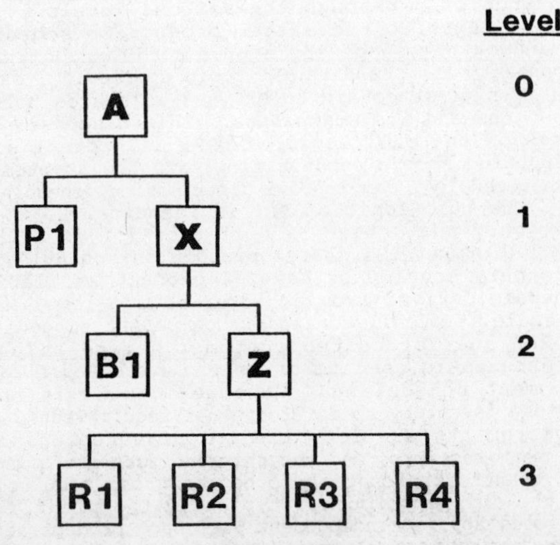

FIGURE 2.

Each transition from level to level in the structure tree represents a stage in the manufacturing process of Product "A". One or more products are manufactured or procured at each stage in the process. In this example, the final stage results in the final product, Product "A". There is an implied procurement stage below the bottom level of the structure tree. If the rate of flow of material from level to level is controlled or determined by the higher of the two levels, the material is "pulled". If the rate of flow of material from level to level is controlled or determined by the lower of the two levels, the material is "pushed". Briefly stated, top-down is equivalent to "pull" and bottom-up is equivalent to "push".

One might easily conclude from this simple example that if scheduling and execution are demand driven, that they would always use top-down, pull technology. That conclusion is valid, but it does not exclude the use of push logic in many environments. The exclusive use of pull logic is not always the best way to run the business. Long throughput times in manufacturing and long vendor leadtimes require push execution at some stage(s) in the manufacturing

process in order to maintain responsiveness to customer demand. Push scheduling and execution may also be necessary to insure the best allocation and utilization of critical resources, particularly those that are in short supply and/or common to most end products. Push execution authorizes production or procurement independent of and/or in anticipation of higher level material needs. Push scheduling considers other factors besides higher level material needs in the planning of anticipated production or procurement needs. Pull scheduling logic will always be necessary to anticipate the needs created by customer demand. However, it is not always sufficient in creating stable, executable schedules that best meet the needs of some businesses. Pull often requires a little push.

MATERIAL REQUIREMENTS PLANNING

MRP is a pull scheduling tool. Its top-down, backward scheduling logic is a natural for converting customer demand into anticipated, lower level material requirements. However, the basic, order-driven logic of MRP generates schedules that defy the smooth flow of product, when executed by the exclusive use of pull authorization. Pull authorization is not given for a component item(s) until the release or authorization of an order to produce the parent or higher level item. MRP logic, on the other hand, assumed that the components would already have been provided by the earlier release of orders for the components. The authorization to produce or procure components must precede their parent item's need date by the components' respective replenishment leadtimes if they are to be available as scheduled by MRP in support of smooth product flow. Since authorization comes from the lower level in anticipation of higher level needs, the execution must utilize push logic.

Execution of the MRP schedule is managed bottom-up in anticipation of higher level needs. Execution problems arise when higher level needs change after lower level execution has already begun, or when lower level execution cannot or does not proceed as scheduled. These problems are not a result of flaws in the basic scheduling logic, and very few of them can be solved by better scheduling logic. Their disruptive impact on product availability can be buffered by embellishments to the scheduling logic, but the problems remain. In fact, they are usually amplified because many of the buffers expand the replenishment leadtime, which increases the likelihood of changes within that leadtime.

The source of most higher level changes is customer demand. Improved management of customer demand within the cumulative replenishment leadtime is the ONLY SOLUTION. All other "treatments" of this problem provide only temporary relief, increase costs and usually increase the problem. The solution has two parts. The most obvious is to acquire better knowledge of what the customers want, how much and when. This is often more difficult than the more subtle second half of the solution, that is, to reduce the replenishment leadtime. However difficult or unattainable the solution may seem, pursuing the solution will yield positive economic benefits. Embellishing the scheduling logic to maintain buffers will both exact and perpetuate additional costs and/or investments.

Increasing safety stock in finished goods inventory for make-to-stock products and in level-one inventory for finish- or assemble-to-order products is the most popular "treatment" for buffering demand changes. This symptomatic treatment of the problem increases inventory investment and authorizes production before it is truly needed, which also increases the leadtime, distorts priorities and consumes resources before they are really needed. In addition, every time the dosage of safety stock is changed the result is just like another change in demand. That is, the treatment has become the same as the problem and increased its detrimental impact.

There are two key factors that degrade the execution of lower level MRP schedules, namely the reliability of the manufacturing process and the validity of the schedules. The solution to the problem is obvious, improve process reliability and schedule validity. However, past approaches have been

to treat the symptoms and ignore the diseases.
Embellishments to the scheduling logic have ignored
the obvious and aggravated the problem. Tedious
schemes have been devised to create allowances for
scrap and off-spec material. Those allowances usually
create unneeded inventory, increase leadtimes and
consume scarce resources which could have been used to
generate profits instead of waste. Elegant methods
have also been devised to supplement, after the fact,
the inability of MRP to anticipate anything but
average reliability problems. If the reliability
problems were eliminated there would be no need to
release invalid MRP schedules, or would there?

Basic MRP logic treats each item independently,
except for its demands. It does not consider any
joint impacts or interdependencies other than those in
the structure of the bills of material. It ignores
aggregate capacity constraints and economies which may
be derived from sequential production of similar
products. It provides a time-phased picture of
material requirements that is valid only when there is
adequate capacity available. Even a valid schedule
may not be the best schedule for a particular
environment. There may be additional economies
available from grouping and sequencing products at
intermediate levels in the product structure. This
grouping cannot be accomplished by MRP. In fact,
unless the grouping can be accomplished at the top of
the product structure, MRP cannot even accomodate the
grouping to yield a valid schedule at all levels in
the product structure. Additional tools are necessary
prior to the use of MRP to group and schedule some of
the items in the product structure and to insure
capacity availability, if MRP schedules are to be
valid.

This principle has been recognized for some time
and responsibility for its fulfillment has been
delegated to the Master Production Schedule (MPS).
Capacity availability checking and/or end-item
grouping and sequencing are in common practice. Some
intermediate grouping and sequencing is also done
within the time intervals of the MRP schedule.
However, there are environments where grouping and/or
sequencing of intermediate level items must be done
explicitly. MRP cannot be used to schedule production
of these items, but it can be used to schedule
availability of their components. It can also be used
to aggregate and offset the higher level demands that
must be met by these intermediate schedules. These
intermediate schedules constitute push planning.
Intermediate (lower) level item schedules control the
planned availability of higher level items. The same
is true when grouping and sequencing are performed
within the MRP time interval using a short-interval,
operations scheduling function. The flow of material
is being determined at an intermediate level and
pushed to higher levels.

This is not an indictment of MRP logic, it is
intended to clarify a variety of different ways in
which it may be applied, and their implications on the
scheduling and control of product flow. The basic
logic schedules discrete lots by netting requirements,
sizing production lots, and offsetting those lots to
generate the lower level component requirements
necessary to produce those lots. As the lot size
increases, the THROUGHPUT TIME OF THAT LOT is
increased, and the replenishment leadtimes for all the
parents of that component are also increased.
However, the TOTAL THROUGHPUT OF ALL LOTS will also
increase, if changeover or setup time(s) for the lot
that is increased are significant. Increasing the run
length or lot size of a single item is detrimental to
the smooth flow of ALL items in the schedule. The
only solution to achieve smooth flow AND maintain
total throughput is to eliminate as much of the
non-productive setup or changeover time as possible.

For many jobshop or make-to-order environments it
may not make sense to reduce the lot size, whereas, in
most repetitive/flowshop environments it is imperative
to reduce lot sizes. However, throughput will
increase in any environment if the setup or changeover
times are reduced. It should be recognized that as
lot sizes decrease, the number of lots must increase,
if the overall production rate is to stay the same.
Discrete MRP becomes more and more tedious to manage
as the number of lots increase (lot sizes decrease).
In repetitive environments it loses its applicability
all together in terms of scheduling individual lots,

but the basic logic remains sound. If the top-level
requirements used to drive MRP are changed from
production lots to production rates, the basic logic
can be used to plan component production and/or
procurement rates. In this application there is no
netting or lot sizing, unless a component is produced
or procured in large lots and inventoried.

The value of MRP, as a scheduling tool, is
directly proportional to the complexity of the product
structures of the products to be scheduled. However,
its value as a vehicle for the communication of
schedule changes is totally independent of that
complexity. Experience also indicates that basic MRP
logic is, and will remain, the logic of manufacturing.
New applications which utilize this logic will
probably continue to be developed as manufacturing
processes change and the understanding of existing
processes increases. The apparent direction of these
applications is to combine or supplement the basic
pull logic, primarily with push techniques that
consider interdependencies and aggregate resource
requirements, to create schedules that fit the process
AND represent the best strategy for running the
business.

DISTRIBUTION REQUIREMENTS PLANNING

The APICS Dictionary defines Distribution
Requirements Planning (DRP) as "the function of
determining the needs to replenish inventory at branch
warehouses." It further states that, "Frequently, a
time-phased order point approach is used where the
planned orders at the branch warehouse level are
exploded via MRP logic to become gross requirements on
the supplying source. In the case of multi-level
distribution networks, this explosion process can
continue down through the various levels ... and
become input to the master production schedule.
Demand on the supplying source(s) is recognized as
dependent, and standard MRP logic applies." That is,
DRP is a first cousin to MRP and it shares both its
strengths and its weaknesses. This discussion will
focus on the pull logic of DRP, its potential for
disrupting smooth product flow, and how supplemental
push technology can improve distribution schedules.

The pull logic of DRP is identical to that of
MRP, only the driver is different (or is it?). A
Level-0 or Level-1 master production schedule, or a
secondary Level-0 or Level-1 product availability
schedule derived from an intermediate-level master
schedule, typically drive MRP component scheduling.
Booked and forecasted customer demand at branch
warehouses is used to drive the pull logic of DRP
shipment scheduling. Customer demand is netted
against inventory to determine net requirements, those
requirements are lot-sized to plan replenishment
shipment receipts, and the shipment lots are offset by
the transportation time to become gross requirements
at the shipping source, typically the plant. This
logic is applied independently to each product at each
branch warehouse where it is stocked. The resulting
schedule does not consider the aggregate impact on
plant inventory or other distribution resources. It
simply calculates shipping requirements by product by
location and transmits those requirements as dependent
demands on plant inventory.

Additional tools which consider the aggregate
impact on shared resources are necessary to validate
these shipping schedules. Car loading or truck
loading programs group many products by location to
schedule carload/truckload shipments and plan the
resources necessary to execute the shipments. The
prerequisite for smooth product flow through both
production and the distribution network is the ability
to make and ship very small lots very frequently at
the rate they are demanded. The total volume of
demand at each branch warehouse must be adequate to
allow frequent shipments in economical
truckload/carload quantities. If the mix of
individual product demands is not consistent from
branch to branch and the frequency of shipments to
each location is not quite high, production must be
flexible enough to economically change its mix to
match the mix of upcoming shipments. When the mix is
inconsistent, the volume does not allow frequent
economical shipments, and/or production is not
flexible enough to react to frequent mix shifts, the

independent pull logic of DRP must be modified or supplemented to achieve valid shipment schedules that reflect the best way to run the business.

The independent lot sizing of distribution shipments for individual products assumes that plant inventory or production can economically absorb the impact of those lots as scheduled. The lumpy dependent demands for a given product are placed randomly on the plant by each stocking location with the expectation that inventory or scheduled production will be available to meet the demand. The timing of those lumps depends on the accuracy of the projected branch warehouse customer demands. A relatively small inaccuracy in projected customer demand can move those relatively large lumps and create a significant impact on plant schedules or inventory availability. There are a variety of ways to deal with this lumpy demand problem. Increased volume will decrease the relative size of the lumps and improve the predictability of customer demand. More accurate demand projections will reduce the number of lumpy demand shifts. Innovative packaging, material handling and shipment methods may also have potential in reducing the minimum shipment sizes of individual products. Improved production flexibility will minimize the economic impact of reacting to needed schedule changes.

The remaining alternatives are to buffer or embellish the scheduling logic, or to supplement the basic pull logic of DRP. Increasing safety stock at the branch warehouse increases inventory, lengthens replenishment leadtimes on other products, distorts priorities and consumes resources before they are truly needed. Adding safety stock at the plant to buffer the impact of dependent branch warehouse replenishment demands has the same detrimental effect on performance as increasing branch safety stock. It also violates the basic principle that safety stock is only used to buffer fluctuations in independent demand during the replenishment leadtime. It is sometimes possible to modify the lot sizing logic to yield smaller lots and thus reduce the impact of the lumps without giving up significant material handling and/or freight economies. However, because each product in each location is scheduled independently, no provision can be made for aggregate economic considerations without supplementing the basic pull logic of DRP.

Joint consideration of customer service, production and distribution concerns can best be accomplished at the plant level in the material flow heirarchy. The lumpiness of demands on plant inventory and schedules can be significantly reduced by eliminating all branch warehouse lot sizing from the DRP logic. The distribution requirements at the plant level would then represent net requirements to satisfy customer demand at the branches, offset by the replenishment leadtimes to the respective branches. In a flexible manufacturing environment, products could be grouped into planned shipments taking full advantage of available aggregate distribution economies. Production would then be scheduled to meet these shipping schedules with minimal plant inventory, but still satisfying customer service objectives. In a less flexible manufacturing environment, with significant economies available from long production runs or cyclical product sequences, production would be scheduled first. Production runs would then be allocated for shipment to branches to minimize plant inventory and satisfy customer demand. The allocation process would create an equal time-supply for each product in all branches. That time-supply would represent the planned interval between production runs for that product. In either case, shipment schedules would take the greatest possible advantage of available aggregate economies in both distribution and manufacturing, while maintaining customer service. Shipment schedules would then be pushed from the plant level to the branches. The branch availability is scheduled by the aggregate scheduling at the plant level, not by DRP lot sizes.

KANBAN

Kanban is widely recognized as a pull type execution tool. It is NOT widely recognized that Kanban is also a push scheduling and execution tool.

The pull system logic of Kanban assumes that a container(s) of parts will be available at the supplying workcenter(s) when the request is made to pull the parts up to the using workcenter. The question is, "How did they get there?". The answer is by the push system technology that is used to plan the number of Kanban's needed to support the pull system and the push logic of the production Kanban that authorizes replacement of each container at the supplying workcenter as a previously produced container is pulled up. The number of containers authorized to be in the outbound stocking point of the supplying workcenter is the number of Kanbans in the system for each part.

The equation used to calculate the initial number of Kanbans (see Figure 3.) reveals why this pull execution technique works. It can also be used to illustrate why MRP, without safety stock at every level, cannot be executed using pull technology. The numerator of the equation represents the number of units that will be consumed during the queue time and the production time for that part in the supplying workcenter, plus an allowance for the overall efficiency of that workcenter. The denominator converts the number of units to the number of containers or the number of Kanbans. The WIP inventory that is authorized by the Kanbans represents the expected usage of that part during its replenishment leadtime AT THE SUPPLYING WORKCENTER. That WIP is the same as the amount of safety stock that would be required to permit the pull execution of an MRP generated schedule for the same part, if and only if, the MRP lot sizes of all parts using that workcenter were equivalent to the number of units per container. Realistically speaking, that would be far too many lots. If lot sizes were increased to yield fewer lots, the safety stock requirements would be excessive. Therefore, we must use push execution for MRP schedules, or must we?

CALCULATING THE
NUMBER OF KANBANS

$$n = \frac{D\,(T_w + T_p)\,(1 + a)}{c}$$

n – total number of Kanban cards

D – average production rate per day (derived from the level master schedule, or parts schedules derived from it)

T_w – waiting time of Kanban cards (queue time for a part in decimal fractions of a day)

T_p – processing time (time required to make a part in decimal fractions of a day)

c – capacity of the standard container for the parts (the goal is less than 10% of daily requirements)

a – the policy variable which provides an allowance for the inefficiency of the workcenter producing the part

FIGURE 3.

Further investigation of the Kanban equation raises the question of how the demand rate was calculated. By definition it was derived from the master schedule. That derivation is simply MRP logic, without time-phasing, applied to a FIXED monthly demand rate in the master schedule. If that rate is changed from month to month, the number of Kanbans must be changed accordingly. This results in a change in the authorized WIP. If WIP goes up, the workcenter must produce enough containers in excess of demand to meet the added needs. If WIP goes down, production must be postponed until excess WIP is consumed. If the total workload from all parts made in the supplying workcenter changes additional changes will need to be made to capacity. All of these changes are disruptive to the smooth flow of product, thus demand must be fixed to avoid continual interruptions in product flow. If demand cannot be fixed for a reasonable period of time, such as a month, Kanban is not an appropriate tool.

The amount of WIP authorized by Kanban can also be quite excessive if the queue time or inefficiency of the workcenter are too high, or if the unit production time is excessive. The queue time is a function of the number of products produced in the workcenter, and the container size, processing time and setup time of each of those products. The number of products is more of a capacity issue, but all of the remaining elements of the queue time are related to the manufacturing process. Unless they are reduced to some acceptable minimum level, Kanban will require an unreasomnable investment in inventory. The efficiency factor is also a function of the manufacturing process. Its major element is quality, doing it right the first time with no scrap or rework. A non-zero efficiency factor acts just like safety stock, it creates inventory in anticipation of "uncontrollable" problems.

Stable schedules, reduced setups and improved process reliability are the cornerstones of Kanban success and applicability. In the MRP vs. Kanban controversy, there is no controversy. Both Kanban and MRP require the support of additional aggregate planning tools that insure capacity availability and represent the best strategy for running the business. MRP logic is used to set demand rates in those environments suitable for the application of Kanban. Stable schedules, reduced setups and improved process reliability will also improve performance in environments where Kanban is not appropriate. The technologies are compatible where they are used jointly, and there is no competition if Kanban is not appropriate.

ENVIRONMENTAL FLOW PROBLEMS

The ideal continuous flow environment is simply that, an ideal to be rigorously and relentlessly pursued. Success is measured in terms of progress toward the ideal, not the perfection or realization of the ideal. It has been demonstrated that scheduling technology can be misapplied to disrupt that flow. These disruptions stem from a lack of understanding of both the manufacturing process and the tools that are used (or not used) to create those disruptive schedules. The manufacturing process may also possess disruptive characteristics which are beyond the capability of current technology to solve. When the process is more art than science, conditions that yield only first quality product may be very difficult to duplicate consistently and economically. This condition can usually be relieved, but not always eliminated.

Current technology may also dictate that some processes be conducted in batches. This may be entirely a function of the production process, as in some chemical reactions, or it may be a function of technology and economics, as in the case of high setup or changeover times, the inability to measure flow that requires batch measurement, bulk transportation facilities, etc. Beyond technological innovation, there is a scheduling philosophy which can minimize the disruptive impact of batch processes. That philosophy is to limit the impact of the batch by flowing product through all those stages in the process that are not batch constrained. The result will be a pulsed flow of individual products, but smooth total flow is still achievable. The classic example is the make-to-order or finish-to-order environment. The key is matching the demand (and shipment) rate to the production rate. Matching individual product demand to individual product batches is a natural in a make-on-demand type marketplace. Make-to-stock markets require that demand between production runs equal the batch run length or some multiple thereof.

An example of a batch constrained environment is shown in Figure 4. This example also illustrates the use of both push and pull scheduling technology to create an intermediate level master schedule that is consistent with the best strategy for running the business. The best strategy for running the business is to maximize the utilization of the bulk production facility that makes Item Z and a family of similar products. The changeover time (lost production time) on the bulk facility can be minimized by sequencing the production of the family of bulk products. The

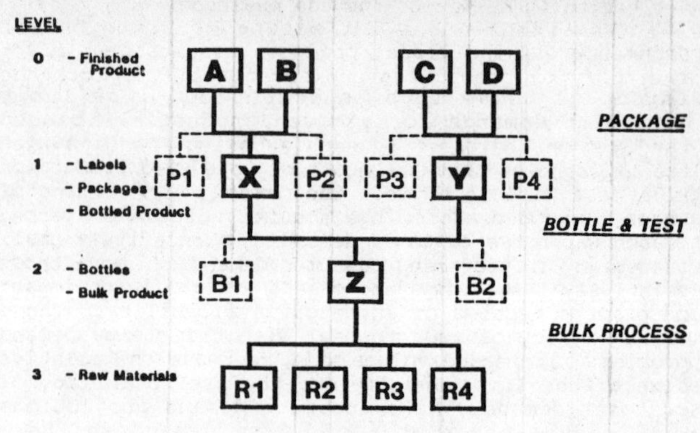

FIGURE 4.

schedules must minimize this lost productivity and meet the demand from customers for a variety of package size and brand name products like Items A, B, C and D. The master schedule, the "master of all other schedules", in this example is the schedule of the bulk facility. This facility requires a batch reaction process and the batch size is the same for each product.

The scheduling process takes place in four stages and uses a variety of scheduling tools. The first stage is master schedule requirements generation. Projected demand for finished products, A, B, C, D, etc., is netted against available inventory and offset by the production leadtime to create gross requirements at the next level down. Those gross requirements are accumulated by bottle size for each bulk product, netted against available inventory, and offset by production and quarantine leadtime to create gross requirements for the master schedule. Available inventory is all on-hand and scheduled on-hand product that has passed the bulk processing stage. The tool used in this stage is MRP logic with lot-for-lot lot sizing rules. Requirements are not lumped by lot sizes at each level, they are netted and given a time-phased offset, which translates them into demand on the bulk facility.

The second stage of the scheduling process determines the number of batches of bulk product needed to meet the translated demand, considering the need to sequence the runs of bulk product to minimize changeover time. The resulting master schedule, if it is feasible, will meet projected customer demands and achieve maximum bulk facility utilization. The sequenced runs, in multiples of the facility's batch size, drive all of the remaining product schedules at all levels in the manufacturing process. The third stage is the allocation of the bulk runs forward through the processes of bottling and packaging to the finished products. This allocation should create an equal time supply of products at each higher level in the product structure. That time supply, the run length in days of supply, represents the length of the cyclical production sequence. That is the amount of time before that product will be produced again. The intent is for all finished products made from the same bulk product to run out at the same time, the time of the next scheduled run for that product, without breaking the master schedule sequence of bulk products.

It should be noted that the schedule for each bulk product is firmed up by the second stage. The third stage firms up the schedule for those items directly on the where-used chain of each bulk item. The remaining items in the product structure are scheduled in the fourth and final stage. This stage can utilize classical top down MRP logic to schedule the remaining items, giving consideration to the firm planned orders created in the second and third stages. The MRP logic will accumulate requirements for items common to more than one product. It will also indicate any exception conditions created in earlier scheduling phases. These exceptions may result from lack of capacity to meet demand and maintain sequences simultaneously, or they may indicate remnants which were created when run lengths were rounded to multiples of batch size. Execution of all of these schedules, with possible rare exceptions, is done in a push mode. The scheduling used a combination of push and pull techniques.

SUMMARY

Pull is almost always in need of a little push. The challenge in scheduling is creating or determining the appropriate environment for the application of the appropriate tools. The disappointment is the waste of talent and rhetoric in an attempt to establish universal supremacy where none exists, and the wasted effort and detrimental impact of tryng to make inappropriate tools buffer or hide the real problems. The objective is excellence in manufacturing by pursuing all the opportunities to improve schedule execution.

Rich Heard is the principal counselor and educator of R.C. Heard & Co., a management counseling and education firm. Prior to forming his own company Rich was associated with the Manufacturing Industry Client Education program of Arthur Andersen & Company. His fifteen years in industry were concentrated in process and semi-process manufacturing. His responsibilities have included the design, development and implementation of management systems in the areas of manufacturing planning and control, distribution, forecasting, and stores inventory management. He has developed and conducted numerous seminars on both manufacturing planning and control and M.R.O. stores inventory management.

Rich holds a Professional Engineer degree and has done post-graduate work, both in Operations Research at the Colorado School of Mines. He is certified at the Fellow level through the APICS Certification Program. Rich chaired the APICS Process Industry Task Force. He currently serves on the Editorial Review Board of the APICS Production & Inventory Management Journal, on the Inventory Management Committee of the APICS Curricula and Certification Council, on the Process Industry SIG Steering Committee, and on the APICS Zero Inventory Crusade Committee. Rich is a past president of the Colorado Chapter and former national officer in APICS. He is co-author of the APICS Bill of Material Training Aid and the APICS Special Report Manufacturing Planning and Control in Process Industries. He is a frequent chapter, regional and national speaker for APICS and other professional societies.

JIT AND MRP—CAN THIS MARRIAGE BE SAVED?

Ed Heard, CPIM*
Plossl & Heard

FOREWORD

A basic premise of JIT manufacturing is that the key to real manufacturing success is the continuous integrated search for excellence in all phases of manufacturing operations. Although modifying closed-loop MRP systems to accommodate JIT-type scheduling practices is clearly a step in the right direction, there is some danger that MRP/JIT control systems will be promoted and perceived as shortcuts to full-scale JIT manufacturing. The purpose of this paper is to describe what can and cannot be done with MRP/JIT control systems and to stress the importance of process improvements in achieving truly significant performance advances.

RECENT DEVELOPMENTS

The zero inventory crusade met some initial opposition from forces in the PIC field with vested interests in closed-loop MRP systems. The developers, promoters and purveyors of manufacturing control system software were not thrilled to be told that "the Japanese were accomplishing miracles without sophisticated computer systems". But, when it became obvious that JIT was attracting a great deal of attention, the race was on. Software vendors vied for the best seats on the bandwagon.

The competition has taken two forms. There has been a genuine effort by some vendors to adapt their software for use in JIT manufacturing environments. That competition is healthy and manufacturing can only benefit from it. The other way in which vendors are competing for seats on the bandwagon is not so healthy. Pick up almost any manufacturing oriented trade magazine these days and look for the software ads. Chances are that those ads will attempt to appeal to people interested in JIT manufacturing in one way or another.

One common ploy is to incorporate something vaguely Japanese into the "eyecatching" portion of the ad. Some ads are not even remotely bashful. They take the meat axe approach. Not only do they use a strong JIT "eyecatcher" but the message comes through loud and clear in the ad text--the software being advertised is your ticket to JIT manufacturing. Therein lies the problem.

THE PROBLEM

JIT manufacturing requires not only excellent planning and execution, but it also requires an excellent environment. (See Figure 1.) What is the environmental nonsense--more

of Heard's heresy? The importance of the environment follows from a very simple notion. The manufacturing environment exhibits certain characteristics that are not influenced by planning and execution tools. More importantly, the environmental characteristics determine how effectively those tools can be used. (See Figure 2 for a list of those characteristics.)

The environmental characteristics are the same things JIT folks call ROCKS in the materials RIVER--plant layout, setup procedures, housekeeping, yields, materials handling, etc. No planning or execution tools can eliminate those rocks. But the rocks can limit the effectiveness of planning systems and execution tools. Advertising of the type described above merely further propagates the easy answer myth. But, there are no shortcuts to JIT manufacturing.

ENVIRONMENTAL IMPORTANCE

Maybe this environmental nonsense is not heresy after all. Haven't the process folks been trying for years to convince us that time-phased MRP is a little much for some of their plants? Likewise, haven't the repetitive manufacturing folks been telling us that work orders and dispatch lists are not really suited for their environments? Everybody has to plan and control priorities and capacities. But, the environment has a lot to do with what kind of planning systems and execution systems are needed to do the job and how well they will work.

ENVIRONMENTAL CHARACTERISTICS

QUALITY CONTROL OR MANAGEMENT

MAINTENANCE PROCEDURES

PROCESS IN USE

FACILITIES LAYOUT

TOOLROOM OPERATIONS

SETUP DESIGNS

SETUP SCHEDULING

PRODUCT DESIGNS

VENDOR RELATIONSHIPS

PURCHASING PROCEDURES

MATERIALS HANDLING

PRODUCT VARIETY

FIGURE 2

Could it be that the interactions between the environment and planning and execution tools are far more subtle than we have formerly understood? Excellent planning systems and execution tools are CONDITIONAL, not objective, terms. Planning systems and execution tools can only be described as poor and good relative to a specific environment. A planning system that is poor in one environment may well be excellent in another. Likewise, execution tools that are highly effective in one environment may be worthless or even overkill in another.

AN OBVIOUSLY INFERIOR PLANNING SYSTEM

Now for a truly heretical thought. If the environment determines how well planning systems and execution tools work, maybe the shortest route to improved performance is to concentrate on improving the environment. After all, if the environment is simple enough, it should not be all that hard to control. Could that be why Kanban, which has often been called an "obviously inferior planning system", gets such good results for Toyota?

DETERMINANTS OF MANUFACTURING EXCELLENCE

PLANNING SYSTEM	ENVIRONMENT	EXECUTION TOOLS	RESULTS
POOR	POOR	POOR	POOR
		GOOD	POOR
POOR	GOOD	POOR	POOR
		POOR	POOR
GOOD	POOR	POOR	POOR
		GOOD	POOR
	GOOD	POOR	POOR
		GOOD	GOOD

FIGURE 1

More to the point, Kanban is not and never has been a planning system anyway. It is an excellent execution tool for certain excellent manufacturing environments. It is no solution for poor environments. But then, neither is any other planning or execution tool. There are no planning and execution solutions to poor environments—— poor environments can only be improved by attacking environmental problems.

KANBAN IS NOT JIT

Kanban is not a solution to environmental problems. It is a mechanism that can be used in highly simplified environments to request parts, authorize production and movement of those parts, and control the level of work in process. In a sense, Kanban is used in highly simplified environments for the same purposes that dispatch lists, input-output reports and move tickets, are used in more complex environments.

Kanban is not JIT. Confusing JIT with Kanban is roughly equivalent to equating automobile engines to transportation. Engines are used to power automobiles. In turn, the automobile is ONE form of transportation. But, no knowledgeable person equates the two.

JIT MANAGEMENT PHILOSOPHY

JIT is a whole-company operating philosophy for long-run growth, survival and excellence in the face of worldwide competition. It incorporates simultaneous campaigns against waste and for the flexibility needed to respond to changing market conditions. Specific directions implicit in JIT include continuous efforts to reduce defects, inventories, production space requirements and labor content in the final product.

Long-run survival and growth can only occur if adequate profit levels are maintained. Profit levels can only be maintained by raising prices or increasing volumes. Raising prices is not a feasible approach because it drives customers away. Sometimes volumes increase simply because the market grows. But the idea is to increase market share——not just to grow at the market rate. Only then is long-term survival assured.

JIT MARKETING STRATEGY

Market share can only be increased by outperforming the competition. The marketing mix——product quality, service, price and availability——must be clearly superior. Still further, the only way to be absolutely sure of outperforming the competition is to be better than they are on ALL four criteria.

But the market share strategy for maintaining adequate profits can only work if costs are minimal. From a whole-company standpoint, that involves designing manufacturable products, introducing, producing and distributing them with little wasted time, material and effort, and doing all this at minimal cost.

JIT PRODUCTION STRATEGY

Total costs in a manufacturing-based company are limited to the costs of material used in the product, wasted material, manpower and overhead. Since overhead includes all plant and equipment, it is clear that long-term growth and survival implies a continuous search for excellence—— the highest quality at the lowest cost. It is also clear that TRUE lowest cost production implies minimum manpower, equipment, facilities and material relative to given levels of output.

To achieve true lowest cost production requires the virtual elimination of all waste. Quality must become near perfect, and materials must move, not sit. People and machinery must be used for JUST-IN-TIME PRODUCTION. They should make ONLY what is needed when it is needed. Early production and excess production imply that more material and people are being used than are needed. Likewise, late production or under production results in late deliveries, excessive shipping costs, etc.

JIT MATERIALS FLOW STRATEGY

If materials are to move not sit, they must flow like water. This, in turn, implies that material flow paths must be short and well-defined——highly structured. The focused factory concept is used to structure and define flows for products and product families. Group Technology (GT) cells are used to apply the same principles for parts and part families. In both cases, equipment must be dedicated to the production of groups of parts or products and rearranged in compact configurations to promote short constant movement.

The need for near constant flows implies a continuous battle to identify and permanently eliminate sources of disruptions. Since work-in-process and other inventories hide problems, they must be reduced to absolutely minimal levels thus heightening problem visibility and reducing carrying costs. Because large batch sizes are clearly inconsistent with constant material flows, every effort must be made to reduce setups to permit changeovers at will. Sometimes this means machinery and tooling improvements. In other cases, it may mean additional people for get ready work, teamwork, practice, etc.

Materials don't move when machines are down for repair so preventive maintenance takes on increased significance. Unexpected defects cause coordination problems, waste material, and play havoc with smooth material flows. Consequently, much effort must be devoted to understanding what causes defects, finding those causes and eliminating them permanently. Statistical Process Control, Quality Circles and other small group improvement approaches are often quite effective in eliminating the real causes of defects.

JIT EXECUTION STRATEGY

Producing parts before they are needed is inconsistent with the JIT philosophy. This has several ramifications for current practices. Individual incentive plans which encourage production independent of need are clearly not viable in a JIT environment since over or early production can easily result. Likewise, supervisory evaluations based on capacity utilization also becomes inappropriate. The issue is whether there is an immediate need for the parts being produced, not whether the workers meet or exceed standards nor whether the machines are fully utilized.

Production to need and constant material flows sound like inconsistent goals. It certainly dramatizes how balanced capacities must be in a JIT environment. Too much capacity results in people standing around. Too little starves downstream work centers. Fortunately the capacity balancing problem actually becomes simpler in a JIT environment due to the highly structured nature of the material flows. When the output end of the production process is tightly controlled and upstream workers are only authorized to produce in response to a pull signal, areas with too few and too many people are highly visible.

Level ouput schedules require the minimum number of workers for given volumes. Running highly structured and tightly linked production processes with minimum work-in-process requires immediate and accurate feedback from "users" to "makers" of parts. Flags, lights, cards and all kinds of other signaling devices can be used to provide this feedback and at the same time provide exceptionally tight control over the amount of work-in-process.

JIT AND CUSTOMER SERVICE

Historically, forecasting has been a real problem for most manufacturers because of long manufacturing lead times. Under JIT operation, the highly structured constant flows and pull system execution permit very short manufacturing lead times. In some cases, the reduction in manufacturing lead times is sufficient to permit formerly make-to-stock manufacturers to become make-to-order manufacturers. In other cases, the reduction simply gives the JIT user tremendous advantages in the market place and in leveling the production schedule.

Level output schedules seem at first glance to be inconsistent with responsiveness to market needs. But level output scheduling does not imply constant production of the same quantity of every item every day throughout the year. It does imply constancy over very short periods and carefully calculated minor changes between periods.

The idea is that short manufacturing lead times permit leveling the schedule with a very high degree of confidence that what is being produced is what is needed.

JIT SCOPE AND LONGEVITY

JIT is an all-encompassing manufacturing management philosophy. It reaches into areas that have previously been considered sacrosanct and challenges accepted practices. Why can't products be made more manufacturable? Why wait until designs are complete to start Value Analysis? Why carry so much service parts inventory? Why not spare capacity instead to make what is needed when it is needed? Does it cost more to tie up money in inventory or in capacity? Why are functions so segregated on the shop floor? Why can't the same guy that runs the machine "check its oil and kick its tires" every day?

JIT operation sounds great but it doesn't come overnight. Progress comes in bits and pieces one step at a time. Indeed, JIT is not a project or a program; it has no end. It is a forever commitment to continuous improvement and it takes everybody from bottom to top to make it work. The rewards are individual and corporate growth, prosperity and ever-increasing industry-wide respect.

JIT SHORTCOMINGS

JIT management philosophy is all encompassing. But for some areas, operational details are scarce. This is especially true for the many information intensive activities necessary to run a manufacturing business. How should the order entry function operate? How should materials be planned? How should purchase commitments be recorded? How should vendor performance be tracked? How should vendors be paid? How should engineering changes be handled?

Coordination, integration, and simplicity are emphasized in the JIT management philosophy. Ways to simplify manufacturing processes and material flows and thus coordinate and integrate manufacturing activities are also stressed. But what about the business activities described above? There are no inherent provisions in JIT for the coordination and integration of the various manufacturing interface activities.

MRPII ADVANTAGES

MRPII emphasizes teamwork. Coordination and integration of manufacturing and the various interfacing activities is necessary for effective and efficient company operation. The ability to operate using a single set of numbers is essential. But a commitment to operating with a single set of numbers imposes stringent information processing and data base maintenance requirements. These capabilities are an integral part of modern manufacturing control systems.

MRPII systems are designed to facilitate the coordination and integration of manufacturing and the various interfacing activities. Explicit mechanisms for supply and demand management in both single and multi-plant environments are provided. Ways to maintain bills of materials, routings and the other necessary data base components are also incorporated. Indeed, the ability to run a manufacturing company from a single set of numbers is one of the major advantages of MRPII.

CONCEPTUAL COMMONALITIES AND DIFFERENCES

Both approaches emphasize integration and coordination of manufacturing and the various interfacing activities. They differ, however, in terms of how integration and coordination are to be achieved. The MRPII approach is informational while the JIT approach is physical.

The informational approach is very general. It assumes that the necessary activities can be coordinated no matter how complex the manufacturing environment. The structural characteristics of the manufacturing process and the materials flows are considered relatively unimportant.

By contrast, the physical approach to coordination emphasizes manufacturing process and material flow organization. It is basically a MAKE THE PROBLEM SIMPLER approach. The idea is to simplify and integrate the physical processes and material flows to the point where coordination is not very difficult.

JIT/MRPII CONFLICTS

Both JIT and MRPII emphasize the importance of level master schedules. They differ, however, in terms of how schedules are to be leveled. The MRPII position is that master schedules need to be level in terms of capacity requirements. The JIT position is that master schedules should be level in terms of capacity and material requirements. (See Figure 3). A master schedule which is level in terms of material requirements will always be level in terms of capacity requirements. But the reverse is not true.

LEVEL CAPACITY SCHEDULE

		WEEK		
ITEM	1	2	3	4
A	250	150		
B		100	200	
C			50	150
D				100
TOTAL	250	250	250	250

LEVEL MATERIAL AND CAPACITY SCHEDULE

		WEEK		
ITEM	1	2	3	4
A	100	100	100	100
B	75	75	75	75
C	50	50	50	50
D	25	25	25	25
TOTAL	250	250	250	250

FIGURE 3

Under MRPII, execution is seen as simply a logical extension of the planning process. Work orders, dispatch lists and input/output control are the major execution mechanisms. Work orders are the primary mechanism for coordinating dependent material requirements and for determining capacities. All three mechanisms are heavily dependent on data collection and information processing capabilities. Data must be collected after every operation so that the progress of work orders on the floor can be monitored and output can be measured. Substantial information processing capability is needed to track work orders and update priorities. Work in process is limited by controlling the rates of input to gateway operations and manipulating capacity as necessary.

Under full-blown JIT operation, material flow patterns are highly structured and clearly defined. Flows are primarily one way with little backtracking and few crossovers. Capacity requirements are determined based on the rates of flow necessary along the various flow paths. Work orders are not used. Various signaling mechanisms such as Kanban are used to control the rates of flow and indicate current priorities. Various forms of physical control are used to limit work in process—standard containers, limited number of Kanban cards, etc. Little data is collected and not much information processing capability is needed for execution.

THE MARRIAGE

The conflicts above are undeniable. Nor are certain potentially complementary characteristics of JIT and MRP. Both stress the importance of the master schedule and planning. MRPII systems provide the information processing capability necessary for effective planning—let's not forget the importance of the "what if" capability. JIT emphasizes the importance of level capacity requirements AND material requirements. MRPII emphasizes the importance of short lead times. JIT provides a way to make them possible through its emphasis on focused material flows.

JIT and MRPII emphasize the importance of vendor management. The blanket order has long been an established MRPII precept. JIT provides a mechanism for leveling material usage, MRPII provides a means for determining the requirements for that material. JIT provides a means for reflecting actual usage; MRPII provides the information processing and communication capability necessary to transmit that information to vendors.

Teamwork is emphasized in both cases. MRPII facilitates teamwork at the functional level. JIT emphasizes the importance of integrating operating, inspection, maintenance, changeover and materials responsibilities at the worker and supervisory levels. It also emphasizes the role of the worker in improving the process.

Marriage of the complementary features of MRP and JIT is clearly attractive. But it is just as clear that some means must be found to overcome the apparent conflicts.

GOLDEN ANNIVERSARY EDITION

What would a manufacturing plant that successfully married JIT and MRP look like after a few years? It would be extremely well organized with clearly defined short straight material flows—focused factories, GT cells, overlapped operations, etc. There would be no store room. Instead, there would be clearly defined stockpoints on the floor. Processes would be extremely reliable and there would be few quality problems.

Standard containers would be used to transport small lot sizes. A visible signaling system would be used to communicate priority changes and "pull" containers from stockpoint to stockpoint on the floor. These "pulls" would occur almost continuously as a result of mixed model final assembly scheduling and would cascade all the way through to sole source vendors. Work in process would be physically limited. There would be very little labor and inventory transaction reporting.

Material requirements will be planned with a daily bucket rate-focused MRP system. (See Figure 4). Work orders would not be used. Production planners would adjust individual part work in process levels and modify run rates to accommodate out of balance conditions due to demand level and mix changes and minor quality problems. Capacities would be adjusted by individual supervisors based on projected part run rates. See Figure 5 for an illustration of the contrast between the priority and capacity management functions under MRP and JIT.

SILVER ANNIVERSARY EDITION

What will a plant look like on its way to a full-scale JIT and MRP marriage? Since JIT is effectively a long term project, it is inevitable that it will operate in a dual-mode during that evolution. All parts will be made under work order control. Lot splitting will be the rule rather than the exception. Small lot parts will flow through the plant. Large lot parts will go back and forth to the storeroom between levels of the product structure.

Although machines will be functionally arranged at first, GT cells will be introduced and flow will ultimately become the rule rather than the exception. The two types of operation and the two types of parts will be matched and segregated to the extent feasible.

	1	2	3	4	5	6	7	8	9
REQUIRED	50	50	50	50	55	55	55	55	55
SCHEDULED	50	50	50	50	50				
ON HAND	20	20	20	20	20	15	20	20	20	20
PLANNED		50	50	50	60	55	55	55	

FIGURE 4

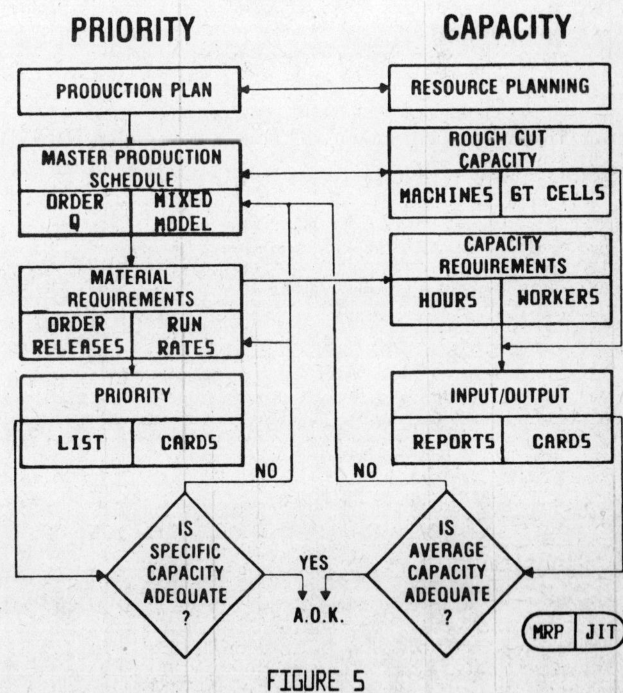

FIGURE 5

The type of labor reporting being used in a work area will be dictated by whether it is a functional department or a GT cell. Traditional inventory transactions will be used for large lot production with tollgates or checkpoint reporting being used for small lot production. Initially, weekly bucket MRP systems will be used with ultimate conversion to daily buckets. Period work orders will be issued for all parts. Multiple lot sheets or cards will be issued for small lot production and will be used to "pull" parts to the next tollgate. Conversion rate factors will be used to indicate how many partial batches should be run during the period and how large those batches should be.

Standard containers will gradually be introduced into the process. As master scheduling leveling capability improves, standard container quantities, lot sizes and master scheduling quantities will be coordinated. In the interim, lot sheets will be used to control container quantities and hence limit work in process. All inventory and labor transactions will be reported against period part work orders.

SUMMARY AND CONCLUSION

Certainly the marriage appears to be logical. Will it work? It will work to the extent that the adopters recognize the importance of the environment. Attempts to combine the planning capabilities of MRP with the pull system execution features of JIT without simplifying the manufacturing process are doomed from the start. It takes excellent planning systems and execution tools AND an excellent environment to get excellent results. The success of individual JIT and MRP marriages will be governed by the amount of effort dedicated to improving the environment.

ABOUT THE AUTHOR

Ed Heard is a principal in Plossl and Heard, a manufacturing management counseling and educational services company based in Columbia, South Carolina. He currently conducts Just-In-Time manufacturing seminars and provides counseling and educational services for a variety of major manufacturing companies. He has an extensive background in materials management that includes a unique combination of hands-on practical experience and academic know-how. He has conducted materials management seminars throughout the U.S. and has been consulting, publishing and educating for fifteen years. Ed is a frequent speaker at local professional society meetings and at national conferences and seminars. He is certified at the Fellow Level by APICS and is active in both APICS and IIE. He is a prolific author and has published in production and inventory management, project management, data processing and accounting trade and academic publications. Ed earned MBA and DBA degrees in production management at Indiana University after working in materials management at Rockwell Manufacturing Company during the middle sixties.

INTEGRATING JIT WITH MRP—AN UPDATE

J. N. Edwards, CPIM*
Rath & Strong, Inc.
J. W. Anderson
Stanadyne Diesel Systems

INTRODUCTION

Last year a paper was presented highlighting how JIT was integrated with MRP. In that presentation we covered the background of MRP and JIT and how we handled the integration of the two approaches where JIT was in fact a "parameter setter" for MRP.

Now after a year of experience we have gained some additional insights. These include a better understanding of the roles of JIT and MRP as well as how to refine the two systems to handle such areas as multi-plant MRP, both batch and flow control, and the interfaces between MRP and JIT.

JIT and MRP INTERFACE UPGRADE

A year of added experience has helped better define the roles of JIT and MRP, for JIT is dealing with the process while MRP is concerned with the planning. This year of experience has created the new addage of "Simplify, Simplify, Simplify" to go along with last years' presentation quoting Mr. Cho's statement on the Elimination of Waste. "...anything other than the minimum amount of equipment, materials, parts, and workers (working time) which is absolutely essential to production..." JIT represents a philosophy that among other things attempts to reduce lead times to zero and lot sizes to one. As such, bill of material levels are eliminated or rethought. Decisions to stock material at different levels because of lot sizing are also altered. A JIT process improvement requires that past practices be reexamined, or to quote Ed Parish of Black & Decker, "Don't get trapped by the MRP metality."

On the other side of the JIT coin, not every process can be simplified to "zero lead time" and a "lot size of one." Therfore a manufacturing control system must be able to handle lot control parts when required as well as handle parts on a flow basis. Whenever a flow can be established, a candidate for "Just In Time" and "Pull" control has been created. The longer the flow, the deeper the overall pull system can be used. To date, lot controlled parts (lots greater than todays usage) still have to be "delivered" to a "stock" area and theby remain on some kind of due date or "push" system.

Finally, the use of "cycle plans" and material flow charts have become an important part of establishing how a process can be planned and controlled by MRP and JIT. The remainder of this presentation will cover how Stanadyne has made further gains in incorporating JIT principles into their overall Program.

THE CASE STUDY

Like many U.S. companies, Stanadyne is wasting no time adapting compatible Production Control techniques, such as KANBAN to their MRP system. To achieve real success in this area, we found it necessary to manufacture under the philosophy of Just-In-Time. That included:

1.) perfect quality
2.) shortening setups and/or
    dedicating machinery

3.) reducing lot sizes
4.) shortening lead times
5.) the focused factory approach
6.) leveling/stabilizing schedules
7.) designing/structuring for
    manufacturability
8.) reducing breakdowns
    (preventative maintenance)

There have been many changes in our manufacturing culture. We began under the job shop philosophy, and now use repetitive manufacturing techniques.

As we made the transition from job shop to flow shop, our manufacturing processes were streamlined to permit line flow operation. As we examined this "new" technology, it became apparent that our manufacturing system would need an overhaul if it was to support the shop floor. Four areas of our manufacturing system received considerable attention.

They were:

1.) the Inventory - from stockrooms
    to material flow
2.) the MRP - from single plant, job shop
    to orderless and multiplant
3.) the Bills of Material - from design to
    manufacturing structure
4.) the Execution systems - from word-of-
    mouth to KANBANS

This paper will attempt to describe our approach in each of these critical areas, explaining in moderate detail, the mechanics behind each conversion.

THE COMPANY

Stanadyne Diesel Systems is a division of Stanadyne, Incorporated, and manufactures precision diesel fuel injection systems for a wide variety of domestic and international customers. There are three primary product lines.

They are:
1.) Diesel Fuel Injection Pumps
2.) Diesel Fuel Injection Nozzles
3.) Ancilliary Products
    Fuel Filters
    Water Separators
    Fuel Heaters

Production rates for the various product lines range from 100 to 10,000 units per day, and manufacturing takes place in four plants in Connecticut and North Carolina. We also have a service parts distribution facility in Garrett, Indiana.

THE INVENTORY SYSTEM

Perhaps the most significant change in our Inventory system has been in our perception of inventories. Rather than inventory being held in a stockroom for subsequent use on 'JOBS', the system has been redesigned to accomodate inventory in constant motion or FLOW. The addition of a floor onhand classification that we call INPRODUCTION has provided three significant improvements. The first improvement has been the ability to receive finished components directly to the floor rather than to a stockroom. Although the previous restriction was imposed by our inventory valuation technique, we can now satisfy the accounting valuation and manufacturing flow requirements. Material can now flow naturally and have full valuation on the floor. The second improvement has been the ability to have material on the floor that has not been reserved for a specific higher (BOM) level assembly. The INPRODUCTION classification is a pool of material available for any higher level need. Our manuafacturing lines are designed such that commitment to the higher level is made as far toward the end of the process as possible, making allocation at or before issue as impractical as it is undesirable. The third improvement is the use of the inventory classification in place of a level in the Bill of Material. Rather than issuing the component(s) as some semi finished assembly which would later be issued as the final assembly, the blank configuration is issued to Inproduction as itself (same part number), remaining there under it is committed _physically_ to the higher level assembly. Figure (1) is provided to demonstrate the basic material flow and the material classifications involved. The entire material flow network comprises many of these basic modules used at three primary manufacturing categories.

They are:

    1.) Blanks
    2.) Components
    3.) Assemblies

MATERIAL FLOW

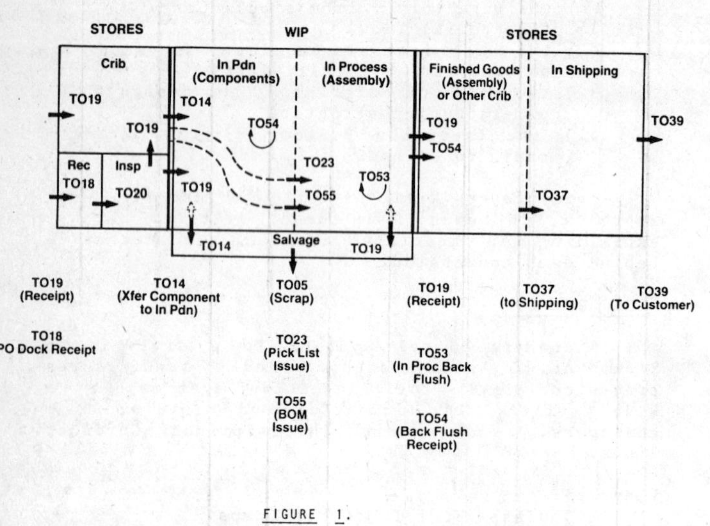

FIGURE 1.

Through years of engineering work we have restructured our products using as many common BLANKS as possible. In many cases we have moved operations from raw material, first operations to the finishing operations on components. This effort has allowed us to dedicate many machines that were subjected to numerous changeovers, large lot sizing, and long lead times.

At the COMPONENT level(s), inventory can flow up the Bill of Material, several levels at a time, without being routed through a stockroom. Inprocess and Inproduction BACKFLUSH transactions are used to track the inventory through these various levels of manufacture. (Inventory transactions will be described in some detail in a latter section of this paper.) With the introduction of multiplant MRP into our manufacturing system, the need to capture all inventories, including that on the trucks became apparent. Another classification, INTRANSIT, was developed to fulfil this new requirement.

INTRANSIT TO and INTRANSIT FROM each plant in the network is maintained to give timely visibility of the rapidly moving inventory at each location. Our system uses both REAL (MRP netted) and PSEUDO (not netted) inventory classifications. In our multiplant configuration, the "buckets" indicating the FROM intransit inventory are REAL since the inventory belongs to the receiving plant, and the TO intransit inventory is PSEUDO since it is a _memo_ inventory. The TO intransit inventory is visible under the SENDING plants' inventory and the FROM intransit inventory is visible under the RECEIVING plants' inventory. The RECEIVING plant uses the SENDING plants count for the INTERPLANT RECEIPT transaction. Discrepancies in counts are handled after the fact and only on items where counts differ by an ABC determined percentage. INTERPLANT ISSUES are made to an INTERPLANT ORDER generated by MRP or by a parts planner. Material is received from vendors using the traditional dock-to-stock method, except that material can be received directly to the floor (ONHAND - INPRODUCTION).

Purchased and/or raw material is received at the dock and placed into a PSEUDO inventory bucket ININSPECTION. Although we are very interested in receiving certified material from all of our vendors, we have only signed three vendors to date. Material is received to a REAL ONHAND location following inspection. The purchase order is accordingly reduced by the quantity received. The various transactions used to FLOW our inventory accomodate both batch and repetitive manufacturing.

Our manufacturing operations continue to be hybrid. We have our high dollar-volume parts processed on lines using repetitive techniques, and our lesser parts processed in batch on both dedicated and general purpose machinery. To effectively control these diverse activities, two techniques reside within our manufacturing system. Neither of the techniques use manufacturing orders. Instead, they are scheduled by part number, quantity and due date. However, the batch processed parts use the issue-to-make (commit at issue to the higher level) and the line flow parts use the issue-as-is (commit on the floor or upon completion) approach. The line flow parts have their components consumed by two types of BACKFLUSH transactions.

The first transaction is the ONHAND BACKFLUSH. It is used to handle inventory transactions derived from production counts as well as from stockroom receipts of blanks, components, or finished goods. After entering the completed part number and a quantity, the Bill of Material is referenced for its components. The ASSEMBLY is added to a specified onhand location, and the components are subtracted from INPRODUCTION (an onhand location). The onhand location used for the assembly may be a stockroom or INPRODUCTION. In the latter case the inventory flows up the Bill of Material while remaining on the floor. This INPRODUCTION backflush continues so long as the assembly part number is common to two or more higher level assemblies, or until the part is to be transferred to another plant. The ONHAND or INPRODUCTION backflush has an additional feature, in that it always attempts to relieve all or part of the quantity for the ASSEMBLY from INPROCESS. Any quantity it cannot relieve from INPROCESS is extended by the BOM quantity-per and reduced from INPRODUCTION. Components not existing in the INPRODUCTION are posted to an exception report, and the differences handled manually. In this mode it may be used as the final transaction in a series using the other BACKFLUSH.

The second BACKFLUSH transaction is used with the INPROCESS inventory 'bucket', and is never used to receive to ONHAND. In a manner similar to the onhand backflush, inventory can be moved up the BOM without passing through a stockroom. The Inventory system is used in place of conventional Shop Floor Tracking.

By strategically including SOC (stage of completion) part numbers in the Bill of Material and applying inventory transactions to them, material is tracked at bottlenecks and/or significant value-added points in the process. SOCs are also used at each department such that the MRP is used not only as a material planning technique, but also as a detailed shop floor scheduling system. Units planned in MRP are

conveniently converted in manufacturing hours and
manpower required. This "new" inventory system
when joined with our modified approach to MRP
fulfils the need for Parts Tracking , as well as
for Material and Capacity Planning systems.

THE MRP

The term MRP will be used in this paper to
describe gross to net explosion logic. It does
not refer to the broader concept of MRP II.

Our MRP began like most systems available
from the large software houses offering such
products. It processed requirements and
replenishments level by level in the BOM. It was
status driven, that is, replenishments follow a
progression from unexploded (status 1) to
complete (status 6). The full progression is:

```
1 = Unexploded
2 = Exploded
3 = Signalled
4 = Approved
5 = Issued
6 = Complete
```

The MRP has been modified, however such that
orders are masked from the shop floor. Order
quantities are clustered into weekly buckets and
presented as schedules to the shop floor.
Requirements are calculated after netting
ONHAND and INPROCESS (instead of ONHAND and
ONORDER). Replenishments are calculated from
various MRP management policy data (yield, fixed,
minimum, maximum, and multiple quantities).
Repetitive and batch processed parts are handled
differently:

Status	Batch	Repetitive
1 = Unexploded	X	X
2 = Exploded	X	X
3 = Signalled	X	X
4 = Approved	X	
5 = Issued	X	
6 = Complete	X	X

MRP netting has been made sensitive to
Status such that status 5 replenishments are not
netted. They are covered by INPROCESS in the
netting logic. Status 2 and 3 replenishments are
netted as well as INPROCESS. They are replanned
both in TIME and QUANTITY so that they reflect
when issues are needed. This scheme allows MRP
to plan and replan repetitive parts without
regard for orders since they are never approved
nor issued relative to a given replenishment
(status 4 and 5 not used for repetitive parts).
Issues are planned based on the quantity
INPROCESS. Inventory receipts consume the oldest
replenishment first, automatically, without
entering an order number. The output of the MRP
is fed into subsytems depending on the type of
part. For example, parts made from raw stock
have an independent scheduling system which
calculates production hours by department within
the schedule. Rates of production are calculated
for each part even though they may be run in
batch. Repetitive parts are organized, and rates
of production are calculated for each family, in
our Repetitive Scheduling system. Multiplant MRP
is performed in the true context, i.e. a single
planning event for all plants within the system.

Our multiplant MRP generates INTERPLANT
orders that are also used for over/under
reconcilliation of shipments.

The planning process is described as follows:

Since the MRP is net change, there is an
activity file which activatesthe necessary
PART/PLANTS for replanning. The file is
organized by low level code.

1. The activity file is read and a
   PART/PLANT is retrieved.

2. Requirements for that part at that plant
   are accumulated.
3. Inventory is netted.
4. Replenishment are calculated using MRP
   policies.
   The replenishments are inserted under the
   activity plant.
5. The BOM, or on default, the partmaster,
   is referenced for the source.
6. If the source is different that the PLANT
   read from the activity file,
   a requirement with identical due date and
   quantity for each
   replenishment is inserted under the
   source plant.
   In this case the PART and source plant
   are inserted into the
   activity file for later processing. If
   the source plant and the
   activity plant are the same, then the
   part is exploded and a
   requirement for each component is placed
   under the activity plant.
   Each component PART and activity PLANT is
   placed in the activity file.
7. The next activity record is read and the
   process continues.

Although the traditional ordering policies
are available to us, we have settled on the
PERIODS of SUPPLY logic for our repetitive
parts. This gives us the effect of requirements
in weekly buckets. In conjunction with the
PERIODS of SUPPLY policy, we use the MULTIPLE
quantities option, where the multiple is assigned
using STANDARD CONTAINER quantitites. The
MULTIPLE quantity feature has the additional
benefit of reducing nervousness in the planning
process. Lead times for KANBAN scheduled parts
is simply set to zero. For parts processed in
lines, two techniques are used to establish lead
time or the effect of lead time. The first
technique is to vary lead time based on demand
such that a constant quantity INPROCESS is
maintained. The second technique uses a data
base parameter - FIXED INPROCESS. Using this
quantity the repetitive scheduling system
calculates issues based on maintaining this fixed
quantity INPROCESS. Much like a garden hose can
hold only so much water, so to our manufacturing
lines can hold only a fixed quantity of parts
(without overflowing).

THE BILLS OF MATERIAL

History

Stanadyne first entered their Bills of
Material into electronic files during the 1960s.
This was under a part numbering system quite
different than todays. Part numers were
significant and we followed only a few of the
rules used in todays structuring. In 1970 the
files were converted to the DBOMP data base to
allow rudimentary Bill processing. Even these
BOMs followed the Design Engineering structure
with little regard to manufacturing flow. Our
products were designed to Customer's
specifications, and new part numbers were issued
with each new model. Part numbers proliferated.
There was little standardization.

The Change in Thinking

In 1977, with the introduction of
significantly higher volumes in the Automotive
Diesel Market, we began to implement 'new'
processing techniques. With these techniques
came the obvious review of what parts could be
manufactured as families of parts. Changeovers
became a constraint on capacity, and the process
of consolidating part numbers, standardizing,
began.

Restructuring

During 1980, the concept of structuring with
Blanks, Components, and Assemblies reached us.

Every part we made or purchased, which had manufacturing operations in house, was assigned a Blank part number. Later, Raw Material was added to the BOMs.

Our strategy has been to standardize from the bottom - up. We have dramatically reduced the number of parts made from raw material. The impact of this is apparent when screw machines can be dedicated to a single Blank used in a family of parts. There are no setups. Lead times become short without lot sizing. And they can be scheduled using a KANBAN.

The future is bright. We have a new product which is a standard pump, the operating parameters of which are controlled through software. It's a microprocessor controlled, diesel fuel injection pump.

Although standardization may not be the wave of the future, it is allowing us to benifit from short changeovers (dedicated machinery), short lead times (reduced lot sizes), and improved flexibility (parts dedicated to higher levels late in the process). And to do this without massive capital expenditures for the latest manufacturing technology.

The Bill of Material structure, and the appropriate manufacturing process can at least delay, until the culture is ready, implementation of the ultimate job shops under Computer Integrated Manufacturing.

THE KANBANS

KANBANS continue to spread throughout Stanadyne. They have been primarily used to schedule common BLANKS and COMPONENTS, but have been creeping into final assembly as well.

Their success must be attributed to many people at Stanadyne, but primarily to the people that actually make the parts. The intense interest in improving quality, and the many clever ideas that have been spawned from Quality Circles, have created the conditions required to make KANBANS work.

The introduction of Statistical Process Control (SPC) at Stanadyne has proven to be an excellent process control technique, as well as an introduction to a different approach to manufacturing.

KANBAN and MRP

As described in last years paper, KANBAN and MRP mix well. MRP schedules a using operation and KANBAN schedules the supplying operations. (Figure 2.) As our process quality and reliablility improves, we have implemented KANBANS as the scheduling technique. The strategy remains one that uses KANBANS at the cutup of raw material first, progressing up the BOM to the Master Production Schedule. (Fig.3)

SUMMARY

The Just In Time or Zero Inventory Crusade is as exciting to us as it was a year ago. We've matured a lot in our understanding of when and how to make use of Just In Time principles.

We mentioned earlier that we are still a hybrid shop. Some of our processes have not achieved the levels of perfection required to implement KANBANS, and by their very nature may never. But we will strive toward the goals of zero lead times, lot sizes of one, short setups, and the often elusive stabile schedule. We'll do it just because its good management practice. We'll do it because its common sense.

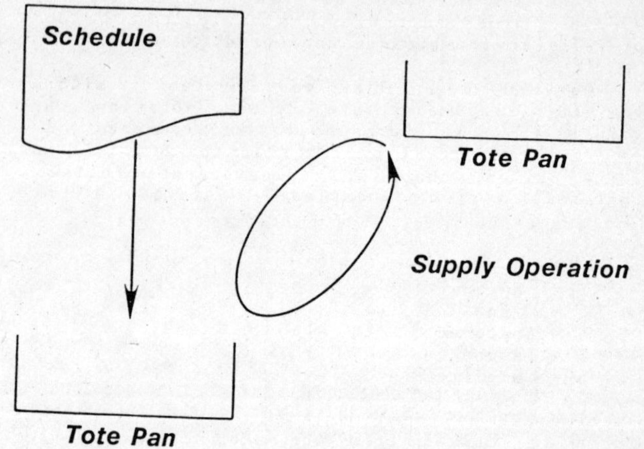

FIGURE 2.

STRUCTURE

SCHEDULE

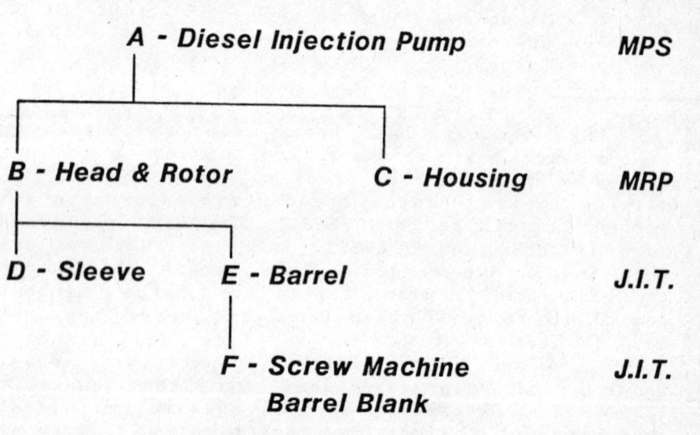

FIGURE 3.

IMPLEMENTING JIT/TQC

Charles G. Andrew, CPIM*
Charles G. Andrew & Co.

FIGURE 1

MRP II JOURNEY (overview)

STAGES IN MRP JOURNEY	PERFORMANCE RESULTS TO BE EXPECTED			
	Delivery Reliability	Manufacturing Throughput Time	Flexibility Replenishment Period	Stock Ratio
1 Today Define Scope and Objectives				
2 MRP I Gain basic control				
3 MRP II Integrate control and improve productivity				
4 MRP II EXTENDED: Achieve continuous productivity improvement JIT - TQC - People				

The just-in-time techniques and total quality control practices (JIT/TQC) are now beginning to receive, and deservedly so, serious coverage in the literature. But while we may now know what JIT/TQC is all about, precious little has been put forth for practitioner guidance on the how to of implementing the new approaches successfully in Western World manufacturing firms. And, based on the author's study mission experience in Japan, that real-world application gap is crucial to profitable survival.

This paper fills that gap by addressing the implementation issues of moving manufacturing ahead on the JIT/TQC journey. Implementation, Japanese-style, is contrasted with the efforts of major North Atlantic manufacturers who are revving up their productivity machines--just-in-time. An implementation framework, based on successful experiences in Japan, the USA, and Europe, is outlined as a road map for others who wish to step up to JIT/TQC. Recommendations for specific improvement actions in the areas of planning, product development, processing, and procurement as well as quality and workforce management (the Four P's Plus) are provided as "handles" for change that the new JIT/TQC concepts represent.

The bottom line is that you do not have to be Japanese to move up to JIT/TQC. But manufacturing professionals do need an effective approach to put the "zero inventory concepts" into practice step-by-step. This paper provides guide posts to make that journey to JIT/TQC successfully.

PERSPECTIVE: THE JOURNEY TO JIT/TQC

It was not too long ago that the gurus stated unequivocably that "there is nothing beyond MRP". Then a number of practitioners demonstrated that you could integrate marketing, manufacturing, and finance under one umbrella, MRP II, Manufacturing Resources Planning. Relating MRP II to the strategic thrust of an organization was the next logical step. And at each stage there were those who said: We have now completed the journey.

They were wrong. They will continue to be proved wrong because productivity improvement in manufacturing is a continuous journey. As the late Joe Powell put it: "Change is sweeping the world. The latest design on one drawing board becomes instantly obsolete as soon as a newer design is started on the next. You have to run like the wind just to stay in place, let alone get ahead. And in today's world the prize does go to the swift."

And that is what happened when JIT/TQC burst on the scene the past five years or so,--and caused loads of consternation in the old MRP camps. There was a lot at stake in terms of fixed notions and fixed investments, both threatened by the newer JIT/TQC techniques. What that thinking totally missed was that humankind is on an improvement journey and manufacturing is no exception.

Given some constructive thought, it becomes quite apparent that JIT/TQC, in real world practice, is truly an extension of the MRP II philosophy. Figure 1 represents a conceptual framework with just-in-time and total quality control as the ultimate destination--at least in terms of today's thinking. On the JIT/TQC journey there are at least four stages through which most manufacturing firms will progress and with each stage we can set targeted performance results to be achieved in at least four critical measurement areas:

- delivery reliability
- manufacturing throughput
- factory flexibility
- inventory stock levels

From a point of inadequate control (during the first stage), an organization will need to step up to MRP I. This is a big control system, appropriate because firms about to enter the second stage will most likely have huge inventories which are "out of control." Complex inventories mandate complex solutions (MRP I), and productivity can then improve.

The third stage in the journey addresses familiar MRP II territory. As the inventory becomes manageable, financial controls and marketing policy are integrated with manufacturing planning; an organization's total resources are directed towards an overall strategic game plan. Productivity improvements in this stage are noticeable and quite rewarding. In particular, inventories begin to decrease dramatically. And that sets the stage for JIT/TQC.

You see, when you don't have very much inventory you don't need a massive P&IC system. That's a basic principle taken from systems thinking and engineering control practices. To illustrate: you must have a very complex control system for a NASA space launch, but the planning and control required for a trip to the local supermarket is obviously much simpler. So it is with manufacturing. When inventories are high, the control system must be complex. Otherwise manufacturing operations are "out of control". When inventories have been reduced substantively, well, then you just don't need as complex a P&IC system.

No, the MRP system does not go away! In fact, MRP must be fast response. But a lot does happen to simplify it. Levels in the bill of material become fewer, stockrooms tend to disappear, production moves from batch to flow, quality levels are extremely high so buffers and rework are substantially reduced--the point becomes clear. When inventories are reduced the planning becomes easier and execution/control out on the shop floor are much more straightforward, handled by the line on the basis of orderly hustle to meet the plan. In effect, the factory, our productivity machine, becomes simultaneously flexible to the marketplace and stable in the shop. Such a factory has reached today's state of the art, JIT/TQC, what we call MRP II Extended.

> GUIDELINE: Manufacturing firms wishing to move up to JIT/TQC should assess their present capabilities, see what the state of the art is for present practices. Thoughtful and ultimately effective productivity improvement journeys will tend to follow four stages, from "gaining control" with MRP I through MRP II and finally on to JIT/TQC (MRP II Extended).

JIT CONDITIONS AND THE FOUR P'S PLUS

The first time you view a Japanese factory that has reached the JIT/TQC stage you are in total wonderment. You know something is different, totally different than you've ever experienced before. And then the light dawns--where is all the inventory? It is different, even a little bit "scary" for those raised in Western World manufacturing where queues, buffers, and safety stocks were traditional ways of problem solving. But what you finally learn, and today can affirm from readings on Japanese manufacturing techniques, is that the lack of inventory is the result of innovative production planning/thinking and truly sound shop floor practices. Based on our own experience in Japan and confirmed by ongoing implementations in the West, we have compiled a list of conditions for just-in-time production. These include:

- "zero" inventories
- make/buy to schedule
- co-makership
- mixed model assy.
- batch size "one"
- single digit S/U

- L.T. = processing time
- MPS -> no surge
- focused factory
- management by sight
- PPM quality levels
- neat housekeeping

It is instructive to note that the Japanese took a different approach to productivity than the Western World. While the Western World was busy with planning and control systems, the Japanese attacked what in retrospect was the heart of the problem--the shop floor. This is where the rubber meets the road, where chips are cut, where parts go together and where product is made. In a word, the shop floor is where the action is--planned results are achieved. The Japanese approach was to work towards simplifying the productive system with the result that less complex manufacturing planning and control support would be required. Most Japanese factories we saw did have an MRP based planning system. But they appeared to be far simpler (fewer levels, fewer whistles and bells) than those typically found in the West. The concentration of effort in Japan over the past 20-25 years has been on improving shop floor practices, simplifying shop scheduling, and streamlining the factory.

In assessing this situation with Western manufacturers the major opportunity we saw, and had to problem solve, was how to move these organizations, most of which had basic MRP systems and thought in terms of large, computer-based P&IC systems, through the journey to JIT/TQC. We found six managerial handles which we labeled the Four P's Plus. Let's look at each of them.

1. Planning. Shaping up the planning system and its use presents improvement opportunities in three areas:

- a baseline standard MRP system should be in place, or the existing one upgraded so the organization has proper ordering and overall priority capabilities to support flow production.

- integration of marketing, production, and financial planning represents a fertile area--in particular, the design/use of the measurement system along integral lines will be particularly productive.

- the management of the master production schedule is the third key area and the objectives here should be the elimination of surges (a level MPS), a short firm period in the MPS resulting from rapid throughput, both providing maximum factory flexibility, schedule stability within the firm period, and visibility/commitment for resource management.

2. Product Development. With this P we find productivity improvement achievements stemming from:

- structuring to facilitate final assembly scheduling as well as commitment and orientation planning.

- policies, procedures and good practices to smoothly introduce engineering change on a timely basis.

- design for producibility in both the inside factory and with outside vendors.

- standardization--product simplification pays!

- effective, non-disruptive new product introduction and old product phase out, a team effort.

3. Processing. This is a critical P and an area on which the Japanese have focused their early attention. Conversely, it is that very area where Western World manufacturing has suboptimized. Processing improvement, on an integral basis with both product design and planning procedures, should strive for:

- standard methods
- process control for TQC
- process flexibility
- workforce participation
- layout--go to flow
- single digit setup
- multi-machine operation
- rapid material transfer

4. Procurement. Here the co-maker concept needs to be put into practice to achieve closer alliance and hand shake relationships with vendors--in place of the old, adversarial style of purchasing management. The benefits include shared productivity gains through the extra strength of including vendors on a collaborative basis in design and production team efforts.

5. Workforce Management. Long neglected in the P&IC literature is the fruitful topic of workforce management both on the factory floor and in support organizations. Again the Japanese excel here and early data from Japanese managed factories in the West indicate that a style which features strong top-down leadership and direction, together with participative detail planning and skillful execution from the bottom-up are a potent force for workforce productivity. Peopleware may be viewed as a soft issue, but proper organizational leadership, communication, and motivational stimuli can provide positive, rock hard results.

6. Total Quality Control. In the minds of many the quality issue pervades all organizational activities. And they are totally right. Companywide Quality Control (CWQC) programs and improvement efforts dealing with MRP II Extended go hand in hand. We view quality as pervading the whole organizational environment. Indeed, it is difficult to imagine a successful MRP II operation, let alone JIT/TQC, without an extraordinarily high level of quality in products, processes and management practices. TQC actions which provide the sound basis for productivity improvements include the goal of PPM (defectives in terms of parts per million), building inspection into the process, making every operator responsible for quality of his/her work, reliability assurance at the source to avoid incoming inspection (Ship to WIP), and so forth. In this view quality is a policy, it is an attitude, it is a total way of life that helps drive an organization, productively.

GUIDELINE: The first step towards JIT/TQC is to benchmark factory operations/controls to surface key improvement possibilities. The Four P's Plus will be used by astute managements to thoughtfully shape, then execute the productivity journey to JIT/TQC.

IMPLEMENTATION, JAPANESE STYLE.

The purpose of our study mission to Japan was a little different than the stated goals of other groups' visits. We were relatively certain that we understood Japanese manufacturing techniques, although we did want to affirm our knowledge/grasp of the concepts. However, our prime purpose was to explore an area that had received little attention in Japanese manufacturing literature, but was of the utmost importance--how to implement JIT/TQC was the priority goal of our study mission. To get a flavor of what we learned, we will look at three different aspects of the implementation issue at three organizations who received us during our stay in Japan.

1. Fugi Xerox, Suzuki. This factory which is relatively new is among the 20 top automated metal cutting operations in Japan. A major up-grade of the MRP system was underway. Although the organization has about 350 employees with less than 125 indirects, management had dedicated 10 full-time people to the MRP upgrade project. In addition, there was significant on-site support from the hardware/software vendor who was also dedicating substantial full-time resources to the project. The goals were ambitious, the timeframe of one year tight. However, our group came away from Fugi Xerox with the distinct impression that the MRP project would happen and be successful within the allotted time. Their commitment said so.

Lessons: What we learned was straightforward; the strong management direction, massive resourcing to accomplish the purpose, and consensus style decisioning by those charged with the responsibility for the project were key ingredients. Management would not abandon this project or change direction part way through--the objectives were clear and the dedication at all levels outstanding. On a happy note --we saw nothing at Fugi Xerox which said you had to be Japanese to duplicate their project intensity.

2. Hitachi and the MST Campaign. At Hitachi we looked first at the overall corporate strategy for productivity improvement and then tested their approach at plant level. As can be seen in Figure 2 the MST (minimum standard time, minimum stocks) Campaign had the twin objectives of cost reduction and lead time shortening. The vehicle was integration of production technologies and Hitachi simultaneously attacked three areas:

- engineering technology--CAD/CAM, standardization

134

- manufacturing technologies: automation, robotics, operation improvement and quick set up, etc.

- control techniques, featuring synchronization with leveled production scheduling and an emphasis on visual control in the factory.

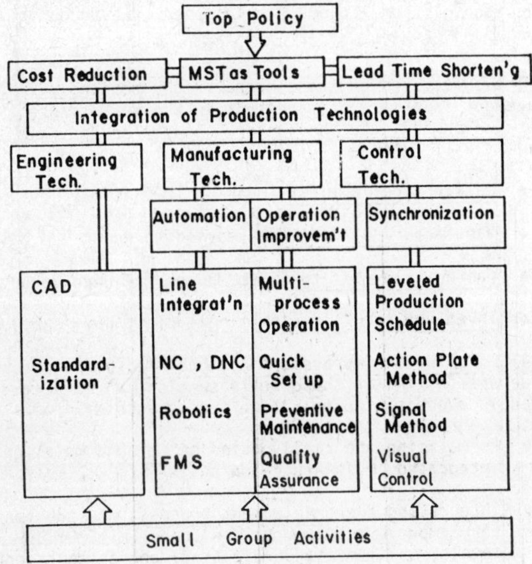

Fig. 2 Promotional Activities of MST Campaign

Lessons: Once again it became amply clear that successful Japanese manufacturing firms autocratically set policy/ direction at top level and then, as shown in this schematic, allow small group improvement activities to "make it happen". The dramatic effectiveness of this approach is clear--from 1978-80 the implemented base of MST grew from 16% of the factories to about 90%. The implementation at plant level followed general MST guidelines, but there seemed to be plenty of latitude allowed to meet individual situations. Another strength of the Hitachi approach was management's measurement of key productivity areas through the use of many simple indexes. To illustrate, two performance indicators for engineering were: the number of designs made with CAD vs the total number of designs; the number of common parts vs the total number of production parts. The effectiveness of these simple, easily understood measurements cannot be overemphasized. One final lesson. Info system improvements were generally run through project groups while manufacturing/engineering technology improvements were considered line responsibilities with assistance from staff provided only upon request.

3. Sharp--Clear Vision of the Future. The first reports of those visiting Japanese manufacturing factories in the late 70's and early 80's indicated that one of the Japanese strengths lay in their ability to make manufacturing operations really strategic. This was positively affirmed in discussions with people from Sharp. The organization had a clear vision of their product/market combinations out in the future and were continually planning on how manufacturing could support their strategic thrust into the global marketplace. This was best illustrated by their approach to new product introduction. The emphasis on designing for producibility and standardization of parts/ components was powerful. Of equal importance was the understanding/consideration of design and development people with each of the Four P's Plus. We found a detail level of knowledge of PIC procedures and practices throughout the engineering design teams and, surprising to us, right to the top.

Lessons: We confirmed here the importance of coordinated team work, and empathy from function to function as opposed to suboptimization. The strategic positioning of manufacturing operations as a vital, contributing partner--not just a second class adjunct to the business--in the productivity battle for marketplace position was sharply in evidence. The organizational result was a clear vision of mission, addressing the future with confidence.

WESTERN WORLD FIRMS REV UP--JUST-IN-TIME

While many North Atlantic manufacturers have been thrown on the defensive by the astounding productivity of Pacific Basin competitors, an increasing number of U.S./ European firms have taken the offensive, fighting back by effectively implementing the JIT/TQC techniques. These firms are the pathfinders. Their JIT/TQC experience can be instructive in speeding up our own programs.

In the paragraphs which follow, we will describe four specific action programs which have wide applicability for firms undertaking the JIT/TQC journey. These programs are based on actual implementation efforts, both in the U.S. and Europe. Sufficient information is given so the central core of each program can be readily understood. The first program addresses action-oriented education; the last three are set in a time continuum. Actual application will depend on the individual organization, its goals/objectives, the state of the art of its manufacturing control system and production practices, and management style. Thoughtful manufacturing managements will want to consider adapting elements from each of these programs as they have been tested and have yielded dramatic productivity improvement results.

1). Program for Senior Managers. The importance of top management leadership and direction in a major improvement program has been well documented in the West. Our study mission to Japan validated the thesis that knowledge-able top-down direction is a key ingredient in Japanese implementation success. But it is also true that the heavily crowded agendas of Senior Management make it most difficult to schedule top management education. Compounding the problem is the fact that many top management people feel they "already know enough"--although, in point of fact, Senior Management does have to be brought up to speed in terms of awareness and commitment so they can handle the massive change in the organization which JIT/TQC mandates. What is required is a creative approach to top management education.

In response to this need we developed a unique and innovative educational program designed especially for factory and general management--to speed up productivity improvement progress and gain needed breakthroughs at both factory and product division levels. Given the state of world-class competition today the imperatives of the situation call for a guided, self-directed learning experience, action-oriented with built-in measurement through the tangible results that attendees will achieve. Here's how it works.

- an opening seminar to generate awareness and provide a forum for early action planning

- in-plant time (about two months) to further identify detailed improvement targets, outline project plans, obtain organizational consensus/commitment

- a follow-up workshop to share and review plans, assess progress, and reaffirm commitment

- an implementation phase of ten to fourteen months; the improvement is put into place/results achieved

- a final, post-implementation workshop during which Senior Managers share results of the successes

The program leans heavily on peer/manager commitment-- a very strong incentive--as well as direction/support from the highest levels. For example, invitations to attend are extended in one instance by the Board of Management. The sharing of improvement targets, action plans, and actual results among the Senior Managers deepens commitment at peer level. The following outline of the opening seminar will give a flavor for the approach:

- Segment One: Strategies for Improvement. Guided by a top-notch faculty, cases are used to address both the technical side of improvements as well as the management-of-change issues involved.

- Segment Two: Overview of Others' Experience. Emphasis is placed on a Japanese case, an outside Western World experience, and an in-company project--all of a successful nature, designed as positive learning experiences.

- Third Segment: Application/Plant Visits. Strategies and techniques for improvement are reinforced through a minimum of two on-site plant visits to world-class manufacturers. Participants are grouped according to planning, product structuring, process/methods, and procurement. Each group (with a facilitator) acts as its own "instructor" to make the learning self-directed and experiential.

- Fourth Segment: Action Plans/Commitment. The development of product/market objectives, factory targets, and first scope action plans is the climax of the program. To underscore the importance of this activity, the results are formally presented, and accepted, by a most Senior Executive who brings closure to the opening seminar.

The program is powerful. Its focus on manufacturing improvement significantly deepens awareness and brings about the critical element of commitment through its action orientation. The high visibility of the program and the fact that Senior Managers actually develop/publish objectives, targets and first scope action plans bring enthusiasm levels and "can do" attitudes to a high pitch. Experience has shown that these attributes are translated back at the plant into effective action. Many people talk about the need for top management education and commitment--this program really does something/gets commitment!

2). Initial Improvement Actions--Short-Term. One of the most effective change agents for an organization is that it experience early success in its improvement journey. We recommend, and have found effective, a number of early actions that can be done in literally a matter of weeks to demonstrate results, start the journey on a positive note. These actions include:

- installation of performance measurements

- detailing the characteristics of the existing factory, its processes and control system

- initiating management team workshops to discuss improvement possibilities and develop "points that need attention"

- reduction of batch sizes--cuts of 50% may be feasible, will "force shop floor action"--gets results

- install cycle counting to get control of stocks

- benchmark quality levels--surprisingly few factories really have a handle on this important area

- initiate actions to reduce throughput lead time by attacking queues, bringing processes under control, moving towards flow layout, asking "why" 5 times

- initiate spic/span housekeeping--this is probably the easiest early action, one that is most visible, will be highly rewarding, signals big change

- review and apply existing procedures; most factories simply do not adhere to existing standard practices; just by applying the "orderly hustle" of what's already in place can achieve results.

3). Breakthrough Action Program--Intermediate Term. A Breakthrough Action Program can be defined as a major effort which brings about improved results, in orders of magnitude, in factory performance in ten to fourteen months. Here the Four P's Plus are used by management as handles to generate improved productivity performance. For example, in an effort to improve process control and resulting product quality the Breakthrough Action might be to build inspection into the operation as a means of laying the groundwork for PPM quality levels. Co-maker relation-

ships with a small selected number of key vendors might be initiated together with an effort to reduce the number of suppliers to more manageable proportions. In the product structure area three concurrent actions might be undertaken: the installation and use of formal BOM update/ change procedures, improvements within the existing structures/configurations, and the initiation with the engineering design folks of a product development-for-producibility approach.

The objectives of these breakthrough actions will be improvement in orders of magnitude in the performance results which indicate the factory is well on the journey towards MRP-II Extended (JIT/TQC). Thus:

- delivery reliability--nearing 100% at mix level

- manufacturing lead time--moving to under ten days

- factory flexibility--firm MPS period under a week

- inventory stock levels--single digit/days supply

4). Follow-on Improvement Actions--Medium/Long Term. Here we are talking of those actions which can be accomplished in a one to two year time frame, such as:

- formalizing and really using MPS ground rules on an integrated, multi-function basis

- integrating the development process into the factory improvement program to achieve minimum BOM levels, maximum standardization, and product modularity at the end of the production process

- achieving mix model capability at the final assembly line--this forces a number of positive actions in contributing operations and with vendors

- radiating co-makership to 75% of the suppliers

- initiating and then radiating small group improvement activities as part of the plan so that improvement actions are recognized as a line responsibility, become a continuous "way of life"

- achieving a flexible/team-oriented climate with the workforce: education, cross training, worker involvement, enlightened management-worker relationships

- "eliminating" stock stores; start with reduction!

- "eliminating" incoming inspection--ship-to-WIP

- focusing the factory so the shop has a few, clearcut tasks and performs each at high level.

> GUIDELINE: The JIT/TQC (MRP-II Extended) journey is a longer term effort and involves a significant amount of change. Fortunately, early incremental steps and near term breakthrough actions can bring about substantial improvements during the first year. Success breeds success and follow on programs should be thoughtfully designed to build on/expand early breakthroughs.

MUCH MORE THAN JUST A CONTROL SYSTEM

One of the deficiencies in the MRP crusade was a lack of sensitivity to shop floor, manufacturing process, quality, and workforce issues. Indeed, these were essentially accepted as "givens", or viewed as "not pertinent" to the MRP main stream. The theory of the case stated that all you needed to do was develop a big MRP system to plan the complex mess we called the factory. But just imposing a complex P&IC system on old manufacturing processes and production techniques did not always bring results. In point of fact, in the writer's personal experience as production manager for an electronics firm, some of the best productivity gains achieved were the combined result of changes on the factory floor to process layout/methods, re-design of product structures to facilitate manufacturing and enhance standardization, and implementation of orderly,

yet simple planning and control techniques. On more than
one occasion we violated the advice of MRP gurus and the
MRP rule book. But we got results!

JIT/TQC is much more than just an improved control
system. From one vantage point, JIT is a better way to
carry out the detailed scheduling/execution of production
activity and vendor control. And in the closed loop MRP II
schematics that shop floor/vendor control loop have always
been the weakest links. The most instructive writings on
schedule execution have appeared recently and are largely
based on Japanese manufacturing practices.

As noted earlier, the Japanese have stressed shop
floor/vendor action in their improvement programs and have
largely executed these improvements through the line organization. We will need to do the same if we are to reach
JIT/TQC status. What does this mean?

First and foremost, the focus of our implementation
efforts must switch from staff imposed to line driven.
Grandiose projects conceived by experts outside operations
are not likely to lead to JIT/TQC. Reversing the Taylor
model, staff serves line by advising, educating, assisting
when requested--never by imposition or through control.
This leads to the need line operations have for direction
from the top. Management's job is to set overall goals/
objectives with a strategic context. Operations does the
detail planning and implementation. Thus, the improvement
project needs to be formalized; not only must the productivity path be clear, but the method of making the jour-
ney--formal project planning/control--must be in place.
Finally, productivity means people and the improvement
effort must be shaped to take into account the relevant
change issues, being sensitive to the human side.

It took Toyota about thirty years to achieve
pre-eminence in world class manufacturing; Western World
manufacturers have the opportunity by learning from others
to materially reduce that time frame, but implementing
JIT/TQC will not be easy. The journey requires arduous
effort and managerial vigilance. But it can be successful
--improve our ability to compete by gaining an "unfair"
competitive advantage. And in the long run that means
marketshare growth and profitable survival.

GUIDELINE: The JIT/TQC journey forces us to think
through our implementation in terms of factory charac-
teristics/ organization which is much more than just a
P&IC system. In point of fact, we must consider planning systems, product development, processes/layouts/
methods, procurement approaches, workforce management,
and PPM quality levels (the Four P's Plus) on an integral basis as we thoughtfully re-charge our productivity
machine. With these "handles", JIT/TQC implementation
can succeed.

ACKNOWLEDGEMENT

While the content of this paper is the writer's
responsibility, a large number of people/firms have contributed in this effort. Among the folks at the General
Electric Co., Richard Kennedy and James Goedhart have been
particularly supportive. J.E.B. de Groot of Philips (B.V.)
collaborated closely over the past three years in developing the basic MRP II Extended concepts and with him we were
able to implement these ideas/approaches in actual practice
in consumer goods factories.

ABOUT THE AUTHOR

Charles G. Andrew, CPIM* is founder and President of
Charles G. Andrew & Co., a firm specializing in management
counseling and education in the United States and Europe.
He was formerly Production Manager for a leading electronics firm during which time he designed, implemented,
and operated an effective, state-of-application, closed
loop MRP system. Prior to this, Mr. Andrew was a Management Consultant with Peat, Marwick, Mitchell & Co., specializing in production and inventory control systems, and
management controls. Mr. Andrew began his business career
with the Continental Group where he held managerial positions in manufacturing, marketing, and systems.

A frequent speaker and lecturer, Mr. Andrew is a mem-
ber of APICS, ASQC, and DPMA. A past President of the
Hartford-APICS Chapter, he has served the Society as found-
ing Chairman of Seminar I and several National capacities.
Mr. Andrew has published in the P&IM Journal and P&IM
Review and is certified by APICS at the Fellow level.

Mr. Andrew is Assistant Professor of Management,
Graduate School of Business, University of Hartford, where
he teaches courses in Business Strategy, Information
Systems, and Production Management. A graduate of the
University of Pennsylvania, Mr. Andrew holds B.S. and
M.B.A. degrees from the Wharton School.

THE MARRIAGE OF MRP AND JIT—IS IT POSSIBLE?

Milt E. Cook
Kim Muinch, CPIM
Hewlett-Packard Company

The objective of this presentation is to describe the possibilities for the marriage of MRP (Material Requirements Planning) and JIT (Just-In-Time).

On the surface, there appears to be a natural marriage between the two; MRP attempts to drive inventory balances to zero; so does JIT.

The speakers will contrast MRP to JIT looking at their basic objectives and functions to determine if the marriage is practical.

Many people feel that JIT is a replacement for MRP. The speakers hope to convince you that JIT is a natural extension of MRP.

Enhancements must be made to MRP in order to maximize the real benefits of the marriage, since most MRP packages are designed for discreet manufacturing environments.

To date, JIT has been primarily implemented in repetitive manufacturing environments.

Let's begin with a review of MRP and its objectives.

MRP is a set of priority planning techniques for planning component items below the product or independent demand level. Its objective is to determine:

* What to order
* How much to order
* When to order
* When to schedule delivery
* Are priorities current for:
  - Inventory Planning and Control functions?
  - Capacity Requirements Planning functions?
  - Shop Floor Control functions?

MRP is a very simple concept and can be effective when properly implemented. MRP systems are being installed at a very fast pace in almost every manufacturing plant.

The techniques have not changed much. However, our knowledge of how to use the techniques has steadily increased as a result of the experience gained from the thousands of installations of MRP.

There have been four major phases during the evolution of MRP:

1. A better ordering methodology.
2. Priority planning.
3. Closed loop MRP.
4. Manufacturing Resource Planning: MRPII

There are two fundamental techniques for materials planning and control: Order Point and MRP. There are other methods which are variations of these two.

MRPII evolved from the closed loop system. MRPII has these characteristics:

1. The operation and financial system are one and the same.
2. It has a "What if" capability.
3. MRPII is a "whole company" system, involving every facet of the business - including sales, production, inventories, schedules, cash flow, etc. - are the very fundamentals of planning and controlling a manufacturing business.

Our profession and systems have been evolving over the past 20-25 years. APICS has been a powerful force in this process. We began formalizing PI&C, then established Materials Management, followed by MRPII. We are now moving into the execution of our plans through JIT and process automation.

There are many tools available today for effective manufacturing and business control. You must pick the right tool to get the job done, whether it is Order Point, MRPII, or JIT. The trick is to pick the right one for your situation. Things are changing very fast today and things are different company to company. You must pick the tool that gives you the best possible customer service and fits within your budget.

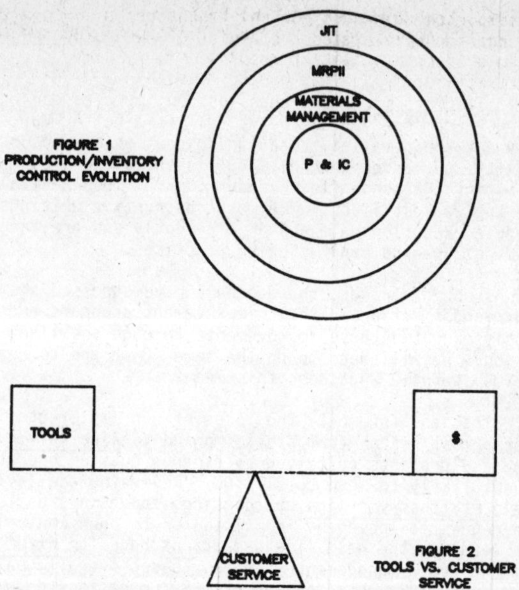

FIGURE 1
PRODUCTION/INVENTORY
CONTROL EVOLUTION

FIGURE 2
TOOLS VS. CUSTOMER
SERVICE

In order to select the proper tool(s), you need to analyze the process of your company from one end to the other and examine the total flow. Only when this has been done will it be clear which tools fit the best.

JIT is a philosophy which, simply described, suggests that a manufacturer produces only what the market demands only as it demands it. JIT, which is often used interchangeably with "stockless production", "synchronized production" or "zero inventory", is comprised of a number of elements which taken together yield improved asset utilization, inventory reductions, higher quality, lower unit costs, and better customer responsiveness. The objective of JIT is to have only the correct part in the correct place at the correct time. Does this not sound like MRP?

MRPII mainly brought marketing and finance into the closed loop system. With JIT we are extending into all of the organizations of a manufacturing company.

The foundation of success with JIT is an emphasis on quality. Quality must be achieved in all organizations to make JIT work.

All business requirements must be included in the usage of JIT in order for it to be effective.

With the requirement for automation that JIT precipitates, engineering must be involved in order to design products that can be produced with ease and flexibility by manufacturing. We have always realized this, but it was not as important as it now is with JIT. Since more of our operations will be automated, we must put much more emphasis on maintenance. We need new systems to schedule preventative maintenance, track equipment, spare parts, etc.

The following illustration contrasts the functions within a manufacturing company necessary to make MRPII and JIT effective:

THE MARRIAGE

MRP & JIT

Planning
Purchasing/Traffic
Finance/Accounting
Production/Inventory Control
Quality
Sales/Marketing
Human Resources
Information Systems
Design/Industrial Engineering
Plant/Maintenance
Manufacturing

The organizations required to support both methodologies are the same. JIT facilitates and demands the linkage of all functions within a manufacturing company into one team. There is no question that we have always

needed this teamwork, but we have not done very well at
making it happen. Our ultimate goal as manufacturers must
be to deliver a quality product to our customers with very
little lead time. If we don't, someone else will.

The elements of JIT are:

* Housekeeping
* Quality through process repeatability
* Reduced setup times
* Small lot sizes - down to one, optimally
* Preventive maintenance
* Reduced inventories (uncover problems)
* Reduced space
* Capacity control
* Multifunctional workers
* Excellent preproduction preparation
* Pull system

By reviewing this list you can see why JIT is a philosophy. Why could you not do any or all of these items in
an MRPII environment? The point is not whether MRPII or
JIT is better; it is how they complement each other.

REPETITIVE MANUFACTURING VERSUS JUST-IN-TIME

A distinction needs to be made between the terms
"Just-In-Time" and "Repetitive Manufacturing". JIT as
used here is a manufacturing philosophy which strives for
excellence. "Repetitive" describes a particular type of
manufacturing process in which the same product or similar
products are fabricated repeatedly to a schedule.

Many manufacturers are repetitive without practicing
JIT. Differences in planning and control tools for a
Just-In-Time environment are more a function of repetitive
process characteristics than of JIT itself. However, JIT
normally extends the assumptions to stabilized schedules,
level production and demand-pull production control.

Now that we have separated the two where do we begin
to implement?

BEGINNING WITH JUST-IN-TIME

To effectively implement Just-In-Time requires simultaneously concentrating on the elimination of waste and on
respect for people. Elements of Just-In-Time include reduced setup times, quality at the source, small lot sizes,
demand pull production control, level schedules, group
technology, concensus management, employee involvement,
and long-term supplier relationships. Because Just-In-
Time is a total manufacturing program, a manufacturer can
start with any one of these elements and move towards a
JIT environment. The element that each customer attacks
first determines the most critical systems need.

As an environment evolves to Just-In-Time, systems
will require changes to support the new manufacturing process. These needs will typically be identified after the
success of some pilot projects. The systems will be
adapted to meet the needs of the environment as it
evolves, not the other way around.

An example of this process is illustrated in
Figure 3. After investing heavily in JIT education, a
Hewlett-Packard manufacturing division initiated a pilot
project by implementing a demand pull system on the final
assembly line for one of HP's printer families. Obstacles
that had to be surpassed included linearizing the material
flow, establishing dock-to-stock inventory receipts, elimination of stockrooms, education of the workforce, re-
layout of the floor and modifying the current materials
system.

Significantly, the materials system did not become a
major stumbling block for over a year. Eliminating other
obstacles forced the system inadequacies into prominence
several months later.

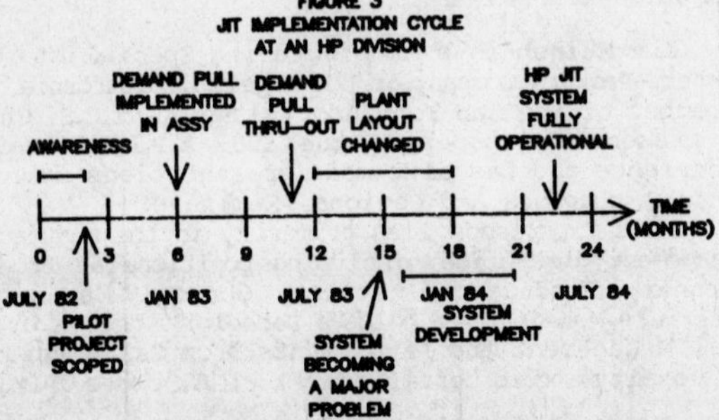

We need to look at a few of the possible systems
changes that may need to be effected once they do become
an issue in your implementation.

The functional effects on applications systems to
support JIT can be summarized as follows:

Production Planning - High level production planning
is essentially the same in either batch or repetitive
environment. It is still done in dollars and usually at
the product family level. Flexibility in modeling is key;
the benefits of using spreadsheets on personal computers
are rapidly being recognized.

Master Scheduling - In a repetitive environment the
major difference is that <u>rates</u> of production are established for given periods as opposed to individual work
orders with due dates.

Just-In-Time dictates that not only are production
rates established, but that in an environment with a mix
of products, that the schedule be leveled as much as
possible. Mixed-model, leveled production scheduling is
achieved when set-up times are low and batch size is minimized. Furthermore, JIT assumes that production rates can
be fixed over a reasonable period (i.e., 20 days) to
minimize variability in schedules that would disrupt
smooth material flow and what is supposed to be a uniform
balanced plant load.

Engineering Data - Structured bills of material are
collapsed to a flat "parts list" for JIT, since materials
flow through the process and stocking of subassemblies is
not significant.

JIT also suggests that new products are designed for
manufacturability. Group technology and parts classification are central to streamlining the manufacturing operation. They become more important in a JIT environment.

MRP - MRP becomes a gross explosion of requirements
based on the established rate per day and the materials
list. WIP is small and turning constantly so that netting
against it becomes meaningless. Gross requirements for
purchased parts are fed to the purchasing systems as
requisitions. In situations where some parts are fabricated those requirements must be translated into fabrication schedules which are distributed to fab areas.

Inventory Control - In a JIT environment the concept
of demand pull eliminates the need to issue materials to
the floor. When demand for material is generated by a
downstream operation (and only then) the upstream operation produces to fulfill this need. Buffer stocks between
operations are eliminated as is the concept of "pushing"
inventory from raw materials into WIP. In a JIT environment materials are consumed from a raw and In-Process
Inventory.

Balances are maintained for inventory locations on
the production line. As product is completed, a post-
deduct transition relieves inventory locations of the
components used based on quality completed, option configuration and revision level.

Cost Accounting - Several aspects of cost accounting
are different with JIT. There are no work orders against
which to cost. Material movement transactions and exceptions are summarized on a periodic basis and passed to the
general ledger. Material variances focus on scrap; extra
usage can be valued quickly by a physical count or in many
cases a base level WIP can be established.

Purchasing - Purchasing must recognize that materials
will be ordered and delivered on a regular and more frequent basis. Capabilities for blanket orders and
scheduled releases against those orders are important to a
JIT environment. Typically the JIT manufacturer will be
sharing longer forecasts with suppliers as well and ultimately will desire the ability to automatically release
purchases.

Shop Floor Control - The need for a sophisticated
shop floor control system is virtually eliminated with JIT
where visual inspection of the shop floor is a much more
effective tool. Variable routings and prioritized work
orders give way to fixed routings and self-scheduling
demand pull of materials.

Capacity Planning - Capacity planning typically plays a major role in a repetitive environment. Because production moves through a standard sequence, it is usually easy to identify and model the bottleneck operations. The capacity of the production process itself is only part of the preproduction chain, however. The capabilities to model vendors' capacities and their flexibility to change production rates will also become crucial in the JIT environment.

Order Processing - Order Processing can be more or less sophisticated depending on the degree of repetition on the demand for option and specific configuration to meet customer orders. If specific customer orders must be matched to particular production units before the units can be built, then the environment calls for a more sophisticated order processing and production scheduling system which can broadcast option requirements to the supplying locations to meet the demand. (Actual production of the option is triggered by demand pull, however.)

Quality Monitoring - Total quality control is a fundamental building block of JIT. Eliminating rework from the system to smooth the flow requires perfect quality at each step. Monitoring the process/product defects and correlating the results to identify problems is the key to eliminating sources of bad quality.

Machine Maintenance - Good housekeeping and appropriate maintenance eliminates machine down time which would otherwise impede the smooth flow of materials.

In general, application systems are much simpler in a JIT environment. They play a lesser role in controlling the floor and a greater one in planning and managing the smooth operation of production.

What you should realize by now is that this list included all of the same system modules as MRP, with the only exception being Shop Floor Control.

John L. Warne, President and Chief Operating Officer, Omark Industries, Inc., at a seminar in Los Angeles last May stated, "You still need MRP for the macro planning with JIT." His company has reduced the use of the computer by about 25 percent in manufacturing. This frees up capacity for other applications. At the same seminar speaker Peter R. Zirbel, Arthur Anderson & Company, told us, "MRP is still required with JIT, but you must turn off many of its features."

Whether it is MRPII, JIT, or a combination of the two, manufacturing companies need to have a stable overall operating strategy:

* What markets to serve and how to serve them.
* What products to be provided.
* What must be produced.
* How to financially justify the investment being made.

JIT is a logical extension of the MRPII concept. We have carried the MRPII concept onto the shop floor control for the execution of the business plan which creates the marriage of MRP and JIT. The following illustration shows this marriage:

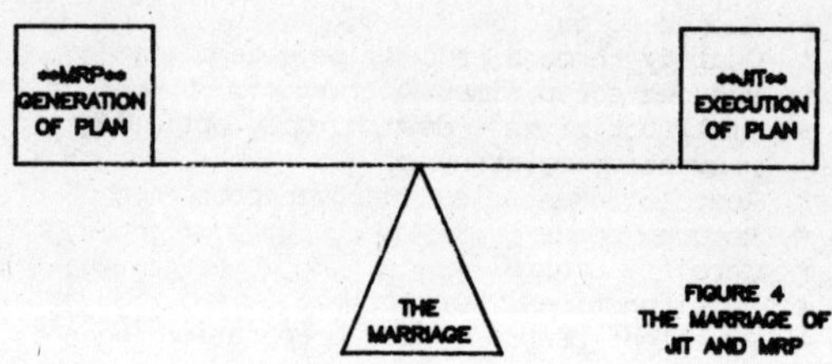

To quote John Proud, Xerox Computer Services, "Expeditors have operated a pull system for many years." The result has been that: 1) they have tended to concentrate only on the "hot" orders, 2) and they have left a mess when all the dust settled.

We can no longer allow a mess when all the dust settles or no longer debate what is right - MRPII or JIT. We need to get on with the job and reestablish our productivity growth.

The marriage of MRP and JIT is not only possible - it is absolutely mandatory!

MRP is a priority planning technique, not an execution tool. If misused as an "order launching" device where orders are "pushed" onto the factory floor, a "mess" is created.

This "mess" (waste) can be avoided through the use of JIT as the execution tool, mainly because of its "demand pull" characteristics, where only those materials that are actually needed on the factory floor are "pulled" only when they are needed.

BIBLIOGRAPHY

Shingo, Shigeo, Study of Toyota Production System from Industrial Engineering Viewpoint, Japan Management Association, May, 1982.

Hall, Robert, Zero Inventories, Dow Jones-Irwin, 1983.

NOTE: The authors would like to acknowledge the efforts of the following people:

John Albin, Hewlett-Packard Company
Jim Heeger, Hewlett-Packard Company
Ray Ybarra, Hewlett-Packard Company

BIOGRAPHICAL SKETCH

Milt E. Cook is a Manufacturing Specialist for the Hewlett-Packard Company in Westlake Village, California. He is a member and officer of the San Fernando Valley A.P.I.C.S. Chapter. He presented papers at several A.P.I.C.S. national conferences. He is a frequent speaker at chapter meetings and has been a contributor to the A.P.I.C.S. journal.

Milt has had two manuscripts published in the Auerbach Publishers' Computers in Manufacturing publication. He serves on the instructional staff of California State University at Northridge, teaching PI&C techniques. He has 23 years experience in production/inventory control fields and holds a degree in Business Management from Pepperdine University.

Kim Muinch is a Manufacturing Specialist for the Hewlett-Packard Company in Los Angeles, California. He is a member of the San Fernando Valley A.P.I.C.S. Chapter. He presented a paper at the 1982 A.P.I.C.S. National Conference and has also made presentations at several A.P.I.C.S. chapters and Regional Seminars.

Kim's experience lies primarily in the manufacturing management discipline, including positions as Production Planner, Production/Inventory Control Manager, and Materials Manager. He holds a Bachelor's degree in Financial Management and Investments from California State University and is certified by A.P.I.C.S. as a CPIM.

ZERO INVENTORY AND MRP
Henry H. Jordan, CMC, CPIM*
Center for Inventory Management

ZERO INVENTORIES is the emerging production and inventory management philosophy. And no one can argue against its goals of eliminating all waste of time and materials.

MRP, MATERIAL REQUIREMENTS PLANNING, as the name implies, is a system which plans what components and materials are required, how many and when.

The ORDER POINT SYSTEM is generally applicable to finished goods stock inventory items and service parts, where the normal demand on the inventory is independent and unrelated to the demand for higher level assemblies.

MRP is applicable to components and materials of end products. Such demand can be calculated on basis of the end products scheduled for production.

MRP is time-phased with every requirement quantity planned for a specific date.

This time-phasing capability of the MRP system can be applied also to independent demand items and is then referred to as a TIME-PHASED ORDER POINT SYSTEM.

MRP LOGIC

The MASTER PRODUCTION SCHEDULE states what end products are required, how many and when.

These end product requirements are then exploded using the BILLS OF MATERIALS (product structure) of each end product. Bills of materials must be accurate and properly structured. The explosion calculates the gross requirements, by date and quantity for all components and materials needed to produce the end product. This is done level by level starting with the highest level in the product structure and ending with the lowest level for each item.

The MRP SYSTEM then reviews the individual item master records to determine the quantity on hand in each time period. These are subtracted from the gross requirement.

It also reviews all open orders for each item, both manufacturing orders and purchase orders as applicable. The quantity scheduled for delivery during the specific time period is also subtracted from the gross requirement.

The balance represents the net quantity required during each time period to meet the demands of the MASTER PRODUCTION SCHEDULE.

This net requirement is offset by the LEADTIME for the item and stated as a PLANNED ORDER by the date the order must be released to meet the required due date.

Net requirements for future time periods may be summarized by the system for low unit cost items with high preparation costs per order to arrive at the optimum lot size for manufacturing or purchasing.

SUMMARY OF MRP INPUTS

1. End product requirements by date and quantity as stated in the MASTER PRODUCTION SCHEDULE.

2. Bills of materials (product structure) stating what components and materials will be required to make the end product.

3. Inventory status stating the availability of each component or material, as well as the scheduled delivery dates as reflected in the open manufacturing orders or open purchase orders.

4. Leadtimes for manufacturing or purchasing of each component and material.

5. Specific policy, such as "lot for lot", for calculating the optimum lot size for each component and material.

MRP OUTPUTS

There are three types of outputs from the MRP system:

1. Action Notices

2. Material Requirements Plans

3. Manufacturing Resources Plans

MRP ACTION NOTICES

Whenever the MRP program is run, action notices are produced for an item (component or material) when it is time to:

1. Release an order

2. Expedite an order

3. Reschedule an order

4. Change the order quantity

Each notice states what action is required. The number of different action messages should be limited. Too many messages tend to be confusing. These are the basic messages which are useful:

Planned order due for release

Expedite open order due on xx/xx (date)

No open order to cover requirement

Scheduled receipt not needed on xx/xx (date)

Inventory above maximum level starting on xx/xx (date)

MATERIAL REQUIREMENTS PLAN

Whenever an action notice is generated by the MRP system, a Material Requirements Plan is produced for the item.

For each time period beginning with "past due", the quantity is displayed for:

Gross requirements

Scheduled receipts

On hand

Planned order release

The time periods may be shown as days or weeks in the near term and months or quarters in the future.

FREQUENCY OF MRP ACTION NOTICES

The frequency of running MRP is not dictated so much by the computer capability, but by the time available to the individuals who must review and process the action notices. Most companies have found it practical to run MRP weekly with special runs whenever there is a significant change to the Master Production Schedule during the week.

Considering the time available to take the required action, it may also be desirable to limit the generation of action notices. This can be done by installing filters in the system based on time spans and dollar values.

For example, action notices for rescheduling a purchase order delivery to a future date could be suppressed, if the revised delivery date is within seven days of the existing date and the quantity is below a certain dollar value.

The rationale is that it may take that long to notify the vendor and change the date, and, considering the dollar value of the delivery, the impact on inventory investment is really not that significant.

MATERIAL REQUIREMENTS PLAN APPLICATIONS

In addition to the Material Requirements Plan for the Action Notice, the plan can be produced on request for special applications.

For capacity requirements plannning, particularly in the case of a critically limited capacity in a specific work center, it may be desirable to review other items requiring the same type of set-up, or only a minimum

change over time. This will enable the production
planner to schedule items to maximize throughput by
minimizing set-up times.

It should be recognized that MRP, per se, is not a
capacity requirements planning system. MRP assumes
infinite capacity. The outputs of MRP must be the
inputs to the Capacity Requirements Planning System and
the loop must be closed by feeding back information from
that system and the Production Activity (Shop Floor)
Control System.

In the case of purchased items, significant cost
savings may be achieved by aggregate buying of different
items at one time. The Material Requirements Plan for
items in the same commodity group may provide
opportunities for the buyer to obtain discounts which
far outweigh the cost of carrying additional inventory.

MANUFACTURING RESOURCES PLANNING

The MRP System can serve as the basis for
Manufacturing Resources Planning. This is frequently
referred to as MRP II.

The analysis of future requirements reflected in the
Material Requirements Plan can be of significant value
in planning both manufacturing and vendor capacities.

By substituting a Bill of Labor for the Bills of
Material, manpower requirements can be determined.

By converting quantities to dollar values,
time-phased financial planning can be accomplished. Of
considerable value is a cash flow projection based on
the Materials Requirements Plan.

MRP LOT SIZING

Considerable discussion centers on the value of an
MRP System in light of the success the Japanese have
achieved in reducing manufacturing leadtimes, production
costs and inventories.

JUST IN TIME and ZERO INVENTORY are concepts which
are being heralded today.

There is relatively little understanding that MRP
can support both the JUST IN TIME and the ZERO INVENTORY
concepts.

Minimize set-up costs, provide sufficient
manufacturing capacity, line up reliable vendors with
short leadtimes, make sure the plant makes what has been
scheduled and MRP will result in achieving the goals of
the JUST IN TIME and ZERO INVENTORY concepts.

As a matter of fact, the MRP logic is based on the
JUST IN TIME philosophy. The system tells you exactly
what and how many you need, and no more, and exactly
when you need it, and not before.

The key to reducing leadtimes and inventories is
found in the correct application of lot sizing
techniques.

TECHNIQUES FOR LOT SIZING

There are nine techniques for lot sizing.

Select the right technique for each item as the MRP
system calculates requirements at each level of the
product structure and you achieve the optimum results.

FIXED ORDER QUANTITY

A fixed order quantity specified for an inventory
item. This policy is applicable to low unit cost
items where the set-up (ordering) costs are simply
too high to buy or make the net requirements in each
time period.

LOT-FOR-LOT ORDERING

Ordering the exact quantity required in each time
period. This policy will achieve the JUST IN TIME
and ZERO INVENTORY concepts. Of course, it may not
be economically feasible to apply it to every item.
However, application to high usage value "A" items
can produce spectacular results.

FIXED PERIOD REQUIREMENTS

Ordering a specified number of time periods of
demand based on the net requirements of the item.
Although considered by some experts as "primitive",
it is a simple and effective technique.

ECONOMIC ORDER QUANTITY

Since the calculation of the economic order quantity
is based on annual usage and assumes that the rate
of such usage is uniform throughout the year, the
Economic Order Quantity technique is really not
applicable to an MRP system.

PERIOD ORDER QUANTITY

This technique determines an order quantity by
calculating the economic order quantity, dividing
that quantity into the annual requirement to arrive
at a frequency of ordering. By dividing the
frequency of ordering into the number of weeks or
months in the year, the ordering interval is
determined. The system then calculates the order
quantity by adding the net requirements within the
time span of the previously calculated ordering
interval. This technique is not applicable to MRP
systems, since it is derived from the classic EOQ
formula and totally ignores the nonuniform and
discontinuous requirements generated by the MRP
System.

LEAST TOTAL COST

This technique calculates an order quantity within a
planning horizon which would balance the cost of
set-up (ordering) and the cost of carrying
inventory. It is the most practical of the lot
sizing techniques using the part-period balancing
concept.

PART PERIOD BALANCING

This technique uses the same basic logic as the
Least Total Cost technique, but then takes a
look-ahead and a look-back to determine if an
adjustment to the lot size should be made. It
involves an additional mathematical routine of
questionable value in the face of changing end
product requirements in the Master Production
Schedule within the planning horizon.

LEAST UNIT COST

The technique also uses the part-period balancing
approach and solves a series of equations to arrive
at the order quantity with the lowest "unit cost"
(Set-up cost plus inventory carrying cost per unit).

WAGNER-WHITIN ALGORITHM

A superior mathematical technique for determining
the optimum order quantity, but so complex that it
is of little real value to most practitioners.

SAFETY STOCKS

The MRP philosophy is to minimize safety stock,
except for highly critical items with long leadtimes.
It is far more economical to plan in terms of "safety
capacity" (i.e. the capability to make more when needed)
rather than progressively increasing inventories and
further decreasing available production capacity by the
addition of safety stock requirements at each level of
the product structure.

"Safety time" can be used and added to the leadtime
to compensate for fluctuations in deliveries of
purchased items. However, it must be recognized that
safety time, like safety stock, will increase
inventories and lengthen the overall delivery leadtimes.

TIME-PHASED ORDER POINT

This technique is in fact the use of the MRP system
for planning and controlling independent demand items.

Instead of arriving at the gross requirements by the
level by level explosion of the bills of materials based
on the end product quantities stated in the Master
Production Schedule, the independent demand requirements
are derived from a forecast.

The subsequent planning and control steps are
identical to those for any other item managed by the MRP
system.

MRP REQUIREMENTS

Successful MRP system implementation depends first
of all on a solid understanding by the user of how the
systems works and how to manage it.

It also depends on timely and correct input
information in all of these areas:

Dependable Master Production Schedules

Accurate inventory records

Valid leadtimes for manufacturing and purchasing

Sound safety stock decisions

Effective order quantity policies

Reliable vendors

Effective capacity requirements planning system

Realistic production schedules which can be met

Closed loop feedback of production and
purchasing order status information

ADVANTAGES OF MRP

No technique which has been developed during the
past twenty-five years offers a greater opportunity for
timely delivery in an internationally competitive market
place than MRP.
Properly conceived and implemented it can achieve
the goals of JUST IN TIME and ZERO INVENTORY concepts.
Improperly applied and used it can be the nemesis of
manufacturing operations.

MRP AND ZERO INVENTORIES

MRP does support the ZERO INVENTORIES concept.
Minimize set-up costs, provide sufficient
manufacturing capacity, line up reliable vendors with
short leadtimes, make sure the plant makes what has been
scheduled and MRP will result in achieving the goals of
ZERO INVENTORIES.
As a matter of fact, the MRP logic is based on the
JUST IN TIME philosophy. The system tells you exactly
what and how many you need, and no more, and exactly
when you need it, and not before.

ABOUT THE AUTHOR

HENRY H. JORDAN, CMC, CPIM* is a Certified
Management Consultant (CMC) specializing in inventory
management, production planning and control, purchasing
and physical distribution. He is Chairman of the Center
for Inventory Management and Managing Partner of
Consulting Services Incorporated.
Listed in WHO's WHO in Finance and Industry and
WHO's WHO in the South and Southwest, he has been a
management consultant since 1969. Prior to that time he
has had more than twenty years experience as Vice
President - Manufacturing, Manager of Production and
Inventory Control, and Director of Procurement in
industry and government.
He is the Chairman of the Inventory Management
Committee of the APICS Curricula and Certification
Council. He is the author of the System Implementation
Handbook. He is also an author and editor of the
Production and Inventory Control Handbook and is on the
editorial board of the Journal for Production and
Inventory Management. He is a member of the Institute
of Management Consultants, the International Materials
Management Society, and the American Management
Association. He is also a senior member of the American
Institute of Industrial Engineers and is the author of
numerous articles on production and inventory management
including the APICS Training Aid on Cycle Counting for
Record Accuracy.

OBJECTIVE

As Manufacturing Resource Planning--MRP II--has evolved and matured, an increasing amount of writings, software, training, and consulting has developed to support the planning, scheduling, and inventory control aspects of the Manufacturing and Distribution functions of modern business. While APICS focused on MRP II, parallel but separate developments were being made in Statistical Quality Control, Automation, and Group Technology in other Manufacturing disciplines. Japan, using a more "holistic" approach, was working on a Manufacturing strategy led by the developments within Toyota, which came to be known as Just-In-Time Production--JIT. Both of these activities reached full development by the pioneering practitioners and advisors about 1975 and began to be studied, copied, and installed in increasing volume over the next ten years. Out of Israel a computerized scheduling development--Optimized Production Technology or OPT--was taking place and reached the U.S. in the person of Elihu Goldratt and his associates in Creative Output, Inc. in 1979. However, the impact of those three activities has been one of competition and conflict among those having a vested interest in each approach. It is about time we put the controversy to bed, understand what is really behind these acronyms, and recognize each as valuable contributions as well as compatible concepts and techniques that can be put together to achieve even greater results than any one alone.

THE DEVELOPING PROBLEM

The U.S. came out of World War II as the industrial leader of the world. However, those of us that go back that far can categorize manufacturing in 1950 as a rather crude and informal area, largely overlooked by the movement toward "scientific management." In spite of some significant efforts by early pioneers such as Taylor, Galbraith, and Ford, it would have been difficult then to put manufacturing, with the possible exception of the automotive assembly line, in the professional category of Engineering or Finance and fields such as Law or Medicine. It has been said of those days that management looked at manufacturing as something rather unimportant that took place between a booking and a shipment. Not that manufacturing equipment, processes and industrial engineering were not given consideration. It was the planning, scheduling, work flow, and control that had been overlooked. And yet in 1950, the U.S. was the best in the world! Between 1950 and 1960, specialists began to contribute to separate manufacturing activities, the separation reflected by the supporting technical societies, such as APICS, MHI, PMA, SME, AIIE, ASQC, TIMS. These efforts were stimulated by the success of the Operations Research approach that had drawn multidisciplinary scientists into problem-solving activities during World War II. Traditionally manufacturing had not attracted these kinds of skills. Out of this creative chaos began to emerge an alphabet soup of techniques which literally exploded with the impact of the computer and the bright young talents of the high-tech culture in the 1960s.

The Japanese came over here and studied all of this very carefully. They then went back home and put together bits and pieces they called:

    SMED - Single minute exchange of die
    POKA - YOKE - Fool-proofing
    KANBAN - a card oriented scheduling method
    etc.

into a coherent manufacturing strategy (JIT). In the U.S., the APICS Society pulled together our disintegrated tools:

    ROP - Reorder Point
    EOQ - Economical Order Quantity
    MRP - Material Requirements Planning
    DRP - Distribution Requirements Planning

    CRP - Capacity Requirements Planning
    SFC - Shop Floor Control
    etc.

into a coherent planning, scheduling, and control strategy (MRP II). Our technical peers in PMA, ASQC, SME, and AIIE were doing the same in their disciplines. However, in the U.S., it became increasingly difficult to keep each discipline in its compartment--the overlaps and interfaces were many and critical. And professional rivalry was rampant. In the mid-east, Elihu Goldratt and his associates were the latest of a long list of missionaries called "finite schedulers" who, up to 1979, had been a largely discredited and unsuccessful group. Creative Output concentrated with greater understanding of the poorly developed field of scheduling and came up with OPT.

The computer hardware and software world, as they got their act together, looked on with the thrill of opportunity leavened by the agony of confusion. What did it all mean and which band wagon should they get aboard? These willing apprentices to the manufacturing sorcerers began to recognize that the operative word was "integration" and threw their acronym into the soup: CIM or Computer Integrated Manufacturing, to represent the EDP community's view of the Manufacturing world.

To make sense of all of this, it is best to look first at JIT, then MRP II, and finally OPT. CIM will not be covered here as it seems important to determine how we manufacture, plan, schedule, and control before we rush to integrate or automate! There are many systems that are, can, and should be computerized and an integrated data base is a valuable resource for any approach. However, until we have a better understanding of manufacturing as a whole, we risk at worst "automating, or programming, a mess" and at least failing to apply the old but still sound principal of Industrial Engineering: "study the method and improve it before setting the standard."

JUST-IN-TIME PRODUCTION

The Japanese started out on quite a different approach than the U.S., and under the title "Production Engineering," combined all the technical manufacturing skills that we would separate into Production and Inventory Control, Quality Control, Manufacturing (Process) Engineering, Industrial Engineering, Material Handling, and Purchasing. They looked at low cost manufacturing as the only objective and came up with three guiding objectives or principles.

1. Eliminate Waste--waste being anything that does not add value to the product.

2. Produce Only What is Sold--if you don't need it now, don't make it now.

3. Henry Ford Was Correct--the assembly line concept of working on one unit at a time and "balancing the line" is the most efficient way to produce, <u>including fabrication and component production</u>.

Inventory was looked at as waste rather than an asset. Any problem in manufacturing that added cost required inventory to get around it. The attitude was to solve each problem (in the U.S. we invoked Murphy's Law assuming such problems are inevitable), stressing the system by reducing inventory until problems literally shut down production. The JIT concept was to solve each problem, as they were identified, rather than add back the inventory. Productivity was the objective and inventory the <u>measure</u> of how well progress was being made in reducing the cost of manufacture, hence the other name for JIT: Zero Inventory. However, JIT is a Manufacturing strategy not an inventory control technique and it is the development of such a strategy that had been missing.

Obviously the goals of zero waste, make only what has sold, and zero inventory are unachievable in the near term, if indeed ever, but continual movement toward these goals produces savings at each step and those who listened to the JIT case histories at the 1983 APICS national in New Orleans heard of productivity gains of 40% and inventory reductions of greater than 50% as typical one-to-three year pay backs. The non-cultural elements of the Japanese approach in JIT have been distilled and reported by the Repetitive Manufacturing Sub Group in APICS and have a compelling logic:

1. Avoid interrupted work flow

- Decrease set-up time (SMED).
- Control quality at the source (SQC).
- Eliminate machine breakdown (PM).

2. Eliminate material handling and stocking

- Rearrange equipment according to product flow (Group Technology or Flexible Manufacturing Cells).
- Reduce space between operations (minimize material handling)
- Eliminate stocking points and deliver to next operation (Reduce levels in Bill of Material, extend Routings).

3. Synchronize Manufacturing

- Cross train operators (Flexible manning).
- Match machine speeds to Master Schedule (Uniform Plant Loading).
- Master Schedule each item sold each period (schedule only what is needed).
- Eliminate queues and banks (zero lead time).
- Work with vendors to embrace JIT and deliver more frequently (Cooperative Purchasing).

4. Switch to "pull" scheduling

- Operations make (replace) only what is used (KANBAN or equivalent).

Note first that KANBAN is only a technique and also cannot be used until most of the other elements of JIT are successfully in place. KANBAN is not a synonym for JIT, just as Critical Ratio is not MRP II.

The essence of JIT is to simplify and eliminate through a process of problem solving, with a clear strategy as to what Manufacturing should ultimately look like. Note also that the JIT approach does not use automation and robotics until all that can be done to rearrange, synchronize, and balance operations is complete. Initial savings are indirect labor (stockroom personnel, material handlers, planners, controllers, inspectors, etc.). These functions do not "add value" to the product. Direct labor reduction occurs subsequently when the automation phase takes place. JIT makes automation easier and more effective, but is not the main thrust. The key point is that JIT changes and optimizes the environment, rather than focusing on the system, automation, or computerization. In focusing on the process, it may not adequately address the planning strategies and activities, but the results are impressive.

- Indirect factory labor--sharply reduced.
- Scrap and rework--sharply reduced.
- Lead times move from months to weeks to days.
- Space is freed-up--up to 2/3 reduction.
- Inventory drops--better than 50%.
- Forecasting is easier--shorter lead times.
- Distribution inventory reduced--less safety stock required; more frequent shipments.
- Shop floor control virtually eliminated.

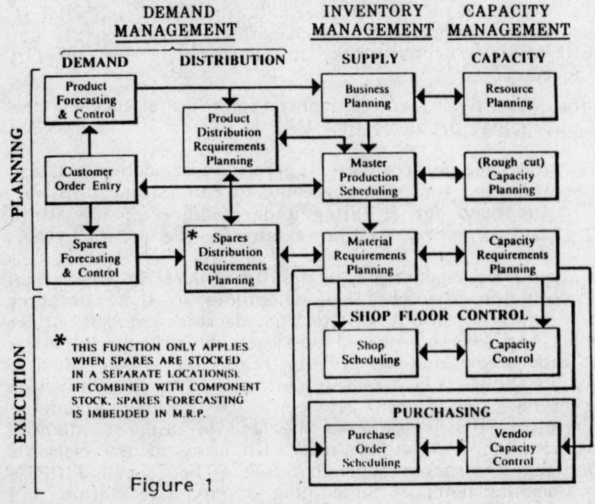

Figure 1

MANUFACTURING RESOURCES PLANNING

The Production and Inventory Control specialists in the U.S. focused on Customer Service and Inventory Control and developed a comprehensive group of techniques between 1960 and 1975, with evolving computer assistance. These techniques were finally integrated into a planning and scheduling strategy for all types of Manufacturing. Figure 1 represents MRP II as a matrix of these functions divided into a planning and execution phase and grouped into Demand management, Supply Management (Scheduling), and Capacity Management activities. Most of these activities are missing in the writings on JIT, perhaps because they are assumed to be in place. Demand Management is required for any manufacturing strategy, regardless of what scheduling system is used. Likewise every manufacturing operation must have a Production Plan and a Master Schedule. Capacity Planning is increasingly important to more closely synchronize the operations to the load placed on manufacturing by the Master Schedule. The critical planning interface between planning and execution is the Material Requirements Planning (MRP I) function. If we recognize MRP II as a planning strategy and JIT as an execution strategy, then MRP I becomes the JIT/MRP II interface.

Figure 2 shows a typical MRP I output which under the traditional MRP II concept is a material planning and scheduling system. It not only plans material requirements but also maintains the need date (due date) for each component supply order so that each order will arrive "just-in-time" for usage by the next level (ultimately the end item scheduled by the Master Production Schedule).

M.R.P. Output

Gross To Net Requirements Planning_________LENS ASSEMBLY

OH = 30   SS = 10   LT = 4 weeks   CLT = 9 weeks   OQ = 4 periods

	PAST DUE	1	2	3	4	5	6	7	8
DEPENDENT REQUIREMENTS				60				50	
INDEPENDENT REQUIREMNTS		10	10	10	10	10	10	10	10
GROSS REQUIREMENTS		10	10	70	10	10	10	60	10
ORDER RECEIPT			100 *				90 **		
PROJECTED AVAILABLE	20	10	100	30	20	10	90	30	20
ORDER RELEASE			90				100		

* SCHEDULED RECEIPT   ** PLANNED ORDER

Figure 2

Under traditional MRP II concepts there are three levels of scheduling:

1. Master Scheduling - quantity and date for completion of end items (high level assemblies or planning bills of material).

2. Material Requirements Planning - scheduling the completion and start date of the components and raw materials dependent on the Master Schedule.

3. Shop Floor Control - scheduling the operations performed on a component between MRP start and finish dates--often called Priority Sequencing.

As we have seen, under JIT Shop Floor Control becomes unnecesssary since parts go from start to completion in less than a day. Master Scheduling is required by JIT and in fact becomes more sophisticated. MRP I does not go away but becomes progressively simpler. To understand the impact on Material Requirements Planning, it is necessary to consider the 6 elements of MRP I:

1. On hand balance
2. Lot sizing
3. Safety Stock
4. Lead Time
5. Gross Requirements (the demand plan)
6. Scheduled receipts/planned orders (the supply plan)

The JIT approach involves a program dedicated to:

1. Eliminate on hand by moving completed components directly to the next user without going in and out of stock.

2. Eliminate lot sizing by reducing setup to the point where lot sizes of one generate no manufacturing cost (time) penalty.

3. Eliminate safety stock ("just-in-case" inventory) by removing all causes for safety stock:
   - Reliable delivery at moment of use
   - Zero defects
   - Zero machine breakdown
   - Zero material handling

4. Reduce lead time to days or less, by speeding up throughput and eliminate causes for move and wait time.

5. Smooth out gross requirements by making only what is needed (literally making everything sold every period).

6. Eliminate any difference between requirements (demand) and orders (supply) because of elimination of lot sizing and synchronization of production to the Master Schedule.

Figure 3 shows the MRP output after JIT has had its effect. Eliminating lot sizing at the Master Schedule has

MRP OUTPUT

Under J-I-T Production

Gross to Net Requirements Planning - Lens Assembly

OH ≡ 0   SS ≡ 0   LT ≡ 1 Day   CLT ≡ 2 Weeks   OQ ≡ 1 Piece

	Past Due	1	2	3	4	5	6	7	8
Dependent Requirements		15	15	15	15	14	13	12	12
Independent Requirements		10	10	10	10	10	10	10	10
Gross Requirements		25	25	25	25	24	23	22	22

Figure 3

smoothed out the dependent demand. The demand line, gross requirements, will be the same as the supply line, scheduled receipts, and "netting" and "net requirements" disappear. If the lead time disappears, MRP is too slow for scheduling and KANBAN takes over. Is MRP still needed? Very much so. First it will take years to achieve full effectiveness of the JIT approach (remember Toyota took 15 years), and we need to bridge that time with an effective scheduling methodology (MRP). Also MRP I was initially developed for job-shop manufacturing whereas JIT was generated in a repetitive manufacturing environment. Some plants or products that have "job-shop" characteristics (erratic low demand and highly option-sensitive customer configurations) may never be suitable for the full application of all aspects of JIT. Professor Schonberger in his excellent book "Japanese Manufacturing Techniques" makes this point very clearly. Where JIT can be fully applied, MRP becomes increasingly simplified and acts as the transition tool until its scheduling function vanishes as KANBAN becomes feasible. But even under full JIT production, the "gross requirements generation", exploding the Master Production Scheduling through a bill of material for the purpose if material planning (vendors) and as input to capacity planning (manufacturing), will always be needed.

OPTIMIZED PRODUCTION TECHNOLOGY

While MRP II was under development in the U.S. and JIT in Japan, Elihu Goldratt was developing his approach to Computer Integrated Manufacturing. The heart of his efforts is a proprietary computerized scheduling algorithm. Although just how that "brain" works has not been divulged, we assume that it is a very fast optimization technique having its foundation in linear programming concepts. Such an approach will in effect do sophisticated Master Scheduling and Rough Cut Capacity Planning in an integrated manner. These are separate routines in most MRP II installations. To understand OPT, it is best to divide it into its two major components (a simplified view):

1. The Brain of OPT--the optimizing Master Scheduling/ Capacity Planning System working on critical parts using critical operations.

2. The Serve System--which uses enhanced MRP methodology to finish the job on non-critical parts/operations dependent on the output from the Brain.

Figure 4 is Creative Output's representation of how OPT works. A full description of OPT is presented in a series of articles written by Bob Fox of Creative Output in Inventories and Production magazine November 1982 through April 1983. Essentially the traditional MRP II data base is constructed (bills of material, routings, market requirements, inventories, and work center data). Next the system is used in an analytical mode to identify bottleneck operations or resources. Those bottleneck operations become the initial resources to be planned by the Brain.

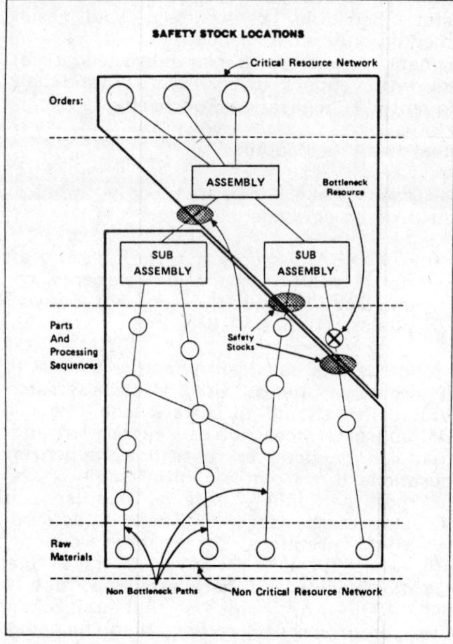

Figure 4

The rest of the resources, the non-critical operations, will be planned by Serve. The routed Bill of Material is then split, identifying those parts in the BOM that use the critical resources. Those parts and resources are then given to the Brain to develop an optimum schedule, using some three dozen parameters that can be set by the user to define the constraints. The Brain, although it "finitely loads" the critical (bottleneck) operations, avoids the pitfalls of the previous "finite loaders" by identifying these constraining resources and provides a "what-if" basis for increasing the capacity of critical resources and identifying new constraints--an elegant tool for capacity management.

In the first place, this advanced and quite complex tool ran up against problems that MRP II faced:

- the need for complete, current, and accurate data
- the need for "smart" people to run "smart" systems
- the need for a better understanding of the manufacturing process than existed in the U.S. in 1980.

OPT could be considered a significant leap in sophistication, but the planners and schedulers in U.S. industry had not even caught up to the demands of MRP II, a simpler and less integrated approach which even today is not understood well enough to realize its potential. In order to apply OPT, Creative Output had to face this lack of readiness for "smart" systems. OPT added an educational effort that recognized the lack of understanding of Manufacturing and had to deal with many of the elements addressed in greater depth by JIT. The so-called OPT's Ten Commandments of Scheduling started out stating that the goals of Manufacturing are to make money by simultaneously:

1. Increasing Throughput
2. Reducing Inventory
3. Reduce Operating Expenses

with the financial impact of simultaneously increasing:

1. Net Profit
2. Return on Investment
3. Cash Flow

The Ten Commandments are:

Scheduling

1. The utilization of a non bottleneck resource is not determined by its own potential, but by some other constraint in the system.

2. Activating a resource is not synonymous with utilizing a resource.

3. An hour lost at bottleneck is an hour lost for the total system.

4. An hour saved at a non bottleneck is a mirage.

5. The transfer batch may not and many times should not be equal to the process batch.

6. The process batch size should be variable and not fixed.

7. Capacity and priority need not be considered simultaneously and not sequentially.

8. Murphy is not an unknown and his damage can be isolated and minimized.

Cost Accounting--Performance Measurement

9. Plant capacity should not be balanced.

10. The sum of local optimums is not equal to the optimum of the whole.

It would take considerable time to match each OPT Ten Commandment to the JIT elements. Suffice it to say that JIT proceeds one step further than OPT and does synchronize operations and eliminates a lot of "Murphys" that OPT recognizes as restraints (setups, queues, and lack of balance, for example). Using OPT in a JIT environment would be far simpler and easier to run, would simplify the software, but it may be the ultimate software answer. However OPT, like JIT, does not address all the planning support activities of MRP II, since OPT focuses primarily on Master Scheduling, Material Requirements Planning, and Capacity Planning, integrating these to a far greater degree than MRP II.

SUMMARY

It should now be apparent that the Manufacturing function has become an area requiring considerable knowledge to adequately understand. It is not an overstatement to say that Manufacturing is becoming a profession and requires much more education and "lab" experience than the academic world has recognized. Until the educational requirements of a profession are available from the academic world, we have a critical scarcity of "smart" people. Yet those few professionals--too often specialists--are developing a growing number of "smart" systems. Unfortunately, manufacturing specialists and management did not recognize, until JIT arrived on the scene, the need for a manufacturing strategy to parallel and implement the rapid development of market and product strategies. As a result, we had no manufacturing framework to hang MRP II onto. Too many of the technical resources made available to Manufacturing have been technique-happy mechanics viewing parts of the whole, but failing to understand the complete subject and properly fit all the techniques and mechanics into a conceptual framework that can lead to the most cost effective operation. The conflict between MRP and KANBAN is a case in point--specialists in scheduling arguing about techniques while failing to address the Manufacturing process and understand when one or the other approach is desirable.

Let us suggest that JIT is the closest we have gotten to-date in the development of a Manufacturing strategy. Its impact on world-wide manufacturing attests to its effectiveness. Its logical approach can be understood by even simple folk, good basic blocking and tackling, to use a sports analogy. It doesn't take smart people to run a JIT facility, but it requires smart problem solving to repeal Murphy's Law. The resulting operation can and is run by simple people with simple systems. Recognize, however, that JIT evolved in repetitive manufacturing operations applying process industry concepts (who have long been under a JIT philosophy) to that environment. The more complex manufacturing operations are classified as job lot manufacturing or job shops and JIT is only just beginning to invade that field. MRP II evolved in the U.S. directing the "smart" people towards planning and scheduling job shops rather than overall problem solving. These complex manufacturing companies represented both the greatest need and the greatest opportunity. Quality improvement, setup reduction, preventative maintenance, and selective opportunities for group technology would have done much to avoid the current demise of some of those job shops, but those concepts failed to get the attention given to MRP II. As APICS broadened its horizon towards repetitive manufacturing, it was that group of innovators that "discovered" JIT and urged the U.S. to improve the Manufacturing environment, by developing and implementing a Manufacturing strategy before applying all of the MRP II methodology that had been applied to the job-shop world.

If we listen to that wise statement, we will not throw out MRP II, but use it more intelligently. Much of it can be simplified even in job shops if we are smart enough to rethink our Manufacturing process! But do not throw MRP II out. It represents the most thorough Planning and Scheduling strategy developed to-date and is a necessary complement to the implementation of a Manufacturing strategy.

Where does that leave OPT? In my opinion, OPT is one of those frequent situations in technical fields of developments that are ahead of their time. It is not surprising to find the best applications of OPT have been relatively simple and well thought-out repetitive manufacturing operations who went into OPT after significant experience in using formal systems. OPT is at this time the "smartest" system and requires real professionals to use it properly. As you might expect, it is expensive and consumes a lot of computer horsepower and time when applied to complex job-shop operations. If JIT concepts can simplify those kinds of Manufacturers and we can develop the required competency to use it, OPT could broaden its impact significantly and become the thrust of the future.

We need to then rethink our priorities in Manufacturing:

1. Develop a long range Manufacturing strategy.

2. Develop a tactical plan to start on the journey to implement that strategy.

3. Make sure that each step of the tactical plan generates major pay-backs, but never stop. No one has been even close to exhausting the productivity gains and inventory reductions that are possible, including Toyota.

4. In this journey start to collaborate and integrate with our peer disciplines in Manufacturing, namely, Q.C., ME, IE, Material Handling, Purchasing, and develop a coordinated attack. Manufacturing is an elephant and we can no longer be like the blind people trying to understand it by describing only the part that each of us touches and feels.

5. Distill out of MRP II those functions that are required as bridges to the future (even though they may change) and sophisticate only those that are permanent and fully developed functions.

6. Look to OPT first as a simulation and modelling tool and then as an advanced approach to Master Scheduling/Capacity Planning.

Those of you who have one inventory turn per year have a long journey, those at 26 turns a year also have a long journey. A modern automotive assembly plant turns 100 times. Are we going to sit back and merely say that our business is different? How about doubling your turns each year? You can't do that with MRP II or OPT alone. It must be done using a JIT approach and using applicable smart systems from MRP II and OPT as required. Someone somewhere is probably working on something that will make OPT look like a model T. It may well come out of the field of Artificial Intelligence. But it is still people who problem solve, manage, and use the systems and we must pace the development to the level of competence of our people and make them smarter before we smarten up the systems. We can go a long way with the simple fundamentals of JIT, but farther if we add MRP II and OPT. To regain the leadership in the world, parallel our systems development--a task in which we are already the world leader--with our JIT efforts. They are not in conflict but partners in progress toward low cost manufacturing.

JUST-IN-TIME: A GOAL FOR MRP II

Walter E. Goddard
Roger B. Brooks, CPIM*
The Oliver Wight Companies

Fourteen years ago APICS launched its successful and now famous MRP Crusade. That effort completely changed the way most U.S. manufacturing companies plan and buy material and make products. MRP has since developed into Manufacturing Resource Planning, MRP II, a planning and operating system that envelopes all of the functions of a manufacturing company. MRP II's acceptance and success are driven by the need to eliminate confusion in creating, converting, and communicating higher-level company strategies into detailed workable tasks.

APICS has now embarked on a second and more ambitious crusade in search of manufacturing excellence. The incentive is competition; the APICS banner is Zero Inventories. This crusade's objective is to inspire greater manufacturing performance by constantly striving to improve. It has no boundaries short of the "elimination of waste in the process of adding value to product." It was inspiried by the functional, quality, and price advantages held by Japanese products in American markets. The Zero Inventories Crusade resulted from closer scrutiny of the why's and how's of a number Japanese manufacturing companies.

APICS is now posturing itself to lead U.S. Industry to more efficient and productive manufacturing by promoting many of the methods used in Japan. This can be most effective only if APICS explains these Japanese practices. We must understand what they are, how they work, and where they are applicable. Only then can the practitioner select those that are superior to his and spread their use.

Today, our society has a vast body of knowledge that characterizes our profession. If the Zero Inventory Crusade is to be successful, its precepts and ideas must be added to this body.

Confusion abounds today. It is common to hear the APICS membership ask, "What's the difference between Zero Inventories, Just-in-Time, and KANBAN?", "Are JIT and MRP II compatible?", "Why am I implementing MRP II when my management wants JIT?", "If I put in a pull system, do I still have to do MRP?", "Does JIT just apply to repetitive manufacturing?", and "Aren't JIT and pull the same thing?"

Leadership comes from strong direction not confusion. If APICS is to fill the leadership position in this ongoing effort, it's time to sort out these issues and clear the air.

To contribute to this effort, we are addressing the following issues: What is JIT? What is MRP II's role with respect to JIT? How does Kanban relate to JIT? And, what are push and pull?

JUST-IN-TIME

To some people, Just-in-Time means having the right part at the right place at the right time. It also means "just enough." That is, exactly the right quantity - no more, no less - and not only with respect to parts but with respect to tooling, capacity, money, and energy. JIT means even more. It means no matter how good you are or how good you get you should constantly strive to improve. JIT is HUSTLE. Constantly working to make the product better, faster, more productively and with less resources. It means meeting the competition and squeezing them by seizing a design advantage, a quality advantage, a cost advantage, or a service advantage and passing it on to the customer. Use this to gain market share, achieve a volume advantage, and squeeze the cycle again and again.

JIT is an American Institution with a Japanese name. Henry Ford did it when he pushed the automobile industry forward with the assembly line. McDonald's did it when they standardized the fast food industry. And Joe Orlicky did it when he invented Material Requirements Planning.

But the breakthrough of today becomes the operating standard of tomorrow. To hustle means to work harder and smarter - to be leaner, meaner, quicker, and better every day.

In the 1950s and '60s U.S. manufacturing was king - we had the products, we had the know-how, and we owned the market. But some of us became complacent and in the following decade we just got out-hustled. The Japanese captured our markets with better products of higher quality at lower prices. We walked away from complete industries, and now certain (American) authors claim the re-industrialization of American Industry is meaningless - this of course is total foolishness.

The television market is America's. The small car market is America's. The shotgun market is America's. As are the commercial aircraft, office duplicating equipment, computers, cameras, shipbuilding, and other markets that we have, lost, or want. All we need to do is design a better product, make it better, at higher quality and lower cost than anyone else. It takes guts, dedication, and a true desire to be the best. As Oliver Wight said, "In business there is no par just competition." This is what JIT is all about.

It means we must focus our efforts to make every action, every investment, every second, and every person make the maximum contribution. Eliminate anything and everything that does not contribute, and when we're done, do it again - better, and then again even better.

MANUFACTURING RESOURCE PLANNING (MRP II)

To manufacture a product is to change something into something else. To convert iron ore into steel is manufacturing, as is the assembly of electronic, metal, and plastic parts into a computer. Companies that are involved in this coversion are manufacturing companies. The actual process of conversion is called "adding value to product."

No matter how simple or complex a product and its process are, a manufacturing company must perform certain activities in addition to adding value to be successful. This includes resource planning: equipment planning, material planning, financial planning, tooling planning, and people planning.

If a manufacturing company's product and process are extremely simple, like horseshoe nails, performing these functions can all be done and coordinated "on the back of an envelope" or in a single person's mind. But, they must be done. As the product and the process become more complex, these activities quickly encompass massive amounts of data that must be processed in very short periods of time. This requires a computer-supported operating system. Without this capability the manufacturing process itself becomes uncoordinated and confusing.

Manufacturing Resource Planning has been developed by manufacturing practitioners to address the planning and orchestrating of a manufacturing process and all of its related support functions. MRP II encompasses logically correct planning and control activities related to material, capacity, finance, engineering, sales, and marketing. MRP II is universally applicable to any manufacturing company regardless of its size, location, product, or process. Some manufacturing companies must focus on capacity, others on material, yet others on the conversion process itself. This does not mean the other functions are not necessary, but most likely, simply easier to perform. MRP II has been called by first-time observers "organized common sense." This is a correct and succinct analysis. More importantly, the popularity of MRP II results from its track record. It has enabled managers to operate thousands of companies in a cross section of American industry more professionally.

JIT AND MRP II

MRP II is "organized common sense" in the form of a planning and operating system for all of the functions of a manufacturing company.

JIT is "the elimination of waste in the process of adding value to product." Why is there misunderstanding? Why would anyone ever say "I'm doing JIT so I don't have to do MRP II"?

The two concepts are absolutely, without challenge, compatible. MRP II attacks and eliminates confusion through effective planning and scheduling. Confusion is wasteful. Thus, MRP II must be considered not only an element of JIT, but a structure that promotes the JIT concept. It is more than coincidence that the U.S. companies that are setting the pace with JIT "American style" are those with effective MRP II systems: Black & Decker, Omark Industries, Instron, American Sterilizer, Corning Glass, Tennant, Hewlett-Packard, Tektronix, etc. It is also more than coincidence that a number of Japanese companies are using MRP II "Japanese style" as part of their JIT program.

In spite of what should be obvious, questions do exist. Some MRP II enthusiasts tend to focus on the planning and execution of the manufacturing process, while some of the JIT enthusiasts tend to focus on the physical manufacturing process itself. Excellence in manufacturing requires both.

Activities that can improve the physical process include: proper material handling, revised plant layout, group technology, multipurpose machines, multiskilled operators, robotics, housekeeping, set-up reductions, improved product design, preventive maintenance, etc. As important as these activities are, we will not concentrate on them. Rather, we will describe how to use MRP II to its full potential in achieving JIT advantages.

If MRP II is to be faulted, it is in its ability to create a valid simulation of what is actually happening regardless of how well or poorly the business is being run. It is robust in the fact that it can handle manufacturing lead times of any length, and lot sizes, queues, and safety stocks of any quantity. It does not judge these values, rather it accepts them as givens and responds as if they were true.

Herein lies how you must use MRP II to achieve JIT. Take lead times as an example: in an MRP II system planning lead times can be set as long or as short as the practitioner desires. Yet, to set them too long will result in excessive WIP inventories and also extend the cumulative lead time of finished goods, forcing the need to forecast finished products when no such need is necessary. Setting them too short, on the other hand, may allow enough time to actually build the product, thus creating a steady state expedite mode and missed customer orders. Thus, the lead time input into an MRP II system must properly represent the manufacturing process or waste will result.

Note that MRP II does not cause or force the lead time to be reduced. The incentive for reducing lead times must come from the practitioner. Lead times are made up of set-up time, run time, wait time, move time, and queue time. Reducing any one of these elements favorably impacts lead times. Since queues normally comprise seventy to eighty percent of most manufacturing lead times, they offer the biggest potential for lead time reduction. MRP II provides essential information for reducing queues. The Capacity Requirements Report projects the required capacity for each work center. The Capacity Input/Output Report monitors the size of the queues and the demonstrated capacity for each work center. With this information, the practitioner can determine the minimum queue size and then adjust the demonstrated capacity to achieve it. As these capacities are being adjusted, the planning lead times for the parts effected should be simultaneously adjusted in MRP II to reflect the reduced queue times.

For middle manager practitioners to really take full advantage of MRP II's capabilities with respect to JIT, they need a top management group that is willing to set the goal and provide strong, enlightened leadership. Top management must set JIT as policy, understand its requirements, and authorize and openly encourage its achievement. The creation of a policy by the general manager and his staff stating that all manufacturing lead times must be reduced to a certain number of days by a certain date in the future might be used to communicate this goal. This policy statement obviously does not cause the lead times to be reduced, but it does give their reduction proper priority.

In true JIT fashion, once the goal has been achieved a new goal will be established - constantly forcing re-evaluation and improvement. Pursuing this approach it can be readily seen that the other planning inputs of MRP II fall into play.

Management should attack waste elimination on more than one front. For instance, at the same time the lead time goal is set, they should establish goals for order quantities, set-up times, and inventory levels.

Order quantities for purchased and manufactured parts in an MRP II system are input by the practitioner. Again, MRP II generally accepts a wide range of ordering policies and quantities, from a discrete quantity of one to fixed quantities of thousands to an array of dynamic algorithms. It treats these as givens and does not judge their applicability or value. Should the practitioner assign an order quantity/policy to a part that forces MRP II to order more than the quantity required, the residual will be held for future consumption. MRP II will always try to drive the inventory balances to zero, but it remains the responsibility of the practitioner to allow this to happen.

Cost trade-offs between inventory carrying costs and set-up costs (or price breaks) are usually at the heart of order quantities larger than one. JIT philosophy encourages the practitioner to avoid this cost trade-off by reducing the set-up costs to absolute minimums. As stated earlier, this requires attention to the physical process. The practitioner can use the information in MRP II to assist him in this effort. Sorting the item master file by order quantity will identify the greatest opportunities. A similar approach can be used for set-up times on the routing file.

Safety stocks, like order quantities, are inputs by the practitioner to an MRP II system. Any quantity is acceptable to the system, and once input MRP II will always try to keep that amount in inventory. Safety stock inventories are never planned to be used and are, thus, planned waste. Again, MRP II can help the practitioner spot these wastes by sorting the item master file. Each part whose safety stock is to be reduced or eliminated should have its demands or supply analyzed for uncertainty. Where no uncertainty exists, the safety stock should be eliminated. Uncertainty of demand is often reduced and in some cases eliminated through lead time reduction. This is most desirable and should be pursued as part of a lead time reduction effort.

The practitioner must be very careful when evaluating those parts with safety stock to cover uncertainty of supply. Often times a supplier appears unreliable due more to our poor scheduling than his. In cases of unreliable suppliers, a team of your engineers, buyers, schedulers, and quality assurance people can often provide the necessary understanding and communications to correct the problem. This team should focus on reducing lead times, improving quality, and delivery reliability. Again, if the supplier can achieve any of these, safety stock can be reduced or eliminated. Safety stock for uncertainty of supply is almost always excessive.

MRP II provides the information necessary to properly focus your resources. Additionally, after physical action is taken to realize an improvement, MRP II retains it for ongoing benefits.

This multifront approach makes JIT the goal of many departments outside of Production and Inventory Control. JIT is a total company goal that must be managed within all of the functional areas of a manufacturing company. Design engineering, process/manufacturing/industrial engineering, quality assurance, marketing, sales, maintenance, personnel, data processing, purchasing, material control, finance, and manufacturing all must become team players for the company to realize a more competitive position through manufacturing excellence.

<u>JIT, KANBAN, PUSH, PULL</u>

Because the term Just-in-Time came from Toyota, and because many people have heard or read that Toyota is using a Kanban system, linkage has occurred. They think JIT means Kanban; or Kanban is the only way to achieve JIT. Not so!

First, Kanban is only a part of Toyota's manufacturing system. It is not a stand-alone segment. Toyota's system also encompasses production planning by top management,

a computer-supported master production schedule, a bill of
material explosion, set-up reductions, quality improvements,
product design changes, etc.

The Kanban portion of the system is used for two
purposes: to reorder certain components and to trigger
the movement of jobs in the factory. For reordering
material, it works identically to a two bin system. When the
first bin is empty, that triggers the need to reorder
material. The assumption is: "If we have used it, replace
it as we need it." This is a "push" planning system as it
replenishes material expecting to need it. Only when a
company is using a component repetitively can such a
material planning system work well.

In contrast MRP II's logic is: "If we have used it,
don't replace it until it's needed." This is a "pull"
planning system. MRP II replenishes inventory only if more
is required. The MRP II approach does not require
repetitive manufacturing but works equally well in a
one-of-a-kind or even in a once-in-a-while manufacturing
environment.

Additionally, MRP II recognizes the need to reschedule
and works to keep the due date and need date for an order
equal. Kanban does not offer this feature.

On the factory floor, there are two ways for the
physical movement of material to occur. If the job is
moved to the next work center upon completion, this is
called a "push" system. You are expecting that the next
operation needs it. If the job is not moved until it is
requested by the next work center, this is called a "pull"
system. You wait until a job is needed.

Toyota uses the Kanban cards to trigger the movement
of material. The consuming work center requests more
material from the feeding work center via the Kanban cards,
i.e., a pull system.

The concern over which movement system is better is
of far less importance than whether you are working on the
right job. If the wrong job is worked on, it makes little
difference whether it remains at the upstream work center
because the downstream does not need it, or whether you
have physically moved it to the downstream work center.
Working on the wrong job but not delivering it to the next
operation is hardly a worthy goal.

If the right job is worked on, then where it's
physically stored is of little consequence. Prematurely
moving it to the downstream operation is insignificant.
Working on the right job is overwhelmingly the most
important thing to do. The goal is minimum inventory
regardless of when it's moved.

Push versus pull in the factory is like the "Emperor's
New Clothes." It is being presented as if it's a
significant issue. We need to pull the charade of
importance off of the Emperor and push the right issues
into the spotlight. What remain are two very critical
issues - generating valid schedules and then executing
them on time.

Toyota and other Japanese companies are successfully
achieving JIT. The Kanban approach is part of their
efforts. Other Japanese firms as dedicated to JIT are
using MRP II.

JIT is the goal. Excellent resource planning and
excellent scheduling must be implemented to achieve it.
The question is: "Which is better, MRP II or a Kanban
system?" Both can be effective. However, MRP II is not
restricted to repetitive manufacturing.

SUMMARY

In an effort to reduce confusion related to JIT,
MRP II, KANBAN, PUSH, PULL, etc., we offer the following
observation:

JIT is the elimination of waste in the value-adding
     process.
ZERO INVENTORIES is APICS' name for the JIT philosophy
     (also known as Stockless Production).

MRP II is a planning and operating system that envelopes
     all of the functions of a manufacturing company.
KANBAN is one part of Toyota's planning and operating
     system (applicable to repetitively manufactured
     parts).
PUSH is to take action in anticipation of a need. Applied
     to either material planning (reorder point) or
     physical material movement (dispatching).
PULL is to take action upon request. Applied to either
     material planning (MRP II) or physical movement
     (Kanban cards).

Therefore:

JIT is not MRP II.

JIT is not KANBAN.

JIT is not PUSH.

JIT is not PULL.

JIT does not require repetitive manufacturing.

JIT is Stockless Production.

JIT is Zero Inventories.

JIT is our search for manufacturing excellence.

CONCLUSION

We import many things from Japan. The slogan,
Just-in-Time, has come from there. But JIT cannot be
bought. Striving for excellence is a philosophy, a
dedicated effort to improve. It's dependent on people not
a culture; it's an attitude not an algorithm; it's a
never-ending challenge not a fixed target. It's the old
American spirit.

The same applies to MRP II. You can buy hardware and
software but you can't buy Class A. Using MRP II in a
superior manner requires a "can do" attitude and a correct
understanding of what it is and how it works from the
general manager to every operator.

Let's all sign up for the crusade. Just-in-Time is a
worthy goal.

Walt Goddard is the President of Oliver Wight Education
Associates. He worked in manufacturing for nine years
and held the positions of manager of management
systems, production control manager, and inventory
manager. Since 1970, Walt has conducted courses for
top management people as well as for the designers
and users of MRP II systems. He has assisted with the
installation of many Class A MRP II systems. Walt has
long been active in APICS. He is past President of
the Fairfield County Chapter and is presently a member
of the Granite State Chapter.

Roger Brooks is Executive Vice President of Oliver
Wight Education Associates and President of Roger
Brooks, Inc. Prior to going into the consulting and
education business, he held several positions at
Hyster Company in Portland, Oregon. He was responsible
for the successful implementation of their MRP system.
As an educator with hands-on experience, he conducts
courses for top management people as well as the
designers and users of MRP II systems. Roger is an
APICS Certified Fellow, and has served as Director
of Education and Research for the Portland APICS
Chapter.

JIT VS. MRP—EXPLODING THE MYTHS

Alan E. Loebel, CPIM
Harris Corporation

OBJECTIVE

The objective of this paper is to explain the real differences between the Just-In-Time (Zero Inventory) approach, and MRP. There are many who believe that changing all lot sizing to "discrete" in an MRP system, will make a JIT system out of it. This paper explores the philosophies inherent in JIT. The concept that everything not directly adding value to the product being manufactured is a waste, is the simple yet elegant basis for JIT. Further, philosophies relative to storage space, queues, scrap, WIP and lot sizing will be contrasted to the philosophies embedded within the typical MRP system.

BACKGROUND OF MRP

Order point systems predated MRP. When 1st generation computers became available in the late 50's and early 60's we computerized the order point, economic order quantity and statistical safety stocks that we'd been calculating manually.

MRP based systems, including early attempts at what is today known as MRP/II, have grown in popularity in the United States over a period that started in the early 60's. These systems began as relatively straight forward material planning tools. Over the ensuing years, all of the systems with the word "planning" in their title have evolved. There are Market Planning, Production Planning, Master Planning, Material Requirements Planning, Rough Cut (or Resource Requirements) Planning and Capacity Requirements Planning, to name but a few.

This emphasis on the planning aspects, and the attendant de-emphasis of the execution aspects of manufacturing, has contributed heavily to the lack of progress in attaining either the "control" promised in the term "Manufacturing Control System" or the increased inventory performance that theoretically should result from these kinds of systems.

EVENT DRIVEN SYSTEMS

Ed Heard calls MRP/II systems "event oriented feedback control systems". This translates into planning systems that require feedback, particularly when things don't happen as planned, don't happen at all, or things happen that weren't planned. This feedback, in turn, precipitates replanning, the results of which are no more likely to be executed as planned than was the original plan. The lack of "control" in this scenario should be evident.

How did this happen? What were the strategies that brought us to the point where a few companies have made excellent use of MRP, a bunch have made good use of it, but the vast majority are in about the same shape they were in before they started?

PROBLEMS TO BE OVERCOME

We established rules for lot sizing. This evolved from the heyday of operations research in the 50's when we thought we could run the factory on statistics and averages. Our reason for lot sizing? To balance inventory costs against large set up costs. Let's save that one for later.

Things were unpredictable. We needed protection. Vendors told us how long it would take them to deliver, and then it took longer. We established manufacturing planning lead times, which didn't materialize. If our vendor's lead times didn't hold up, why should ours be any better? We, too, are vendors to our customers.

Demand was unpredictable because we couldn't get the customers to order what we wanted to build, or what we forecast they would order.

We planned for queues, or buffers of work at each work center to protect against the variability in the lead time and the fact that events couldn't be predicted too well and we needed protection against interruption of the manufacturing process.

These are only examples of what we did. We assumed some things (vendor lead times, forecasts, etc.) were not changeable in large part, and proceeded to develop systems and techniques to cope.

BACKGROUND OF JIT

No discussion of JIT would be complete without mention of Japan, even though most of us are sick of hearing of their great strides in productivity.

Japan took a proactive view instead of a reactive view. JIT is only one of several philosophical and strategic methods used. And it didn't just appear magically one day. It evolved over a relatively long period of time.

After World War II a strategy was established: eliminate unemployment through industrialization. The goal was to attain full employment through use of this strategy. However, an additional strategic element was added: dominance. The Japanese recognized that they were at a disadvantage in several areas, but two were of major proportions. They had little space and they had almost no raw materials. Therefore they focused their efforts on a few key industries, with world market dominance their strategic target and goal.

To attain these goals they employed a 3 prong attack.

ATTACK ON QUALITY PROBLEMS

First was quality. Most of us remember when the term "made in Japan" was cause for chuckles. Japanese quality was so bad during the late 40's and early 50's that a law was passed requiring manufacturing origin to be prominently displayed on all products to protect the unwary consumer. Rumor had it that a Japanese city was renamed "USA" so that "made in USA" could be stamped into products made there.

Quality problems were to be attacked with such ferver that their competition would not be able to produce a product as reliable, at a competitive cost.

ATTACK ON PRODUCTIVITY PROBLEMS

Next came productivity. The Japanese recognized early that low costs and high productivity are partners. The most talented engineers in Japan are more likely to be found on the shop floor than in the design engineering activity. It is said that most Japanese foremen are degreed industrial engineers. It was also recognized that stability of manufacturing work load can be a huge contributor to increased productivity.

NIH (NOT INVENTED HERE)

Finally, they made a conscious decision to avoid major Research and Development projects with their attendant risks and costs. To accomplish this they signed licensing agreements to import the needed technology in the markets where they intended to attain dominance.

SUCCESS SHOWS

It wasn't until the early to mid 70's that we began to hear about the Japanese and their tremendous strides. We knew that their quality had improved dramatically, but we knew it as consumers, not competitors.

Japanese automobiles began to make real inroads into American life. Companies like Toyota and Nissan acquired reputations for excellent quality. These reputations were based on solid "frequency of repair" records never before seen in this country.

Cameras from Japan became the standards of the world. Names like Nikon, Canon and Minolta became household words.

Other electronics businesses such as television receivers, stereos and more recently, video cassette recorders, came to be more and more dominated by the Japanese. No one would say that with RCA, Zenith and many others, the Americans are out of electronics. But most major American electronics companies import large portions of their products from what we euphamistically call "off shore" suppliers. And names like Sony and Quasar (formerly an American company) continue to be more dominant as time passes.

OBVIOUS DIFFERENCES

The differences in cultures, styles and values between the United States and Japan have been repeated time and time again. I will comment on them here only to the extent necessary to finish setting the stage for exploding the myths.

Culture, style and value are only part of the picture. Other differences also contribute substantially to the scenario.

The Japanese are in it for survival. And where survival is at stake, there is a tendency to learn, and learn quickly.

THE SIZE FACTOR

As mentioned earlier, Japan is a small country. Their entire square mileage is roughly equivalent to that of the state of California. Crammed within their borders is a population equal to approximately one half of ours. This space problem was the main contributor to the development of techniques that have received a lot of publicity, such as "focused factories" and "Just In time Production."

The United States, on the other hand, is the land of plenty. Space is a resource that has never been a problem. So, as opposed to "focused factories" we build huge plants to manage complete vertically integrated businesses. This is not inherently good or bad; only a fact. These businesses have a tendency to become overly burdened with extra layers of overhead and bureaucracy, and are therefore much more difficult to manage than focused factories.

BUSINESS AND LABOR

With survival the name of the game, a spirit of cooperation exists between business and labor in Japan that makes most American business people stare incredulously.

They have labor unions, but everyone labor and management alike, belongs to them. In key industries, compensation plans include salary and bonus for everyone. The objective is to tie the health of the company to the health of the individual. And it works.

We have spent years developing an adversary relationship between labor and management that has left deep scars and gross mistrust of each faction by the other.

NATURAL RESOURCES

Japan has almost no natural resources. This affects the people in two major ways. First is the expense of importing almost everything they need. This became only too apparent with the energy crisis of 1973. They have no oil or coal, and their energy costs exploded almost overnight. Second, is their need to maintain a balance of payments. To bolster the economy, there is an absolute need to export goods at least equal in value to what they import. Due to the lack of natural resources, this means manufactured product. In this case survival was the mother of invention.

MRP AND JIT TOGETHER

One of the most popular myths is that MRP and JIT can't exist together. Wrong!! There is absolutely nothing in either technique that precludes using the other. As a matter of fact, the term "synchro MRP" is used to describe the combining of the 2 philosophies.

To begin with, it must be remembered that MRP (and MRP/II) is basically a planning (and replanning) system, having little association with the actual manufacturing process. JIT, on the other hand, is almost exclusively an excecution system that doesn't concern itself with planning.

Furthermore, JIT is only one of several building blocks needed to begin to approach the elusive "zero inventory" position.

This doesn't mean that it can be done without some changes being made. One obvious change to attempt that is not as beneficial as it might intuitively seem, is to change all lot sizing rules in the MRP system to "discrete" or "lot for lot." Those trying this have quickly discovered that it has a tendency to

dramatically increase already long computer run times, and in many cases to exceed size restrictions on files containing the MRP generated planned orders. A better approach is to continue to plan larger quantities in MRP, and spoon feed the manufacturing process. Perhaps MRP could be planning in weekly time increments, but the line could be fed hourly or daily.

Another change needed is in the lead time area. Most MRP systems have weeks or days as the smallest time increment for lead time offset. When JIT techniques begin to work, actual lead times will be less than the MRP systems can cope with. A recommended approach is to liberally utilize phantoms or pseudos in bill of material systems, changing the "shape" of the bills from "narrow and deep" to "wide and shallow." Now, a leadtime offset from final assembly due date or ship date can be used for a required date for <u>all</u> components, instead of the classic level by level offset. This is not a "cure all" technique, but is suggested to demonstrate that most objections to JIT and MRP co-existing can be countered with reasonable solutions.

Exploding this myth should not be construed to mean that MRP and JIT can co-exist in all environments. Some basics are required. These basics are relatively level production, repetitive manufacturing, dedicated resources and short setup.

ARE PROBLEMS INEVITABLE?

Another popular misconcept is that problems in the manufacturing process are inevitable, and as a result interruptions are bound to occur.

In MRP implementations, particularly earlier ones, we took this seriously, and built buffers into the systems. It was not always apparent what these buffers really were.

Queues at work centers were desirable to protect against running out of work. We were (and in most cases still are) worried about people slowing down if they fear running out of work.

Lot sizes were desirable to spread the costs of long and expensive set ups over a larger volume of parts, until the inventory carrying costs increased past the point of savings established by the lot size.

Safety stocks were desirable because they protected against fluctuation in supply (downward) or demand (upward). It was also desirable because lead times couldn't be depended upon.

In fact, queues, lot sizes and safety stocks are all inventory, in one form or another. The JIT attitude is that of Toyota: "The value of inventory is disavowed." The belief is that rather than protecting against disruption in the manufacturing process, inventory hides problems, and therefore contributes to, and in some cases even causes the disruptions.

Contrasting this idea to our classic position, one begins to see that to embrace the "inventory is bad" attitude, takes a complete reversal of conventional American manufacturing thinking patterns. We have to attack the problems more diligently than we ever have. Japan's Nippondenso has reportedly called inventory "the root of all evil," certainly a stronger position than that attributed to Toyota. But it is very descriptive about their attitude.

Disruptions in the manufacturing process are not inevitable, but we can't stop them if we're looking at the symptoms instead of the disease.

GROUP TECHNOLOGY

GT has been reported as one of the "elimination of waste" techniques utilized to help reduce inventory. A myth that has quickly popped up, is that GT is only applicable to a few select businesses. Wrong!

While it is true that gruop technology is not universally applicable, it can be used in far more types of manufacturing environments than may be immediately apparent. In it's simplest form, GT is an assembly line concept, but not limited to assembly types of operation. For instance, it could be used in a machine shop.

As an example, a simple machine shop might consist of work centers containing mills, drills, lathes and grinders. Each work center has a queue of material in front of it, and experiences time delays getting this material from one place to another within the

department. Capacity imbalances between equipment
types are common, but difficult to spot.

The same department, layed out on GT lines, would
have the machines rearranged to be dedicated to a
certain family of parts. This family is typically
determined by geometry. For instance, one line of
machines might be dedicated to cylindrical parts
between 1 and 4 inches in diameter.

Several things happen in the above scenario.
Setups can be converted to changeovers or partial
setups, usually drastically reducing the time required.
This, in turn, allows smaller lot sizes, even using EOQ
type formulas. Lead times compress to an almost
unbelievable point. To go from months to days is not
unreasonable in extreme cases. Capacity imbalances
stick out like a sore thumb. Indirect labor has been
reduced because the need for material handlers and
expediters has been greatly reduced.

It is a rare manufacturer that doesn't have at
least a few processes that lend themselves to GT. The
paybacks can be tremendous. We have complained for
years that 80% to 90% of our lead times were queue and
move time. GT gives us the opportunity to take a giant
step toward reducing those numbers.

Even in cases where the concept is obviously and
admittedly applicable, resistance is often encountered
because of the perceived cost of rearranging an entire
factory. There are all flavors of GT, some much more
expensive than others. The simplest and cheapest I've
seen was a huge machine shop where no physical
rearrangement of equipment was made. The machines were
simply painted different colors. The "pink line" was
for parts of a certain geometry, while the "blue line"
was for parts of a different geometry. This particular
machine shop had demonstrated a reduction in lead times
in the neighborhood of 75%! And this was done without
moving one machine.

SCRAP IS GOOD

The heading above may look ludicrous, but that is
what we practice in this country. Despite our recent
interest in quality circles and such hype as ""quality
is job one," as a country, we pay workers to produce
scrap. Most pay systems include calculations for
volume of output (earned hours, etc.) but not volume of
quality output. In many electronic businesses, a
substantial percentage is added to the calculated
standard product cost, just to cover rework activities.
Rework is not only expected, but it is accepted as a
normal part of doing business.

In a JIT situation, there are no buffers to cover
mistakes. Flow of material is expected and needed
to keep the production lines going. In this
environment, quality is everyones job. Establishing
such an environment takes a tremendous amount of trust
in people. Labor and management in the United States
have historically been adversaries as opposed to
partners. To truly implement what the Japanese call
"Jidoka" will take more than just a commitment by
management.

We have long recognized the irony of never having
enough time to do things right the first time, but
always having enough time to do them over.

JIT IS THE SOLUTION

The myth that JIT is the solution to all of our
problems has caused much gnashing of teeth, and has
sent the MRP software vendors back to the books in an
attempt to dig up information that proves their
products can help to attain JIT.

It is doubtful that any American manufacturer can
completely convert to JIT production, yet it is likely
that every American manufacturer could find some part
of his or her business where the JIT principles are
applicable.

Kenneth Wantuck identified 14 basic elements
grouped loosely under two major headings, that taken
together, represent the Japanese approach to improved
productivity.

Elimination of Waste

o Focused Factory Networks
o Group Technology
o QC At The Source
o JIT Production

o Uniform Plant Load
o Kanban PC System
o Minimized Set Up Time

Respect For People

o Lifetime Employment
o Company Unions
o Attitude Toward Workers
o Automation/Robotics
o Bottom Round Management
o Subcontractor Networks
o Quality Circles

It can be seen that JIT is but one technique among
many. This is not to say, however, that JIT cannot be
installed by itself. The answer to the question "is
JIT applicable to my business?" is "probably, to some
extent." If your master schedules are relatively
stable, or can be made so, if the manufacture of your
product is relatively repetitive, or can be made so, if
some portion of your resources are dedicated, or can be
made so, if your setup times are short, or can be made
so, if your quality is good, or can be made so, then
JIT is for you in one form or another.

CONCLUSION AND SUMMARY

While the differences between cultures, management
style, philosophies and values, vary substantially
between Japan and America, we cannot be deterred from
utilizing techniques that have proven viable to the
Japanese.

The Japanese have toured the world, cameras and
recorders in evidence, investigating the techniques
found useful by other people. They have returned home
with the new ideas and concepts, and modified them to
meet their own needs. They didn't discard techniques
out of hand with the simple excuse that "it won't work
in our culture."

Dave Garwood recently reported that the Japanese
are "aggressively and enthusiastically" learning how to
implement MRP/II. If you think they're tough to
compete with now, wait until they utilize American
planning techniques coupled with Japanese values
relative to inventory, waste, group technology, etc.

What we need to do is to get aggressive ourselves
to solve what have appeared to be insurmountable
problems.

Rather than bemoan the setup costs we have to
cover with lot sizes, we should investigate group
technology to slash those lot sizes to a fraction of
what they are.

Rather than accept bad quality, we should begin to
attack it at the source. Refuse to pay for the
creation of scrap. Get the people who produce products
involved in better quality. Quality circles are a good
start, but fall far short of doing the job. The
Japanese call it "quality at the source" and take it
seriously. We cannot entertain JIT production and Zero
Inventory schemes until quality is much better than it
is. As long as we telegraph to our employees that a
certain amount of scrap is okay, we're doomed to
mediocrity.

Rather than argue and cajole, we must truly solve
the age old problems that exist in communication and
cooperation between Marketing, Engineering and
Manufacturing. It certainly isn't difficult to realize
that the high cost and low productivity resulting from
products that look good on paper but can't be
manufactured, put us at a huge disadvantage in world
markets.

These quality and manufacturability issues are but
representative of the issues we must face. Despite
recent well publicized productivity increases, we are
still complacent. We need to be shaken up a little.
Japanese superiority in manufacturing knowhow and
quality, must be made a myth!!

RECOMMENDED READING

For those desiring to become more familiar with
the details of concepts introduced here, several good
articles and books exist.

A 2 part article entitled "Production Control &
Japanese Productivity" by Robert W. Hall in the
September/October and November/December 1981 issues of
Inventories and Production makes excellent reading.
   Also excellent, are Nick Edwards' and Jeffrey
Anderson's "MRP And Kanban - American Style," and Ed
Heard's "Why MRP/II Won't Get Japanese Level Inventory
Turns," both published in the APICS 26th International
Conference Proceedings.
   The above articles will, in turn, lead you to
still more recommended reading. Good hunting!!

ABOUT THE AUTHOR

Alan E. Loebel, CPIM

   Al is presently Manager, Manufacturing Systems for
Harris Corporation, a multi divisional manufacturer of
electronic equipment, headquartered in Melbourne,
Florida. In his capacity on the corporate staff, he
functions as an internal consultant to the divisions of
Harris in matters relating to Manufacturing Systems of
all kinds, with emphasis on MRP/II.
   Prior to joining Harris, he held various line and
staff positions in materials management and data
processing. These positions include Director of
Management Information Systems for the Bostitch
Division of Textron, Senior Consultant with Arista
Information Systems and Materials Manager for Cutler
Hammer, Inc.
   Al is certified (CPIM) by the American Production
and Inventory Control Society (APICS) and is a frequent
speaker at APICS meetings.

LINKING MRP AND JIT: THE BEST OF THE OCCIDENT AND THE ORIENT

W. A. Sandras, Jr., CPIM*
Hewlett-Packard

MRP systems are very good at macro-planning. They can project labor and machine capacity requirements, cash commitments, material usage, and even engery and space requirements. A kanban system does not provide this information directly. On the other hand, a kanban system is very good at shop floor control and execution, while shop floor control systems within MRP are very complex and become more and more burdensome as lot sizes approach one. Despite the philosophical and system differences between MRP and JIT (or kanban), 16 months of experience at Hewlett-Packard's Ft. Collins Systems Division (HP/FSD) has shown that it is feasible AND desirable to link MRP and kanban together. The weaknesses of MRP are complimented by the strengths of kanban, and the weaknesses of kanban are complimented by the strengths of MRP. While the linkage between MRP and kanban is not extremely difficult, the changes tend to permeate a wide variety of systems. Some people also feel a tendency to modify the philosophies of JIT to fit well with MRP systems, rather than achieving a proper link that utilized the philosophies and strengths of each.

HP/FSD

Most of us visualize JIT or kanban in use with high volume products manufactured on dedicated progressive assembly lines. Familiar examples include Toyota, several HP divisions, and a handful of other companies. Less common but equally valid is the use of JIT in job shop, product independent production processes (see 1983 proceedings article titled "Continuous Flow Customized Production"). HP/FSD manufactures desktop computers. Some of the products are near the high end of the personal computer market while others are in the CAD/CAM or computer aided engineering market. In addition we produce a wide variety of software products. Today, approximately 20% of all production output of the facility is manufactured using only JIT processes. Another 20-30% of the output is in a transitional stage to JIT manufacturing processes. By the end of 1985, virtually all products manufactured at HP/FSD will use a JIT manufacturing process. By way of comparison, HP/FSD has 33,000 part numbers, 180,000 product structure records, and 500 vendors. We use an HP3000/Series 64 computer for MRP and use standard off the shelf MM3000 MRP software from HP. (Most of HP's approximately 50 divisions throughout the world are investigating or converting to JIT processes).

PRODUCTION PROCESSES

Figure 1 shows three types of production processes in use at HP/FSD. Process A and B are JIT processes, while process C uses traditional batch workorder production techniques. Process A is used for higher volume products, and is best described as a dedicated progressive assembly line approach to manufacturing. In practice, the "dedicated" lines are somewhat flexible and can build a narrow variety of similar products if they all go through the same work stations. Process B denotes product independent assembly lines using traditional workbenches or closed loop transporters. Process C is traditional batch manufacturing using workorders. Nearly all products currently using process C are in the process of being converted to JIT lines using process A or B. Today, several products have been converted to the JIT approach, while other new products have started out with the JIT philosophy. Only a small percentage of production will remain as traditional batch production. As Figure 2 shows, batch production will be continued only for prototype and out of production service parts. Mature, stable, higher volume products will use process A, while products with lower volumes and rapidly changing volumes will use process B. At HP/FSD, the top 75 products, excluding software, have a production rates from over 300 units per day for the top products down to 2 per year for the lowest volume products. While it is practical to make nearly all of these products using a JIT approach, the familiar repetitive manufacturing JIT approach is obviously not applicable to all of the products. Notice that process A and process B are both true JIT or kanban approaches - A is repetitive and B is job shop. Only process C will remain using workorders and batch philosophies.

COMMON LINKS

In many instances the system changes are identical for repetitive and job shop JIT links to MRP systems. However, in some instances the systems changes required for the repetitive JIT link are not the same as those required for job shop JIT link. Examples of identical changes are found in the areas of production planning by rates rather than batches (Fig. 4). Other consistent changes occur with the eventual use of kanbans to authorize vendor material deliveries (Fig. 5); changes to

PROCESS	TYPE	SYSTEM	MATERIAL	AREA NOW	PRODUCTS
A	DEDICATED	PULL	KANBAN	none	MATURE HIGH VOLUME
B	FLEXIBLE	PULL	KANBAN	9000 line	LOW VOLUME IMMATURE/DECLINING PILOT
C	FLEXIBLE	PUSH	WO/COP	PL11 lines	PROTOTYPE OOP PARTS

FIGURE 2

FUTURE PRODUCTION

A (30%) ↑	DEDICATED PROGRESSIVE ASSEMBLY LINE	
B (60%) ↑	GENERIC ASSEMBLY LINE	
C (10%) ↓	BATCH LINE	

FIGURE 1

ORDER PROCESSING/SHIPPING

	PRODUCT TYPE	BUILD TO	OPTIONS	BOOKING	SHIPPING
A (30%)↑	MAKE TO STOCK	KANBAN FGI	NO OPTIONS / PACKAGED OPTIONS	NO BOOKING or TO DAILY RATE	SHIP FROM FGI
B (60%)↑	MAKE TO ORDER	KANBAN ORDER / KANBAN FGI	FEW/MANY OPTIONS / MODULAR	BOOK TO DAILY RATE	SHIP FROM PRODUCTION
C (10%)↓	BOTH MAKE TO ORDER & TO STOCK	FGI, ORDER	MANY OR FEW ANY TYPE	BOOK TO RUNS	SHIP FROM FGI (COLLECTION OF ORDER PIECES)

FIGURE 3

MATERIAL ORDERING (from Vendor)

	STOCK REQ.	MACRO PLAN	RECEIVING	TO VENDOR	INVOICING
A (30%)↑	MRP & KANBAN RELEASES	MRP PLANS	PAPER & PAPERLESS DECENTRALIZED	PO's IO's KANBAN ORDERS	PAY EACH RECEIVING or BY PERIOD
B (60%)↑	MRP & KANBAN RELEASES	MRP PLANS	PAPER & PAPERLESS DECENTRALIZED	PO's IO's KANBAN ORDERS	PAY EACH RECEIVING or BY PERIOD
C (10%)↓	MRP RELEASES	MRP PLANS	PAPER CENTRALIZED	PO's IO's	PAY EACH RECEIVING

FIGURE 5

MATERIAL (Stocking, Handling, Flow)

	TRIGGER	WORK STATION REPLENISH	REPLENISH SOURCE	ON HAND UPDATES
A (30%)↑	KANBAN	KIT REPLACE PARTS CONTAINERS AT WORK STATION	LINE STOCK WAREHOUSE	POST DEDUCT (BACKFLUSH)
B (60%)↑	KANBAN	KIT	LINE STOCK WAREHOUSE	POST DEDUCT DEDUCT AS USED DEDUCT BEFORE USE
C (10%)↓	PULL DECK COP	TOTE BOXES COP	CENTRAL WAREHOUSE	DEDUCT BEFORE USE

FIGURE 6

ACCOUNTING

	METHOD	LABOR	MATERIAL	VARIANCE	OVRHD ALLOC	STANDARDS
A (30%)↑	BY PROCESS	COLLECT BY PERIOD	COLLECT BY PERIOD	BY UNITS & CYCLE COUNT	BY THRUPUT TIME, MATERIAL & LABR CONTENT	BY INDUSTRIAL ENGINEERING STUDY
B (60%)↑	BY PROCESS	COLLECT BY OPERATION	COLLECT BY PERIOD	BY UNITS & CYCLE COUNT	BY THRUPUT TIME, MATERIAL & LABR CONTENT	BY INDUSTRIAL ENGINEERING STUDY
C (10%)↓	BY BATCH WORKORDER	COLLECT BY WORKORDER	COLLECT BY WORKORDER	BY WORKORDER	BY WORKORDER, MATERIAL & LABR CONTENT	BY HISTORICAL WORKORDER CLOSES

* LABOR + OVERHEAD ALLOCATION = VALUE ADDED

FIGURE 7

pay accounts by period rather than by receipt and much of the change to process accounting from batch accounting practices is the same for both JIT situations (Fig. 7).

UNIQUE LINKS

One notable example of a different link is in the use of post deduct logic or backflush (Fig. 6). On a functioning repetitive assembly line, material moves

PRODUCTION PLANNING

	SCHEDULING	QUANTITIES
A (30%)↑	LEVEL SCHEDULES	DAILY RATE
B (60%)↑	VARIABLE & LEVEL SCHEDULES	DAILY RATE
C (10%)↓	VARIABLE & LEVEL SCHEDULES	BATCH RUN QUANTITY

FIGURE 4

ENGINEERING

	PRODUCT	PROCESS STEPS	MFGABILITY RATING	POSSIBILITY of AUTOMATION
A (30%)↑	MINIMUM BUILT–IN OPTIONS	FIXED ROUTINGS	HIGH	HIGH
B (60%)↑	MODULAR OPTIONS	VARIABLE ROUTINGS	MODERATE	MODERATE
C (10%)↓	BUILT–IN NON-MODULAR MODULAR	HAND CRAFTED VARIABLE or FIXED ROUTINGS	LOW	LOW

FIGURE 8

PERSONNEL

	PERFORMANCE
A (30%)↑	HIGH QUALITY TIME STDS/MAINT LINE BAL TEAMWORK/IDEAS
B (60%)↑	HIGH QUALITY MEET TIME STDS/FLEXIBLE TEAMWORK/IDEAS
C (10%)↓	HIGH QUALITY MEET STDS BY WORKORDER

FIGURE 9

through a fixed routing rapidly and predictabily. It is sufficient and timely enough to relieve inventory balances for the components as each product is completed. Post deduct or backflush logic works well for repetitive processes and substantially reduces the paperwork involved and the number of transaction processed. With job shop, product independent processes, material moves through variable routings and often not as quickly or in the same volumes. Post deduct logic will often work if the thruput time is short enough, but one can often avoid the post deduct side effects and use instantaneous deduct approaches. Other differences may be in the approach to setting labor standards; in how the bills of material are structured; in how material is stored, requested and presented to production workers; and in how production is initiated.

USEFUL FEATURE

One of the most useful features an MRP system can
have to facillitate the link of MRP and kanban is the
ability to store multiple on hand balances by location for
the same part. With MRP systems, planned material is
usually issued according to a picking list generated from
a workorder. Workorders are impractical as lot sizes
approach one, that is, as just in time manufacturing
becomes closer to reality. Without workorders the concept
of a traditional pick list is invalid. How then can
material be issued to the production line (initially from
the warehouse but ultimately directly from the supplier)?
During the initial stages of JIT, material may be stored
in a warehouse and on the production line. The material
stored in production is not work in process, but is
actually another storage location. Production obtains
material from the floor location through the use of
kanbans, not workorders. As a kanban is circulated, the on
hand balance of the floor stock is reduced. The on hand
balance of the floor stock can also be reduced through
post deduct logic. It is important that post deduct logic
be applied to a specific location however, to simplify the
ability to cycle count other locations such as the
inventory locations in the main warehouse. Also, during
the transition from workorders to kanban, the multiple on
hand balance feature allows materials to retain control of
the bulk of the material dollars in a central warehouse,
yet still have production line stock. The ultimate goal of
course is to have only production line stock, in absolute
minimum amounts.

PRODUCTION AUTHORIZATION

Ideally, a shipment from FGI would initiate a kanban
authorization to build another unit. However, until we
can perfect a way to stabalize order rates, manufacturing
cannot be coupled directly to the incoming orders.
Manufacturers typically decouple themselves with finished
good inventory for higher volume low option products, or
with order backlog for lower volume higher option
products. Some manufacturers rapidly adjust capacity with
a hire and fire policy, thus having the workforce absorb
the order fluctuations. HP follows a lifetime employment
policy, and therefore we use only FGI or order backlog to
smooth production rates. As Figure 3 shows, products
using process A will replace units shipped out of FGI.
The ultimate goal of course is to replace units one at a
time. Today, HP/FSD builds at a specific rate per day
(Fig. 4), and adjusts the rate monthly as units are
shipped above or below expecattions. The kanban limits can
shut the line down however, as maximum FGI limits are
reached. This approach is in use today and proves quite
effective for software products. In process B, orders are
released from order backlog according to a planned rate
per day (Fig. 4). If shipments are stopped or fall
behind schedule, kanban limits automatically slow down the
release of material to prevent work in process buildups
beyond the authorized kanban limits.

PRODUCT STRUCTURE

Product structuring effects engineering, production
and materials. Products using process A might someday
consist only of a single level bill of materials. In
theory, other structure levels are not required since the
product is assembled on a progressive assembly line with
fixed routings. In practice, while the product structure
can certainly be simplified, multi-levels may still exist
to document service parts, to assist production assembly
documentation, repair manuals, and engineering design.
Products using process B will find it difficult to use a
single level product structure if the products are of a
modular design.

MAKE YOUR OWN MATRIX

There are nearly 100 boxes on the nine figures
contained in this article. Naturally, a full discussion of
each is not possible in a short article. A few of the
considerations in linking MRP and kanban have been briefly
discussed. Carefully study of the figures will point out
areas of required change. Not all changes required for
HP/FSD may apply to your company, and undoubtedly you will
be able to add other boxes. Try to edit and build upon
the matrix of changes presented in this article to develop
matrix specifically for your company. (We would be
interested in obtaining a copy of your matrix -
undoubtedly your insight will help us to update our own
matrix.)

CONVERSION FROM MRP TO JIT—A CASE STUDY

Russell G. Copeman, CPIM*
Double A Products Company

INTRODUCTION

This presentation is a case study of two plants that are in the process of making the change from MRP controlled job shop to "just-in-time" manufacturing. In one plant the internal manufacturing is 100% "just-in-time" while the purchase components and planning functions are operating under MRP. In the second plant, both "just-in-time" and MRP approaches are being used in the manufacturing area.

Whereas MRP is a technique that accommodates uncertainty in complex situations by providing a closed-loop model that can react quickly to changing inputs, "just-in-time" is a philosophy which is based on reducing complexity rather than accommodating it.

Classic "just-in-time" only works in a repetitive manufacturing environment and in such an environment, MRP has a very limited role. Although many companies aspire to a repetitive manufacturing environment, most older companies find themselves in a more complex job shop environment where simple visual systems and pull type controls will not work.

In this transition between job shop/complex and repetitive manufacturing/simple, there must be a marriage of MRP and "just-in-time". This is particularly true in the area of shop floor control systems where the basic assumptions of the approaches are in conflict. Because both approaches depend on unified programs, it is difficult to take a piece out of either system and have it work in isolation.

The presentation will cover step-by-step the changes that have occurred in these plants in moving from job shop toward repetitive manufacturing methods. It will also discuss the changes that were made in the MRP system to accommodate "just-in-time".

The preceding paragraphs are essentially the abstract that I submitted to APICS for this presentation. They are a little misleading. As a company we are not trying to install a '"just-in-time" system . We are also not trying to have "Zero Inventory". What we a trying to accomplish is to set up our manufacturing plants using a philosophy of flow manufacturing operating in the simplest manner that we can conceive.

COMPANY ENVIRONMENT

Before explaining what we have tried to do, it is important that you understand something of the background of the Company so that you will understand why we've tried the things we have and have a feel for whether or not they are appropriate for other companies.

The Company produces a series of proprietary product lines for the industrial hydraulics market. These products are normally considered commodity items and have tens of thousands of cataloged options. They are sold in a market that has come to demand a one-hour to six-week lead time.

The Company's manufacturing processes include all forms of metal cutting and assembly. The parts involved are relatively simple, but require extremely close tolerances. Typically a part had 10 or more process steps, and lot sizes were predominantly under 50 pieces even when lot sizes were large enough to cover a six-month supply.

In the early 1970's , the Company's operations were organized along departmental lines, and were set up in a job shop configuration.

BACKGROUND

During the late 1960's and early 1970's, the Company's response to the classic problems of poor service, poor inventory utilization, poor utilization of capital equipment, and poor labor efficiency was to attempt to apply state-of-the-art materials techniques. Specifically, we tried the following.

-We installed a computerized inventory system in 1968.

-We installed computerized routings in 1968.

-We installed a critical ratio rescheduling system in 1969.

-We established a central dispatch system in 1970.

-We established a finished goods warehouse in 1971.

-We installed a computerized capacity planning system in 1972.

-We installed a rough-cut capacity planning system in 1973.

-We developed operation simulation capability in 1974.

-We installed a partial MRP system in 1974/1975.

These techniques were successful to the extent that we actually showed some improvement in performance at a time when our product line offering was exploding. Unfortunately, not only were our product lines becoming complex, but so was our data acquisition and data processing requirements. A good indication of this was the fact that we changed our mainframe computer six times in 12 years.

By the mid 1970's, we started to wonder if just maybe we were chasing the wrong targets. Maybe we were chasing effects rather than causes. Then in mid-to-late 1970's, we came across the Group Technology and Kanban concepts and concluded that we were chasing the wrong targets. We were using our computerized systems to accommodate complexity rather than spending our time simplifying our operations.

It became obvious that cost was more related to complexity of operations than it was to direct labor, that complexity was related to throughput time, and that Group Technology was the key to throughput time reduction.

From a manufacturing point of view, the ideal operation would be to make only one type of part and to make it one piece at a time on a single type of machine in a time frame that was less than the lead time required by our customers. This would mean:

-no forecasting,

-no scheduling,

-no capacity planning,

-no work-in-process,

-no safety stock inventory,

-no setup changes, and

-no need for reports.

Unfortunately, this ideal had two minor problems. First, it was unattainable; and second even if it were attainable, we would have to work into that position from where we started. That meant we had to find ways to control thousands of long throughput parts while we tried to make them seem like a few short throughput parts.

This was a major problem because Kanban-type visual control systems will not work until throughput time is drastically reduced. That meant that until we reduced throughput time, we must depend on a forecast-based push system like MRP to control our operations.

It was our intention to use the Group Technology approaches to reduce our throughput time. Unfortunately, Group Technology is not a technique. It is a philosophy. This meant that its implementation must be an evolutionary development rather than a revolutionary development, and that in turn meant that we were faced with continuing to develop our MRP II systems while we started our Group Technology indoctrinations.

What happened in the late 1970's and early 1980's was that while we were redesigning a number of product lines using Group Technology concepts, building a new product-focused plant, and twice laying out our Michigan plant; we were also installing a new MRP II system, a new Distributed Requirement Planning system, and a standard costing system. The rest of this article is devoted to what happened during this period of the late 1970's and early 1980's.

PREPARATION

The first steps toward short-lead-time, flow-type repetitive manufacturing started as a result of attending the SME group technology seminars in Atlanta in 1976. After these seminars, a deliberate effort was made to find out more about Group Technology approaches. Most of what we found had been published in the United Kingdom or Europe and much of it was concerned with coding systems.

Although the long term advantages of the Group Technology approach appealed to some of us in the manufacturing area, the thought of selling a multiple-year coding job to engineering as a prerequisite to getting some results in manufacturing did not seem very realistic. However, in our search for examples of companies that had made Group Technology approaches work,we had come across The Langston Company who had started without going through the coding stage. We felt that our product lines had enough parts commonality that we too could start in manufacturing without first going through the coding process. We felt that the only way we were going to be able to sell this approach to the whole company was to set up an example whose results were undeniably favorable.

FIRST PROJECT - MICHIGAN GROUP TECHNOLOGY

This first project was started in 1977 in our Michigan plant. We set out to change our existing job shop layout with its five departments (turning, milling, drilling, grinding, and bore finishing/deburring) into three departments (a bar line department, a specialty lines department, and a cast parts department). Our requirements included the following.
- Each part must be made complete within one department.
- Material must only flow in one direction in a department.
- Parts families should be used as a basis for material, tooling, and process rationalization.
- A department should be staffed to take care of its own minute-to-minute problems without the help of a staff department.
- The labor force should be flexible enough to allow it to follow the load in a department.

This project spent more than two years in the Manufacturing Engineering Department before we ever moved the first machine. The following things were done during that period.
- We reduced the number of bar stock materials we used by 30 percent.
- We reprocessed 75 percent of our manufacturing routings.
- We reduced the number of unique tools we used by 5 percent.
- We rewrote and negotiated a 50% reduction in our direct labor job descriptions.
- We laid out the entire manufacturing area at least five times.
- We reorganized all departments so as to allow for the move of inspectors, dispatchers, manufacturing services engineers and general labors into the manufacturing lines.

These personnel reorganizations were really based on three considerations. These considerations were:
- supporting the Group Technology restructuring,
- separating short-time frame operating functions from longer-time frame planning functions, and
- pushing decision making responsibility as close as possible to the point of activity.

The actual changes moved parts of the Inspection, Maintenance, Manufacturing Engineering and Materials departments into the Group Technology manufacturing departments forming multi-functional teams. Basically those functions that control the hour-to-hour activity in manufacturing were moved under the control of the line manufacturing superintendents. These functions included patrol inspection, but not quality assurance; routine maintenance, but not major machine repair; routine reprocessing, but not new process development; and internal line dispatching and rescheduling, but not order release or master scheduling.

After going through all of these planning steps, we started our equipment moves in the fourth quarter of 1979 and completed all equipment and organizational moves by August 1980.

1ST PROJECT RESULTS

In less than two years, we saw the following results.
- WIP was down 61% in material and 67% in labor.
- Raw material was down 36%.
- Throughput time was down 58%.
- Individual machine rescheduling was down 80%
- Scrap rate was down 42%
- Direct labor productivity fell and then rebounded to 31% above the starting point.
- Setup time as a percentage of total direct labor was up 100%.

This project was the success that we needed to sell the concept. After getting through the three-to-four month start-up period, the morale improvement was startling. For the first time, most of the shop floor

personnel felt they had control over their environment. This made them amenable to further changes.

CONVENTIONAL CHANGES

During this same period, we were continuing to develop our conventional systems. Specifically, we did the following.
- We developed a finished goods control system during 1976/77/78.
- We developed a master scheduling system in 1979/80.
- We developed a real-time order entry system in 1979/80.
- We installed a new closed-loop MRP system in 1981/82.

At no time during this first Group Technology project did we think about running the manufacturing area without conventional shop floor systems. However, part of our lot size reduction justification was based on parts family setups which meant that we wanted to release manufactured parts in families. This is something that the conventional MRP system is not set up to do. In fact that approach violates the basic assumptions upon which MRP systems are based. An MRP system uses product relationships as a basis for decision making, and we were looking for a system that would release work based on a process relationship. We spent considerable time with APICS groups, SME groups, and our MRP software supplier discussing how we might accommodate parts family releases within an MRP system. We did not come up with a good answer.

What we finally did was to use the MRP system to release lots in a normal manner with completion dates, and allowed the shop to group parts and schedule any sequence they wanted so long as the completion dates were not violated. This meant that we had significantly reduced our rescheduling capability. However, with throughput time reduced to four-to-five weeks, we did not have as much need for rescheduling and it worked fairly well.

2ND PROJECT - FOCUSED MANUFACTURING

While the Group Technology project was going on in the Michigan plant, we were in the process of developing a new generation of product for one of our major product lines. In keeping with our discussions on parts and process rationalization, the engineering group did an outstanding job of designing a product that allowed us to take advantage of parts family manufacturing. Further, the design reduced the number of "standard" options to be produced and made it possible to produce all non-standard options as quick conversions from the standards.

We decided to use this product as the basis for a focused-manufacturing project. As a result, we designed and built a plant in North Carolina to build this product line. In this facility, we used equipment which was dedicated to specific parts families. This plant was started up using a closed-loop MRP system with complete work order and standard cost disciplines.

By mid 1983 we had completed our start-up and were in a full production mode. In looking at the operation, we discovered that with a few changes, we should be capable of assembling any mix of products on any day and with one exception, no manufactured part should require more than a week's throughput time. At that point, we decided to attempt to run that manufacturing operation with a visual shop floor control system.

In November 1983, we crossed over from an MRP work order control system to a visual Kanban-type system on the shop floor.

CHANGES IN MRP SYSTEM

There were a number of changes made to the MRP system to accommodate the visual systems used in the shop.

First, all manufactured parts had their lead times set to zero. This meant that as long as we had a single piece of stock for a part number, the system would not attempt to release a work order. Therefore, no parts appeared on the New Orders - Make report and nothing would appear on the Reschedule - Make report. The only work orders produced were one work order per department per week for the purpose of labor reporting. Purchased parts, however, had appropriate lead times in the files and continued to be treated in a normal MRP mode.

The second change was in the information that we entered into the order/demand field of the MRP system to

generate gross requirements. Where we had originally
entered discrete model orders out to an eight week time
fence and then used a forecasted family-planning-bill
requirement for the next ten months, we now use only the
family-planning-bill requirement which is entered on a
week-by-week basis at the production plan rate. This is
possible because the assembly operation has the parts
available to build any model mix on any day and the
Kanban-type floor system automatically requests
replacement parts as needed. This means that we do not
need to plan for specific-model parts but only for
specific operating levels. For that reason, family
planning bills which establish an operating level are
sufficient to drive the MRP system for manufactured parts.

With purchased parts, we violated the normal MRP
practices and used a two-week safety stock. This safety
stock is used to make up for the day-to-day build mix
change which is not accommodated by using average mix
family planning bills as the system driver.

The last change in our system approach affected both
the MRP system and the finished goods DRP system. Because
the manufacturing plant has the capability of producing
and shipping the models required by the finished goods
warehouse in a time frame that is shorter than the
biweekly review period used with the DRP system, it is no
longer necessary to place purchase order information on
the DRP system because that information would be removed
before the next review. Therefore, rather than place
hundreds of purchase orders into both the DRP and MRP
systems and adjust them for receipts and acknowledgments,
we simply note what we need weekly on a single sheet of
paper and send it via facsimile to the Carolina plant. We
then adjust the on hand balances when shipment is made
from the plant and received by the warehouse.

2ND PROJECT RESULTS

After six months of operating in this mode, we have
seen the following results.
- Work orders have been reduced by more than 80%.
- Labor data collection and entry has been reduced
  by 50-60%.
- All parts allocation reports are no longer used.
- No kit picking lists are run.
- No parts kitting of any kind is done.
- Order/demand field updates were reduced by
  approximately 80%.
- Finished goods ordering transaction time has been
  reduced more than 80%.
- Manufacturing part stockouts have been reduced to
  two parts over six months.
- Inventory turn has been improved.

In addition to the reduction in overhead activities,
the new systems have had very good acceptance on the floor
and have generated a great deal of interest at other
company operations.

3RD PROJECT - MICHIGAN JUST-IN-TIME

As a result of the successes in the Michigan
Group Technology project and the North Carolina focused-
manufacturing project, a second Michigan project was
started in late 1983. This project separated the
manufactured pump product lines from the other product
lines manufactured in the Michigan plant and set them up
as repetitive manufacturing lines and cells using visual
control systems similar to those used in the North
Carolina plant. This project required another complete
rearrangement of the Michigan plant.

The equipment moves are currently under way and we
expect all equipment moves, organizational changes and
special material handling systems to be completed by late
August 1984.

We currently expect the results of this project to be
similar to those of the North Carolina project with one
exception. Because the distribution warehouse is adjacent
to this manufacturing operation, we intend to extend the
visual systems and do away with the need to use any
computerized ordering systems to replenish finished goods
stocks on these product lines.

FUTURE DEVELOPMENTS

We are currently designing a number of next
generation product lines that will allow us to replace
current products with products better suited to short-
throughput repetitive manufacturing.

We are also looking at augmentations to our MRP
system that will allow us to use such things as overlapped
processes and backflushing. The nature of the product
lines in the Michigan plant is such that we may always be
forced to use some form of work order controlled
manufacturing on part of the product lines. For that
reason, we are working to set up our MRP system so that it
will accommodate both work order controlled manufacturing
and repetitive manufacturing.

In the area of purchased parts, we are not currently
trying to develop "just-in-time" suppliers. Most "just-
in-time" supplier programs now underway are only the
traditional effort to push inventory back onto the vendor.
If the supplier is not set up to manufacture in a "just-
in-time" mode, his only recourse to "just-in-time" supply
pressures is to stock the user's parts and make small
shipments at the expense of additional handling and
stocking cost. This unfortunately occurs without the
offsetting savings that come from repetitive
manufacturing. The net effect is that the supplier's
total cost increases and someone is going to have to pay
for that increase. Our plans are to finish our internal
developments and then work to educate our suppliers to the
savings and shipment reliability improvements they can
gain by working to become a true "just-in-time" supplier.

SUMMARY

The phrases "Zero Inventory", "just-in-time", Group
Technology, and Kanban are confusing. Sometimes they
appear to be techniques, and sometimes they appear to be
philosophies. Combined they are a philosophy which
encompass a group of techniques and approaches which are
directed toward simplifying manufacturing operations.
They encompass an entire company. They affect engineering
design, types of processes, types of tooling, vendor
selection, quality control, systems development,
organizational structure, etc. If properly applied, this
philosophy can result in a major productivity increase. A
productivity increase not measured as direct labor
efficiency (although this does occur)-but measured in
major overhead reductions.

We have found that an adoption of this philosophy of
simplifying operations is not as easy as plugging in a
computer. To be successful, it requires a complete change
in the way we view our problems, and their potential
solutions. We must change our perspective from one of
finding complex solutions to complex problems to one of
removing the complexity from complex problems. This takes
education and this education takes time. Further, for
this education to be effective, it needs concrete examples
of the benefits this change in perspective can accomplish.

Our Company is trying to change its perspective. We
are doing this with education and with project examples.
We appreciate the fact that our complex problems will not
disappear overnight. Because these problems will not
disappear quickly, we must continue to accommodate them
with conventional approaches such as MRP until the day
arrives when we no longer need such complex computerized
methods.

We believe that good MRP users may be survivors-but
good repetitive manufacturers will be winners. For that
reason, we are working on surviving with good MRP systems
while working to become winners who do not need complex
systems in the long term.

It is an interesting trip.

ABOUT THE AUTHOR

Russell G. Copeman is the Vice President of
Manufacturing for the Double A Products Co., a subsidiary
of Brown and Sharpe Manufacturing Company. While at
Double A Products he has also worked as Plant Manager,
Materials Manager, and Product and Inventory Control
Manager. In total, he has spent more than 17 years in
the Production and Inventory Control area.

He earned a B.S. in Mechanical Engineering from
Georgia Tech, and a M.S. in Industrial Administration
from The Krannert School at Purdue University. He is
certified at the Fellows Level in APICS; he is a
Certified Manufacturing Engineer in SME, and he has
chaired The Integrated Manufacturing Committee of the
Michigan Technology Council.

ZERO INVENTORY (JUST-IN-TIME)
Ruth A. White
Joy Manufacturing Company
Kenneth G. Christovich
SKF Industries, Inc.

OVERVIEW

Zero inventory is the quantitative measurement of a successful Just-In-Time (JIT) relationship between a manufacturing customer and its supplier. Manufacturers traditionally carry safety stocks of critical supplies and components as protection against a supplier's erratic delivery performance and inconsistent material quality as well as the enemy within; that is, poor planning and inaccurate inventory records. In past healthy economic periods with low interest rates and abundant cash, inventory costs were accepted as reasonable insurance premiums against poor supplier performance and planning inaccuracy. In the contemporary economic environment buffer stock is an expensive, wholly unacceptable business practice. Companies must implement formal factory operating systems so as to reduce parts inventory levels.

Successful Material Requirements Planning (MRP) Systems improve inventory accuracy and planning capability, so that companies have good purchase requirements information. Nonetheless, purchasing practices do not change significantly, because, while the buyer is better managed, the supplier community remains as unreliable as before. Thus buffer stocks are still needed. Purchasing must still place orders which protect against late deliveries and shortages and is at the mercy of supplier stated lead times.

Suppliers with long lead times force the manufacturer to place its firm planned time fence further forward of the due date into the period where basic schedule changes are still likely to occur in response to changing demand. Because these orders are being placed for schedules which are still planned rather than firm committments, shortages or overages will occur. In short, the planning information is not really used for purchasing to its fullest extent because, typically, suppliers are unable to react.

The primary goal of Just-In-Time is to develop suppliers who have formal planning systems which are able to use the buyers planned order information to shorten lead times and improve delivery performance. The mechanics of communicating are very straightforward. The buyer either electronically or through a print out transmits planned order requirements from its MRP system which are entered into the front end of the suppliers MRP system (Fig. 1). Therefore, both supplier and customer are sharing the same information through the entire planning horizon. This makes it possible

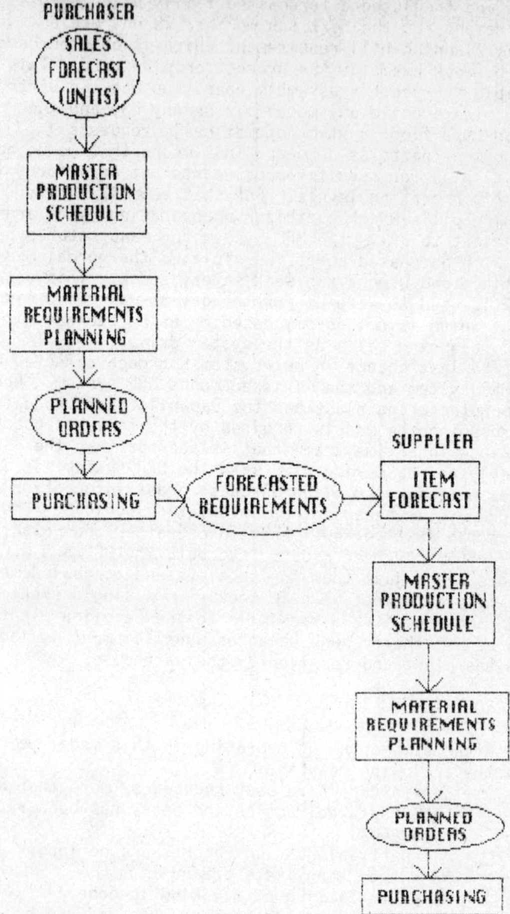

for the supplier to reduce the lead time on firm orders down to its own manufacturing lead time, because material requirements have already been placed from the planned orders information received from the customer. The integrity of the forecast obviously improves as we approach the due date.

Just-in-time means far more than delivering a quantity of parts when required. Any vendor can simulate just-in-time deliveries through reserve stock programs, expediting and product allocations to customers who complain first and loudest. The true just-in-time concept means much more. This paper explores the broad concept of just-in-time supplier relationships and presents the mechanics and benefits of one such relationship achieved between Joy Manufacturing's Coal Machinery Division and their major bearing supplier, SKF Industries, Inc.

Joy and SKF have found that the same Just-In-Time principles which work in the auto industry also provide significant benefits in their relationship where Joy's product is custom, highly engineered underground mining equipment using a wide range of bearings in relatively small quantities (at least in comparison to the auto industry). Traditionally, SKF and Joy did business on an annual contract basis. Every year, Joy's Corporate Bearing Committee sends SKF and its many competitors a request for quotation on all parts which Joy Engineering approved. The quote document included an estimated annual usage for each part with a

162

blank line for the price to be typed in. All of the invoice price quotations are entered into the computer and the best three prices for each part are selected as approved for contract purchasing during the coming year. Freight and other costs are not considered. The Basic Work Standard (BWS) for the year is the average of the three invoice prices and buyer performance is based in large part on purchase price variations from standard. Therefore, all three suppliers got some of the business, but for every bearing bought from the highest price supplier, one had to be bought from the lowest price supplier to offset the variations against the standard. Since it was Joy's policy to have three active suppliers for each part, a supplier could generally figure on getting a one-third share, all other things being equal. Joy got annual price committments and since competitive pricing was stressed, was able to hold invoice prices down. Each supplier who wanted to supply bearings at these price levels was assured a share of the business. But, is this the best we can do?

Since the bearing suppliers did not know precisely which sizes they would receive orders for and how many parts would be ordered for what time periods, they quoted Joy a standard lead time which included raw material lead time. That meant thirty-two (32) to thirty six (36) weeks after receipt of order. Thus, Joy had to commit firm orders far in advance of their firm scheduling period and could wind up ordering too many parts. Excessive inventory became a problem. On the other hand, during growth periods, Joy might have ordered too few parts and would wind up short of bearings. This made scrounging for additional bearings and expediting necessary. As soon as this happened the tendency would be to order extra part.

<u>MRP SYSTEMS WORK TOGETHER</u>

Since Joy uses MRP II to plan purchases it seemed that planning information could be useful to develop a relationship with suppliers by more effectively communicating planned requirements to the supplier in advance of issuing the actual purchase order. The primary goals are reduction of lead time and zero inventory. SKF's Roller Bearings Division was eager to discuss the possibilities since they too were using MRP II to manage their business at a "Class A" level of proficiency. After several meetings SKF and Joy entered into an agreement which has resulted in a vastly improved relationship with benefits for both. Lead times are cut by two thirds, inventories are reduced by as much as 80% and purchasing is more efficient and less costly. SKF is now sole source on products included in the agreement and margins are more stable which improves profit planning for SKF. What follows are the authors critical comments on traditional purchasing philosophies compared to the Total Value Purchasing (TVP) concept which is the basis for Just-In-Time.

<u>TRADITIONAL PURCHASING PHILOSOPHIES</u>

Management must abandon traditional purchasing rules which mandate dual sourcing and price buying. These rules serve only short term goals and foster antagonistic relationships.

* We buy/you sell
* "Cherry Pick" the quote for the lowest prices
* No advance notice of orders to be issued
* Pit one supplier against the other
* Poor communications (don't tell them any more than you have to)
* Order extra (just in case)
* Keep your supplier base big (more competitive pricing)
* Quality is the factory's problem
* If Engineering puts them on the spec., they must be okay

All of these are geared toward squeezing down invoice prices. In fact, a "price war" will eventually ensue. Sooner or later, you know when suppliers are beaten down on price. Lead times stretch out as suppliers are reserving capacity for more profitable business. Delivery reliability will deteriorate as suppliers honor higher profit orders before your orders. Some suppliers compromise on quality to try to salvage profits.

The mechanics of this approach to purchasing are simple. Send the drawing and specs to three or more suppliers, receive their bids, and buy from the lowest bidder. Let's say you receive bids from three suppliers. Supplier A is foreign. Supplier B is in another state, and Supplier C is within the home state.

COST ITEM	A	B	C
Invoice Price	$46.00	$51.00	$51.50
Shipping	3.00	2.00	.50
Import Duty	5.00		
Total Purchase Price	$54.00	$53.00	$52.00

Normally, we would choose Supplier C, with the lower purchase price or we might even choose Supplier A if we only looked at the invoice price.

This approach assumes "all other things are equal". But we know from experience that quality varies from supplier to supplier. This necessitates costly incoming inspections. Some suppliers ship materials which are rejected and we must absorb the expense of getting credit for the bad parts and then shop for replacements, or we may order extras as a hedge against rejects. Suppliers who ship early affect inventory levels and cash flow. Suppliers who ship late cause shortages on the shop floor and require costly expediting. We tend to carry inventories or bring material in early to protect ourselves against the late shipper. While these costs are difficult to quantify for individual parts, we all know the costs are there. They are a drain on profit and a drag on productivity. If purchasing spends all of its time expediting orders and issuing debits for mistakes, they are not visiting key suppliers and developing quality sources. The problem with this traditional approach to purchasing is that we judge the buyer performance by their ability to pinch pennies on the invoice and ignore the other costs as "somebody elses problem". The rub is that "somebody else" - Quality Control,

Accounting and Production - are the same company, so the costs still show up on the income statement.

TOTAL VALUE PURCHASING (TVP)

If we are serious about our search for excellence, we must adopt new prinicples of purchasing and supplier relationships. This implies that both supplier and buyer must make the philosophical and financial committment to enter into a long term contract agreement that establishes ongoing open channels of communication, mutual trust and integrity. The supplier and buyer must join together and work as a team toward mutual goals rather than separate goals. The supplier, in fact, becomes an extension of its customers' own operations.

Total Value Purchasing (TVP) stresses value analysis which goes far beyond invoice price. We must recognize the potential cost of poor quality and delivery performance and strive to develop sources which assure a known level of superior reliability in terms of both quality and delivery. Beyond this, the supplier must also be able to provide ongoing technical support. We must be willing to pay a higher invoice price for some items if we expect to buy the best. Purchased product loses its source identity in the final assembly and becomes a part of the finished product. Each part must measure up to the same standard of design quality and reliability as the whole. No manufacturer would accept otherwise. Remember we are looking for the exceptional value which contributes to the bottom line.

COMMUNICATIONS COME FIRST

The brainstorming started with the SKF Field Sales Engineer, Jim Duchene and co-author, Ruth White. White recognized that Joy Purchasing was seeing little benefit from Joy's MRP system because bearing supplier lead times were so long. White questioned "Why?" Was it a capacity problem or maybe related to poor planning? Duchene knows SKF uses MRP to manage the factory operations, and suggested that perhaps Joy and SKF could use their systems to improve communications. They agreed to bring their companies' management together to discuss opportunities to improve the relationship through each others' committment to the principles of Manufacturing Resource Planning (MRP II).

SKF was represented by Marketing and Materials Management at the first meeting held at the Joy plant in March of 1983. Joy's Purchasing and Materials Managers and key members of the MRP implementation team described Joy's system and clearly communicated their expectations of a Just-In-Time supplier. The primary supplier selection criteria are the following:

* Supplier management at the highest level must understand and be committed to the JIT relationship.
* Supplier must be interested in becoming knowledgeable about your business.
* Supplier should be a proven leader in its industry in terms of product design technology applications and service engineering.
* Supplier should have an MRP system which works and should have data which supports a grade of "Class B" user or better.
* Supplier should be engaged in the implementation of a Statistical Quality Control (SQC) approach to improving quality and productivity.
* Supplier must evidence solid financial position and a stable labor relations environment.

SKF responded enthusiastically to the initial meeting, made a presentation of their MRP status, and invited the same Joy personnel to visit the SKF plant to continue discussions and work out the details of the JIT relationship.

SKF demonstrated a strong desire toward committment and evidenced capability in all key areas. SKF's Management is clearly committed to the development of better relationships with their customers. They have been involved for over two years in the implementation of Statistical Methods for improving quality and productivity, embracing the philosophies of Dr. W. Edwards Deming, as described in his widely published, "Fourteen Points for Management." A tour of SKF's plant confirmed their committment toward quality and productivity. SKF's goal was to enter into a long term agreement which increased share and stabilized margins. Joy was looking for shorter lead times, fewer reschedules, less expediting and reliable delivery of quality bearings. The agreement was incorporated into the Joy fiscal year 1984 contract in September of 1983.

MECHANICS

At the beginning of each month, White sends Joy's planned order report to SKF's forecasting analyst who enters all of Joy's projected requirements for the next twelve months into the item forecasting module of SKF's MRP System. SKF creates a master schedule around the Joy requirements. Since Joy is sharing MRP planning information with SKF who is incorporating it into their MRP planning, no firm orders have to be issued until SKF is ready to cut steel. Only requirements within twelve weeks of the due date are considered firm. The JIT contract has been in effect for a year and the results are impressive. Both SKF and Joy are reaping the benefits:

* Lead times are reduced by nearly two-thirds.
* Reschedules on firm orders are eliminated.
* Expediting is limited to unanticipated service requirements. Wasted energy is recaptured at both Joy and SKF.
* Inventories are reduced by as much as 80% at Joy. SKF doesn't keep stock "in case" Joy needs them.

* With smaller inventories, parts stores are
  better managed so obsolescence will be
  eliminated. Costly warehouse space
  requirements will be reduced.
* Traffic planning has been improved.
  Shipments are consolidated so as to
  reduce freight costs to Joy and improve
  shipping productivity for SKF.
* Price variances for the Joy fiscal year are
  zero.
* Fewer purchase orders are issued
  reducing paperwork and clerical
  processing for both Joy and SKF.
* Purchasing dollars committment is reduced
  by more than 50% which improves cash
  flow analysis.
* SKF productivity improves as good
  planning input eliminates the need for
  short runs that were needed to respond to
  unplanned "At Once" requirements.
* SKF's share of the business increased.
* Profit margins are more stable because
  prices are based on a known product mix.

Since Joy purchasing now communicates
with only one bearing supplier in place of three,
and does less expediting and rescheduling, White
spends more time visiting key suppliers working
with Joy's Value Engineering, Design Engineering
and Quality Control departments to reduce the
total cost of Joy operations.

Joy and SKF are well on their way for Zero
Inventory/Just-In-Time delivery and they are
enjoying a win/win relationship as they continue
their search for excellence.

THE CHALLENGE FOR THE FUTURE

It has been the authors' experience, through
the development of this concept, that cost savings
and productivity gains achieved in the JIT
customer/supplier relationship through Total Value
Purchasing far outweigh the savings achieved
through the traditional purchasing approach.
Overemphasis on invoice price serves only the short
term. We cannot afford the costs of poor quality and
delivery, and yet, in our quest for the lowest price,
we destroy our supplier's incentive to supply the
best quality, to improve methods, or to strive toward
better management of operations to assure reliable
deliveries. How can we expect a supplier to work
toward support of our long term goals if we offer
only short term rewards in exchange; i.e., the next
order, this year's contract; little or no profit.
Seeking out the superior suppliers, joining together in
mutual goals, trusting and _working_ on strong
communications serve the long term objectives of both
supplier and customer.

To be successful, companies must work together
to insure that they remain competitive in the future.
The current competitive environment does not have
room for the generally accepted mediocrity of the
past. There is no such thing as an "acceptable"
number of rejects, "acceptable" adherence to
specifications, "acceptable" delivery performance, etc.
It is our passive acceptance of deteriorating standards
which has made American industry wasteful and
non-competitive. If it is our intention as
manufacturers to improve productivity and quality
and our competitive position in the world market, we
must make our suppliers a part of the team. We
cannot tolerate or encourage mediocre performance
by suppliers and strive for excellence as a
manufacturer. We are not alone and separate in our
search for excellence. We are a team and must work
as a team. The parts our suppliers ship to us, we in
turn ship to our customers, who ship in turn to their
customers. All of us share the responsibility of
supplier and customer and must support the drive to
make Anmerican products more competitive. The
world market will turn its back on us if we fail to
strive for excellence.

Ruth A. White is a Senior Buyer and Corporate Bearing
Chairwoman for Joy Manufacturing Company. She is
responsible for the purchase of bearings and
hydraulics for the Joy Machinery Division; in addition
to her duties at the location of manufacturing
underground coal mining equipment, Ruth chairs a
committee for all Joy locations and coordinates the
negotiations of bearing purchases for the entire
corporation. Ruth's thirty years of service with Joy
Manufacturing Company has given her experience by
holding positions in Accounting, Data Processing,
Receiving, Warehouse, Machine Shop Expediting,
Material Control and Purchasing. Ruth is dedicated to
turning the Purchasing functions into a Materials
Management profession of the future. Ruth and her
husband, Floyd, are enjoying 35 years of marital bliss
and have three children and eight grandchildren.

Kenneth G. Christovich is Marketing Manager for the
SKF Roller Bearings Division, SKF Industries, Inc.
located at Hanover, Pa. He has developed the role of
Marketing within the MRP II environment. This
includes the development of a "closed loop"
forecasting system used for Master Scheduling and
Financial Planning. He has formed a Marketing
approach to customers which stresses the benefits of
purchasing from an MRP II vendor and has linked
SKF's "Class A" system to customer systems. He
obtained his B.S. degree in Business
Administration/Marketing from Villanova University.
He attended outside formal MRP education from Oliver
Wight Education Associates, Inc.

JUSTIFYING JIT IN SERVICE INDUSTRIES

C. David Wieters
University of Texas at El Paso

OBJECTIVE

This paper will illustrate the diminished role that inventory savings can be expected to play in justifying JIT in service industries. Support for this contention will be based on comparison of the motor vehicle industry to selected service industries. Upon accepting this proposition within the constraints of the available data, we will turn to a discussion of alternative characteristics of JIT that may serve to justify the introduction of these concepts into service organizations.

INTRODUCTION

In the last few years the topics of quality circles, KANBAN, Total Quality Control, and Just-In-Time have permeated the management and PICS literature. Driving forces of foreign competition based on quality and productivity along with rising interest rates and associated inventory carrying costs have made changes in manufacturing imperative. Most of the attention has been focused on applications in repetitive manufacturing applications.

The U.S. economy has a growing service base with the percentage of personal consumption expenditures approaching 50 percent. The 1981 census indicated that service employment had exceeded government employment and was nearly on a par with manufacturing. While the initial focus of JIT on manufacturing was appropriate and must be continued in order to avoid further loses of markets and industries to foreign competition, the importance of the service sector demands consideration whenever a new approach, concept, or innovation is introduced. A critical requirement of any new approach prior to implementation is justification. While repetitive manufacturers may be able to justify JIT almost solely on cost savings resulting from reduced inventory, it is less likely that services will have as easy a job of economic justification.

INVENTORIES: MOTOR VEHICLE INDUSTRY VS. SERVICES

In this section we will use inventory as a percent of assets to measure the importance of inventory and turns as a measure of inventory productivity. These ratios for the motor vehicle industry will be compared to similar ratios for selected service industries. Data were obtained for 1982 from the Standard and Poor's Compustat data base. In Table 1 we see that inventory can be of major importance to some service industries--wholesalers and retailers. With the exception of retail eating places, retailers invest as much or more in inventories than the automotive industry. Given the same opportunities to reduce inventory, retailers could justify JIT on inventory cost savings to much the same degree as the Big Four. In the wholesale industry only dealers in scrap and dealers in petroleum products invested slightly lower percentages in inventories than the automotive industry. Potentially all wholesalers could utilize inventory cost savings as justification to the extent used in the automotive field. This is not to imply that inventory cost savings will be sufficient justification in these industries or in the motor vehicle industry, only that comparable economic importance of inventory exists.

The hotel/motel, communications, financial services, health care and educational, shipping, natural gas distribution, and miscellaneous personal services are clearly in a weak position to use inventory savings to justify JIT. The other factor that determines if inventory reduction is a viable justification is the current productivity of inventory as measured by inventory turns. If an organization has minimal investment in inventory and already is achieving high turns, the cost saving opportunities are small.

TABLE 1
THE IMPORTANCE OF INVENTORY BY INDUSTRY

INDUSTRY	INVENTORY/ASSETS
HOTELS-MOTELS	.012
TELEPHONE COMMUNICATIONS	.017
COMMUNICATIONS SERVICES	.056
RADIO-TV BROADCASTERS	.123
COMMUNICATION INDUSTRY OVERALL	.021
SAVINGS & LOAN ASSOC.	.016
FINANCE SERVICES	.031
PERSONAL CREDIT INSTITUTIONS	.114
PERSONAL FINANCE SERVICES OVERALL	.043
NURSING & PERSONAL CARE FACILITIES	.015
EDUCATIONAL FACILITIES	.042
HOSPITALS	.055
HEALTH CARE & EDUCATION OVERALL	.051
TRANSPORTATION SERVICES	.021
AIR TRANSPORTATION	.040
TRUCKING-LOCAL & LONG DISTANCE	.055
RAILROAD-LINE HAUL	.065
FREIGHT FORWARDING	.087
WATER TRANSPORTATION	.108
SHIPPING INDUSTRY OVERALL	.056
NATURAL GAS-TRANSMISSION & DISTRI.	.073
SERVICES:ADVERTISING AGENCIES	.025
SERVICES:EQUIPMENT RENTAL & LEASING	.028
SERVICES:MISC AMUSEMENT & RECREATION	.036
SERVICES:DATA PROCESSING SERVICE	.045
SERVICES:AUTOMOTIVE REPAIR & SERVICE	.048
SERVICES:COMPUTER PROGRAM.& SOFTWARE	.053
SERVICES:BUSINESS SERVICES NEC	.064
SERVICES:COMPUTER RELATED SVCS NEC	.065
SERVICES:CLEANING & MAINTENANCE	.087
SERVICES:DETECTIVE & PROTECTION	.106
SERVICES:PERSONAL	.112
SERVICES:RESEARCH & DEVELOPMENT	.119
SERVICES:MANAGEMENT CONSULTING	.129
SERVICES:MOTION PICTURE PRODUCTION	.173
SERVICES:LINEN SUPPLY	.233
SERVICES:RACING INCLUDING TRACK OPER'N	.323
MISCELLANEOUS SERVICE OVERALL	.106
MOTOR VEHICLES & CAR BODIES	.183
RETAIL:EATING PLACES	.045
RETAIL:FUEL & ICE DEALERS	.149
RETAIL:DEPARTMENT STORES	.176
RETAIL:FURNITURE STORES	.243
RETAIL:AUTO DEALERS & GAS STATIONS	.252
RETAIL:WOMENS READY TO WEAR	.252
RETAIL:MOBILE HOME DEALERS	.287
RETAIL:GROCERY STORES	.304
RETAIL:LUMBER & OTHER BLDG MATERIALS	.325
RETAIL:STORES NEC	.392
RETAIL:VARIETY STORES	.412
RETAIL:APPAREL & ACCESSORIES STORES	.435
RETAIL:MAIL ORDER HOUSES	.442
RETAIL:SHOE STORES	.445
RETAIL:HOUSEHOLD APPLIANCE STORES	.457
RETAIL:DRUG & PROPRIETARY STORES	.475
RETAIL:JEWELRY	.480
RETAIL:SEWING & NEEDLEWORK STORES	.609
RETAIL INDUSTRY OVERALL	.248
WHOLESALE:SCRAP & WASTE MATERIALS	.125
WHOLESALE:PETROLEUM & PETRO PRODUCTS	.135
WHOLESALE:LUMBER & CONSTRUCTION MAT'L	.229
WHOLESALE:NONDURABLE GOODS	.242
WHOLESALE:HARDWARE,PLUMBING & HEATING	.276
WHOLESALE:DURABLE GOODS	.298
WHOLESALE:DRUGS & PROPRIETARY	.345
WHOLESALE:ELEC.APPARATUS & EQUIPMENT	.346
WHOLESALE:METALS & MINERALS	.348

TABLE 1 (CONTINUED)

INDUSTRY	INVENTORY/ASSETS
WHOLESALE:GROCERIES & RELATED PRODUCTS	.362
WHOLESALE:MACHINERY & EQUIPMENT	.379
WHOLESALE:ELEC.PARTS & EQUIPMENT	.393
WHOLESALE:AUTOS & PARTS	.456
WHOLESALE:SPORTING & RECREATION GOODS	.528
WHOLESALE INDUSTRY OVERALL	.289

(Source: Standard & Poor's Compustat, 1982)

A COMPARISON OF INVENTORY TURNS

Yoshio Ohya, general manager at Nippondenso Co. is quoted in the March issue of INC. as indicating that his company carried seven hours of raw material, nine hours of WIP, and eight hours of finished goods inventories. This implies three days or less of inventory or 83 turns based on a 250 day work year. The distribution of types of inventories is particularly important to service industries. Service industries, especially retailers and wholesalers, are primarily finished goods oriented. As a consequence many JIT techniques may have limited application to services, or require exceptionally creative adaptation. However, before dealing with that issue, let's consider the inventory turns in the selected industries.

Table 2 shows that five of the nine service industries have higher inventory turnover rates than the motor vehicle industry. Only wholesale and retail have marginally lower turns than the motor vehicle firms. This result is similar to the relative inventory investment patterns found across these industries. In combination this information permits a rough projection of inventory cost savings potential by industry.

TABLE 2
INVENTORY TURNS BY INDUSTRY

INDUSTRY	TURNS
HOTELS-MOTELS	48.6
TELEPHONE COMMUNICATIONS	18.0
RADIO-TV BROADCASTERS	6.1
COMMUNICATIONS SERVICES	5.3
COMMUNICATIONS INDUSTRY OVERALL	15.2
NURSING & PERSONAL CARE FACILITIES	50.1
HOSPITALS	13.8
EDUCATIONAL FACILITIES	7.1
HEALTH & EDUCATION OVERALL	14.8
TRANSPORTATION SERVICES	66.6
TRUCKING-LOCAL & LONG DISTANCE	25.3
AIR TRANSPORTATION	25.3
FREIGHT FORWARDING	18.1
RAILROADS-LINE HAUL	8.8
WATER TRANSPORTATION	4.7
SHIPPING INDUSTRY OVERALL	14.2
NATURAL GAS-TRANSMISSION & DISTRI.	11.5
FINANCE SERVICES	12.5
SAVINGS & LOAN ASSOC.	8.7
PERSONAL CREDIT INSTITUTIONS	5.9
PERSONAL FINANCE SERVICES	9.9
MOTOR VEHICLES & CAR BODIES	7.4
WHOLESALE:PETROLEUM & PETRO PRODUCTS	13.8
WHOLESALE:GROCERIES & RELATED PRODUCTS	12.7
WHOLESALE:SCRAP & WASTE MATERIAL	8.6
WHOLESALE:NONDURABLE GOODS	7.8

TABLE 2 (CONTINUED)

INDUSTRY	TURNS
WHOLESALE:DRUGS & PROPRIETARY	7.5
WHOLESALE:METALS & MINERALS	7.2
WHOLESALE:LUMBER & CONSTRUCTION MAT'L	6.7
WHOLESALE:HARDWARE,PLUMBING & HEATING	5.1
WHOLESALE:ELEC.APPARATUS & EQUIPMENT	3.7
WHOLESALE:DURABLE GOODS	3.6
WHOLESALE:AUTOS & PARTS	3.5
WHOLESALE:MACHINERY & EQUIPMENT	3.4
WHOLESALE:ELEC. PARTS & EQUIPMENT	3.2
WHOLESALE:SPORTING & RECREATION GOODS	2.7
WHOLESALE INDUSTRY OVERALL	7.4
SERVICES:CLEANING & MAINTENANCE	33.7
SERVICES:ADVERTISING AGENCIES	25.6
SERVICES:AUTOMOTIVE REPAIR & SERVICE	17.9
SERVICES:BUSINESS SERVICES NEC	17.3
SERVICES:DATA PROCESSING SERVICES	16.5
SERVICES:MISC AMUSEMENT & RECREATION	11.9
SERVICES:COMPUTER PROGRAM. & SOFTWARE	9.5
SERVICES:PERSONAL	8.5
SERVICES:EQUIPMENT RENTAL & LEASING	8.2
SERVICES:DETECTIVE & PROTECTION	7.6
SERVICES:COMPUTER RELATED SVCS NEC	5.4
SERVICES:LINEN SUPPLY	5.3
SERVICES:RESEARCH & DEVELOPMENT	4.5
SERVICES:MOTION PICTURE PRODUCTION	3.9
SERVICES:MANAGEMENT CONSULTING	2.0
SERVICES:RACING INCLUDING TRACK OPER'N	1.9
MISCELLANEOUS SERVICES OVERALL	6.3
RETAIL:EATING PLACES	25.4
RETAIL:GROCERY STORES	10.2
RETAIL:FUEL & ICE DEALERS	6.1
RETAIL:DRUG & PROPRIETARY STORES	5.8
RETAIL:WOMENS READY TO WEAR	5.6
RETAIL:DEPARTMENT STORES	5.1
RETAIL:HOUSEHOLD APPLIANCE STORES	4.8
RETAIL:AUTO DEALERS & GAS STATIONS	4.4
RETAIL:APPAREL & ACCESSORIES STORES	4.0
RETAIL:LUMBER & OTHER BUILDING MAT'L	4.0
RETAIL:VARIETY STORES	3.9
RETAIL:MOBILE HOME DEALERS	3.7
RETAIL:SHOE STORES	3.4
RETAIL:FURNITURE STORES	3.3
RETAIL:STORES NEC	3.1
RETAIL:MAIL ORDER HOUSE	2.6
RETAIL:SEWING & NEEDLEWORK STORES	1.8
RETAIL:JEWELRY STORES	1.5
RETAIL INDUSTRY OVERALL	6.0

(Source: Standard & Poor's Compustat, 1982)

JIT POTENTIALS

Assuming the 83 turns quoted earlier and a conservative 25 percent cost of carrying inventory, what are the potential savings and return on assets of a JIT program? Table 3 tabulates the carrying cost savings and the savings to assets ratio. The ratio of operating income to assets is shown as a reference point. These pretax and depreciation figures estimate the justification power of inventory savings may provide a JIT program.

In all cases some inventory savings could be achieved based on the given assumptions. In the motor vehicle industry the potential is over four percent of assets. One manufacturer of hardware has reported that a first year investment in JIT cost $200,000 and led to a $20 million reduction in inventory. The first year savings in carrying costs were estimated at $7 million based on a 36 percent annual carrying cost. For this company the savings represented approximately 2.7 percent of assets and resulted from reductions in WIP and finished goods. Clearly in a manufacturing setting such inventory related cost savings will serve as effective justification to management. Industries with smaller inventories will have comparably smaller savings opportunities. Moreover, application of JIT techniques may be proportionately more expensive to implement.

If we exclude the wholesale and retail industries, we find a smaller inventory base with which to work--1 to 10 percent of assets as compared to 18 percent in the motor vehicle industry. The potentials of .1 to 2.4 percent savings on these smaller stocks is just not as impressive. Furthermore, the JIT tools that address internal inventory issues are largely empty opportunities for service industries. Only JIT purchasing techniques apply in a direct manner. For these reasons JIT in service industries will thrive only if a broader conceptualization of the JIT philosophy is developed. In order to pursue this line of reasoning, we first review the group of concepts that are associated with JIT. Then an attempt will be made to reframe these ideas into a service oriented environment.

TABLE 3
POTENTIAL INVENTORY COST SAVINGS VIA JIT

INDUSTRY	SAVINGS ($MM) * see note below	SAVINGS PER ASSET DOLLAR	INDUSTRY OPERATING PROFIT PER ASSET
WHSL:SPORTING & RECREATION	$ 15.8	.128	.050
WHSL:AUTOS & PARTS	111.6	.109	.225
WHSL:ELEC.PARTS & EQUIP.	134.9	.094	.118
WHSL:MACHINERY & EQUIP.	56.8	.091	.060
WHSL:ELEC.APPARATUS & EQUIP	63.4	.083	.186
WHSL:METALS & MINERALS	43.9	.079	.111
WHSL:DRUGS & PROPRIETARY	147.8	.078	.113
WHSL:GROCERIES & RELATED PDS	243.1	.077	.152
WHSL:DURABLE GOODS	117.6	.071	.120
WHSL:HARDWARE,PLUMB.& HEAT.	37.9	.065	.083
WHSL:NONDURABLE GOODS	200.7	.055	.098
WHSL:LUMBER & CONSTRUCTION	1.9	.052	-.026
WHSL:SCRAP & WASTE MAT'L	47.5	.028	.105
WHSL:PETROLEUM & PETRO PDS	67.0	.028	.111

WHOLESALE INDUSTRY AVERAGE SAVINGS PER ASSET .066

INDUSTRY	SAVINGS ($MM)	SAVINGS PER ASSET DOLLAR	INDUSTRY OPERATING PROFIT PER ASSET
RETAIL:SEWING & NEEDLEWORK	28.7	.148	.223
RETAIL:JEWELRY STORES	136.0	.118	.088
RETAIL:DRUGS & PROPRIETARY	537.3	.110	.193
RETAIL:HSHLD APPLIANCES	10.6	.108	.109
RETAIL:MAIL ORDER HOUSES	28.7	.107	.113
RETAIL:SHOE STORES	202.4	.107	.229
RETAIL:APPAREL & ACCESSORIES	20.6	.103	.250
RETAIL:VARIETY STORES	1648.5	.098	.140
RETAIL:STORES NEC	127.5	.094	.164
RETAIL:LUMBER & BLDG MAT'L	177.0	.077	.109
RETAIL:MOBILE HOME DEALERS	2.6	.068	.008
RETAIL:GROCERY STORES	1493.1	.067	.150
RETAIL:AUTO DEALERS & GAS	15.5	.060	.190
RETAIL:WOMENS READY TO WEAR	45.6	.059	.245
RETAIL:FURNITURE STORES	34.1	.058	.095
RETAIL:DEPARTMENT STORES	2474.3	.041	.111
RETAIL:FUEL & ICE DEALERS	174.5	.035	.143
RETAIL:EATING PLACES	69.8	.008	.180

RETAIL INDUSTRY AVERAGE SAVINGS PER ASSET .057

INDUSTRY	SAVINGS ($MM)	SAVINGS PER ASSET DOLLAR	INDUSTRY OPERATING PROFIT PER ASSET
SERV:RACING INCL TRACK OPR'N	$ 7.1	.079	.173
SERV:LINEN SUPPLY	5.1	.054	.147
SERV:MOTION PICTURE PRODUCTION	367.7	.041	.093
SERV:MANAGEMENT CONSULTING	43.0	.032	.129
SERV:RESEARCH & DEVELOPMENT	2.4	.028	.056
SERV:PERSONAL	10.1	.025	.133
SERV:DETECTIVE & PROTECTION	14.6	.024	.173
SERV:COMPUTER RELATED SVCS	8.5	.015	.381
SERV:CLEANING & MAINTENANCE	1.1	.013	.212
SERV:BUSINESS SERVICES NEC	30.0	.013	.226
SERV:COMPUTER PROG. & SOFT.	3.7	.012	.081
SERV:AUTO REPAIR & SERVICE	22.4	.009	.196
SERV:DATA PROCESSING SVCS	11.2	.009	.225
SERV:MISC AMUSEMENT & RECREA.	25.9	.008	.118
SERV:EQUIP. RENTAL & LEASING	5.6	.006	.206
SERV:ADVERTISING AGENCIES	.4	.004	.097

MISC. PERSONAL SERVICES AVER.SAVINGS PER ASSET .024

INDUSTRY	SAVINGS ($MM)	SAVINGS PER ASSET DOLLAR	INDUSTRY OPERATING PROFIT PER ASSET
NATURAL GAS-TRANS. & DISTRI.	924.9	.016	.155
WATER TRANSPORTATION	47.0	.025	.117

TABLE 3 (CONTINUED)

INDUSTRY	SAVINGS ($MM) * see note below	SAVINGS PER ASSET DOLLAR	INDUSTRY OPERATING PROFIT PER ASSET
FREIGHT FORWARDING	5.9	.017	.105
RAILROADS-LINE HAUL	748.7	.014	.091
TRUCKING-LOCAL & LONG DISTANCE	57.8	.010	.172
AIR TRANSPORTATION	239.4	.007	.062
TRANSPORTATION SERVICES	.6	.001	.164

SHIPPING INDUSTRY AVERAGE SAVINGS PER ASSET .012

INDUSTRY	SAVINGS ($MM)	SAVINGS PER ASSET DOLLAR	INDUSTRY OPERATING PROFIT PER ASSET
HOSPITALS	100.9	.012	.173
EDUCATIONAL FACILITIES	2.7	.010	.217
NURSING & PERSONAL CARE FAC.	1.5	.002	.133

HEALTH & EDUC. AVERAGE SAVINGS PER ASSET .010

INDUSTRY	SAVINGS ($MM)	SAVINGS PER ASSET DOLLAR	INDUSTRY OPERATING PROFIT PER ASSET
PERSONAL CREDIT INSTITUTIONS	218.7	.027	.117
FINANCE SERVICES	316.7	.007	.047
SAVINGS & LOAN ASSOC.	1.2	.004	.064

PERSONAL FINANCE AVERAGE SAVINGS PER ASSET .009

INDUSTRY	SAVINGS ($MM)	SAVINGS PER ASSET DOLLAR	INDUSTRY OPERATING PROFIT PER ASSET
RADIO-TV BROADCASTERS	186.6	.029	.133
COMMUNICATIONS SERVICES	46.8	.013	.150
TELEPHONE COMMUNICATIONS	645.0	.003	.165

COMMUNICATIONS AVERAGE SAVINGS PER ASSET .004

INDUSTRY	SAVINGS ($MM)	SAVINGS PER ASSET DOLLAR	INDUSTRY OPERATING PROFIT PER ASSET
HOTELS-MOTELS	7.1	.001	.143

* Savings are based on assumed 83 turns and an inventory carrying cost of 25 percent of dollar value.

(Source: Standard & Poor's Compustat, 1982)

JIT RELATED CONCEPTS

Just-In-Time encompasses a variety of concepts, techniques, and assumptions or beliefs. For example, JIT assumes that the following goals are desirable:
1. Lot sizes, purchased or manufactured, should be as small as possible,
2. Machines must run reliably,
3. People must perform reliably,
4. Inventory should be minimized since it is inherently wasteful and bad,
5. Quality must be high and consistently achieved,
6. Production plans should be level and stable.

In order to achieve these goals pressure is applied to:
1. Minimize setup or change overs between jobs,
2. Develop cooperative teams of employees,
3. Develop a high commitment to total quality control on the part of all employees,
4. Develop and manage operations so that challenging goals can be achieved consistently and reliably,
5. Assure equipment reliability via an effective preventive maintenance program, and
6. Assure reliable employee performance via training and development of a strong individual commitment to the organizational goals.

Many of these ideas lead to reduced inventories. However, when reduced inventory is insufficient to justify the program we must emphasize other merits of JIT.

ALTERNATIVE JUSTIFICATIONS FOR JIT

The idea of constant improvement and attention to any barrier to smooth production is a key attribute. A commitment to reduce change over time, to eliminate breakdowns and defects, to abolish stockouts and lost material, to minimize material handling, and to establish high moral and cooperative team work all contribute to cost savings. These savings may be harder to document than inventory reductions but they may be substantially more important. Less rescheduling, more reliable delivery date quotations, better service time for customers

American Production & Inventory Control Society

translate into smaller scheduling staffs, and loyal
customers.

Consider a hospital as a subject for JIT analysis.
Inventory accounts for about 5½ percent of assets and
inventory turns about 14 times in this industry. Some
service demand is highly predictable, e.g. dialysis
schedules, while other services have highly erratic
patterns, e.g. emergency department activities. Many
procedures require team work and highly reliable equipment performance. Change overs occur in operating rooms,
X-ray setups, bed changes, and other processing facilities. Total quality control fits well in this health
care environment. Reliable team performance is critical
to the success of the organization. JIT fits this
service environment.

In hospitals, as in a factory, the system is not
stressed during lulls in demand. It is during periods of
peak demand that a system shines or not. Change overs of
an operating room is not an issue when there are three
idle facilities available. But in cases of peak loads,
holiday weekend traffic accidents for example, the flow
through bottleneck operations such as X-ray, emergency
departments, operating, catscans, or other facilities
could be critical. JIT analysis could lead to improvements that would allow a hospital to provide a higher
level of health care with fewer units of these expensive
facilities.

In hospitals the most obvious inventory is in the
form of patients. Minimizing the queues and transportation of patients could have a significant impact on the
productivity of the hospital and also improve the quality
of health care. Anyone who has observed or experienced a
waiting line for X-ray or an operating room can attest to
the dysfunctional aspects of WIP in the halls. Similar-
ly, the compression of admitting/discharge procedures
coordinated with housekeeping becomes a means of providing the same number of effective beds with fewer actual
beds and associated space. Furthermore, reduced queues
could have the following benefits:

1. Shorter average hospital stays,
2. Reduced cross infection,
3. Reduced space requirements, and
4. Less confusion and hence potential for errors.

As in manufacturing, queues could be reduced by tighter
I/O control, e.g. consider a KANBAN approach to dispatching patients to X-ray.

The constant improvement crusade of JIT would direct
energy to resolving the causes of many just-in-case
policies and practices found in all organizations. In a
hospital there is a potential to perform tests beyond the
minimum required medically. Some of these could fall
into the just-in-case category while others could be to
assure that there was no mistake, quality problem, in
prior tests. Creative and persevering analysis might
well reduce the number of these tests to the benefit of
the patient and the freeing of lab resources.

Service industries are even more sensitive to the
quality of interpersonal skills than manufacturers.
Moreover, engineered hardware oriented solutions to
problems are more difficult to apply in the service
sector.The team aspects and individual commitment to
quality that is inherent in JIT will potentially contribute more to services than it has to manufacturing.

The message of JIT is not that organizations have not
been concerned with the problems discussed but rather
that we have solved them with inventory or other
buffering devices which tend to bury the problem. These
inventory and buffering techniques represent commitment
of resources ahead of time. Early commitment of
resources reduces flexibility and a percentage of these
efforts will turn out to be in error or will have
prevented efforts on more relevant tasks. A third
benefit of JIT is shared with many of the motivational
theories of management--MBO, job enrichment, and
participative management. JIT seeks to enlist all
members of the organization in the cooperative search for
improvement. This is not a new goal for management. A
major contribution of recent JIT programs is the
demonstration of impressive successes. Such tangible
results provides credibility for the system of concepts.

SUMMARY

While most service organizations will not find
physical inventory reductions a major source of financial
justification, there are other significant attributes of
JIT that offer rewards to these firms. Improved service
is a major competitive strategy for these industries.
The system wide approach of JIT has as great or greater
role in services than in manufacturing. Productivity of
our service sector becomes evermore critical as it gains
a larger segment of our economy. The general goal of
providing prompt, quality, custom designed service to

ABOUT THE AUTHOR

Dr. C. David Wieters is Associate Professor of
Management at The University of Texas at El Paso. His
primary teaching and research interests are in the areas
of production/operations management, production control,
and purchasing and materials management. His educational
background includes a B.M.E. degree from Cornell
University, a M.B.A. from The University of Rochester,
and a D.B.A. from Arizona State University. He has over
seven years of industrial engineering experience with
Eastman Kodak Company and IBM. He is a Certified
Purchasing Manager.

A PROGRAM FOR COMMUNICATING JUST-IN-TIME CONCEPTS TO SMALLER MANUFACTURING VENDORS

Jan R. Williams
Alexander Grant & Company
Harry S. Tice, Jr., CPIM
Stanadyne Diesel Systems

ABSTRACT

Smaller manufacturers often first consider just-in-time production concepts at the urging of major customers who are significantly larger than their own company. These manufacturers generally are uncertain as to the exact meaning and implications of JIT, and are cautious as to the impact of JIT on a smaller business. This presentation describes the vendor relations program of a major repetitive manufacturer who has adopted just-in-time concepts, and describes what this customer expects of his vendors. The presentation then looks at these requests from the point of view of the small manufacturer and uses specific examples to show how smaller companies not only can meet these requirements, but also can use just-in-time concepts to improve product quality and operational effectiveness in their own business.

The major manufacturer in this presentation, Stanadyne Diesel Systems, is a high volume supplier to the automotive industry. Many of the company's suppliers are smaller manufacturers with sales less than $25 million annually. In order to implement just-in-time concepts, the company has developed an educational approach and joint programs to bring vendors into the fold. These programs focus on the dual challenges of:

- Meeting the unique scheduling challenges of JIT.

- Developing the product quality levels necessary to support JIT.

REACTIONS TO THE JUST-IN-TIME CRUSADE

We have heard an enormous variety of reactions to the just-in-time crusade, ranging from enthusiasm to skepticism and downright hostility. Virtually everyone agrees that the benefits claimed for just-in-time are worth striving for, but many are taking a close look at the techniques of JIT to separate the real benefits from the empty jargon. We believe that JIT is a valid way to run a manufacturing business, and that in the future for many companies it may be the only way.

To set the stage for our presentation we would like to consider three of the popular pieces of folk wisdom regarding JIT:

1. JIT is exclusively for automotive companies.

   This is not correct, although it is true that the automotive companies were in the forefront of JIT implementation in America. In our experience, JIT concepts have spread to many of the basic industries and companies in America. A quick scan of the programs for JIT flights at APICS conferences will confirm this point.

2. JIT is for the big boys.

   This is true. Our bigger companies have been first in reaping the benefits of JIT; put another way, large industry has been the entry point for JIT into our economy. The important point, as we will illustrate, is that JIT in practice involves networking concepts that tend to push JIT in some form down through the multiple layers of vendors and suppliers which both support and depend on large industry.

3. JIT is just a flash-in-the-pan.

   This does not seem likely, both because JIT makes so much sense, and because so many large companies already are committed to the basic concepts. What

is likely is that JIT concepts will be tried out, modified and tuned to a variety of situations. Terminology probably will change. We expect that the basic concepts will be with us in some form for quite some time.

THE PLAN OF THIS PRESENTATION

We will describe our approach to just-in-time for the smaller manufacturer in four stages:

1. First, we will describe certain aspects of the small business environment.

2. Second, we will describe Stanadyne's definition of JIT and the approach the Company has developed to orienting JIT vendors.

3. Third, we will discuss the impact of JIT on smaller manufacturers: the strategies available to vendors faced with JIT, the information systems implications and needs the smaller business faces, and some of the practical constraints and advantages inherent in the smaller business.

4. Finally, we will discuss the payback for the smaller vendor, and a program of steps these manufacturers can pursue in adjusting to JIT.

In discussing the smaller manufacturer, certain aspects of a small business will affect the acceptance and implementation of JIT concepts and practices. These include:

Production Volume - Volume obviously is lower for a smaller manufacturer. This affects the way he looks at everything from tooling options to the amortization of overhead expenses.

Capitol - The smaller manufacturer must ration his capitol very carefully. Cash flow may be his biggest concern.

Expertise - Small business does not normally have access to experienced technical expertise in fields like production and inventory control. The management team is likely to be the Chief Executive plus one or two key assistants.

Resources - The small company simply does not have the "arms and legs" to take on special projects. Implementation of new concepts or procedures must be spare time projects or will require outside resources.

Flexibility - Here the small business possesses a decided advantage. An entrepreneur-driven organization can act quickly and take advantage of opportunities and new techniques as they arise.

Innovation - Once again the small business has an advantage. Often the leaner organizations are more innovative, if only because they must be to survive and prosper.

Equipment - The smaller business usually does not own the specialized equipment of bigger competitors. This may be an advantage, in that the small business has no incentive to stay with production techniques tied to older equipment.

Dependence on Key Customers - Here is one of the key points of our presentation. The small business is often very much dependent on key customers. If a major customer declares that JIT is the way of the future, our smaller vendor faces some fascinating challenges and decisions.

OVERVIEW OF STANADYNE

Stanadyne, Inc. is a multi-faceted corporation involved primarily in manufacturing complex metal components. A major unit within the Stanadyne organization is the Diesel Systems Division which manufactures the majority of distributive diesel injection pumps used in the United States. The Diesel Systems Division also manufactures a variety of support items including injection nozzles, fuel filters, water separators, and fuel heaters.

Stanadyne's major customers include John Deere, Caterpillar Tractor, International Harvester, Detroit Diesel Allison (GM), Oldsmobile, Kubota and Onan. Most of these accounts have adopted some form of just-in-time philosophy and the trend is gravitating towards 100% of the Company's customers.

STANADYNE'S NEEDS

In order to meet the new market trend of JIT all companies must take a much harder look at how this encompasses an entirely new method of manufacturing and scheduling work through production facilities.

A BRIEF OVERVIEW OF JIT

Most people equate JIT with results such as lower inventory, faster response, and better quality resulting in a lower overall cost. JIT certainly encompasses all of these features, and more, leading to significant productivity improvement.

Generally accepted practice is to view JIT as two distinctly separate but interelated facets:

1. The elimination of waste and scrap, and

2. Respect for people in the work force.

There are five basic credo that must be embraced to make JIT work.

1. Open Kimono - Everyone must have complete visibility of all the problems so they may be solved. This exposure is difficult for many people to accept since there is a definite vulnerability as the weakest part of a facility becomes painfully evident.

2. Totally in Sync - JIT requires as many operations as possible receiving and feeding simultaneous quantities to reduce throughput time and eliminate queues. This may require the actual slowing down of some machinery. A new method of equipment justification must be developed that includes these factors.

3. System Entirety - Every phase must be optimized. Improved scheduling cannot be implemented without improved quality, which cannot be improved without process control, which requires trained people, which are a result of management commitment.

The barriers that divide design engineers from manufacturing personnel must come down. Every person can contribute to problem solving; this has happened in many manufacturing plants.

4. Keep it Simple - Despite its title this is the most difficult credo to enforce. There seems to be some aura of mystique, some need to complicate simple ideas.

5. JIT not Just-in-case - Make no more of anything that what is need now! This certainly flies in the face of all the economic lot sizing techniques drilled into us from our first exposure to manufacturing.

Predicated on accepting the five basic credo, we may now examine the nine elements of JIT:

1. Focused Factories - Treat large integrated factories as small separate distinct units - perfect for small manufacturers.

2. Group Technology - Group machinery in a logical sequence to manufacture products rather than by function. Train personnel to work within the group and work as a cohesive unit.

3. Uniform Plant Load - Build a product mix of some parts every day to minimize disruption in lower levels responding to swings in Master Scheduling.

4. Negative Feedback - Relates to a pull-through trigger demand system, what many refer to as KANBAN. Output required drives the input. This ensures that resources are applied against true requirements, nets WIP and creates demand only when required by a higher level component or operation. Note that this does not require any computer to function. KANBAN (means card in Japanese) may use any means of trigger, such as functional containers, signal pieces, or cards, and is used extensively in repetitive manufacturing.

5. Minimum Set up Time - The backbone of economic lot sizing is predicated on set-up time. Therefore, if set-up time can be reduced, lot sizes can be made smaller. Theoretically, a zero set-up time allows an economical lot size of one (1) piece. Set-up time is a generally disliked, wasteful necessity that is born with grit. If we applied the same learning and study techniques to reducing set-up time, we discover that about 50% is wasted by not having the tools necessary at the change-over site. Another 25% of the time is wasted because we do not practice, routinize and improve methods. Approximately another 15% can be eliminated by incorporating features such as uniform die-closures, uniform locating pins, swing and hinge bolts. It is interesting to note that 75% of the time can be reduced by people, not large cash expenditures. Time and motion studies as simple as taping a set-up and reviewing it by several employees discloses many areas of time savings.

6. Preventive Maintenance - Each operator is responsible for his own machine; PM, cleanliness and function. Since many failures exhibit signs prior to major problems, many are averted by proper attention by operating personnel. Only major repairs are performed by non-operating personnel.

7. Quality - Operator-controlled quality using techniques such as statistical process control eliminates making lots salted with rejects to be picked out or reworked. Inspectors do nothing to improve quality, only monitor a process after it is too late.

8. Suppliers - A new relationship must evolve between suppliers and customers. A spirit of cooperation replacing antagonism will create a symbiotic atmosphere. Since JIT and KANBAN do not lend themselves readily to multiple sourcing, we must embrace a former heresy - the single source. The mutual trust and dependence formed is demanding on both parties. Each must be thoroughly open with the other. The price for all the business brings great responsibility. A supplier may never let his customer down since no alternatives exist. Pricing of goods must be by negotiation to determine a fair profit at a reasonable cost. The customer's requirements must be available. The supplier's cost accounting must be open to scrutiny.

Supplier's quality must deliver virtually 100% good parts.

9. Span of Control - Although narrow, tall spans of control ensure fast execution, they inhibit good planning. Since JIT execution is self starting, the planning function becomes far more important. A case in point - some Japanese companies only have five levels of hierarchy top to bottom in automobile plants. Some American companies have that many levels in the hourly payroll alone.

Every person in a JIT plant is involved in planning to avoid problems later. True this "consensus" technique takes longer, but production problems are minimized.

How many of your new product start-ups exhibit numerous engineering fixes? Have you heard the expression "don't buy a product the first year it is out because the "bugs" haven't been removed"?

Why do we perpetuate this situation? Our competition may start up later, but they will make money from day one.

A. *Sorting the Wheat from the Chaff*

By process of elimination, Stanadyne selected those suppliers of commodities that by their past performance of delivery, quality and service had demonstrated superiority over their competition. This means the top 50% of the vendors.

B. *Certification*

Each of the selected suppliers had a quality audit preparatory to certification. This replaces incoming inspection. Lists of items to be corrected now are being addressed and the first candidates are just about ready.

C. *Quality Controls*

A three-day intensive seminar was held at Stanadyne to introduce the fundamentals of SPC (Statistical Process Control) for top management personnel of the Division's 30 top suppliers. A mathematics instructor from a local college covered theory of profitability, theory of central tendancy (bell-shaped curve), and control parameters defined by X and R charts.

As a result of this approach, six suppliers have opted to incorporate SPC (three more already were in the process but came to the seminar anyway). Nine out of 30 clearly shows the trend of the future.

D. *Scheduling*

Purchase orders are placed only as a means of providing the legal instrument between two parties. All quantities are scheduled by separate means. The defined time fences per a JIT agreement permit planning many months into the future but limit exposure to the most current demand.

E. *JIT Agreement*

The Stanadyne Purchasing and Release Control System (SPARCS) agreement is an attempt at simplifying the "business" end of the relationship between supplier and customer. The greatest departure from standard practice is the elimination of invoices and subsequent matching.

The packing slip becomes the invoice and receiving report. Another departure is that certification is eliminated in most cases with the agreement standing as a blanket certification.

F. *Expertise*

There is little, if any, available in this uncharted area. We are learning by evolution. Come on in, the water's fine!

STRATEGIES AVAILABLE TO THE SMALL VENDOR

The small vendor faced with a shift to JIT by his biggest customer has four available strategies:

1. *Avoidance* - A supplier can reject business from JIT-oriented customers; after all, who has time for all this new-fangled nonsense? Not only will this strategy cost business in the short run, but what if the JIT concept catches on and spreads?

2. *Built-in Buffer* - A supplier can supply his customer just a little at a time from his finished goods warehouse. This is hardly likely to pass muster in a program such as Stanadyne's, and is likely to cause an impressive variety of trouble in any JIT program. For one thing, specification changes will be strictly at the vendor's expense!

3. *Split Mode* - A vendor can operate his plant in a combination of styles, with JIT co-existing with traditional concepts. In effect, this will be necessary since not all a vendor's customers will be on just-in-time. While it is possible to accomplish, the sophistication required to run a shop in a split mode may be well beyond the reach of a small manufacturer.

4. *Just-in-time Operation* - In our estimation, the small manufacturer will be best off if he runs his entire shop in a just-in-time mode and interfaces with traditional customers through stockroom buffers, either in finished goods or in raw materials.

SYSTEMS IMPLICATIONS OF JIT

Just-in-time is predicated on closer communication between customer and vendor. An important aspect of this communication is the transfer of scheduling information. Many companies have moved to a computerized release schedule delivered to vendors electronically, sometimes going to the point of placing their own terminal in a vendor's office. The potential for the proliferation of customer systems in a small vendor's office is serious. Today's small business is often a microcomputer environment if it is computerized at all, and it is poorly equipped to handle the technical challenge of interfacing with multiple customer systems.

On the positive side, JIT concepts offer the possibility of simpler manufacturing control systems as businesses begin to function more like process flow shops. As overall lead times shrink, a smaller producer may avoid the need for detailed job tracking and may find that a flat bill of materials structure is sufficient for his needs. These factors make it more likely that he can control his operation using straight-forward (and cheaper) microcomputer-based systems.

PRACTICAL CONSIDERATIONS

Conversion to just-in-time requires a total commitment by the organization starting at the very top. Even in a closely managed smaller business it may be difficult to introduce new concepts to the entire organization. Both the financial function and the quality control department face potentially disconcerting changes in their responsibilities and operating procedures.

Depending on a plant's particular production process, the change in physical facilities may present a challenge. While most JIT changes are procedural, some concepts like quick-change tooling may require some investment and a gradual phase-in.

Education of plant personnel is the biggest single requirement and is a significant challenge. Because of the practical resource limits we discussed earlier, the small business operator may find it difficult to retrain his entire management team and workforce.

PAYBACKS

The basic payback from JIT is very simple - the business will be more profitable. Improved quality, reduced rejects and rework, and reduced inventory levels all lead to lower costs and more effective use of capitol.

There is also a more fundamental reason for adopting JIT concepts. As we discussed earlier, a customer on JIT is seeking to reduce his list of vendors and build long-term relationships with a select group of suppliers. In many industries, adaptability to JIT already is necessary to retain old customers and to acquire new ones.

HOW TO PROCEED

We believe there is a series of steps smaller manufacturers must take to adjust to JIT. These include:

1. Accept the fact that JIT requires a new way of looking at the production process, rather than business as usual with some different trimmings.

2. Focus first on educating the key person or people in the Company. There generally are only one or two "drivers" in a smaller manufacturing company, and they must fully understand the concepts and sign on to the program.

3. Use the resources of your large customers as much as possible. Most companies implementing JIT have an outreach program like Stanadyne's. Take all the training they offer, but also look for ways to draw on their engineering, quality and information systems departments.

4. Take the opportunity to broaden your contacts and information flow within the customer's organization. JIT is based on open, frank flow of information and on a good faith relationship. This may initially require significant work to develop and maintain.

5. Develop a formal overall action plan for conversion to JIT. A change of this magnitude is too important to leave to informal activities and happenstance.

6. Concentrate on training the entire organization, focussing on supervisors, but getting the word to all employees. JIT will affect every person and job in the plant.

7. Think through the changes to your manufacturing process. Draw a picture of your material flows and highlight each change from current to future practices.

8. Identify and summarize key production resources, including both machines and labor skills. Key resources here are those required pieces of equipment or job procedures which will change the most under JIT. Develop a realistic plan for effecting change in these resources.

9. Define your systems and information needs, and develop a realistic plan for meeting those needs.

10. Communicate with your customers, both JIT and non-JIT, and keep them informed of your plans and progress.

11. Identify key supply components, contact your vendors, and investigate ways to implement JIT on your raw materials supply side.

Jan R. Williams is a Partner in the firm of Alexander Grant & Company and is responsible for Management Advisory Services in the New England area. He is certified at the fellow level and has been a frequent speaker at chapter meetings, APICS and BPICS international conferences and regional meetings. Prior to joining Alexander Grant, Mr. Williams was with Price Waterhouse in Madrid and in Boston; he also has held a variety of materials management positions with the General Electric Company and the Millipore Corporation.

Harry S. Tice is Corporate Director of Purchasing at Stanadyne Diesel Systems in Windsor, Connecticut. He is a CPIM and also certified as a CPM by the National Association of Purchasing Mangers. Mr. Tice has held positions both as Materials Manager and as Purchasing Manager; before joining Stanadyne, he was with Tally Industries and the Echlin Manufacturing Company.

JUST-IN-TIME/TOTAL QUALITY CONTROL—
PROCESS INDUSTRIES INVENTED IT

Michael P. Novitsky, CPIM
Michael P. Novitsky & Associates

The American Production & Inventory Control Society's (APICS) current ZERO INVENTORY CRUSADE is a spinoff from the Just-in-Time/Total Quality Control (JIT/TQC) concepts being applied first and most successfully by major Japanese producers and more recently, by Western World manufacturers. However, as we explore the many issues that make up the JIT/TQC picture, we see a striking similarity to approaches used in many of our oldest Western World industry groups, commonly called PROCESS INDUSTRIES.

In his latest book, "Japanese Manufacturing Techniques", Richard Schonberger points out:

> "The ultimate is not assembly line (repetitive) production but continuous production, which is found in what are often known as Process Industries"....."The Japanese Just-in-Time system simplifies by making unit processing as much like continuous processing as possible".

The first step is to define what makes up the Process Industry manufacturing environment, then we can see how the JIT/TQC applications have been hard at work for many years before the modern Japanese production world got such big press about what they were doing.

THREE TYPES OF PRODUCTION

The APICS Dictionary defines the three different types of manufacturing processes as:

> JOB SHOP....departments or work centers...organized around particular types of equipment...eg. drilling, forging...products flow...in batches...SYN: intermittent production.

> REPETITIVE MANUFACTURING: Production of discrete parts...ususally at...high speeds and volumes. Material tends to move in a sequential flow.

> PROCESS MANUFACTURING: Production which adds value by mixing, separating, forming...in either batch or continuous mode.

The definitions attempt to differentiate between the three distinct types of production processes one would find inside a factory or plant. It should be noted, however, that it is common to find more than one type of production process inside a single factory.

Let us now look more closely at what makes up the Process Industry-type production environment.

PROCESS CHARACTERISTICS

There are some common ingredients which make up the typical Process plant, such as:

A. Capacity is well defined:

There usually is not much flexibility in changing the output rate of work stations or the overall factory.

B. Dedicated storage facilities:

The nature of the raw materials (usually liquid or powder) dictates the type of storage vessel and the specific items that can be stored in each.

C. Short manufacturing lead times:

Because of the flow-production, the process time is generally quite quick, compared to the other two types of manufacturing processes. (Can be as short as minutes, as in the case of some chemical reactions and petro-chemical operations).

D. Product yields vary:

It is not always possible to control the amount of end product and, at times, it may be difficult to control the type/grade of the end product. Eg: certain types of plastics.

E. Routings are fixed:

The product being generated, in many instances, may predetermine the work centers that must be used, not allowing for a choice in routings.

F. Work-in-process (WIP) is not significant:

There is generally little WIP to warehouse or to keep track of.

We have set the stage for further discussions of what Process-type manufacturing is all about, and we can now evaluate how the JIT/TQC principles might apply.

JIT/TQC PRINCIPLE #1: Eliminate Waste

Within a Process environment, there is an extremely high priority (because of the impact on Cost & Profit) on reducing waste, with the goal to eliminate it completely.

Of special consideration is the pressure to avoid:

a. REWORK: Many of the process-type products can be adjusted by adding combinations of ingredients or adding more heat or pressure. An example would be the blending of wines and spirits, to achieve a specific alcohol content, taste-level, fragrance, color, body, etc.

Such flexibility enables the production department to salvage what might otherwise be scrap in other product processes.

b. MAINTENANCE DOWNTIME/DISRUPTIONS: Because of the high investment in capital equipment and the pressures to insure continuous flow of product, there is a high priority on keeping the plant running at maximum output. Absorbing overhead costs through production volumes also pressures management to reduce/eliminate work flow stoppages through planned preventive maintenance. Some process plants operate continuously three shifts per day, seven days per week, and 360 days per year, shutting down for five days for major equipment maintenance.

JIT/TQC PRINCIPLE #2 Establish good housekeeping practices; clean shop floor with minimum materials.

Process-type firms are involved with a continuous Good Manufacturing Practices (GMP) program that makes good economic sense, even though such actions may also be required by government regulation. The Food and Drug Administration (FDA) and the Environmental Protection Agency (EPA) have set minimum standards for performance but the more progressive firms have also recognized the positive impact on eliminating waste through improved GMP.

JIT/TQC PRINCIPLE #3: Anticipate quality problems to avoid downtime.

There has been an evolving improvement program in Process Industries, particularly addressing the issue of computerized process quality control. This has moved many production processes from an ART to a SCIENCE in process adjustment procedures and has reduced overspecification of products.

Additionally, these firms have become more flexible in responding to raw material variability by planning alternative reactions and, where appropriate, changing formulations.

<u>JIT/TQC PRINCIPLE #4: Make only what is needed right away; the goal is economical operations at any level of production.</u>

Process firms are capacity intensive environments, forcing high priority on Master Production Scheduling (MPS) that capacity-tests on a continuing basis.

The changeover times are not easily reduced and are procedurally constrained, but the numbers of changeovers are lowered through product sequence scheduling.

Because of the nature of the flow production, a product-specific cost calculation is not commonly in place, but, instead, an estimated overhead absorbtion factor is usually applied.

The Process Industry generally does not endorse the "ideal lot size equals one" campaign; however, in theory, the continuous process is "ONE". Zero IDLE Inventory is a more widely-endorsed program direction then the Zero Inventory Crusade.

<u>JIT/TQC PRINCIPLE #5: Lost productive time due to changeovers should be minimized.</u>

The Process-type plants have generally been designed with the latest technology know-how. It is very costly to alter the equipment after the fact, and there may be limitations due to currently available technology.

The standard practice for years has been for engineers to achieve the lowest changeover times during the facility design stage.

<u>SUMMARY</u>

In this paper, we have attempted to support the claim "Process Industries Invented JIT/TQC" and, in that effort, have first defined what the Process Industry is.

Since there are only a few "pure" Process firms but many firms with <u>some</u> process characteristics, we have concentrated our attention on the lessons applicable to the process element inside a manufacturing environment. The current trend is to move our job shop-type processes into a more repetitive, higher volume production mode with the inherent benefits to such a strategy.

Likewise, a move from a repetitive process layout to a continuous process flow means shortened manufacturing lead times, reduced WIP, improved stock ratio, greater marketplace responsiveness, etc.

The concept of JIT/TQC is, indeed, getting much press, with many firms searching for solutions to improve the overall productivity. Process firms have learned much already about the JIT/TQC approach and can serve as a body of knowledge from which the Job Shop and Repetitive manufacturing firms can learn much.

BIOGRAPHICAL SKETCH

MICHAEL P. NOVITSKY, CPIM

The Principal of his own management consulting firm, Mr. Novitsky has had over 15 years of hands-on business experience, both as a Project Leader of an MRP II/DRP II system implementation in a major consumer goods company and as a management consultant working with firms in Europe and North America.

He works with major multi-national firms, developing specific client-oriented education seminars/workshops in a wide range of MRP II subjects. He has also done in-depth, results-oriented counseling in both repetitive and process-type manufacturing environments for clients on both continents.

Formally Manager, Logistics Planning for a Fortune "200" consumer goods company, Mr. Novitsky headed the Project Team and pioneered the application of a closed-loop Distribution Planning System (DRP) for that company's multi-plant logistics network.

A frequent lecturer and contributor to American Production & Inventory Conrol Society (APICS) publications, Mr. Novitsky is serving his third term as National Chairman, Process Industries Special Interest Group. He is a graduate of the University of Scranton with a B.S. degree and is certified by APICS.

NOTES

NOTES

NOTES

NOTES

NOTES

NOTES

NOTES

NOTES